The Plot to Betray America

ALSO BY MALCOLM NANCE

The Plot to Destroy Democracy: How Putin and His Spies Are Undermining America and Dismantling the West

The Plot to Hack America: How Putin's Cyberspies and WikiLeaks Tried to Steal the 2016 Election

Defeating ISIS: Who They Are, How They Fight, What They Believe

THE PLOT TO BETRAY AMERICA

How Team Trump Embraced Our Enemies, Compromised Our Security, and How We Can Fix It

MALCOLM NANCE

New York

Cover design by Amanda Kain
Cover photograph © The Asahi Shimbun / Getty Images
Cover copyright © 2019 by Hachette Book Group, Inc.

Hachette Books
Hachette Book Group
1290 Avenue of the Americas
New York, NY 10104
hachettebookgroup.com
twitter.com/hachettebooks

First Trade Paperback Edition: November 2020
Hachette Books is a division of Hachette Book Group, Inc.

Editorial production by Christine Marra, *Marra*thon Production Services.
www.marrathoneditorial.org

Book design by Jane Raese
Set in 10.5-point Utopia

Library of Congress Cataloging-in-Publication Data has been applied for.

ISBN 978-0-316-53576-2 (hardcover); ISBN 978-0-316-53578-6 (trade paperback);
ISBN 978-0-316-53577-9 (ebook)

Printed in the United States of America
LSC-C

1 2020

Contents

Foreword

For 243 years these United States of America have endured the terrifying forge of enlightened revolution to emerge a new nation filled with chaotic compromises and a spirit of limitless possibility. The successful revolution that bested a global superpower instilled in all who called themselves American an unquenchable passion for liberty, a white-hot ardor for freedom. These peoples—who held dear the experiment of American democracy in a new republic, arrived at these shores to worship the God of their choice, and came together in community when suffering struck—expanded their vision until it reached the Pacific Ocean.

Our founding fathers, though men of flesh and blood often steeped in shameless hypocrisy and sometimes too self-serving in their ambitious seeking of land or comfort, still created a globally unique political ideology, which started with the words: "We hold these truths to be self-evident, that all men are created equal."

In the two and a half centuries since these words were written, we have come to accept the sanctimony of excluding women, people of color, and Native Americans, the latter exposed to violence and disease. Yet the founding fathers boldly wrote this single idea of common equality, knowing that their sins would eventually be exposed to history and that their misdeeds and errors would be undone by their progeny. They drafted these words knowing that time would temper the hot iron of a young, brash, and passionate nation. Given time and reason, America would transform into an enlightened ideal where those words would not just ring true but would be the basis for a nation of all men and women, even of those whose lands had been stolen and those who had arrived in bondage.

In two and a half centuries, America has faced a fractious civil war, unbridled imperial greed, slaughtering world wars, near national starvation, a civil-rights reckoning, an international ideological struggle, and a final embrace of equality and global economic prosperity. From thirteen small states, America became a nation unrivaled in history, one that took in the world's immigrants and refugees to create a country whose greatness is proclaimed in three Latin words: *E pluribus unum.* From many, one.

America is the greatest power the world has ever seen simply because it harnesses the strengths of all those who seek her bounty. A nation where the transgressions of the parents could always be atoned for by the children who stood firm to refine the American promise.

America has been a place where goodness, compassion, and kindness were the noblest of goals, where character, erudition, and empathy were the hallmarks of our national leaders. It held these values dear until the inner hatred of some rejected the simple act of electing a black man as our first citizen. His mistake was to try to bind the nation by giving the poorest health care, the gift of life, and with it a greater opportunity for liberty.

On November 9, 2016, and on every day since the election of Donald J. Trump, a narcissistic scoundrel of a con-man turned opportunistic politician, this once great nation has been on a brakeless descent into a seemingly unending hellscape of national despair. Sixty percent of our countrymen and women, especially those of color, Native Americans, and the poor, are ignored by a scalawag whose only love is for himself and his billionaire friends. It is heartrending that Trump has convinced a cavalcade of sunshine patriots and the misguided desperate to believe that they could be masters above all others if they just embrace hatred and violence and make him their petty tyrant.

Malcolm Nance reveals in these pages how Trump violated the oath of office after having been elected with the assistance of our foreign enemies and a disgraceful alliance of neo-Nazis, white supremacists, and congressional toadies who may best be called fifth columnists. All of these so-called citizens allowed Trump free rein to transform America from a constitutional republic to a constitutional autocracy, with our beloved national contract a mere fig leaf. Nance outlines the long, disgraceful journey into the wretched, putrid bilge of Trump's nascent authoritarianism. It lays bare the plan to enrich himself at the expense of

America's national security and his mad desire to mimic the ironfisted rule of his peers: a ruthless Russian dictator, a North Korean mass murderer, and an assortment of communist autocrats.

I hope I inspired a few of you in my role as Josiah Bartlett, the fictional president in the TV series *The West Wing,* when he said:

> We did not expect nor did we invite a confrontation with evil. Yet the true measure of a people's strength is how they rise to master that moment when it does arrive ... but every time we think we have measured our capacity to meet a challenge, we look up and we're reminded that that capacity may well be limitless. This is a time for American heroes. We will do what is hard. We will achieve what is great. This is a time for American heroes and we reach for the stars.*

I am sure that, informed reader, you will realize you are the heroes we have been waiting for. With your enlightened passion, America will survive.

Martin Sheen
Los Angeles, CA
August 2019

*Reprinted with permission from *The West Wing* creator Aaron Sorkin.

The Plot to Betray America

Introduction

When I first wrote about the Trump-Russia scandal in my books *The Plot to Hack America* (2016) and *The Plot to Destroy Democracy* (2018), I did not suspect that the nation would still, in 2019, be embroiled in what is clearly the greatest scandal in the history of the United States. There has not been one day where revelations about the activities of Donald Trump and his associates related to their activities with Russia was not the top news story in the country.

All during the Mueller investigation, Trump sought to frame his version of the investigation as a "witch hunt" and insisted there was "no collusion, no collusion, no collusion." However, once the actual report was released, a whole new phase of the Trump-Russia scandal was unleashed.

In December 2018, just months before the special counsel's report would be submitted, Trump appointed William Barr as US attorney general, who became his private hit man. When former FBI director Robert Mueller III delivered the report to Barr in March 2019, the news media was initially bamboozled by the new attorney general's four-page memorandum, which concluded "that the evidence developed during the special counsel's investigation is not sufficient to establish the President committed an obstruction-of-justice offense" and also that the report "did not find that the Trump campaign or anyone associated with it conspired or coordinated with Russia in its efforts to influence the U.S. presidential election."

Although a different picture emerged when a redacted version of the report from the special counsel was finally released to the public and Congress in April 2019, the report did not clearly resolve the issue. Granted, Mueller's report provided a road map for Congress to impeach the president, but it never clearly said there was criminal liability.

Mueller may not have indicted Trump (because the Justice Department rules said he absolutely could not), but he also did not pull any punches when he spelled out in his report more than ten instances where Trump likely obstructed justice to avoid further inquiry into a raft of crimes that led to fourteen additional inquiries. Mueller stated that "the Russian government perceived it would benefit from a Trump presidency and worked to secure that outcome" and that "the Campaign expected it would benefit electorally from information stolen and released through Russian efforts." Let that sink in. Trump expected data from Russia and wanted to benefit from the theft by their spy agencies.

It seemed like Trump's goose was cooked until the greatest scandal in the history of America was covered up by the greatest scandal in the history of America. Unlike Comey, Barr had apparently taken Trump's die-hard "loyalty oath." Working with Republicans, Trump has managed to position key people in the Justice Department, the Republican Party, and the Supreme Court in an effort to jury-rig the results of any future court case or impeachment proceeding and to stop the Democratic Party's slow walk toward impeachment. Trump has been, in effect, abusing presidential power at all turns. He has ordered members to quash subpoenas, ignored congressional testimony, and defied the Congress of the United States. What could have been his early exoneration if he had let the Russia investigation run its course instead has opened a new phase of investigations in the greatest case of American corruption.

To date, I have written numerous books on intelligence tradecraft, counterterrorism, the rise and fall of the Islamic State and Al Qaeda, and the fundamentals of the Russian plot to hack the American elections. However, nothing done by the worst terrorists filled me with more horror than realizing that Alexander Hamilton's "unprincipled man"—the American-grown autocrat that the founding fathers had warned the nation about some two hundred years earlier—had finally cheated his way into the Oval Office with the assistance of an ex-KGB officer. This was not only an insult to all Americans living in a democracy but to all of us who have served in America's military and public service to defend her.

THIS BOOK WILL EXPLAIN the elusive one-word question that has permeated the entire Trump-Russia scandal: *Why?* Why did Donald Trump suborn perjury, order crimes, hide secret communications and contacts with Russian assets, and show an undying subservience to the ex-KGB officer ruling as a dictator in Moscow?

I completed my initial draft of *The Plot to Betray America* well before the Mueller report was publicly released. It was satisfying to have Mueller validate everything I had written in this and my two previous books—because numerous right-wing pundits have been insisting all along that the Trump-Russia scandal was a wild, liberal conspiracy theory. It's eerie how easy it was for me, an average intelligence professional, to unravel the Russian operation, as I did in *The Plot to Hack America*. The findings in that book came out six weeks before the election and foreshadowed the Mueller report, including the prediction that there would be an FBI counterintelligence investigation that would critically damage the Trump presidency. In *The Plot to Destroy Democracy,* I learned how horrifically hard it was to pin down Trump on conspiracy charges. He controlled the public relations tools of the nation and had a historical enemy working in his interest. This part of the Mueller report would end up at 448 pages. I did it in 345. However, *The Plot to Destroy Democracy* exposed the fantastical web of ties between Team Trump and both Russian and European anti-immigrant, alternative right-wing political factions. It revealed his desire to join an axis of autocrats led by Putin.

In *The Plot to Betray America,* I detail how Donald Trump, his political team, his family, and his most loyal American followers deliberately tried to get away with the greatest act of treachery in the history of the United States—an open in-your-face betrayal of the oath of office for money, power, and the chance to fundamentally break the traditional American system of government and damage our national security to benefit Trump's allies in Russia, Saudi Arabia, and a newfound friend in North Korea. Trump has tried to make America essentially a Moscow-backed autocracy filled with obscene corruption. Gone is the accountability and image of transparency in a constitutional democracy that so many Americans would find they had taken for granted.

The Plot to Betray America is the story of how equal measures of hatred, ambition, ignorance, and superstition have come to tear America apart. It is a nightmarish tale, two parts political thriller and one part spy novel, of how the formerly hardline anti-Communist Republican Party has turned on a nation's norms and shredded its belief in the Constitution to cover up the crimes of a pathological liar. History has revealed that Trump is a man who could barely construct a comprehensive sentence on tangible policy to the American people but has managed to use the raw power of the Oval Office to subjugate the 60 percent of American citizens who oppose him and to ignore any law that suits him. This man has created a for-profit concentration camp system and was publicly overjoyed when he separated thousands of Central American, Honduran, Guatemalan, and Nicaraguan children from their parents and caged them in desert prisons. The worst part of the story is how easily one-third of the nation has been brainwashed into backing a man who thought the pinnacle achievement of his life would be to construct a building emblazoned with the word *Trump* in Moscow, the capital of our enemy. This American story is a shameful, sorrowful tale the likes of which we should be heartfully embarrassed about.

SECTION I

Organizing to Steal an Election

CHAPTER 1

Betraying the Oath . . . in Plain Sight

On July 27, 2016, when Donald J. Trump, the Republican nominee for president of the United States, approached the podium to deliver a barn-burner speech against his Democratic Party opponent Hillary Rodham Clinton, he knew he was about to betray his nation. Everything America had ever stood for was about to be burned to the ground. When he did this, he had but one goal: to win.

To achieve his victory, he was going to do something no other American in history had dared. He would publicly and brashly demand that a hostile foreign power intercede on his behalf in the 2016 election for president of the United States. Trump's request was simple: he would ask the Russian intelligence agencies to steal the emails of his opponent and release them publicly to the global news media so that he could win the election. It would be a crowning achievement of political performance art that will likely never again be rivaled in American history. It was a singular political move that no one had ever dared to do previously. Before Trump bullied and insulted his way onto the top of the ticket, an outrageous spectacle like this was unthinkable. Unprecedented! This was just the way Trump liked it. He was going to make history.

With all this in mind, Trump stepped forward to the microphone, and in an instant he let the mask slip off, exposing four years' worth of winks, nods, and signed contracts with Putin's Kremlin, and said words that, for any other person, would have been tantamount to treason:

> Russia, if you're listening, I hope you're able to find the 30,000 emails that are missing. I think you will probably be rewarded mightily by our press.[1]

Voilá! It was done. Donald J. Trump, champion of the Republican Party, stood before the world and publicly embraced America's most insidious near-peer enemy. But what did Trump care? He had a race to win, and if it meant using the global media's fiery obsession and insatiable appetite for any news related to Hillary Rodham Clinton's emails, so be it. Perhaps his public confession, where he practically admitted that he was in league with a foreign nation, relieved a secret internal pressure, a pressure that incessantly weighed heavily within him, but which motivated him to achieve a perpetually pressing secret desire: "I *must* be a winner."

With the narcissistic intensity that passes for a soul, Trump revealed to the world that "whatever it takes" would not just be a mantra but the modus operandi for Team Trump. Everyone, from his campaign manager to the fist-throwing supporters at his rallies, would carry out their assigned tasks and do everything and anything to ensure a victory. A ruthless desire for success would guide himself, his family, his advisers, and his followers. Donald Trump would win this election, and he did not care how it was done or what resources were necessary—*whatever it takes*.

Confessing publicly that he likely had been and wanted to work with the assistance of a foreign nation was a delicate affair. Trump had been carefully cultivating his relationship with the Russian government as far back as the 1980s when it was the Communist Party–controlled dictatorship of the Union of Soviet Socialist Republics, the Soviet Union. One could argue *that was then, this is now*. But to Trump, Russia has always been a cultural ally filled with beautiful, sexy women and oil and natural gas billionaires with insatiably good taste in food, cars, and, of course, real estate. Russia was in the hands of a strong, tough leader and a ruthless mafia. At that level, utmost respect was a *must*. Trump fancied himself a world leader like Putin—a man who saw what he wanted and took it, and yet remained beloved by the Russian people. If only Trump could win, then Putin would be his closest friend. Had he not already promised assistance? Yes. His oligarch emissaries, like Konstantin Rykov, had been assisting since the night in 2012 after the reelection of President Barack Obama. That same night Trump demanded in a Twitter message, a tweet, that Americans take to the streets in protest! How could Obama win a second election? Rykov had been watching Trump's Twitter feed and said in a private message that if he wanted to run for president "Russia will help you." Trump responded with a picture of himself on his executive jet giving a double thumbs-up. One week later, he started his 2016 campaign by registering a political action committee called Make America Great Again, reminiscent of Ronald Reagan's slogan of "Let's make America great again."

Putin knew that it would take a great effort on Russia's part; there were real risks. But Donald Trump was *a different American*. Trump saw in Russia a nation filled with men like him. He could build a bridge across the cavern that he believed Obama had fashioned by rejecting Moscow's political moves around the world. Russia was culturally aligned with the American Republican Party: it hated gays, blacks, and all others with the exception of the harried and victimized white race. In Russia women were to be put back in the kitchen, not running for president. The Russians worshipped the same Christian god as the Americans and had formed an informal law enforcement alliance against Islamic terrorism. These were greater similarities than differences. Trump reckoned, Why be enemies?

After Trump betrayed his nation, he stepped back to bask in the afterglow of opprobrium. Many in America were aghast, while others, Trump supporters, were elated with this unabashed betrayal of America in plain view. One could almost hear the collective national gasp as he invited Russia to dump Clinton's emails. Beyond brash and bold, it was insane and political suicide! But Trump had read his audience well, particularly the news media; to them, he wasn't throwing out words of treason but rather dropping an unrivaled mass of newsprint catnip. He had just launched the greatest controversy in American political history, a controversy that contained the only rap journalists wanted to hear—*Hillary Clinton's private emails*. Just imagine if they could get that!

Next to Oprah Winfrey or Beyoncé, Hillary Clinton was the most well-known woman in the world, but she was a highly private one. Virtually nothing was known about how she communicated with her closest friends and family members about the intimate details of her existence. Trump was potentially offering access to that.

Trump had unleashed that which had been offered to him four years earlier. This public statement was the signal of a quid pro quo—something given for something given in return. In return, Moscow only wanted one thing: to lift the crippling economic sanctions imposed by the mutually hated Barack Obama and his then secretary of state Hillary Clinton for Russia's invasion of Ukraine and the seizure of Crimea. To Moscow, Obama was stealing the money of the Russian oligarchy by not allowing anyone who used American banks to deal with Russia. From the oligarchs' point of view, these "stolen" billions were rightfully theirs and the sanctions were theft.

To win, sure, Trump would lift the sanctions, and in addition, he would finally get the hotel he had fantasized about since 1987: Trump Tower Moscow, planned to be the tallest building in Russia with his name across the top in garish gold letters. "Teflon Don" would take the help of anyone who could give it, despite the questionable means.

Since the news media had been aflutter for weeks with news of the Democratic National Committee (DNC) hacking and WikiLeaks's exposure of its correspondence, Trump was well aware that Russian intelligence agencies could provide the coup de grâce to Clinton's campaign. The superspies at the FSB (Federal'naya Sluzhba Bezopasnosti or Federal Security Service), the successor to the ruthless KGB, would take that difficult shot, and in an ultimate act of flattery to Donald, release of the emails would make Clinton's campaign dead on arrival. Trump had already been briefed on information that was flowing in from Russian contacts and being collected by associates both inside and outside his campaign. Whether it be from his close adviser Roger Stone, Julian Assange and WikiLeaks, Paul Manafort, George Papadopoulos, or any of his other sources for dirty tricks, the real dirt on Hillary Clinton would be obtained and shoved down her throat.

Against all odds, he would become president of the United States.

After he had spoken his thoughts about Clinton's thirty thousand emails out loud, a stunned press corps started to ask questions, but none so directly as MSNBC's Katy Tur, a reporter assigned to the Trump campaign, to whom Trump had given the insulting nickname Little Katy Tur. She would be the only reporter to see the statement for what it was—near treachery. Tur stood up and asked Trump what millions of stunned Americans were thinking: "Do you have any qualms about asking a foreign government—Russia, China, anybody—to interfere, to hack into the system of anybody's [*sic*] in this country?" Trump responded snappily with a retort that Obama was a failed president. Tur persisted: "Does that not give you pause?" Cornered, Trump gave Vladimir Putin's entire game away. "No, it gives me no pause . . . If they have them, they have them. We might as well."[2] Trump failed to admit his call for foreign intervention as anything more than a novel way to beat his opponent.

In that instant, every counterintelligence officer in the Western world must have thought "This . . . is treason." While the counterspies were dumbfounded and likely pulling every bit of confidential data on Trump and his contacts with Russia out of their files, the world wondered, Did his appeal to Russia truly technically amount to *treason*? The answer is that it didn't comply with the full legal definition of the word. US Code, Title 18, Section 2381 defines treason as:

> Whoever, owing allegiance to the United States, levies war against them or adheres to their enemies, giving them aid and comfort within the United States or elsewhere, is guilty of treason and shall suffer death, or shall be imprisoned not less than five years and fined under this title but not less than $10,000; and shall be incapable of holding any office under the United States.[3]

Legal scholars will argue that the definition of treason strictly happens only when a war is formally declared by Congress, which was last resolved on December 11, 1941, when the United States voted war against Nazi Germany. To many, it is an archaic word that harks back to the days of the Cold War or the American Revolution. But there are historical and constitutional contexts. From the medieval era, it was codified in English Common Law as "whatever crimes the king or queen says it is." The American legal definition of treason was literally designed to do away with the Crown definition. Its high bar for treachery is enshrined in Article 3, Section 3 of the US Constitution, and it was written so that only the individual betraying the nation would be punished. That way entire families could not be charged. The section says that "Congress shall have Power to declare the Punishment of Treason, but no Attainer of Treason shall work Corruption of Blood, or Forfeiture except during the Life of the Person attainted."[4] Case in point: the betrayal of General Benedict Arnold.

The Case of Benedict Arnold: America's Premier Traitor

Trump is not the first American to attempt to cheat and lie and end up betraying his country, but he should be the last. As CIA director John Brennan once said, traitors often start as unwitting dupes, desperate debtors, or starry-eyed idealists. They are found, cultivated, and often deceived by spies against their nation. It is illogical to think that just because a party to treason is never detected, indicted, or convicted means the crime was never committed. Fortunately, many of them are, but others defect and often escape justice. Donald Trump, you will see, is an altogether different animal.

Benedict Arnold is considered the greatest traitor in American history for his attempt to almost snuff out the bright flame of the American Revolution. His betrayal was to make a conscious choice to sell the American garrison at West Point to the British in 1780. In the beginning a fierce patriot, Arnold put his life on the line many times for the birth of the nation. It would be his own ego and a desire to satisfy his comely and avaricious wife, Peggy Shippen Arnold, that would convince him that all his woes could be solved through the help of her artistic friend Major John André, chief of intelligence for the British forces in America.

As a man who came from a seafaring family in Norwich, Connecticut, Arnold committed his personal fortune to military service in the Continental Army even before there was a United States. A natural adventurer and an aggressive citizen soldier, his strong personality led him to fight alongside Ethan Allen in the Green Mountain Boys in an effort to take Fort Ticonderoga from the British and send the new Continental Army cannons to Boston.

Under the orders of George Washington, Arnold planned and executed a daring and arduous expeditionary mission to seize Quebec City, Canada, at that time the British Continental Command Center and the heart of their forces in the Americas. A daringly asymmetric attack, this force went through some of the toughest terrains on the planet and surprised the city but failed to take it. Though the mission ultimately failed, Arnold did seize the city of Montreal, challenging British supremacy in the northern frontier. Soon after leaving Canada, he created his own private naval force on Lake Champlain that seized and destroyed British forts, all the while engaging in naval actions that caused massive damage to the British navy in the battle of Valcour Island on Lake Champlain.

Arnold would join generals Philip Schuyler and Horatio Gates at the Battle of Saratoga, New York. This action was critical to stopping British general John Burgoyne's attempt to split the American colonies in two. Arnold was a daredevil officer—considered rash, bold, and explosive. At Saratoga, he took a critical counterattack that may have saved the entire battle—at a moment when he was without an actual command. Just minutes before his assault, he had been relieved of his command by General Gates, who thought him too impetuous. After Gates ordered him off the battlefield, Arnold jumped on his horse when he espied a disaster unfolding on the American flank. He rode off, took command of his former troops, and blitzed into the British flanking movement, which would have destroyed the Americans. He saw it coming! His swift action wounded him in the fight—a ball broke his leg bone—yet a maimed Arnold fought like a madman, halting the momentum of the British advance and costing adversaries to this new nation a great loss of life.

After a grueling campaign to take Quebec, he became known as the American Hannibal. He was celebrated when he returned to Philadelphia to recover from his wounds. Arnold had a warrior's heart, but he felt he wasn't sufficiently recognized for his perspicacity and valor. He was not rewarded. It was then that thoughts of treachery first entered his disillusioned mind.

Like many others who betray their nation, Arnold fell into debt: financial vulnerability and desperation often lead to risky acts. Arnold fell in love with a woman well above his station and he gained financial debts. While an adjutant general in Philadelphia, his new wife, Peggy Shippen, led him to take bribes, and he misused army materials and manpower to line his pockets. He bought an exquisite mansion, Mount Pleasant, that overlooked the Schuylkill River and kept Shippen in luxury, as befitted a general's wife.

He drained a considerable amount of his family savings to fund the Lake Champlain campaign, and then was accused and acquitted of stealing logistical supplies sent down from Quebec. As military commander in Philadelphia, he started trading in petty graft, expanding into full-blown corruption, as he usurped profits from ships that made it past the British blockade. These goods needed his official pass to get by American lines. He supplied them—for a cut of the profits. Furthermore, Arnold allegedly shook down businessmen. The most noteworthy accusation concerned the *Charming Nancy*, a ship Arnold held shares in. Arnold was on the take from a trading consortium that needed his passes to get goods from the *Charming Nancy*. When the ship could not land in Philadelphia, they asked him for military horse carts to move the private goods across British lines. Arnold agreed and was paid off, but in this case, he got caught. Arnold would later be given an insignificant military court-martial. Washington, his friend and commanding officer, was ready to overlook this bit of idle corruption to get his best officer back into the field.

Arnold, on the other hand, was offended by the very accusations. An ego of such proportions was dangerous. It was Washington's slap of the wrist, and a treacherous wife, that led him to decide he was no longer of use to America. At his wife's suggestion he contacted Major John André. Arnold used an intermediary named Joseph Stansbury to shuttle communications between himself and André through a secret code system. Mrs. Arnold would often write innocuous letters to André but include Arnold's secret code written in invisible ink.

The British had always known Americans could be bought off, particularly some egoistical officers, but neither André nor the British commander in chief in the Americas, General Sir Henry Clinton, ever considered Arnold as a potential traitor. Arnold initially demanded a payout of twenty thousand pounds or $3.5 million in modern currency. The British would eventually pay out the equivalent amount of $1 million in the end and offer an annual stipend.

It was September 1780 when Washington wanted to put Arnold back into a combat command. Now secretly a traitor, Arnold feigned a wounded leg and asked to be put in command of the critical garrison at West Point instead. Reluctantly, Washington consented. Upon arrival, Arnold started his treachery and issued deliberately conflicting repair orders, which created the illusion that new breastworks were being built while, in reality, he was deliberately weakening the garrison's defenses.

All the while, like a dutiful spy, Arnold passed on general military intelligence, including garrison and combat unit strength reports on all Continental Army activity from Georgia to Rhode Island, to the British. He sent situation reports on West Point's condition, particularly on the massive chain across the Hudson that blocked British ships. He even suggested avenues of attack to take the garrison, which he had left open. Arnold was a useful traitor, but a dangerous pitfall in spy craft is that enemy intelligence officers will eventually want to have a face-to-face meeting to validate loyalty.

On Arnold's own request, Major André arranged to meet him at the house of a man who was duped into thinking a British officer was defecting. At that same time General Clinton was moving British forces to eventually take West Point, based on Arnold's plans. However, George Washington's own spies detected Clinton's preparations to attack West Point, and he had unknowingly passed orders and warnings to the traitor. When Arnold received orders from Washington to defend West Point, he ignored them to make it easier for Clinton to win.

Arnold also provided bonus intelligence. He routinely reported Washington's personal movements around the colonies, including the size of his security detail and the names and locations of his escort units. He had hoped that the entire matter could be settled by having a British raiding party kill or capture the Virginia commander in chief. It was resolved that Washington would be captured along with West Point and most likely killed or forced to surrender the Continental Army.

As providence would have it, Major Benjamin Tallmadge, father of US military intelligence and Washington's spy chief, fortuitously arrived just hours before at the location where Major André was captured. Tallmadge instantly figured out that Arnold was a traitor at the very moment Washington was literally dining at Arnold's breakfast table. When word of the treason finally reached Washington, his only words were, "Arnold has betrayed us."

Arnold had just minutes to escape to the safety of Major André's transport, the fourteen-gun sloop HMS *Vulture*. After his defection, Arnold wrote Washington a letter declaring that he was, indeed, a traitor, a defector to the Crown—and good-bye America. Peggy Shippen, still with an angry George Washington, pretended she had been abandoned by Arnold. He magnanimously allowed Shippen and her child to cross British lines to join him.

Major André was not so fortunate. He was quickly "measured for a noose." A few years earlier in 1776, one of America's first spies, Captain Nathan Hale, was hung by the British. Washington took the loss of this fierce patriot badly, very badly. He was not in the mood to give clemency to a man who was ready to destroy the revolution. General Clinton offered a prisoner exchange, and Washington demanded Arnold's head for André's. Someone was going to die, and the father of the nation did not care which of the two it was. Clinton could not go against his word, and so André was promptly hanged on October 2, 1780, in Tappan, New York.

Several cases regarding treason arose during the American Revolution, likely as a result of Benedict Arnold's plight, and unlike many general constitutional provisions, the clause on treason was made intentionally specific to ensure every latitude was given so that the accused had to commit an act that was clear to all who observed it. Arnold's betrayal met that standard. Since the punishment for treason was death or life imprisonment, the definition served to impress the gravity of the offense. In 1788, the Constitution permitted Congress to establish the legal framework and definition for treason.

Unlike the earlier British version, which focused specifically on the betrayal of trust to the Crown, the US Constitution focused on betrayal of the nation. So, the founders narrowed the scope of treason to two areas: persons of American citizenship who chose to wage war against the United States or those who *willfully* conspired, assisted, aided, abetted, or otherwise directly helped an enemy of the United States in wartime.[5]

In *helping an enemy of the United States*, legal scholars commonly believe the US Constitution was designed to be interpreted and redefined amid changing circumstances in different eras. In the modern era, a person can commit acts that meet the legal definition without ever seeing a foreign enemy, and modern communications could aid and abet a foreign power without ever leaving one's seat at a café via email, social media, or providing material support through the spreading of disinformation or propaganda or by encouraging further acts. After 2014, the FBI and Justice Department brought a wave of indictments and convictions against citizens who sought to join the Islamic State terrorist group ISIS. As the United States was in conflict under an Authorization of Use of Military Force (AUMF), a substitute for a declaration of war, and the War Powers Acts (which allows the president to interdict imminent threats), all were not charged with treason. For example, Adam Gadahn, the American spokesman for the Al Qaeda terrorist group, was never charged but simply hunted down and killed by military action, so no tangible review of his status could be acquired.

Professor Laurence Tribe, the Carl M. Loeb Professor of Constitutional Law at Harvard University, "assumes conspiring with foreign adversaries and domestic accomplices to defraud the American people should constitute a clear case for treason, and therefore indictment." Tribe asserts that the legal barriers to the indictment of a sitting president, for the very act of treason and defrauding the government in elections that may have enabled him to attain the position in the first place, are essentially circular arguments.[6] Tribe believes that offenses that are both impeachable and criminal can, by virtue of their criminality itself, stand out as a reason for indictment. He mentions offenses that are *both* impeachable (because they constitute "Treason, Bribery, or other high Crimes and Misdemeanors," as Article II, Section 4 specifies) *and* criminal (in the sense of violating the federal criminal code), noting that "it's their criminality from the outset and not the removal of the criminally accused from office that subjects the accused to indictment."[7] History will show that, whatever the suspicion, impeachment must be invoked to remove a president from power in order to hold him criminally culpable for any charge.

America's Gallery of Traitors

Arnold was not the first of such betrayals in American history. There were always self-serving charlatans, con men, and traitors who sold the nation's honor for a pittance. Numerous other petty spies, schemers, and double-crossers have cropped up throughout America's history. Back in the American Revolution, a little-known young ensign named William McDermott of George Washington's Continental Army would defect to the British and sell the plans to Fort Washington, north of New York City, for a reward of sixty pounds.[8] Other figures had a great impact on the safety and security of the United States. Within the most secret halls of government, for example, FBI spy hunter Robert Hanssen was a man whose treachery sent numerous Russian spies working for the CIA to their deaths. I should note that those deaths involved being thrown into a furnace alive. His comrade, CIA counterintelligence officer Aldrich Ames, did the same for a small amount of cash to cover debts. Ames betrayed the agency over an eight-year period even as he was supposed to be hunting for internal double agents such as Hanssen. They were both eventually caught and sentenced to life, and the only justice will be that they will likely die in prison.

Many more have betrayed the nation for money, fame, and personal revenge, including well-known spies such as Henry Gold, Jonathan Walker Jr., and Harold Nicholson. Some even defected to the enemy's camp after their betrayals, such as Edward Lee Howard. The most recent and significant traitor to defect to Russia was Edward Snowden. Snowden started as a CIA information technology employee and used that job to gain employment at the National Security Agency (NSA). Snowden's case is a classic example of a whistleblower inadvertently dragooned into Russian service while maintaining the belief that his idea of exposing America's secrets was good for the world. Snowden first fled to China and then on to Russia, where he has found himself, since 2017, under the control of Russian intelligence, who own his apartment and maintain his daily existence. Peter Earnest, veteran CIA clandestine service officer and director emeritus at the International Spy Museum in Washington, DC, said of the significance of Snowden's defection to Russia: "This is an individual with knowledge about a major national security organization [the NSA], one Russia would love to penetrate. He's a pretty smart guy. With only a GED, he was able to secure employment with the CIA, the NSA and Booz Allen, and with it a high-level security clearance. So, he'd be a very useful resource to them."[9] Yet of all the turncoats and traitors, only Julius and Ethel Rosenberg, two avowed members of the American Communist Party who passed on the secrets of the hydrogen bomb to Russia, were tried and executed for treason during the Cold War, a conflict that did not meet the constitutional definition of war.

"Russia, if you're listening . . ."

Was the "Russia, if you're listening" speech really the first indicator that Donald Trump was going to align himself with a hostile foreign power and sell the nation's democratic foundation out to a lifelong foreign spymaster? Requesting that a foreign power use its electronic intelligence agencies to hack into the private servers of a fellow American citizen and then use the results to help him skew an election was pretty damning. But I argue in these pages that this Mayday call to Moscow is one of the least significant acts of betrayal he would later commit as president of the United States.

Trump may not have known that his interactions with Russian agents, assets, and facilitators would lead to the violation of criminal laws and the Constitution and rupture the trust of the nation—perhaps he stumbled into it. In *The Plot to Destroy Democracy* I wrote how Trump transitioned from a useful idiot to an unwitting asset. These are tradecraft terms for a person who is being used by a foreign power but is too stupid to suss it out. As John Brennan, a career intelligence professional, testified before the Senate Intelligence Committee in 2017 on the matter of the Trump-Russia investigation: "Frequently people who go along a treasonous path do not know they are on a treasonous path until it's too late."[10] But after that infamous speech, I believed he was now a witting asset—a person who knew that his actions would benefit a foreign power as well as himself and was fine with it.

Though Trump demanded that Russia release what he believed were emails that it had already stolen from Hillary Clinton, via Russia's hacks on the DNC headquarters, none actually existed. It was a religious belief of the conservative right that Clinton's emails had been hacked and were in Putin's possession. The initial source for that belief was a small obscure conspiracy theory website, believed to be a component of Russia's online disinformation network, called whatdoesitmean.com. This website, which releases carefully crafted propaganda with primarily Russian sources, claimed in a May 2016 article that Russia had indeed hacked Clinton's emails and the Kremlin was "debating" releasing twenty thousand of them. This was a fantastical story that took on a life of its own in the conservative underground until it sprouted up as a discussion point on Fox News (via the website Gateway Pundit) that same month.[11]

Unlike President Richard Nixon's orders to break into the DNC's Watergate headquarters in 1973, the Russian intelligence operation to steal emails from the Democratic Party was far more than just a political crime. It was the first direct public attack to knock down the foundations of American democracy and to damage the principles that uphold our Constitution. One could say it was the opening salvo of Web War II. Web War I was Russia's sustained attack on the Republic of Georgia, Ukraine, and other ex-communist nation states from 2000 to 2015. By stealing the emails, any emails, Russia was well aware that the US news media and Donald Trump would create a spectacle so irresistible, the keyboards of journalists and social media talkers would melt under the relentless pounding of eager fingers. Russia also had a full century of academic study and deep intelligence analysis of America's political system from the Soviet perspective. They knew that America's constitutional republicanism relied on accurate information and an informed electorate to work properly. They also knew that the rich could game the system with money. Cash could allow even the dimmest of personalities to mass-distribute whatever political propaganda could be crafted to win. Through social media, any single individual with the right amount of salacious or controversial information could be equal in influence to the *New York Times* and even provide content desired by the *Times*. Russia had also used its academia to understand that America was weak and susceptible to any external information or conspiracy theory that looked credible and found its way into the news media bloodstream. So, they tasked their spies to use social media to hack the mind-set of the American public, basing their hacking on the distrust of government agencies and discord among white men and minorities and women.

The hacking of the DNC and its aftereffects on the 2016 election are already being portrayed as the third-most significant sneak attack on the United States after Pearl Harbor and 9/11. Yet despite the fact that the fundament of the nation was being torn apart, for many, this threat would be virtually ignored or would not be believed because it came from a source other than Donald Trump's mouth. In fact, both Russia and Trump relied on global news media to make the political effects of the attack as damaging as possible. For Trump, it would catapult him to the presidency. For Russia, it would validate its carefully crafted plan to put a willing asset in the White House. The media's obsession with news related to the emails normalized Trump's often idiotic ramblings and public embrace of the Russian Federation. By the time Trump swore the oath of office in January 2017 and gave his inaugural carnage speech, his followers had come to believe that their loyalty to his love of Russia was purely patriotic, and their devotion to him superseded any loyalty to the Constitution of the United States. Such a transformation from a rabidly anti-Russian party to docile admirers in less than four years was Putin's dream come true.

CHAPTER 2

The Super Villain with a Leash

Anyone who becomes a bad guy, a run-of-the-mill villain, requires a greater villain, a super villain, to turn him—some person or cause that causes an otherwise honest man to carry out the basest and lowest of activities, including betraying other men. For Judas, it was the Pharisee Joseph ben Caiaphas, the leader who beguiled him with thirty pieces of silver to betray Jesus Christ—which guaranteed that Christ would become a historic martyr. With Benedict Arnold, it was his wife's questionable relationship with the chief of British intelligence in the colonies, the young and charming Major John André. To understand how and why Trump would betray the nation of his birth requires a quick retrospective of the Russian leader, Vladimir Vladimirovich Putin.

Putin has qualities that easily impress Trump. Over a decade it has become clear that Trump has not just been an admirer of Vladimir Putin but has even engaged in a kind of love for him, or the kind of man he represents. Trump has adored Putin for his ruthlessness and easy access to his stolen billions. This personal adoration and financial lust is precisely how many traitors are recruited to turn on their own nations.

Putin did not haplessly stumble into power—he murdered his way to it. And he has lately been handling the greatest intelligence acquisition in the history of Russia or perhaps the world: Donald J. Trump. Putin's lifelong calling has been to ruthlessly acquire information, which for him is the greatest source of power and the source of his personal strength. So he became a spy, and after that life, he applied the skills of blackmail, extortion, selective murder, and intimidation honed by his years at the KGB to neutralize businesspeople who did not comply with his orders. Blackmail and extortion, known as *kompromat,* were rife in the years before and after he took the reins of power from the corrupt and drunk Boris Yeltsin.

At the fall of the Soviet Union, Yeltsin presided over one of the largest transfers of wealth in history. Battling off a coup attempt by the hardcore communists to restore the Soviet elite back into power, he started the liquidation of Soviet government facilities and assets, which were sold in the low millions or hundreds of thousands of dollars but were worth tens of billions. From fire trucks to fighter jets, nuclear reactors to oilfields, it would all be sold off at fractions of a penny on the dollar. Soviet collective communism would be enveloped by a mafia-run blizzard of money changing hands and cocoon the nation in a chrysalis of cash, luxury goods, and death. The new government that emerged, led by Yeltsin with Putin as chief of intelligence, manifested as a form of freewheeling criminal capitalism reminiscent of the uncontrolled American gangster and mafia days in the 1930s prohibition era.

After the Soviet empire smashed itself on the rocks of capitalism, Russian society developed into four distinct classes. The top of the food chain is the elite of the elite: the leadership, a group of ex-communists who remain in power, including ex-KGB. Below them are the oligarchs and criminals or Russian mafia. They draw their power from the leadership, which gives them permission to conduct their business. The Russian leadership and the oligarchs are two sides of the same coin. The oligarchs are a middle-aged, savvier group of ex-communists who have used the mafia and their ties to the ex-KGB leadership to transform themselves into capitalist autocrats. The criminal class, just below them, does the street work of creating new lines of capital and spiriting the money out of Russia. At the bottom are the people, who are satisfied with how their lives have materially improved under the new Russian Federation, with better commerce, entertainment, and food. But they are still essentially living like they did during the Soviet era, only with better cars.

Putin transformed Russia so that the oligarchs would have access to the criminals to control business and the general population. It provided a measure of order and centralized control, with the trappings of democracy. To Putin, it was very necessary. The post-Soviet era was rife with hyperinflation scams, Ponzi schemes, and a wild money grab that led to an increase in consumerism. During this period, unscrupulous

Westerners flooded in trying to seize the media, banks, and Russian women, without any respect for Russian society and values.

In 1998, when the country underwent a market downturn, Yeltsin chose Yevgeny Primakov, the former head of Russian intelligence, as his deputy. But instead of a manager who would use the old ways to clear his boss, Yeltsin was rewarded with investigations of himself and his daughter. This would not do. What was the purpose of holding onto power if your own subordinates undermined you?

At the time Yeltsin had heard how a young ex-KGB officer, Vladimir Vladimirovich Putin, had helped St. Petersburg's mayor Anatoly Sobchak form an alliance with the criminal underclass by using strong-arm KGB tactics, which these criminals respected. Additionally, this young man, just thirty-nine years old, was loyal to Sobchak, even though the mayor was under an anticorruption investigation. Yeltsin thought that discrediting him could not be done directly, and Putin's loyalty had yet to be tested. Yeltsin brought him to Moscow and gave him control of the FSB. This agency was the successor to the old Soviet KGB—all that had changed was the first two letters and a massive new multibillion-dollar budget. Nothing else.

Putin immediately figured out he needed to be loyal to the center of power. He had to protect Yeltsin, and then, when convenient, he would step up and replace him. First, he had to stop the investigations. Putin arranged to blackmail the chief of the corruption investigation, the prosecutor general of the Russian Federation, Yuri Ilyich Skuratov. The post Skuratov filled is equivalent to US attorney general. He had risen to fame by exposing a former Soviet slush fund called FIMACO (Financial Management Company), where as much as $50 billion of Soviet state cash was being hidden offshore in an account in Jersey, one of the Channel Islands off the UK coast, in case the Communist Party was ousted from power.

Yeltsin was under siege by Skuratov, and it took the young spymaster Putin to save his bacon. During the Skuratov prosecutions, a videotape was splashed over every Russian TV channel exposing a man who appeared to be the prosecutor in a ménage à trois with two prostitutes. To put the nail in the coffin, the soft-spoken and rarely seen Putin even appeared on national television to hold a press conference confirming that the FSB had identified Skuratov as the man in the video. Skuratov quickly resigned, and the investigations were stopped.[1] This allowed Yeltsin to fire Primakov. The young Putin was installed as the prime minister, just one step below Yeltsin.

Yeltsin stepped down as Russia's leader on December 31, 1999, and Putin was named interim president. Soon after he became president, Putin pardoned Yeltsin and immunized him from all forms of prosecution or investigation. This chaotic chapter of Russian history, during which Soviet communism struggled to evolve into a fledgling democracy, closed with the country reverting to a Stalin-like autocracy.

Soon after assuming the presidency, the formerly quiet Putin suddenly became a raging firebrand against terrorism when four apartment buildings in greater Moscow were bombed in 1999, killing 293. Putin ordered the Russian army to invade Chechnya in order to punish the supposed attackers' base of operations. Evidence would soon surface that the FSB might have carried out these bombings itself when alert residents and police caught a team of FSB officers planting hexogen high explosives in an apartment block. FSB claimed it was a training exercise, but the hundreds of pounds of explosives were real military-grade blocks. The incident was soon forgotten as the Russian population bought the propaganda from a solidifying dictatorship.

A new Putin had emerged. He adopted the visage of a stalwart avenging KGB officer and tough-acting demagogue determined to crush Chechnya and terrorism in Russia. Within Russia, his anti-US stance was also admired. Alexander Dugin, a former communist turned fascist philosopher, would discuss this period in a 2016 YouTube video where he said, "In Russia, pro-American forces almost openly dominated in the 1990s, and only in the 2000s did Putin begin to push aside their authority little by little."[2]

Conservative American politicians in the post 9/11 world also admired his "kill them all" attitude in Chechnya. In 2002, two major acts of terrorism gave Putin his own 9/11, providing further opportunities for him to feign strength in the face of terrorism, while increasing and consolidating his power. Chechen Islamic extremist terrorists seized the Dubrovka Theater in Moscow and executed what counterterrorism professionals call a suicide hostage barricade operation. During the siege, the terrorists held TV interviews. They made it clear they had the capacity to blow up the theater and kill all the hostages. In response, Putin authorized an attack that allowed the Russian special forces, the Spetsnaz, an alpha counterterrorism unit, to use a highly lethal knockout gas to overpower the terrorists. However, this unusual method of attack resulted in the death of 202 hostages by the gas. Only four hostages were killed at the hands of the terrorists.

Two years later Chechen terrorists would lay siege to a school in the Russian village of Beslan and conduct another suicide hostage barricade. They took over 1,100 hostages, mainly parents and 777 children attending the first day of a school celebration. Putin ordered the army to assault the compound, even though it was clear suicide explosives were rigged everywhere. Bizarre tactics were used, including having tanks fire their main guns directly into buildings without regard to the safety of the hostages. In the end, the massacre at the school would kill 334 parents and 138 children, most of whom burned to death after the army forbade that fires they had started be extinguished.

Putin's utter ruthlessness was widely admired by American conservatives. As a counterterrorism professional studying these incidents, I often spoke to US Army Special Forces team members, Navy SEALs, and FBI agents while practicing at the Quantico Shooting Club and found many had starry-eyed admiration for how the Russians had crushed the terrorists without regard for loss of innocent life. They would all talk about the horrible massacre at Beslan and how the Russians did not care for anything other than "killing the tangos," a euphemism for terrorists. A number of military and police "experts" launched new careers by lecturing around the country at conservative forums about the two hostage barricades at Beslan. The consensus from these peers was that America needed to be equally as ruthless. To many American conservatives, Putin's resolve was a sign of a leader they could follow.

Murder Inc.: The New SMERSH Campaign

One aspect of Putin's psyche was that he demanded unwavering loyalty from his subordinates, particularly those in the intelligence community. He reestablished a secret ritualistic punishment routine that had operated during World War I called SMERSH. SMERSH was an acronym coined by Joseph Stalin for an umbrella organzation of three counter-intelligence agencies of the Red Army. Its motto was "Death to spies." During the war, SMERSH troops caught Nazis and their collaborators. The James Bond movie *From Russia with Love* popularized the KGB-era activities of SMERSH. By the time of Putin's reign, the organization had long been disbanded—or had it been? In 2006, when Putin signed a law legalizing targeted killings abroad by his intelligence agencies and military forces, he reactivated an assassination unit, name unknown, that essentially was SMERSH. The unit's goal was to hunt people Putin considered to be traitors, and its hallmark would be high-profile public killings using the worst weapon possible—death by poison.

Putin was not shy about assassinating anyone who criticized or investigated too closely. One such person was Anna Politkovskaya, a journalist, who investigated and criticized the government. She was shot four times just as she stepped out of an elevator—a literal kill box—in her apartment building. The alleged killers, who were supposed to be Chechen terrorists, turned out to be FSB officers and their relatives. None of them was brought to justice, and several politicians who investigated the Moscow apartment bombings were killed as well. The nouveau SMERSH unit was busy.

Political enemies also drew the attention of Putin's assassins. On February 27, 2015, Boris Nemtsov, a longtime opponent of Putin, was shot dead in front of the Kremlin. In an area blanketed with video cameras and police, Nemtsov was conveniently murdered behind a truck that had been strategically parked to block all views of the murder.

Former spies who committed treason held a particular place in the mind of Putin. As a KGB man, he expected 100 percent unwavering loyalty to the state—treason equaled death, without any statute of limitations. Putin said precisely that in 2018: "Traitors will kick the bucket . . . Trust me. These people betrayed their friends, their brothers in arms. Whatever they got in exchange for it, those thirty pieces silver they were given, they will choke on them."[3]

Alexander Litvinenko is a former FSB agent who moved on from fighting the Russian mafia to becoming a popular author who criticized Putin's regime. He wrote a book, *Blowing Up Russia: Terror from Within,* that accused Putin of using the FSB to blow up the Moscow apartments. He was noteworthy for his handsome good looks and television appeal. Apparently, this book and another on the Russian government's control of the mafia were a step too far. Enter SMERSH.

On November 21, 2006, Litvinenko, then living in London, had dinner with Andrey Lugovoy and Dmitri Kolton, two former KGB officers turned private security contractors. At some point, Litvinenko drank a cup of tea, which he was unaware was laced with the highly radioactive nuclide polonium-210. Within days he became violently ill and showed signs of radiation poisoning. He died soon afterward. A British investigation revealed the identity of the poison, an isotope traced back to a Russian nuclear weapons reactor. It was the first deliberate polonium poisoning in history.

Roman Tsepov, a Russian billionaire and former friend of Putin, would also be served poisoned tea during an interview at an FSB office, which led to radiation sickness and death. The poison was likely the same polonium-210. The Kremlin immediately launched an information warfare operation designed to diminish the stature of the victim. "He's a nobody," Putin said in a press conference. He also said he was a man of "low intellect." This insult is also, ironically, one of Donald Trump's favorite phrases.

The Russian state fought Britain at every step to ensure that the killers escaped justice. In fact, Lugovoy was later elected to the Russian state parliament, the Duma, and was hailed as a national hero. This act-reward cycle became part of Putin's intelligence apparatus, a not-so-subtle strategy that made clear to FSB officers that, no matter how much of an abject failure they had been, they would fall under his *krysha* and be given rewards and notoriety—as long as they remained loyal state security officers. In Russia, a person of influence like a major politician or criminal who provides protection is called *krysha*, which means "roof." He repeated this cycle with the comely Anna Chapman, a Russian clandestine service officer living as an "illegal" spy. She was arrested with nine others in the United States. Instead of disgrace, she would go on to become a famous fashion model, TV commentator, and member of the Russian Duma.

Putin's favored murder techniques are literally medieval. He prefers two weapons almost exclusively. If you are a low-value nuisance, you are shot to death. If you are a high-value enemy or a traitor to the state, you get exotically poisoned. In Putin's own words, he warned, "Those who serve us with poison will eventually swallow it and poison themselves."[4] The choice of poison is designed to send a signal that it is the state selecting its most insidious methods to kill you. Some potions act quickly and without warning, while many give the appearance of death by natural causes, such as a heart attack.

Serving poisoned tea and dusting telephone handles and doorknobs with radioactive powders or nerve agents are Putin's specialty. Sergei Skripal, an intelligence officer with the GRU (the Russian military intelligence agency), was exchanged in a spy swap after committing espionage for the West. He settled in Salisbury, England. His daughter, Yulia, continued to travel back and forth to Russia. Putin ordered the most toxic of all Russian nerve agents, Novichok, to be put on a door handle in an effort to kill them both. They were sickened along with twenty-six others but recovered due to rapid medical intervention. Unfortunately, the crystal perfume bottle that was used to bring the poison into the United States was found by two people in Amesbury, United Kingdom: one woman who tested the perfume died of exposure to the nerve agent; another man was sickened.

In 2008 Putin allowed the election of his deputy Dmitri Medvedev to act as a national fig leaf for a shadow third term. For four years Putin consolidated control of the nation and launched his first cultural inroads into American conservatism by sending emissaries to the evangelical community and offering to host conferences on the defense of Christianity, hosted by evangelical megachurch leader Franklin Graham. The FSB was starting to lay out plans for infiltrating the National Rifle Association (NRA) as well. Soon after Putin's reelection in 2012, the Duma adopted laws that limit freedom of speech, curtailing people's ability to organize in protest. Vladimir Vladimirovich Putin, son of Soviet navy sailor Vladimir Spiridonovich Putin, the grandson of Spiridon Putin, cook to both Vladimir Ilyich Lenin and Josef Stalin, would now rule Russia as a single unchallenged leader.

Putin's greatest obstacle to reestablishing Russia as an economic superpower was the nation he had spent his whole life spying on: the United States of America. He had spent his youth confronting America and its European allies in the shadows of the Cold War when he was assigned to a KGB outpost in East Germany, but his decades of dedication to the Supreme Soviet, the legislative bodies of the USSR, fell apart when the nation eventually failed. Still, the successor spy agency, the FSB, where he worked his way to be its director under Yeltsin, could serve the exact same goals the communists desired—to make Russia a dominant power and eclipse America by doing this—yet would require an asymmetric view of the task.

Direct confrontation with America was a fool's game. But now his spy agency had billions in Western-supplied money, intelligence, will, and loyal spies at his command. Eventually, he would learn a lesson that would change the world: with modern Internet technology he discovered that one did not need to overthrow governments with invasions; one could simply make them welcome your invasion by convincing them it was in their interest. His chief of armed forces, General Valery Gerasimov, understood that in the information age, entire nations could be made to believe what another foreign leader told them, and they could be led to ignore their own country's leadership. Gerasimov had said that "the opposing side [is] to be deprived of its actual sovereignty without the state's territory being seized."[5] How? The other side will convince them to give up their sovereignty. Social media and the Internet had finally reached a point of impact such that America could be invaded by an insider threat of its own making. Russian propaganda could now enter America as legitimate news and convince the unwitting and the lazy to surrender themselves because the Internet says it is a good idea. Once a certain critical mass of gullible people believe something, they will adopt the idea as their own and think it was always brilliant and true.

Gerasimov was correct. Why try the command codes of the enemy's atomic bombs when you can control the people and influence them to choose a Moscow-friendly leader? It would prove to be the Trojan horse of the information age.

In America, the Russians' target population would be the Republican Party. Conservatives were always considered self-serving and susceptible to autocrats and would fall in line with a leader. Former KGB officer Yuri Bezmenov lectured the West on the types of people the KGB recruited. Bezmenov's famous quote about how the KGB instructed him offers a look at how conservatives were preferred recruits for spies: "Try to get into established conservative media with a large circulation, reach filthy rich movie makers, intellectuals, so-called academic circles, cynical egocentric people who can look into your eyes with angelic expression and tell you a lie. These are the most recruitable people, people who lack moral principles who are either too greedy or suffer from self-importance. They feel they matter a lot. These are the people the KGB wanted to recruit." The Russian intelligence officers were wary of liberals, socialists, and, worst of all, other communists. Bezmenov said that idealistically minded leftists were not to be recruited or used because "when they become disillusioned, they become your worst enemies."

If Putin could neutralize or even influence the conservatives who were publicly aligning with him, he would make Russia great again. He was good at convincing people to work against their own best interest. It was a skill he had learned as a novice spy in Dresden, East Germany.

Vladimir Vladimirovich: The Baby Spy

Putin's service and time in Dresden working for the KGB as a covert recruiter was a defining period for both his outlook on the Western world and where he first learned to organize intelligence activities and manipulate human failings. Dresden allowed him to practice his ability to identify and cultivate unwitting people. The skills he learned to influence and exploit others were a staple of his training at the Yuri Andropov Red Banner Institute in Moscow a few years earlier (now the Academy of Intelligence or SVR Academy). He had access to multiple sources of human intelligence from the First Directorate of the KGB, the KGB Third Directorate for counterintelligence, the GRU, the HVA (foreign intelligence agency of the German Democratic Republic [GDR]), and the Stasi—the feared GDR Ministry of State Security. Additionally, the Dresden regional district commanding officer, the *residentura,* had direct access to the local police or *volkspolitzei,* who would walk in with information about

Westerners, West German students, businessmen, or others who were found at the train station or crossing the border visiting their relatives in the east. The local cops allowed them to collect potential spies through people with legitimate reasons to be in the east but who respected and did not suspect the local police like they did the Stasi. The KGB Dresden office would have police bring them to the station, and there they would be processed and promised rewards or threatened with punishments.

Dr. Douglas Selvage is a historian, scholar, and international expert on the Stasi and the KGB. He said that one of the KGB's favorite tactics was to use the Stasi and *volkspolitzei* to find a Westerner who had an East German girlfriend. The girl would be pressured, out of national loyalty, to recruit her boyfriend. He would then be handed off to the KGB for development. Most of these activities took place at police stations or at a Stasi remand prison in Dresden, which was located on Bautzner Straße in the northeast residential district across the River Elbe. A former Stalinist secret police (NKVD) and KGB prison, the building was notorious to the locals.

A short walk away is 4 Angelikastraße, the former KGB headquarters where Putin worked from 1985 to 1989 as a young agent. The street was named after nineteenth-century painter Angelika Kauffmann. Located in the Radeberger Vorstadt neighborhood, the three-story villa was owned, before the end of World War II, by the family of Austrian actor Karlheinz Böhm. The KGB later confiscated the house from the Böhms.

Angelikastraße is now a beautiful, elegant tree-lined street, and the former KGB office has become the Rudolf Steiner House, the home of a German society celebrating Steiner, the famous Austrian philosopher and author, who founded the esoteric philosophy of anthroposophy, or the spiritual study of human wisdom. Steiner's thought was to use the scientific method to extend into spiritual development. Steiner eschewed central authority and sought to instruct each of his followers to break free of even his authority through rational thinking and developing the human imagination and expression as a form of self-rationalization. It's ironic that the KGB, the global enforcers of centralized authority and crushing the human spirit, would have preceded his organization in this villa.

The mission Putin performed at Angelikastraße allowed him to recruit top officials, compromise certain Westerners, and gain favor with key people. In Putin's own words in an interview, only "very special people, with special qualities, and special convictions and special character" were suitable for the work of developing human targets and turning them into traitors.

Sources about Putin's time as a junior operative vary. As a low-ranking officer, he would have been delegated to menial tasks—bringing up coffee and doing the tedious fieldwork that senior agents often don't like to do themselves, such as keeping records, maintaining spy networks, and keeping top KGB and Stasi officials informed of their basic operations. Otherwise, it was a full-time job developing human capital for manipulation. From the beautiful neighborhood where Angelikastraße was located, Putin had a lovely workspace with which to do just that, and it did not hurt having a KGB/Stasi prison and torture center across the street.

Putin's time in Dresden was tracked by Stasi researchers who in 2018 found his entry ID card for the headquarters. During his time in Dresden, he cultivated these skills and abilities, through his craft as well as his contacts and access to information, by virtue of his post. A big part of this was learning about potential recruits, as well as adversaries, and how to influence, compromise, or exploit them. Putin's time there, including the formative period of the collapse of both the GDR, which reintegrated East Germany and West Germany into one reunified country, allowed him to realize that his own motherland, the Soviet Union, would collapse of its own weight. History could not save the communist Soviets. It was corrupt and centralized, and the Russian people wanted to throw it off and adopt a more Western lifestyle. The fall of his own command structure and the realization that his East German friends had now technically become capitalist enemies must have been hard to take. The loss of his entire world was difficult and would come to shape his outlook and approach to the Western world.

Putin had particularly useful access to information through his position, which he used to his advantage. In Dresden, these assets worked for Major General Horst Böhm, the last German to serve as regional director of the Stasi. According to Dr. Selvage, both the German Stasi and the KGB resident in charge of East Germany kept a master list of all persons who were agents and assets or who had the slightest contact with all the allied agencies, including the KGB, HVA, GRU, and *politzei.*

All these people could be blackmailed and developed. As the GDR collapsed, Putin retrieved this master list of Westerners and East Germans who were essentially blackmailable as they could be revealed as former foreign spies. Recall that the Stasi managed over 102,000 *inoffizielle Mitarbeiter* or unofficial informants; almost 2 percent of the population was informing on their neighbors. For example, according to his former colleague Usolzev, Putin downplayed what he intended to do on return to Russia by telling peers he was going to lead a humble life. "He had prepared things to make a living as a taxi driver in Leningrad, and suddenly, we saw him become the mayor of the city." A master copy of the file containing all the contacts of the joint intelligence agencies was kept in the Stasi regional offices. Putin was able to steal and retain the list to use privately for his own ends, including to gain favor with Boris Yeltsin.

Russia, in whatever form, would always need a spymaster.

Some believe that Putin saw the post-Nazi cultural strictness of the fascists-turned-communists as a model for how a nation could be controlled from a centralized party but still function with ruthless efficiency. Putin supposedly "internalized" the political model of the GDR and adopted it to what would become the Russian Federation—top-down leadership, capitalist fundaments, and one authoritarian party. Everything else, like press freedoms, democracy, and liberty, would be window dressing. Literally, a Potemkin village would mask the true leader's dictatorial authority. The exercise of centralized, inflexible power as a means for the survival of the state, maintaining its influence and strength, became part of Putin's "strategic DNA."[6]

The Soviet Union, where Putin was born, had strict systemic control over the daily lives of every person. He believed it somehow gave him purpose, which is why as a teen he asked KGB officers how he could join. As previously stated, they advised that he attend university and become a lawyer. Again, he did just that. He understood there was a need for a consumerist society—everyone wanted better quality clothes, cars, and food—but as the son of the chef for Stalin, he admired the KGB's willingness to get the job done, no matter what the cost in human lives. Unlike the West, human rights and humanity itself in Russia were consumables. People needed to die for the common good, be it mafia control, businessman intimidation, or by mass-starving an entire people. If millions were to die—as Stalin had done to his own army or by deliberately causing a famine in Ukraine while stealing the Ukrainians' harvest to give elsewhere—that, to Putin, was just a numbers game played out in pencil and paper.

The Western mind cannot fathom how casually and unimaginatively Russia will kill people or allow people to be killed. It's like running a chicken-processing plant; some of the stock is bound to die. So long as the media is controlled and the deaths are not personalized, it does not pay to name all the farm animals slaughtered.

ALTHOUGH PUTIN MAY NOT necessarily want to resurrect the Soviet Union, he does want to regain its lost importance—and restore the Russian people's pride in their country, often motivated all the more in response to the humiliation of its loss of former relevance and influence after the fall of the GDR and wider Soviet world system.

To effect the autocracy he wanted, he would have to unify the widely diverse groups that had sprung up all over the Russian Federation after the fall of the Soviet Union. He formed a new party called Yedinaya Rossiya, United Russia. According to Russian sources, though often filled with propaganda, this is likely true: there are more than 2.2 million members in Putin's United Russia Party, the ruling alt-right party of Russia.[7] Led by Russian prime minister Dimitry Medvedev, the party was behind the effort to reinvent a new Russia, which was anti-globalist, anti-NATO, and anti-UN and fully supported by Putin.

THE RUSSIAN "KID CHARLEMAGNE"

Putin not only sees himself as a version of Russia's new Peter the Great but has made moves more akin to Charlemagne, the eighth-century unifier of Christian Europe. In his 2013 state of the union address, he put forth a vision designed to not only appeal to the Orthodox Russian congregation but to white, Western Christian conservatives and evangelicals around the world. Putin was recognized as the angelic champion of

Christianity's culture, which he saw as being persecuted. In a speech on December 13, 2013, Putin laid the way for evangelicals and conservatives to see him as the international leader of conservative values:

> Today, many nations are revising their moral values and ethical norms, eroding ethnic traditions and differences between peoples and cultures. Society is now required not only to recognize everyone's right to the freedom of consciousness, political views, and privacy but also to accept without question the equality of good and evil, strange as it seems, concepts that are opposite in meaning. This destruction of traditional values from above not only leads to negative consequences for society but is also essentially anti-democratic, since it is carried out on the basis of abstract, speculative ideas, contrary to the will of the majority, which does not accept the changes occurring or the proposed revision of values.
>
> We know that there are more and more people in the world who support our position on defending traditional values that have made up the spiritual and moral foundation of civilization in every nation for thousands of years: the values of traditional families, real human life, including religious life, not just material existence but also spirituality, the values of humanism and global diversity.[8]

Putin, with the Russian Orthodox Church patriarchy, would put forward a template to unite a new, conservative Europe under a Christian banner. America could come along too. He set his spymasters to develop an intelligence operation to bring the Americans along by making common cause with ideological soul mates across the Atlantic.

A New Anti-Western Russia

"Starting from about 1989, we completely reoriented toward the West. We looked at them as a future paradise. We expected that once we had done all that they demanded, we'd dance for them and they would finally hug and kiss us, and we would merge in ecstasy," said Evgeny Tarlo, a member of Russia's upper house of parliament, on a Russian talk show in 2018. "Instead," he said, "the West has . . . been trying to destroy Russia."[9]

Russia banned high school exchanges in the FLEX (Future Leaders Exchange) scholarship program. Run by the US State Department, it was suspended by Moscow after one child decided to stay in the United States with a gay couple.[10] Then American businesses operating in Russia began encountering hatred. For example, the animosity for the West forced McDonald's restaurants to advertise that its food was "made in Russia, for Russians."[11]

In 2009 things changed in a remarkably negative way with the election of President Barack Obama. The first African American to occupy the White House seemed to immediately drive Russia insane. Obama was a traditionalist and a constitutional scholar and desired most of all to maintain the traditional pillars of presidential power and act as a stalwart steward of American dominance worldwide. He maintained all the positions of the previous US presidents and took a harder line on Russia. Like all presidents before him, Obama was a realpolitik player who made sound decisions based on the best assessments of the intelligence community and scholars and his observations based on his experience as a Harvard-trained lawyer. He had a keen mind when it came to understanding Russia, and he quickly learned that the political and economic intelligence was true: Russia was a threat. Obama's moderate view of the world, and his naïve belief that perhaps the space filler, Russian premier Medvedev, could be molded into an anti-Putin, made him want to come to an accommodation. American conservatives held the same views of Obama that the Russians held. This gave them a commonality that would bind them by 2016.

In Russia, race hatred toward Obama was insane: pictures of Obama eating a banana were shown on All Russia State TV, which reaches 90 percent of its population. Powerful Putin-driven antagonism against the United States began to resurface, a Russian hatred that exceeded that of the Cold War. On a popular talk show on the state-run First Channel, Sergey Mikheev, director of the Kremlin-allied Center for Current Politics, told the show's host that "the United States is experimenting geopolitically, using people like guinea pigs. . . . They treat us all in the same way, threatening not only world stability but the existence of every human being on the planet."[12]

Obama sincerely tried to use all the political and diplomatic power at his disposal to come to an understanding with Russia but not allow them to run rampant. When he offered a concession, his hand would be slapped away. Putin had no interest in Obama. Putin would change Russia's direction and orient it to undermining the Black Plague that was the Obama administration.

Obama's secretary of state was his vanquished opponent, Hillary Rodham Clinton. She had spent decades in and around the White House and had a clear sense that Putin and his oligarchical cronies were not supporters of freedom and liberty. When it came to America and its European allies, Putin was hard at work dismantling democracy.

Clinton saw Putin and the Kremlin for what they were: mischief makers across Europe. She took a hard line on their attempts to undermine the transatlantic alliance, a position Trump, sadly, would work to dismantle in Putin's name just eight years later. Like Obama's good works, Clinton's legacy toward diplomacy and democracy would be smashed out of misogyny and spite.

Operation Grizzly Steppe

It was during the period starting in 2010–2012 that Vladimir Putin was somehow impressed by Donald Trump. Perhaps it was because the TV show *The Apprentice* was a major hit in Russia. Trump was admired by many of the oligarchs, most notably billionaire Aras Agalarov. His son Emin was a popstar who got Trump to do his classic "you're fired" line in his Russian music video. The CIA and FBI would later call the Russian influence operation to elect Trump president by the code name Grizzly Steppe. This mission had several phases, but the first was to exercise influence on American politicians.

As noted earlier, the first person to encourage Donald Trump to run for president was Konstantine Rykov. It was Putin himself who later noted he personally endorsed Trump as US president. In one interview with RIA Novosti, Russia's international news agency, Putin remarked:

"We don't know for sure how it will be after the elections. . . . We don't know whether the presidential candidate Trump will be implementing his intentions, how far will he go in cooperating with us; or whether Mrs. Clinton, if she becomes president, will implement her threats and her harsh rhetoric about Russia."[13]

With this interview Putin balanced his hatred for Hillary Clinton with soft words toward Trump. It was a subtle way of revealing his hand to his preferred candidate. With a Moscow-backed candidate, political influence missions would have to be done in such a subtle way. Putin's United Russia Party could not just come in as an ally to the Republican Party, as it had done in Europe. Moscow would have to use covert intelligence operations to ensure any chance of success. To lead the way, the party increased its information warfare operations, and extremism was mainstreamed.

The Russians had been studying American society for almost one hundred years. They only had six months, from the beginning of 2013, to establish Kremlin agents of influence in or near Donald Trump's camp. The team working the NRA would be tasked to get closer to Trump and shape his message through that group. Alexander Torshin and Maria Butina were already nearing their peak influence on the NRA leadership and had gained access to Trump's son, Donald Trump Jr., an avid shooter of defenseless animals. But the young "liaison officer" assigned to Trump was a very attractive dark-haired woman named Julia Alferova, ex-wife of oligarch Artem Klyshin. Her public job was assisting Trump in getting Miss Universe running, but the details of her day-to-day work are virtually unknown. In July 2013 Trump held his planning meeting in Las Vegas for the November pageant.

Phase I: Rig the 2016 Election

The nature of the operation would be to set up a massive network of coordinating right-wing groups from around the world that would assist with the dissemination of material produced by Russian intelligence. The initial thefts of data would be handled by the cyber bears of the FSB, the GRU, and the Special Communications and Information

Service-Russian Federation (SCIS-RF)— the Russian version of the NSA. Using information acquired through all means of *active measures,* including *kompromat* (blackmail), forgeries, fake news stories, and numerous other forms of media manipulation, the Kremlin would blitz the American and European news media machine, which would lap up every word as true until proven false. It would be the single greatest manipulation since Mao Tse Tung launched the great Cultural Revolution—a billion Europeans and Americans would be bombarded with the "truth" as Vladimir Putin's intelligence agencies saw it. They would be fed so many lies that the truth would become flexible.

Russia used citizens from a variety of professions to identify, cultivate, and eventually recruit unwitting assets who could pass on useful information to the state. They recruited Russian academics, writers, journalists, diplomats, entertainers, and businessmen to meet their US counterparts, impress them with their proximity to the Russian leadership, and place them in positions where these US citizens would feel they were playing a valuable role in the geopolitical stalemate between the East and West.

These were old strategies from the Cold War: to insinuate their intelligence operations the KGB helped in preparing academic conferences aimed at promoting policies favored by the Kremlin. During the Cold War, the KGB and the International Department of the Central Committee of the Communist Party of the Soviet Union would select foreign participants who could lend credibility to the aim of the conference. They used the credibility of the Western participants to pollinate their interests in places where they would otherwise be shunned. Nothing was left to chance as even the topics would be picked and guided by the International Department, but it would be considered an academic and diplomatic effort. Back then no one was fooled because the Soviet Union's propaganda efforts were its only tool.

The USSR also stole information on science and technology operations from academic conferences and computers. The Soviet Union's active measures and human exploitation techniques were deployed to manipulate the markets or other economic targets to benefit the USSR. This included the use of disinformation fed to financial experts, hopefully resulting in a gain for the Soviet Union. However, this effort didn't always succeed because the Soviet Union was so isolated from the global markets.

Today, however, the Russian Federation has money, weapons, and oil as tools to establish its credibility, as well as the previous human influence strategies, which are all used to influence political and economic policies. Not only has the current Russian intelligence apparatus used the same methodologies to steal secrets from developers and engineers around the world, it has also sought to deploy disinformation campaigns with the goal of misleading adversaries about Russian science and technology development, and to damage or hinder the progress or relationships around scientific development for its adversaries, including the United States and Western Europe.[14]

Phase II: Recruit Unwitting Assets

To execute Russia's goal to damage American democracy, Putin ordered his intelligence agencies to launch a massive active measures campaign against the United States. Electronic social media landscaping was never enough, and to an old spy like Putin, he was more adept at using human intelligence and personal influence operations. No spymaster relies completely on faceless people behind computer screens to carry out the most sensitive intelligence operations. From the very start, Putin realized he would need to use prestige and class to manipulate Trump. Trump's ego and desire for luxury presented an easy mark. For a principal contact Putin would use his ambassador to the United States, Sergey Kislyak. From 1981 to 1984, Kislyak was the second secretary of the Permanent Mission of the USSR to the United Nations in New York. Kislyak has held many diplomatic positions since then in Russia and abroad and in 2008 became ambassador to the United States. Like all senior Soviet and now Russian Federation diplomats, American intelligence believed that the role of these foreign ministry officers was to facilitate the identification and recruitment of potential assets or spies.

One of the first campaign contacts occurred on December 2, 2015, when former general Michael Flynn went to Kislyak's residence in Washington, DC. In an interview with *The New Yorker*, Flynn said he knew

Russian US ambassador Kislyak from his "days at DIA." Kislyak was known throughout the intelligence community as one of the chief intelligence collectors in the United States, and Flynn should have known that.[15]

This meeting was arranged by Flynn and attended by his son Michael Flynn Jr. It was described as "very productive"—but to what end? This was a year before the election, and already the Trump team had made a major overture to Moscow.[16] To Putin, this meeting would be seen as coming to kiss the Kremlin ring and receive blessings. A week later Flynn traveled to Russia to sit at the right hand of Vladimir Putin and receive a payment of $42,000 from RT (Russia Today), the state-sponsored Russian television network, for a speech delivered at RT's tenth anniversary gala. To Flynn, it was just dinner and a speech. According to a former Czech foreign minister, Putin and Flynn just exchanged pleasantries: "How are you? Good. What's new?" But the point isn't what was discussed; it's the image shown to the world. To the average Russian, it would look as if Flynn was under Putin's protection, under his *krysha*, that Putin had turned the former head of American military intelligence. It was not true, but as you'll see in chapter 3, optics are everything in television.

Other strategic tasks reveal the objective of the Russian campaigns. In the past, an agent would be tasked to surface forgeries into a news stream via a trusted source or unwitting asset. In the digital age, this would be done with propped-up websites, blogs, or social media outlets. An example of this was the use of digital cutouts like WikiLeaks, DC Leaks, or Guccifer 2.0. Such outlets would draw attention from the news and exploit the viral nature of social media platforms to spread disinformation. Journalists eager to get scoops were easy targets for spreading disinformation and rumor milling, especially as the confines of journalistic ethics gave way to citizen bloggers and those who sought newfound celebrity on social media platforms.

Using these methods, Russia, in 2016, would dominate the global market in government destabilization and information manipulation. Donald Trump would be Russia's crowning achievement. Russian operatives would help him with a broad, deep, and wide-ranging cyberwarfare operation that would tilt an election in America and start the breakup of its foundations. They would use government intelligence agencies, military units, and private intelligence contractors. The point group would be run by Yevgeny Prigozhin, a Moscow restaurateur.

In 2013 Prigozhin would organize and finance the Internet Research Agency (IRA), a Russian intelligence subcontractor troll farm. The task of the IRA was to deeply data-mine the relationships and accounts of American citizens and create propaganda that was personally crafted for the individual Facebook, Twitter, or Instagram user. Prigozhin was the same chef who won a government contract to provide healthy meals for schoolchildren in Moscow but allegedly served them rotten leftover food from his restaurants. His IRA network would come online in 2014 specifically to change the perceptions of Donald Trump in the eyes of the American public.

In the past operations of *kompromat,* wiretaps, photographs, and video were used to create compromising materials that could be used to embarrass a target publicly via newspapers or passed to officials to ruin the target's reputation. In the digital arena, this would evolve to email dumps, videos published to websites, and digital cutouts. Even if the materials were not specifically embarrassing, leaking emails and then engaging in a campaign to accuse the target of malfeasance was sufficient to stir a scandal. Moscow would see to that. For this aspect of the intelligence operation, there would be a series of "dangles": bait—some new, some old—that no potential asset could resist. The goal of these dangles was to co-opt the assistance of Trump and his campaign. Putin would certainly not forget Trump's avaricious children. Still, it would not be a walk in the park with the pooch. But if there was one thing Putin was adept at from his days in Dresden, it was keeping a tight leash on the subjects he handled and bringing them to heel for Moscow.

CHAPTER 3

Trump: The Dog to Be Walked

He may talk like an idiot and look like an idiot.
But don't let that fool you. He really is an idiot.

—Groucho Marx, *Duck Soup*, 1933

Donald Trump most likely came onto the KGB radar officially in 1977 during his relationship and subsequent marriage to his first wife, Ivana *née* Zelníčková. At the time, the country she came from was called Czechoslovakia. This small nation was formed in 1918 at the end of World War I when its Czech and Slovak populations declared independence from the collapsed Austro-Hungarian Empire. Czechoslovakia was invaded by Nazi Germany in 1939, and like much of Eastern Europe, it was "liberated" by the Soviet Union, which then drove it directly into an alliance of communist dictatorships under the umbrella of its anti-NATO organization, the Warsaw Pact. From 1945 to 1992, it operated as a communist dictatorship. For one small moment, the Czechoslovakian people revolted and attempted to embrace democracy in 1968 in what was popularly dubbed the Prague Spring. This rebellion was ruthlessly crushed when the Russians and other Warsaw Pact nations invaded with overwhelming military force and arrested all the planners. The nation would remain occupied until the fall of the Soviet Union in 1989. Until then, it was under the watchful eye of the KGB, which controlled the Czech intelligence agency, the Státní bezpečnost (StB).

Luke Harding, an investigative reporter for the *Guardian*, uncovered a treasure trove of data that indicates Trump popped onto the radar of the Soviet Union's KGB when the StB reported extensively on Trump's relationship with Ivana. She met Trump in 1976 in New York City, while modeling for a skiing event. At the time she was living in Montreal, Canada, with a boyfriend, after having divorced her Austrian husband, Alfred Winklmayr. Her marriage to Winklmayr had enabled her to obtain Austrian citizenship and leave Czechoslovakia without defecting, eventually migrating to Canada.

Donald and Ivana married in 1977 in a high-society wedding. However, Ivana was still a Czech citizen whose family was behind the Iron Curtain, and her movements, activities, and relationships continued to be tracked and duly reported to the StB. In 1997, Czech intelligence files from the communist era were declassified.[1] They give a highly detailed picture of how intimate family information went from Trump to Ivana, to her family, to the StB, and then to the archives of the KGB. The operation was carried out in Zlín, Ivana's hometown. Who do you think was the primary source of information being passed to the StB and by extension the KGB? Ivana's father, Miloš Zelníček.[2]

Of course, information like this would have been rudimentary and of little interest to the Czechs themselves, but when cultivating a potential asset, every piece of data is important. For example, the number of children a couple has speaks to the health of the relationship; the amount of travel informs as to the level of wealth. The family's hatred or love of the target identifies the approach, if any, by which to recruit family members to spy. All information on the Trumps had great value to an intelligence apparatus. In an article entitled "Czechoslovakia Ramped Up Spying on Trump in Late 1980s, Seeking US intel," Harding encapsulated in one sentence what a trained intelligence officer such as CIA director John Brennan, MI6 officer Christopher Steele, me, or any number of intelligence professionals could see: Trump was a bauble to be picked up and kept in the pocket of the KGB. They had direct access to his immediate family. They would know his likes and dislikes, the rumors of infidelity, and the estimated value of his worth and could easily fill out the psychological profile of him and his measure as a man.

When George Herbert Walker Bush, former vice president to Ronald Reagan, former director of the CIA, and also former head of the Republican Party, was elected to the presidency in 1989, the Russians started shaking trees, trying to find ways to influence Bush. It is then when the StB, at the tasking of the KGB, became much more interested in Trump, as he had access to top Americans, such as Bush.[3] Harding confirmed that the Czechs did indeed start a serious intelligence collection operation to expand reporting on Trump himself and his organization. The operation was confirmed by then chief of the Czech secret intelligence service, Vlastimil Danek: "Trump was, of course, a very interesting person for us. He was a businessman, he had a lot of contacts, even in US politics."

Danek later told the Czech paper *Respekt*, "We knew that Trump was influential. He didn't hide that he wanted to become president one day. We were interested in learning more things about him."[4]

According to the German newspaper *Bild-Zeitung* (or *Bild*), which worked with the *Guardian* on the project, an StB field officer named Jaroslav Jansa, code-named Lubos, was responsible for tracking the Trumps.[5] In 1979 the Czechs issued an order to tap their phones: telephone calls between Ivana and her father, Miloš (who was already a human intelligence source), "should be intercepted."[6]

Both the *Guardian* and *Bild* reported that Czechoslovakia's case file on the Trumps was filed under the code names Slusovice, America, and Capital.[7] According to their reporting, the Czechs had extraordinary intelligence that the US media would have loved to have possessed at the time. Apparently, the family sources informed the StB about the Trumps' prenuptial arrangement, which stipulated that Ivana would be paid $1 million if they divorced. Also, that Trump's company was "tax-exempt for the next 30 years."[8] To show the level of intelligence the Czechs had, they even learned that Trump gave donations to both Republicans and Democrats in 1988 in the amount of $10,000 each.[9]

Nuclear Treaty Negotiator

Trump also had personal ambitions to be a major figure on the world stage. He wanted to become the principal negotiator for the Strategic

Arms Reduction Treaty (or START). This was a Reagan-era agreement in which the United States and Russia would draw down their nuclear arsenals. It was a highly sensitive process that both America and Europe held great hopes for. Whoever could pull off dismantling thousands of atomic bombs would essentially become a hero and a Nobel Peace Prize candidate. Unfortunately for Trump, the people negotiating this were Secretary of State George Schultz and Russian foreign minister Andrei Gromyko.

Scott Feinberg wrote in the *Hollywood Reporter* that Nobel Peace Prize winner Bernard Lown said Trump had "Russia mania in 1986."[10] Trump came to Feinberg in 1986 to learn all he could about Mikhail Gorbachev so he could lobby to be sent by President Ronald Reagan to Russia to work on nuclear disarmament and get a Nobel Prize. Lown claims Trump said that if Reagan appointed him to be plenipotentiary ambassador, "within one hour the Cold War would be over!" Lown was astonished and said, "I was not sure about his motivation for why he was doing it. But it puts together sort of a continuum that began way back in '86, with his fixation on Russia—the Soviet Union, then."[11] This sentiment was followed by William E. Geist, who wrote in the *New York Times*:

> His greatest dream is to personally do something about the problem and, characteristically, Donald Trump thinks he has an answer to nuclear armament: Let him negotiate arms agreements—he who can talk people into selling $100 million properties to him for $13 million. Negotiations is an art, he says, and I have a gift for it. . . . The idea that he would ever be allowed to go into a room alone and negotiate for the United States, let alone be successful in disarming the world, seems the naive musing of an optimistic, deluded young man who has never lost at anything he has tried. But he believes that through years of making his views known and through supporting candidates who share his views, it could someday happen.[12]

In a 1984 *Washington Post* article, Lois Romano also covered Trump's ambition to negotiate with the USSR over nuclear weapons:

> This morning, Trump has a new idea. He wants to talk about the threat of nuclear war. He wants to talk about how the United States should

negotiate with the Soviets. He wants to be the negotiator. He says he has never acted on his nuclear concern. But he says that his good friend Roy Cohn, the flamboyant Republican lawyer, has told him this interview is a perfect time to start.[13]

With his usual braggadocio, Trump stated he did not need any education about START or the capabilities of the systems and why they needed to be reduced. Much like he would brag in the future about the capabilities of the Islamic State terrorist group, the Afghanistan war, and global trade, Trump would claim he knew everything there was to know about tens of thousands of atomic warheads and the intercontinental ballistic missiles. To him, all it took was bold, aggressive negotiations, and atomic bombs would—*poof*—disappear, and he would be the hero of the atomic age. Trump stated:

> It would take an hour-and-a-half to learn everything there is to learn about missiles. . . . I think I know most of it anyway. You're talking about just getting updated on a situation. . . . You know who really wants me to do this? Roy. . . . I'd do it in a second.[14]

By early 1987, Trump was making noises in the United States suggesting he could run for president, which happened to coincide with his almost obsessive desire to meet Gorbachev and be the premier arms negotiator. It reflected a trait that was characteristically Trumpian—a man with an oversized ego who felt he alone could fix this and make great changes in the world at a time when great changes were flying past him at a historic rate. During this period détente, a geopolitical thawing of relations, was midstream between America and the Soviet Union, after they had faced off for decades, pointing atomic bombs at each other. During this period one of the greatest musical hits in Western music was the antinuclear war song sung by Sting, former lead singer of the band The Police, titled "Russians," which repeated the refrain: "I hope the Russians love their children too." The song's lyrics burned into the psyche of American adults: "What might save us, me and you, is if the Russians love their children too." The desire for a rapprochement with Russia was popular and topical. The underpinnings of the Soviet Union were already crumbling. An inflection point in global history was clearly coming, and Trump wanted to be praised for being a key part of that history. This insatiable desire to forge a peaceful bond, based on money and real estate development, between America and Russia would become a defining ideological belief for Trump. (In a way, his marrying his first wife, Ivana, who emerged from behind the Iron Curtain, perhaps gave Trump the notion that a lot of hot, buxom Eastern European women, unobtainable in the West, were waiting to be introduced to the world of Trump luxury. His marriage to his third wife, Slovenian Melania *née* Knavs, seems to suggest this.)

Trump signaled his flirtation with Russian affairs and presidential aspirations by spending almost $130,000 to make some controversial views known in the news media. On September 2, 1987, he took out a *New York Times* full-page ad with the assistance of his friend Roger Stone. It delivered an anti-NATO policy and listed a myriad of now-familiar complaints about how NATO was not paying its fair share, how Japan and the Saudis were relying on American money for their defense, and how the little guy was not getting benefits from American defense alliances:

> To The American People . . . on why America should stop paying to defend countries that can afford to defend themselves. . . . The world is laughing at America's politicians as we protect ships we don't own, carrying oil we don't need, destined for allies who won't help.

In this ad, Trump was betting that inciting poor Americans—desperate for some benefit from ending the Cold War—against the elite could work as a bold populist methodology. Trump wrote that wealthy Americans could "help our farmers, our sick, our homeless by taking from some of the greatest profit machines ever created—machines created and nurtured by us."

It could have been written in Moscow, and it likely was. These views were what a textbook intelligence officer would write for an unwitting dupe who viewed money as the basis of everything. No need to ask for atomic secrets when one could, over a pleasant lunch and with the prospect of a possible business deal in Moscow, have a man take out news ads in the *Times*, the *Washington Post*, and the *Boston Globe* and state modest versions of the Soviet Union's propaganda at his own expense! It would directly challenge the Republican Party orthodoxy and poke a finger in the eye of the uber-hawk Ronald Reagan and his ex-CIA vice president George H. W. Bush—and Trump did just that.[15]

In 1988, during the Mikhail Gorbachev "Gorby-mania" that was sweeping the country, Trump was so taken by Russia that he was easily fooled by a Gorbachev impersonator named Ronald Knapp. Knapp suddenly appeared at Trump Tower in a stretch limousine, shaking his hands together in the air like a boxing champ. Trump was so excited he ran down to meet the supposed Soviet leader. Maureen Dowd reported that a local TV man on the scene, Channel 5's Gordon Elliot, affirmed, "There was absolutely no question he bought it."[16] Watching the video that exists clearly shows Trump thought Knapp was Gorbachev. It was also widely shown on the Maury Povich television show, making fun of Trump for being fooled.

In 1988, Czech intelligence's confidential informant, Milos, likely Ivana's father of the same name, reported an interesting factoid that would change how Trump was viewed by both the Czechs and eventually the Russians. Trump had just returned from a visit to the Soviet Union in 1987 (more on that later), and the Russians were likely trying to discern if they had an idiot they could use for influence or if he was a potential player they could cultivate. Milos reported a conversation that could only have come from Trump's lips. Trump had ambitions and that "any false step of [Ivana's] will have incalculable consequences for the position of her husband who intends to run for president in 1996."[17]

As I mentioned previously, Czech intelligence increased their surveillance activities of Trump after it was learned he was interested in running for president, and though they were dubious of his chances, they duly noted his activities. On October 21, 1988, source Milos reported that Trump discussed running for president. The report would go on to state that "despite the fact that it seems to be a utopia, D. Trump is convinced that he will succeed."[18]

Czech files showed that the StB was tasked to recruit Trump, and it made a good faith effort to get him to the country. In 1989, a report filed under a source named A-Jarda revealed an attempt to lure Trump to visit the town of Slušovice, about twenty minutes east of Ivana's village of

Zlín, after meeting a delegation of the Czechoslovakian Agricultural Production Committee.[19] Slušovice was an internationally known collectivist farm and would have been a good cover for an innocent operation of looking at the cows and pigs while cultivating or entrapping a well-known philanderer like Trump. A farm delegation from Czechoslovakia led by František Čuba went to New York in September 1989 and met with Trump and invited him to come to Slušovice. Trump did not visit at that time, but he would eventually get the tour from Čuba, who chaperoned him and Ivana. After visiting their "biotech" and "electronic operations" he stayed in the Hotel Všemina in Slušovice.[20] Trump returned to Zlín and Slušovice in November 1990 with the news of Ivana's father's death.[21] According to Harding, Jansa, the StB main source, was a mere one hundred meters away, still collecting information.

Intourist—Mr. Trump's KGB Tour Guides

Obviously, Donald Trump was obsessed with engaging the Soviet Union early in his business career. Some of this was his desire to be in on important negotiations with the United States' chief adversary, and the other reason appears to be his interest in bringing a Trump Tower to Moscow. Trump's nuke fears led to several early engagements with the USSR. His Moscow visit to the National Hotel was likely arranged by Intourist, the official KGB agency that moved Westerners around Russia. It was run by Vladimir Strzhalkovsky, a KGB officer.

Like most civilians who ignore the perils that surround them, be it swimming in a crocodile-infested river, going up to pet a hippopotamus as it sleeps in an African lake, or getting that better photo of those lions by leaning out an open window, Trump saw money in the Soviet Union. He gave not one thought about those tour guides—the trained KGB intelligence officers who were bringing him into one of the most totalitarian nations in the world.

At its inception, Intourist was a front for the NKVD, the Stalinist secret police. After the semiromantic portrayal of the Soviet Union's founding by American journalist John Reed, in his seminal book *Ten Days That Shook the World,* Americans in the 1920s started becoming interested in visiting the Soviet Union and its communist form of government. A tourism organ was established to guide them and determine who were fellow travelers and could be turned into agents or saboteurs. Their visits could then be turned into propaganda used to portray a USSR that was prosperous, successful, and diverse.[22] Though Intourist was billed as a travel agency, it was responsible for luring foreigners to the Soviet Union to not only propagandize them but to compromise them.

With the KGB running both internal and external security in Russia, foreign visitors were directed to a special bureau that handled their travel and transportation to ensure they did not stray from the strictly controlled path, with tour guides handled by the KGB for gathering and reporting intelligence about each person's behaviors, activities, and sexual desires and/or perversions. Many people wanted to see Russia's cultural charms, but the KGB ensured there was always a chance for sexual opportunities, as seduction and blackmail was a full-time business. And there was Donald J. Trump, being chauffeured around Moscow under the complete control of the KGB.

After the fall of the Soviet Union, the Intourist agency was privatized. In 1992, the British travel agency Thomas Cook purchased a majority interest in the remaining company and renamed it VAO Intourist, but it has remained connected to the Russian government, able to cooperate should Putin express an interest.

Not only did Intourist arrange Trump's first visit to the Soviet Union, but the hotel that was the former flagship of Intourist is now the Moscow Ritz-Carlton.[23] The claim in the Steele dossier that Trump had cavorted with urinating prostitutes was based on his 2013 visit to the Moscow Ritz-Carlton for the Miss Universe Pageant.

Vladimir Strzhalkovsky was the head of the agency at the time of Trump's visit. As the KGB officer who controlled the so-called travel department, he would have overseen Trump's first trip to Moscow in 1987. Strzhalkovsky later made headlines when he became the recipient of the largest severance payment in Russian history totaling $100 million after leaving Russia's largest mining company, Noriksk Nickel.[24] He was appointed CEO of the mining company in August 2008 and pushed out of Noriksk Nickel by an oligarch named Oleg Deripaska. Strzhalkovsky just happened to also serve with Vladimir Putin in St. Petersburg. Ironically, Strzhalkovsky later worked as vice chairman for the Bank of Cyprus before Trump's future secretary of commerce, Wilbur Ross, took the job after Strzhalkovsky's departure in 2015.[25] (Ross, a billionaire, chose to run this tiny bank in the Eastern Mediterranean.)

After Strzhalkovsky left, he claimed the bank was lax in its lending repayment efforts—implying it was designed to launder money. "I have a feeling that people from the bank were running around with bags of money, looking for someone to give the money to and not caring whether it will be repaid or not."[26]

So goes the first of the most amazing series of personal coincidences that would characterize Trump's future administration: loose personal connections to the KGB via money. Who knew that a KGB senior officer who ran Trump's tour of Moscow in 1987 would run the Bank of Cyprus, only to be replaced by Wilbur Ross. That bank was, coincidentally, used by one lobbyist—Paul Manafort—to funnel money to secret companies working for Putin's chosen leader in Ukraine, Viktor Yanukovych. Coincidence, right?

The agenda of the Trump administration and its conservative followers would be joined at the hip to the Russian Federation. Still, there had to be an origin story for Trump's Ahab-like obsession to work with the Russians, and it was a shining tower in Moscow. That story would start in 1986.

The Moscow Tower 1.0

Trump's first real contacts with Soviet leaders occurred in March 1986, the month Trump was introduced to Yuri Dubinin and his daughter Natalia Dubinina at a luncheon hosted by Estée Lauder's son. Dubinin was the ambassador of the Soviet Union to the United Nations at the time of the luncheon and then later that same year became the Soviet ambassador to Washington. Natalia stated in an interview that while they were living in New York, she picked her father up at the airport and took him to Trump Tower where they had lunch. Trump, with the help of his ghostwriter Tony Schwartz, wrote about it in *Trump: The Art of the Deal*:

> 2:30 P.M. A prominent businessman who does a lot of business with the Soviet Union calls to keep me posted on a construction project I'm interested in undertaking in Moscow. The idea got off the ground after I sat next to the Soviet ambassador, Yuri Dubinin, at a luncheon held by Leonard Lauder, a great businessman who is the son of Estee Lauder. Dubinin's daughter, it turned out, had read about Trump Tower and knew all about it. One thing led to another, and now I'm talking about building a large luxury hotel, across the street from the Kremlin, in partnership with the Soviet Government. They have asked me to go to Moscow in July.[27]

These high-level Soviet Russian contacts led to Trump receiving an invitation to come to Moscow in January 1987. Of course, it was arranged by the KGB. Trump also detailed his trip in *Trump: The Art of the Deal*:

> In January 1987, I got a letter from Yuri Dubinin, the Soviet ambassador to the United States, that began: 'It is a pleasure for me to relay some good news from Moscow.' It went on to say that the leading Soviet state agency for international tourism, Goscomintourist, had expressed interest in pursuing a joint venture to construct and manage a hotel in Moscow. On July 4, I flew with Ivana, her assistant Lisa Calandra, and Norma to Moscow. It was an extraordinary experience. We toured a half dozen potential sites for a hotel, including several near Red Square. We stayed in Lenin's suite at the National Hotel, and I was impressed with the ambition of the Soviet officials to make a deal.[28]

Trump and his then wife Ivana arrived in Moscow on July 4, 1987, after Soviet diplomat Vitaly Churkin arranged the trip details with Intourist. Treated as a ministerial-level visit, Trump was wined and dined lavishly. They stayed at the National Hotel in the Lenin suite and carried out the usual tours of the Kremlin, Red Square, the Russian State Library, and various ministries. Trump finally got his meeting in Moscow with Mikhail Gorbachev.[29] Michael Oreskes wrote in the *New York Times* that even when given the opportunity to meet with Soviet leadership, he was more obsessed with arms negotiation than the hotel tower project:

> The ostensible subject of their meeting was the possible development of luxury hotels in the Soviet Union by Mr. Trump. But Mr. Trump's calls for nuclear disarmament were also well-known to the Russians.[30]

It was a splendid visit for Donald: he and Ivana were treated like royalty. His desire to meet with and do business with Russians, even if they were communist despots, was finally being satisfied.

When Trump wrote in his book that he visited multiple locations to scout out hotel locations for the Trump Tower project, it revealed to Soviet intelligence that Donald Trump could be an asset in the United States. For all of Gorbachev's *glasnost* promotions, the American government remained unfriendly to the Soviet Union's interests. The walls were starting to crumble, but the intelligence and political needs of the USSR would still require friendly assets. For this, Trump fit the bill perfectly, for he had something most Americans who visited Russia did not have: money. Though Russia was poor, it had resources and national infrastructure that would always need updating. Whoever made a reverse *glasnost* and could enter the Russian market before the house of cards collapsed could make some money in a region that had been closed for business for almost a century. Apparently, Trump saw this opportunity but miscalculated the need for the luxury by ten years—they were not ready for his brand until after the Soviet Union fell. To him, it was about placing his name on the top of an unclimbed mountain and the prestige of a towering building that would bring luxury and gluttony to a nation that had only women to offer. This was a good start for a man like Trump. On this point, Soviet intelligence officers were watching—and waiting.

The fall of the Soviet Union came rapidly after these meetings, and Trump seemed disinterested until the dust started to settle. By 1996, under Boris Yeltsin, Vladimir Putin helped sell off the assets of the city of St. Petersburg, formerly known as Leningrad. At the same time, Trump applied for the Russian trademark of his name in preparation for Trump Tower Moscow. In that same year, almost a decade after his first trip, Trump traveled to Russia with Howard Lorber to meet with the gatekeeper for Moscow projects, Mayor Luzhkov, a very influential politician aligned with the Russian organized crime world. After that visit, in

November 1996, Trump stated in a news conference his intention to develop a $250 million project in Moscow, which would include a Trump international hotel and a commercial building, Trump Tower. In January 1997, Trump confirmed his plans in *The New Yorker,* and he stated it after meeting in Moscow with Aleksander Lebed, the former lieutenant general in the Soviet army and nominee who ran against Yeltsin:

> We are actually looking at something in Moscow right now, and it would be skyscrapers and hotels, not casinos. Only quality stuff. But thank you for defending me. I will be going again to Moscow. We're looking at the Moskva Hotel. We're also looking at the Rossiya. That's a very big project; I think it's the largest hotel in the world. And we're working with the local government, the mayor of Moscow and the mayor's people. So far, they've been very responsive.[31]

Sadly, for Trump, the environment in the wild post-Soviet world led him to eat his own words. Two years after publicly meeting with Lebed, Trump's application for approval for Trump Tower Moscow was dismissed.

Trump's electoral prospects for president were still in the air as well. A key player in this story was longtime supporter Roger Stone, a partner in the lobbying firm of Black, Manafort and Stone, which specialized in promoting dictators, petty tyrants, and murderers while rehabilitating their reputations in Washington, DC. They were known as the "dictators' lobbyists." Stone quietly served as the chairman of Trump's presidential exploratory committee in the 2000 election season. But Trump bided his time and stayed out of the Bush versus Gore fray, with the presidency still on his mind.[32]

Nance's Law in the Age of Trumpian Unreason

Former Royal Navy intelligence officer and James Bond creator Ian Fleming once wrote a spy dictum that held a lot of water until recently: "Once is an accident, twice happenstance and three times enemy action." It has long been a staple in the global intelligence community, but it was crafted in World War II. Since the beginning of the Cold War, the belief in accidents was eliminated because far too much "coincidence" was taking place in the dark shadows. Many activities were well-planned intelligence operations that found operatives stumbling fortuitously into the arms of foreign intelligence agents far too often. In my career and books, I've amusingly dubbed my own dictum Nance's Law of Intelligence Kismet or "Coincidence takes a lot of planning."

The problem is this dictum, or truism, is no longer much of an espionage joke in the world of Donald J. Trump. Nance's Law in the Age of Trumpian Unreason appears to be a hard-and-fast rule when investigating the relationships between Trump's administration and family and organizations and the Kremlin. Worse yet is that these coincidences are troubling and appear virtually everywhere. By the time this manuscript was completed, Robert Mueller wrote in his controversial report that there were *no coincidences* between the contacts with Trump's team and Russian intelligence agents, assets, influencers, businessmen, and diplomats. He found over one hundred secret contacts that Team Trump tried to hide from the US government. In fact, Trump's campaign would be found to have solicited assistance, expecting to benefit from Russian intelligence activities, while encouraging more nefarious services. Trump's call for assistance in hacking Hillary Clinton's emails was just one glimpse of Team Trump's operations in plain view.

In my last book, *The Plot to Destroy Democracy*, I brought attention to the process used by professional intelligence officers to recruit potential assets and/or agents. If you haven't read that book (and you should), I review, below, this universal set of tools known by the acronym MICE: money, ideology, coercion/compromise, and ego/excitement. It bears repeating here:

M is for *money*: Most intelligence activities will find that money is truly the root of all evil. Almost overwhelmingly, money, usually dangled to relieve targets from a personal debt that they wish to conceal, is a primary motivating factor for most who betray their country. Audrey James, the CIA clandestine service officer, walked into the Russian embassy in Washington, DC, and for $50,000 wrote down the names of dozens of

CIA assets, agents, and officers. Over his time working for the Russians, James collected $1.5 million. His avarice and flashing of the money he collected led to his capture and imprisonment for life.

I is for *ideology*: In some instances, a retrained intelligence officer can turn an asset by using an appeal to the asset's common political and/or social beliefs.

C is for *coercion* or *compromise*: Coercion is used when other reproaches fail, in which case an intelligence officer uses compromising material for the purpose of blackmailing the individual into cooperating. In hostile intelligence agencies, coercion through physical intimidation or abuse is used.

E is for *ego* and *excitement*: In some instances, the occasional methodology that may work is the allure of carrying out an exciting, secret activity without others detecting the betrayal. In other words, the thrill of the game. Intelligence officers around the world use other similar tactics for recruiting people, such as massaging the ego of a self-absorbed individual, stoking the courage of an otherwise withdrawn person, or determining the right balance of risk and reward that satisfies a person's psychological needs for traction, attachment, or emotional support.

The KGB had Trump on its radar and would be using the MICE strategy to bring him under its sway, as his interest in Russia clearly blinded him. He was a potential asset and an exploitable victim worth keeping.

Trump's forty-year development from a useful idiot to a possible Russian asset will be instructive in the depths of corruption: that M (money) can bring a man to the White House who may, in fact, be a wholly owned subsidiary of a foreign government. It would have been easy for the Russians to guide Donald Trump; they knew Trump would get his tower in Moscow even if it required him to sell America for it, and Benedict Arnold be damned, he would!

CHAPTER 4

Swimming in Rubles

The Russian Cash Laundromat

During the 2016 election season, Trump would loudly declare, "I have no business in Russia." It's a clever turn of phrase, but on this point he is a liar. Trump was famous in New York City for working with Russian business partners. He repeated this lie to maintain the false perception that he only worked with good, clean Americans. The truth is he had a good many business deals in the works with Russia. More importantly, he was the kind of man that responded to bribes—both direct and indirect—and was easily misled by flattery, which made him a potential asset for two types of criminal enterprises: organized crime and espionage agencies.

The naissance of his troubles came after Trump made a series of terrible investments in the 1990s; specifically, the Trump Casino in Atlantic City was an immediate bad investment. How? It was almost, literally, an ATM of other people's money because Trump borrowed money on the casino's earnings to recoup all his investments, using the business's cash. The business could never recover from the debt load he created. He literally bankrupted a money-making machine. Also Trump hawked cheap "luxury goods" on the general marketplace—from steaks (Trump Steaks) to wine (Trump Winery) and ties (Trump Collection), made in China using child slave labor. No one wanted these goods, so each venture failed miserably. He then tried a university venture (yes, Trump University) that would eventually be outed and sued as a fraudulent activity. Even his bread-and-butter real estate ventures were fairing badly due to poor management. By 2000, Trump quickly became cash starved, despite frequently claiming he was worth $8 to $10 billion. He was so mistrusted and well known for his chronic lying to investors that only one bank in the world would loan him money, the American subsidiary of the German banking firm Deutsche Bank. However, those loans were suspected of being backed up by unknown investors from Eastern Europe, with even shadier ties—Russian oligarchs.

At the same time Trump was going under, the Russian Federation economy was doing poorly under Yeltsin. Many of the sharks who had made their billions from liquidating Soviet assets wanted to offshore their money to safer havens. The post-Soviet real estate buying boom would start in the early 1990s but only truly explode after 2000 when the liquidation of state assets was essentially in the hands of a few oligarchs. However, tens of thousands of average Russians were finally making money in the new era of "democracy," as we've touched upon briefly, and they wanted to hide it in tax shelters where the state could not get to it easily. Fine houses and luxury apartments all across Europe were bought. Some of that money started to flow into two American cities: Miami and New York City. Florida was obvious because the weather was warm. New York because the market was ripe with old émigrés from the old Soviet Union who would facilitate purchases the Russian way, with no questions asked. They would become the masters of this market. Each of these Russian immigrants had ties to the Old World and could bring dominance in the new one. Of course, some had shady connections to the Russian mafia, but that's how one does business in a rough world. Many of Trump's New York City allies from the former Soviet Union brought their mind-set about dealing with the Old World along with their new money. In his time of greatest financial need (which according to his horrific IRS findings was all the time), they partnered with Trump, pouring hundreds of millions of dollars into real estate whose true value could be hidden well but would appreciate over time. Luxury real estate was a great tax haven for Russian oligarchs, and Donald Trump specialized in just that; as the Russians invested, a raft of new partners and partnerships would come to be joined with Trump. Each one of these individuals working on his projects always seemed to have ties to one of two organizations: the Russian mafia or Russian intelligence agencies.

And like clockwork, every time a connection was identified as being mafia or spying related, Donald Trump would swear he never heard of his former partners.

Trump SoHo

When Trump wanted to build a new skyscraper in early 2000, Trump SoHo, he partnered with several prominent former Russian businessmen. To work with Trump, they formed a company under the name of Bayrock, LLC.

One was Teyfik Arif, born in Kazakhstan in 1953. He resigned in 1991 from the USSR's Ministry of Commerce and Trade (KGB run) after seventeen years, where he held the position of deputy director of its Department of Hotel Management. The US State Department Bureau of Research and Intelligence and CIA reporting asserted that the USSR Ministry of Commerce and Industry was headed at the time by a KGB lieutenant general, Yevgeny P. Pitovranov, and was systematically engaged in commercial espionage in the West.[1]

Arif founded Specialty Chemicals Trading Company when the former Kazakh Soviet Socialist Republic gained independence. It was then that Arif and his brother secured ownership of ACCP, a chromium plant in the Aktobe region of West Kazakhstan. They later established offshore real estate companies to fund high-end developments in Kazakhstan, Azerbaijan, and Turkey.[2] In 1993, Arif worked as a Kazakh "agent on the ground" for Trans-World Group (TWG), the first and largest private company in Russia, which produced aluminum and sold it on Western markets.[3] It was jointly run by British metals trading brothers David and Simon Reuben, as well as Mikhail "Michael" Cherney and his brother Lev.[4] Michael Cherney was suspected of drug trafficking, money laundering, fraud, and sponsoring murder on behalf of a Russian organized crime group run by Mafiosi Vyacheslav Ivankov.[5] *Bloomberg Businessweek* reported that the two brothers "were known for their rough style of doing business."[6] In 1999, Arif left TWG and moved to Turkey, where he partnered with Rixos Hotels, a luxury hotel chain. In 2001 he joined forces with Felix Sater and formed Bayrock, LLC, a luxury real estate development company. It is alleged that Bayrock might be a laundromat for Russian oligarch money.

Laundromat or not, Bayrock, LLC, would provide all the seed money for Trump SoHo, provided Trump lent legitimacy and his brand to the Russians. They would get the golden name in a project that would clear hundreds of millions of allegedly dirty dollars acquired from questionable sources including liquidation of Russian state assets. Trump, himself, would get a new skyscraper with his name on it, at no cost.

Trump was jointly responsible for all decisions made by Arif and Sater, which served them all well. Their relationship was so close that they set up their offices inside Trump Tower just floors away from Donald.[7] As an example of their personal peccadilloes in the business world, Arif, in 2005, was at a birthday party with future president Erdogan and the oligarch Mashkevich. Trump called and wished a happy birthday to Teyfik.[8] It wouldn't be so happy five years later, as Teyfik was arrested in Turkey for running a prostitution ring on a luxury yacht. He was sponsoring parties for rich business partners. The Turks charged him with human trafficking. While charges against the billionaire were dropped, two other men who were in his employ were convicted.[9]

One of the most well-known associates was Felix Sater. Sater was born in Moscow and had changed his name from Sheferovsky because of his checkered past—including time in prison for stabbing someone in the face during a bar brawl. At Trump SoHo, Sater was responsibile for raising money for the company. As an officer of the company somehow his felony record was not revealed to investors.[10]

In a deposition related to the affairs of his Bayrock real estate development group, Trump stated that "Russia is one of the hottest places in the world for investment," and "we [Bayrock and the Trump organization] will be in Moscow at some point."[11] When Trump filed a defamation suit against writer Tim O'Brien, he made statements about his deals in Russia related to the towers.[12] "It would be a nonexclusive deal, so it would not have precluded me from doing other deals in Moscow, which was very important to me," he said, and as if to make his point, he bragged that Trump "Super Premium Vodka is displayed at the 2007 Millionaire's Fair in Moscow!"[13] On Russian advertisements Trump used the face of the founder of the Soviet Union, executioner of the czar's royal family, and all-around mass murderer Vladimir Ilyich Lenin.[14]

Other Russian Money

Of the many other personalities who brought Russian money into Trump's world, there was Tamir Sapir. Born Temur Sepiashvili in the Soviet Republic of Georgia in 1946, he was the son of a Russian army major. A graduate of Tbilisi State University, Sapir attended classes with Stalin's grandson Vasily Stalin. A Jewish Georgian, Sapir worked as an administrator in the Soviet state and processed passports for Soviet Jews who wanted to emigrate abroad. In 1973, he emigrated to Israel. For early Soviet émigrés, those with Jewish heritage were occasionally allowed to leave for Israel, which was also a springboard for emigration to the United States. After living in Israel, he moved to Kentucky but eventually settled in New York City, working as a cabbie. There he partnered with Sam Kislin and invested his $10,000 life savings to open an electronics store in Manhattan on Broadway. Soviet émigrés in the city during the 1970s were few and far between, unlike the massive wave that would arrive after the fall of the Soviet Union in the early '90s. Sapir claims former president of Georgia Eduard Shevardnadze played an important role in his success. He once recalled, "Once USSR's Minister of Foreign Affairs, Eduard Shevardnadze, visited my shop. One of his bodyguards, Murad Kazishvili, turned out to be my childhood friend. Back in the day, an organization existed called 'Council for American-Soviet Trade,' in which over a hundred large American companies participated, among them fortune 500 companies."[15] Sapir parlayed this and his business trading fertilizer and oil between America and the Soviets. He created extensive business ties with his friend Kazishvili's assistance. He accompanied Vice President George H. W. Bush to Moscow, who headed the council and invested in carbamide, an important component in petrochemical processing.[16] Sapir invested his profits in New York real estate when prices were at the bottom. With his own energy and luck, in less than twenty years he went from a cabbie to a billionaire, owning hundreds of properties across the city.

In 2006, Sapir's organization partnered with Trump's organization for the Trump SoHo project. By 2007, Trump referred to Sapir as a "great friend" and hosted his daughter's wedding at Mar-a-Lago. In 2008 Sapir's daughter held a bris ceremony that Trump and his son-in-law Jared Kushner attended and discussed real estate projects with a man named Lev Leviev. Leviev is known as the "King of Diamonds" and is very close to Vladimir Putin.[17] Sapir's daughter married Leviev's right-hand man Rotem Rosen. Sapir passed away in 2014.[18]

Another larger-than-life investor in Trump world was Semyon "Sam" Kislin. He immigrated to the United States in the 1970s, first settling in Boston and then moving to Brooklyn, New York, in 1976. He opened up a small electronics store in Manhattan with Sapir for high-level Soviet dignitaries and KGB agents as clients. Around 1976, Trump purchased two hundred televisions from Kislin on credit for the Commodore Hotel.[19] In 1991, Kislin opened a company with Mikhail Cherney called Trans World Commodities. Kislin served on NYC's Council of Economic Advisors, advising the mayor, until 2001, appointed by Rudy Giuliani, and was a large donor to Trump's campaigns.[20] Both Interpol and the FBI believed that Trans World Commodities was being used to launder millions from Russia to the United States. An FBI report also cited that Kislin belonged to the Ivankov mafia, set up in Brighton Beach. They had global dealings. Kislin sponsored a visa for a Russian contract killer named Anton Malevsky to enter the United States.[21] The FBI also struggled to figure out where mafia leader Vyacheslav Ivankov lived. Journalist Robert I. Friedman tells the story of how James Moody, chief of the bureau's organized crime section, found Ivankov. Moody told Friedman: "We were looking around, looking around, looking around. We had to go out and really beat the bushes. And then we found out that he was living in a luxury condo in Trump Tower."[22] Around 2001, Kislin issued personal mortgages to Russian buyers at Trump World Tower. He also issued a mortgage to Vasily Salygin, who would later become a future official in Ukraine's Party of Regions. Salygin worked during some of the same years as Paul Manafort in Ukraine.[23] A "strategic partner" for Bayrock in handling Trump projects, specifically Trump SoHo, would round out this crew.[24] That would be Alexander Machkevich. He was a mining billionaire who made his wealth during perestroika in Kazakhstan.

According to Israel's *Haaretz* newspaper, he became one of the biggest tycoons to emerge from the Soviet Union.[25] Machkevich, Patokh Chodiev, and Alijan Ibragimov were known as the Trio (Eurasia Group) in Kazakhstan. They met through their mutual relationship with Boris Birshtein, a high-level Russian businessman whose son-in-law would later partner with Donald Trump in the Trump Toronto project. He would later go on to become the majority owner in Eurasian Natural Resources Corporation, one of the world's largest mining and metals companies. In 2011, Birshtein was accused of a $55 million money-laundering scheme in Belgium, which was never proven. He reappears in this story at the inauguration of Trump in 2017.

Trump Tower Moscow . . . Again

In 2005, a longtime Trump associate named Felix Sater quietly went to Moscow to scout out the site of an old pencil factory near Moskva River. A year later Donald Trump Jr. and Ivanka Trump would travel to Moscow and stay at the Hotel National Moscow. Trump's organization repeatedly attempted to register trademarks for Trump, Trump Tower, Trump International Hotel and Tower, and Trump Home in preparation for building a skyscraper on this location.[26]

Sater was a childhood friend of Trump's lawyer Michael Cohen and became an influential associate helping Trump, yet again, attempt Trump tower projects in Russia, as well as Yalta. The deals never materialized, but Sater, who eventually went to work for the Trump organization, successfully helped with Trump SoHo through his Kazakhstan connections. The Khrapunovs, who allegedly invested stolen Kazakhstan money in Trump SoHo, were part of a lawsuit with Sater in New York for money laundering. They also faced charges in Europe and were convicted in absentia in Kazakhstan. They denied these charges. Nonetheless, Sater arranged a meeting between Trump and Ilyas Khrapunov in Trump Tower.

Sater was also involved as tour guide for Ivanka Trump during a 2006 trip to Russia in which he famously stated, "I arranged for Ivanka to sit in Putin's private chair at his desk and office in the Kremlin." None of the deals materialized, but Sater remained in Trump's orbit right up until the election.

All the while Trump was running for president and denying all contacts and deals with Russia, Sater was working on the latest attempt at Trump Tower Moscow. Sater partnered with Andrey Razo, a developer in Russia, and traveled to scout out potential sites, meeting with Andrei Molchanov, whose father was Putin's boss back in the early '90s and is currently a senior vice president of VTB Capital. Sater and Cohen, who joined the Trump Organization in 2006, worked feverishly during the election to bring Trump Tower Moscow to fruition.

Former FBI director Andrew McCabe wrote in his book *The Threat* that there is no difference between crime syndicates operating worldwide and the Russian government. As McCabe saw it, the Russian government was the top criminal syndicate in that country, and by extension, its influence in how money flowed in and out of the homeland enabled the government to exert a certain amount of pressure on those oligarchs who wanted to continue to make money in Russia. Be it New York, London, Tel Aviv, or the Costa del Sol, the invisible strings attached to both the mafia and the oligarchy always led back to the Kremlin. In Russia, you want to be under the *krysha* or protection of a high-powered criminal, as high as possible, and there is no higher *krysha* than Vladimir Putin.

Putin spent a decade replicating his success reining in the mafia in St. Petersburg by doing the same to the oligarchy. By 2010 both the Russian mafia and the elite were brought under an acceptable measure of control. They accepted an amount of profit that made them insanely rich and gave them the ability to operate. Everyone who worked with the Russians wanted to be under his *krysha*. By 2013, it became clear that Donald Trump wanted to be under that roof too.

It was during the period of June to November 2013 that Trump met with his Russian contacts for the Miss Universe Pageant. He was focused on two items he wanted most: the Trump Moscow Tower and access to Russian women. In fact, Trump wrote at the bottom of a letter to Putin that he looked forward to seeing the "beautiful" Russian women. He even met with the richest oligarchs of Russia in private. Soon afterward, he again announced that the Trump Tower Moscow would be built. That said, any financial component of the tower project from the Russian side would be linked to Russian intelligence directly and Putin indirectly.

There is a key Russian apart from Putin and Kislyak in this story, a billionaire aligned with all the scandals, the one ring that bound them all. That would be Aras Agalarov.

Agalarov was born in Baku, Azerbaijan, and moved to Moscow in 1989. There he founded Crocus Group in 1989 and established several companies in the United States as early as 1990, after he moved into property development and opened Crocus Expo International Exhibition Center. He was known for his associations with *vory v zakone*, roughly translated as "thieves in law," the professional criminal class of the Russian mafia.[27]

Agalarov was working with Sherbank and the Russian state-owned Vnesheconombank (VEB), also known as the "bank of spies" for its funding of Russian intelligence operations—both linked to Putin's personal friend. He would be the principal organizer of Miss Universe Moscow with Trump.

Herman "German" Gref served in the USSR armed forces for the internal troops of the USSR Ministry of Internal Affairs (MVD). Gref is a longtime associate and ally of Putin and has known him since the 1990s. He was CEO of Sberbank, Russia's largest bank, under sanctions by the US Treasury. In 2000, Putin appointed Gref as minister of economic affairs, a position specifically created for him. During the 2013 Miss Universe pageant, Agalarov arranged a dinner for Trump at the Nobu restaurant with oligarchs and government officials and introduced him to Gref. Sberbank was one of Agalarov's biggest lenders and was a co-sponsor of Miss Universe. Agalarov sought $1.6 billion from Sberbank to finance Trump Tower Moscow, among other projects. That was before the bank was placed on the sanctions list. In 2016 he was named CEO of VEB and tasked by Putin to clean up bad loans.[28]

Sergey Gorkov was the former CEO of VEB. In 1994, he graduated from FSB Academy with a degree in law. He was also a speaker of Arabic and English. He worked with Bank Menatep and for the Yukos oil company. In 2005 he went to London then returned to Russia in 2006. In 2008 he was appointed director of the Personnel Policy Department at

Sberbank, and by 2010, he was appointed deputy chairman of the board of Sberbank. His promotion also led to Sberbank sponsoring Trump's Miss Universe pageant. In 2016, Putin appointed Gorkov as head of VEB.

Putin is a lifelong practitioner of judo. He used these financial ties to Donald Trump to perform a strategic flip. Russia has a poor economy based solely on oil and weapons sales and has no true allies apart from a motley collection of global strongmen. However, as a result of the attack on the United States, Donald Trump and the Republican Party have been added to his coterie, and Putin is fully intent on bringing about the rule of the autocrats worldwide.

Running for President of . . . Trump Tower Moscow

While running for president, Trump's staff were furiously working on making the Moscow tower deal. Trump himself would spin a fabulous web of lies over the next year denying that any of this was happening. On September 2015, Michael Cohen and Felix Sater discussed designs and the Trump Tower Moscow deal via email. In addition to Cohen and Sater, Dmitry Chizhikov, a senior financial adviser on behalf of Andrey Rozov, a Russian investor, was involved. Rozov was a highly placed Russian developer and CEO of the company IC Expert. In October 2015, Rozov sent a letter of intent to Cohen, a joint agreement for the construction of a building in Moscow to be designated Trump Tower Moscow. On October 12, 2015, Sater and Cohen exchanged emails. Cohen emailed Sater a concept video.[29] Sater reminded Cohen how he was able to get Ivanka to spin on Putin's chair on a 2006 previous trip to Moscow. Sater sent a letter of intent to Cohen outlining the terms of a Moscow tower deal on October 13, 2015. Rozov had already signed it by the time it was forwarded to Cohen for Trump's signature.

By the end of October 2015, Cohen sent back a signed letter of intent with the request that it not be disclosed publicly. In November, Sater emailed Cohen that he was on a plane to the Bahamas to meet Rozov and a very close friend and partner of Putin's best friend. Sater commented to him on how he loved Trump's Putin-Russia reference, and he asked Cohen to send him that part of the press conference so he could hand it over to his associates in the Bahamas so that it would go directly to the Kremlin.[30]

In November 2015, Cohen and Dmitry Klokov, a director of external communications at PJSC, a large Russian electricity transmission company, communicated about the Trump Tower Moscow development deal at least four times. It was Ivanka who pushed Cohen to engage with Klokov. Cohen pushed back, likely because he was already collaborating with Sater to obtain funding for the project.[31]

It was during this period that Trump, Cohen, and Sater floated the idea of offering Putin a bribe. The tower had a preliminary design with a one-hundred-story glass monolith, which had more than a passing resemblance to a Soyuz space launch rocket. It would be located at the site of the Moscow International Business Center. It would be all high class, and the spa would be named Ivanka. To sweeten the deal, they would build a penthouse at the top of the tower worth $50 million and give it to Putin as a "gift" to get the project approved. In the Foreign Corrupt Practices Act, a US law passed in 1977, this is defined as a bribe.

On December 1, 2015, Sater emailed Cohen, asking him to scan a copy of his passport for the Russian Ministry of Foreign Affairs.[32] On December 19, 2015, Sater texted Cohen to send copies of Cohen's and Trump's passports, so visas could be issued by VTB Bank, along with invitations to discuss financing for Trump Tower Moscow. Sater noted that bank CEO Andrey Kostin would be the invitee and would be at all meetings with Putin. This would give the meeting the optics to look like a business meeting instead of a political agreement.[33] No matter how it was portrayed, it showed American citizens working with private representatives of Putin, an ex-KGB officer, and a US presidential candidate.

CHAPTER 5

Team Trump

When I published *The Plot to Hack America* six weeks before the election, it was very clear who the players were on Trump's team that were assisting in his relationship with Russia. I labeled them the Kremlin Crew, an assemblage of the top political hatchet men in the world—a dirty half dozen who would lie and cheat and help him steal an election. They were also his friends. Top of the list was a new player with a relatively clean résumé, US Army lieutenant general Michael Flynn. Commissioned into the US Army in 1981, he was the former director of the US Defense Intelligence Agency (DIA). On July 24, 2012, Flynn took charge of the DIA after serving as the intelligence chief for Afghanistan at the Office of the Director of National Intelligence (ODNI).[1]

While director of the DIA, Flynn traveled to the headquarters of his Russian counterparts at the GRU. The first American military leader to visit, he toured the GRU's facilities and spoke with leaders and personnel. In a *New Yorker* article, Steven Hall, the former head of the CIA's Office of Russian and European Analysis and one of the savviest minds on Russia, called the trip "quaint and naïve." Though it appeared the Russians were open to such a visit from a military official, it was also a chance to perhaps recruit an American spy. To many in US intelligence, Flynn's goodwill went a bit too far. Several months after he returned, Flynn wanted GRU officials to tour the DIA headquarters at Bolling Air Force Base in Washington, DC. DIA senior staff flipped out, and the idea died a quick death. Inside the DIA, members of the Russian counterintelligence section had concerns that the Russians had "turned" Flynn because he was pushing so hard for cooperation with the GRU despite literally decades of experience that cautioned against it.[2]

The flashing lights were not just in the DIA. Former director of National Intelligence James Clapper told NBC News in June 2018 that he had warned Flynn of cooperating with the GRU. He worried that Flynn "may have succumbed" to the friendliness of Russian intelligence officers when Flynn ignored this advice.[3] Still, Flynn persisted in expanding cooperation with Moscow. Following his trip, he asked for more sharing of information with Russia and specifically came to the DIA Counterterrorism Center (formerly JIATF-CT) to produce some reports and briefings at the "releasable to Russia" (REL RUS) level. DIA staffers collectively rolled their eyes. They turned to their computers, put together open source information gathered from TV and news reports, stamped it REL RUS, and sent it forward to the foreign dissemination division for review. In that way, the DIA provided the information according to Flynn's wishes but gave nothing of real significance to the GRU.

General Flynn had a history of breaking protocol and rules, especially those around classified information and personal security. The most glaring was installing a private computer connection in his Pentagon office and sharing confidential information with uncleared foreign nationals in Afghanistan. These security red flags suggested someone who was willing to meet in secret with intelligence officers if he believed he was in the right and everyone else was in the wrong, as many had warned him about with the Russians.[4]

On August 7, 2014, at the insistence of President Barack Obama, Flynn resigned from the DIA. His parting comments included: "Life is like surfing a wave. You can't change the way a wave breaks, but you can certainly change the way you ride it." He retired under heavy pressure from the White House due to his irrational conspiracies and White House suspicions of his involvement with Russian intelligence. He had to resign, otherwise Obama would have had to publicly fire him.[5]

His personal hatred of Obama would lead Flynn to join Donald Trump. Flynn met Trump for the first time in August 2015. Two months later, he would astonish everyone in the intelligence community by appearing on RT in a discussion on America; two months later he attended RT's tenth anniversary gala.[6] Putin was photographed at the table with Flynn seated on his right and the American Green Party leader Jill Stein on the other side. As noted earlier, this signaled to the Russian armed forces that Flynn was in Putin's pocket; any intelligence professional would have known this was the goal of the dinner and would never have attended such an event. Not Michael Flynn. In his speech at the gala, Flynn talked about terrorism in Syria and the civil war and commended Putin for the widespread bombing of Syria by Russian forces. He spoke about Russian foreign policy but would not back up Obama's criticism of Russia's ruthless assistance to Assad by helping them commit mass murder.[7]

Throughout 2016, unnamed Russian officials believed they had developed a strong relationship with Flynn and could use him to influence Donald Trump and his campaign. Obama officials considered him a national security threat, but Flynn continued to be Trump's main foreign policy and national security adviser.[8]

Also, in 2015, Flynn gave a speech for the Russian air cargo company Volga-Dnepr and for Kaspersky Labs, the Russian anti-malware company. Amazing considering that Kaspersky later received notoriety for allegations of installing Kremlin malware on computer systems. Flynn received $11,250 for each speech.[9] In June 2015, Flynn traveled to Egypt and Israel to broker agreements on Saudi Arabian–financed and Russian-backed energy and nuclear deals. Here lay a key node in all his relations among these countries. Flynn did not disclose any of these engagements in government filings or before Congress.[10]

Following a failed military coup in Turkey in mid-July 2016, the government of Turkey asked the United States to extradite Fethullah Gülen, who it believed sponsored the attempted overthrow. Flynn, speaking to an audience at an anti-Islam convention in Cleveland, noted Recep Tayyip Erdogan was an Islamic leader and the military would be a more secular and better government for Turkey.[11] This was a surprising statement since Turkey had just brutally purged the military and government of anyone opposed to Erdogan. Clearly, there was something behind Flynn's embrace of a freshly minted dictator.

Around July 27, 2016, Bijan Kian (Bijan Refiekian), a partner of Flynn's in FIG (Flynn Intelligence Group), spoke with him about working in the interest of Ankara and President Erdogan. Kian partnered with Kamil Ekim Alptekin, head of the U.S.-Turkey Business Council and who had a

Dutch shell company they could use to get into the Turkish government's good graces. They initially called this project the Truth Campaign.[12]

On August 4, 2016, Kian sent an email to General Flynn referring to Fethullah Gülen as a young Ayatollah Khomeini. As proof he noted Khomeini had sought refuge in the West before returning to foment the Iranian Revolution. Supposedly, western Pennsylvania was Gülen's "Paris" before returning to Ankara to stir up rebellion. It was fanciful. This is an especially apt metaphor for Kian to use since Flynn was conspiracy-theory-level convinced that Iran was the center of all evil in the world.[13] For the next several weeks, Kian reported to Flynn visits he had with senior Turkish government officials in the United States and who had traveled to the US to work on the plan. The Turkish government then paid $600,000 into Kamil Alptekin's company. Alptekin pocketed $120,000 (a 20 percent commission) through his subcompany named Inovo and sent the rest to FIG. It was clearly a middle man's payoff of Flynn by the Turks. The intent of the project—now called Operation Confidence—was supposed to eventually lead to "criminal referrals" against Gülen with Flynn's assistance.

The mission to get Gülen with Flynn's help was now moving forward. From September through October 2016, Alptekin and Kian began writing an op-ed that Flynn would eventually put under his own name in the *Hill*, an online and print newspaper focused on DC politics. The op-ed compared Gülen to a terrorist and used some of the wording Kian had used about Khomeini. Flynn was now deeply involved with the final stages of the presidential campaign. In the op-ed, Flynn referred to Gülen as "Turkey's Osama bin Laden."[14] The editorial ran the day of the 2016 election. But Flynn's large deposit of Turkish money and the surprising op-ed were suspicious—too convenient. This later led the Department of Justice to begin the FARA (Foreign Agents Registration Act) investigation. Since all the parties initially lied to agents about the arrangement with the Turkish government before making deals, it was a relatively easy indictment for the Justice Department to trap Kian and Alptekin.[15] I discuss these ties in more detail further on. But it was Flynn who did not reveal that these payments came from a foreign government or that Alptekin helped FIG disguise the money.[16]

Stone and Manafort: Friend to Dictators, Knaves, and Thieves

Dirty tricks master Roy Cohn was likely one of the most influential people in the making of Donald Trump. As the chief counsel to Senator Joseph McCarthy in the 1950s, Cohn was known for playing very dirty and very personal. He had been part of many efforts to destroy liberal political opponents for decades. He represented Trump in his housing discrimination case back in 1973. He used stalling tactics to drag out the process until the efforts by the DOJ were useless. During Watergate, he went on the attack to defend Nixon after Archibald Cox was fired. "Cox was nothing but a Kennedy hatchet man," said Cohn.[17] Cohn said of the Watergate inquiry, "Despite a year of investigation, the president is yet to be connected with a single crime." Cohn was not only admired by a young Donald Trump but also by the young Roger Stone and Paul Manafort. In fact, Manafort and Stone met Trump through Cohn. Stone had an extensive close relationship with Trump dating back to 1979.[18] Paul Manafort met Trump through Cohn in 1980.

Trump always wanted his own personal version of Roy Cohn who would not be his father's consiglieri but his own. He would eventually find that character in a future attorney general, but I will save that for later. However, Trump did come to find a man he could relate to when it came to dirty pool. That was Republican dirty tricks operative Roger Stone. Stone says Trump helped him and his partners set up the office location for their new lobbying firm, Black, Manafort and Stone, using his contacts and pull. Cohn also recommended Trump should be their first client.[19] Fittingly, thus started decades of Stone representing criminals, con men, and warlords.

Roger Stone

Stone was born in 1952 in Connecticut, the son of a well driller. He started making clever political tricks as early as age eight. In 1960 Stone manipulated other students in a mock election between John F. Kennedy and

Richard Nixon.[20] "I remember going through the cafeteria line and telling every kid that Nixon was in favor of school on Saturdays. It was my first political trick." In high school, he manipulated an election for student president by recruiting another student to run against him. "I built alliances and put all my serious challengers on my ticket. Then I recruited the most unpopular guy in the school to run against me. You think that's mean? No, it's smart."[21] He was a Barry Goldwater–supporting conservative in his youth and volunteered for Goldwater's 1964 campaign for president.[22] Active in the Young Republicans Club in 1974, Roger ran for president of the club with the help of his new friend, Paul Manafort.[23] After joining the Richard Nixon reelection campaign, Stone left college and did not graduate.

Stone joined the 1972 Nixon campaign, where he developed his well-deserved reputation for dirty tricks, fake opposition research, and bald-faced lies. He loved that era so much he tattooed Nixon's face on his back between his shoulder blades. Stone engaged in various dirty tricks, including trying to tie a Nixon opponent to a fake group he made up called the Young Socialist Alliance (YSA). His friend Brad Porter had suggested the idea. The first name proposed was the Gay Liberation Movement. Porter facilitated the effort for Stone by creating stationery with the YSA logo to lend authenticity.[24] Stone would fondly recall, "By night, I'm trafficking in the black arts. Nixon's people were obsessed with intelligence."[25] In the presidential campaign Stone recruited a man to be a driver for Democrat Hubert Humphrey in order to spy on him.[26] After Nixon's victory, he was assigned to the Office of Economic Opportunity. Eventually, he joined the office of Senator Bob Dole, but his trickster past caught up with him as well as his swinger lifestyle. He was allegedly fired over soliciting men to perform immoral acts involving his wife.[27]

After his firing, Stone moved over to working for a wide range of conservatives, including the 1980 and 1984 Ronald Reagan campaigns.[28] During the 1980 election, Stone manipulated the polls by backing the candidacy of John B. Anderson, a white-haired independent, helping him to get the nomination of the Liberal Party of New York. This split the opposition to Reagan in the state and enabled Reagan to win New York. That same year Stone formed a lobbying firm with Paul Manafort and

Charlie Black with the intent to work for conservatives and people who were so awful they couldn't be adequately represented in Washington.[29]

In 2000, during the Bush versus Gore presidential election, when the recount came down to a few hundred votes, Stone was one of the leaders at the center of the Florida disturbance called the Brooks Brothers riot. This was an organized group of "everyday protesters" who were in fact all paid white male political operatives. The "protesters" were Republican staffers from DC and elsewhere, wearing button-down shirts and khakis, who laid siege to the Florida secretary of state's office with the mission to disrupt the vote counting and intimidate the government workers. This fake protest was actually organized to stop the recount altogether. They worked for Stone.[30]

In 2008, during the Hillary Clinton primary against a young Barack Obama, Stone created a political action group called Citizens United Not Timid, with the acronym CUNT, to attack her with a legally pronounceable misogynist insult.[31]

As I have mentioned, Stone had long pushed Donald Trump to run for president, starting in 1988,[32] and during the presidential campaign in 2000 under the Reform Party ticket.[33] It wasn't all political dirty tricks; many schemes were for business purposes. Stone, Trump, and others were fined for placing ads in newspapers in the Catskills to lobby against gambling in the area. The purpose was to undermine competition for Trump's Atlantic City casinos. Stone was required to pay a fine of $100,000.[34]

In the 2016 election, Stone claims that he convinced Trump to run for president. Stone was working in the Donald Trump campaign until he left on August 8, 2015. Both sides dispute why he left, with Stone claiming he quit and Trump claiming he was fired. However, for the remainder of the campaign, Stone made several claims to still be in close contact with the Trump campaign.[35] Of course, he was—because likely the "firing" was a ploy to give Stone the ability to do any dirty operation he wanted and say he was on the outs with Trump. It was a classic Stone-like ploy to keep his client's hands clean. But Stone was not the only professional hatchet man on Trump's team. There was a professional with a proven track record of throwing elections to friends of Moscow. He would come to run Trump's entire campaign.

Paul Manafort

Manafort was the son of Paul Manafort Sr., the former mayor of New Britain, Connecticut. Manafort followed his Republican father's work in politics. Their family had a well-established presence in the area stemming from his grandfather's and father's history of development in the area. Paul Jr. would start his path in politics in his teens.[36]

As a lobbyist, Manafort started his work for American politicians in Washington, DC, then moved on to foreign clients. He had served for Republican candidates and presidents as far back as 1976, when he was a delegate coordinator for President Ford under James A. Baker III.[37] He then went on to work on the effort to elect Ronald Reagan during the 1980 election. He would later work in the White House Personnel Office under Reagan. He subsequently worked on campaigns for George H. W. Bush and Senator Bob Dole.

Then he helped found Black, Manafort and Stone in 1980 with Charles Black and Roger Stone. The lobbying firm based in Washington, DC, was known for its work for foreign leaders, parties, and businesses to lobby the US government via PR campaigns and legislation policy. The firm added Democratic party finance chairman Peter Kelly in 1984 and changed its name to Black, Manafort, Stone and Kelly (BMSK). BMSK understood there was money to be made outside the United States in the worst corners of the world.[38]

From 1990 to 1994, Manafort went to work for a group that claimed to represent the people of Kashmir: the Kashmiri American Council led by Syed Ghulam Nabi Fai.[39] Fai was a key figure in a scandal to influence DC that resulted in his arrest on July 19, 2011. He was charged with conspiracy and tax evasion related to the money he received for his efforts on behalf of the Pakistani intelligence agency, the ISI (Inter-Services Intelligence).[40] Fai had been a conduit for Pakistani intelligence to influence American politicians, using Manafort as his American front man. In 1994, Manafort worked for Edouard Balladur, the former prime minister of France. The scandal was over the sales of Agosta 90B submarines from France to Pakistan. Funds from the weapon sale were used to promote the Balladur campaign for prime minister, with Manafort pocketing over $200,000 on the transaction.

BMSK was hired to represent the flamboyant and spendthrift Filipino dictator Ferdinand Marcos at $950,000 per year.[41] Their official FARA disclosure stated the work was to "lobby, represent, and assist with promotion of the political and economic objectives of the principal (Marcos)."[42] Marcos was responsible for stealing billions from the Philippines and torturing thousands of Filipino citizens, yet was receiving support from American officials. Manafort was also a lobbyist for Saudi Arabia from June 1984 to June 1986. He focused on arms deals for the Saudi government. For Saudi Arabia, Manafort was paid $250,412.12 to represent the government of Saudi Arabia to discuss "the proposed arms sale to Saudi Arabia."[43] Manafort personally handled arrangements for Bandar to sit in the vice presidential box for the 1984 Republican National Committee.[44]

BMSK under Manafort was also paid to rebuild the terrible image of the Angolan warlord Jonas Savimbi. The effort by Black, Manafort, Stone and Kelly was started in September 1985 for $600,000 per year. Manafort worked with Christopher Lehman to secure the deal to help Savimbi gain support in Washington since both had worked in the Reagan administration. The firm represented the National Union for Total Independence of Angola (UNITA) on "US media and press strategies, monitored progress of legislation to aid UNITA." The firm was paid $599,990 for twelve months of work, ending on December 14, 1986.[45]

As Savimbi shifted from being a supporter of Maoist-influenced rural agrarian reforms to becoming a staunch anticommunist and ally to the conservative leaders in the United States, efforts to promote him as a champion of freedom brought him into the influential halls of the American government, including meetings with both President Reagan in 1986 and President George H. W. Bush in 1990.[46] Reagan even gave a nod to Savimbi's fight in Angola in his 1986 State of the Union address, and CIA support flowed in.[47] Other African murderers with money appealed to the firm. In Nigeria, BMSK worked with Sani Abacha, beginning in 1998, to promote an image of Abacha as a forward-thinking democracy-oriented leader, despite the overthrow of the Shonekan government and the subsequent brutal oppression and theft of funds from the people. But none of these eclipsed the Zairian dictator Mobutu Sese Seko. The firm worked for Zaire in 1989 on a $1 million per year contract to promote contacts with US officials. Mobutu enriched himself, building palaces and buying a Mercedes-Benz fleet; he embezzled millions while his country's economy crumbled. He had eliminated political opposition for years through execution, torture, and exile. Those he couldn't control through those means were bribed. However, Manafort exploited the view of Mobutu as an anti-Soviet ally across many administrations, from Richard Nixon through George H. W. Bush.[48] By contrast, the Jimmy Carter administration had a tepid engagement with the Mobutu regime.

Manafort Goes to Ukraine

In 2010 Victor Yanukovych, the pro-Moscow Ukrainian politician, was working under the roof of Rinat Akhmetov, a renowned Ukrainian gangster who murdered his way to power. Elected to the presidency with Putin's help, one of his first actions was to take control of the parliament, where he changed the laws so that he could seize and neuter the judiciary. Soon afterward, these changes in laws gave him and his cronies the ability to extort businesses, and those who did not come along were seized by the government and sold off. The entire basis of the government started to reflect Putin's early moves to consolidate the business and criminal classes under his control.

Unbeknownst to Manafort, a national movement rejecting the Ukranian government and against pro-Moscow politicians was brewing. It would be the best thing that ever happened to him. The rebellion—the Ukrainian Revolution of 2014, also known as the Euromaidan Revolution—would make him rich and solidify his role as a global dirty trickster and kingmaker.

On June 26, 2013, Iryna Krashkova, a young Ukrainian woman from Vradiivka, Ukraine, was kidnapped by two policemen and a taxi driver, gang-raped, beaten, and left for dead. When the three men left to find a shovel to bury her body, she escaped. As word spread of other similar assaults, which came to be known as the Vradieka rapes and murders, it formed the basis for a national protest. Protesters gathered at Maidan Nezalezhnosti (Independence Square) in downtown and, over a period of months, occupied the space at varying levels of intensity. When the president withdrew suddenly from taking steps to join the European Union, protesters were further motivated. People were now openly calling Yanukovych's government corrupt and in the pocket of Moscow. The protesters barricaded the square and gradually coalesced into a national Ukrainian movement opposing Moscow.

By Christmas, Moscow had given the Viktor Yanukovych government a financial relief package of $15 billion, which furthered the belief that Russia was buying the Ukrainian government. Mass protests engulfed the country after proof emerged that seven activists had been tortured, killed, or disappeared by the government. On February 20, 2014, President Yanukovych ordered a tax on the protesters. Sniper fire, source unknown, erupted from buildings near the square. Both protesters and police were shot to death by these mysterious snipers. When the shooting stopped, over one hundred protesters and sixteen policemen had been killed. Within a day, the police abandoned the government, and it became clear Yanukovych had no basis of support. The president fled to Russia. At almost the exact same time, Putin ordered his special operations forces to invade Crimea. The justification for this invasion was to protect ethnic Russian citizens from what Putin called "neo-Nazis."

A Thief on the Trump Train

Just when Trump needed an expert in stealing elections and winning at all costs, in walked Paul Manafort. Through his own efforts, Manafort got himself introduced to the Trump campaign team by Thomas J. Barrack Jr. in February 2016. "I'm not looking for a paid job," he wrote to Trump.[49] This was true. He was looking to glom onto a politician to whom he could sell his influence. If pro-Moscow Ukrainians paid well, he must have thought, "wait until Moscow gets a load of this!" When Manafort approached Trump, he was deeply in debt.[50] He maintained an unhealthily expensive lifestyle—a fatal flaw that allowed others to lead him by the nose to his downfall. Manafort had a personal debt of $17 million to Russian oligarch Oleg Deripaska. His financial obligations, plus his lack of a moral compass concerning whom he chose to work with, would prove problematic as he joined the Trump campaign.

On March 28, 2016, Manafort would be hired to hunt delegates for the upcoming primaries. Just over a month later, on May 19, 2016, he would be moved up to campaign chairman. Later, he would be promoted to campaign manager after the firing of Corey Lewandowski on June 20, 2016.[51] Lewandowski said, "Manafort has been in operational control of the campaign since April 7."[52]

Manafort was one of the attendees of a meeting with Russian lawyer Natalya Veselnitskaya in Trump Tower on June 9, 2016, arranged by Rob Goldstone. He was joined by Donald Trump Jr. and Jared Kushner.

Manafort created a super PAC called Rebuilding America Now in June 2016, which raised over $24 million by the end of the election cycle.[53] The PAC was run by Laurance Gay, a former associate at BMSK.[54] Gay was also involved in the Trump inaugural committee, which came under the scrutiny of the special counsel. Multi Media Services Corporation (MMSC) was paid $19 million by Rebuilding America Now. Anthony Fabrizio, a silent owner of MMSC, was a Republican pollster and strategist. Fabrizio had a long history of working with Manafort in other efforts, including Ukrainian elections. Because of his connection to Manafort, he became the pollster for the Trump campaign. Although Manafort was apparently working on the Trump campaign for free, his lawyers received a payment of $125,000 in June 2017 from MMSC.[55] Later, this arrangement would come under fire by prosecutors when it was discovered Manafort lied about the source of funding of the Fabrizio payment.[56]

The RNC was held from July 19 to 21, 2016, in Cleveland, Ohio. During the convention, the Trump campaign called for a change in the Republican platform on Ukraine to a pro-Kremlin position that would reduce support for Ukrainian opposition.[57] J. D. Gordon would say that Trump told him to push the new policy to remove support for arming Ukrainian allies.[58] Manafort would deny being behind the push to change the policy in an interview with MSNBC's Chuck Todd.[59]

Two weeks later, Manafort was under fire for his work for exiled Ukrainian president Viktor Yanukovych. News broke that Manafort had been paid millions to work for Yanukovych. He denied ever working for Ukraine or Russia. He was also accused of not disclosing lobbying efforts for the Party of Regions on August 18, 2016.[60] After the news broke, Manafort was fired. On August 19, 2016, he was labeled a "distraction" for the campaign, and the neo-fascist Steve Bannon took over responsibilities of campaign chairman. After Trump took power, they would claim Manafort had a "very limited role" during the 2016 campaign as campaign manager. After all his efforts for decades of working for the worst of the worst, Manafort was now a nonperson to Trump, a man he had known for decades. Time would prove Rick Wilson's dictum of "everything Trump touches dies" true when Manafort's relationship with Trump would cost him everything he had accumulated, including his freedom.

After Manafort, Trump stopped relying so much on political hit men. From this point onward, he would rely only on homegrown assets. However, the weakest link in any mafia is not the lieutenants, it's the children of the mafia don. The greed of the Trump kids would prove to be both the best and worst part of being a mafia dad.

CHAPTER 6

The Dynastic Crime Family

Sarah Kenzidor, a scholar on global dictatorships and autocrats, succinctly described the role of the Trump children in his White House. "Trump is grooming Jared and Ivanka for a dynastic kleptocracy. This is what you see in autocracies and in mafia states. It's a way to keep corruption going and keep that money flowing." And keeping the money going is precisely what they would do as they purported to serve the people of the United States.

The Trump family are closer to the medieval papal family the Borgias. Like the Borgias, they have cajoled, lied, and forced their way into the center of the state. Once in power, they have felt that all positions, roles, monies, and largesse was theirs. They have no sense of civic duty or responsibility to the nation—only to the family. The Constitution and the laws they swore to uphold are merely lip service to gain access to the intelligence, money, and spheres of influence that would enrich them personally.

The Trump family believes there is no reason that accountability should apply to them. They have no sense that the US government is built on the separation of powers and independent branches of government, which can enforce that accountability.

THE PANAMA PROJECT

Ivana Marie "Ivanka" Trump is the eldest daughter of Donald Trump and former model Ivana Trump. She was born on October 30, 1981. Ivanka was raised in New York as a Presbyterian Christian, primarily by her mother, along with siblings Donald Jr. and Eric. Her parents divorced when she was ten. She attended the Chapin School in Manhattan until she was fifteen, then transferred to Choate Rosemary Hall in Wallingford, Connecticut. After graduating from Choate, she attended Georgetown University for two years, then transferred to the Wharton School at the University of Pennsylvania. Ivanka graduated cum laude in 2004 with a bachelor's degree in economics. In 2005, she joined the Trump Organization as executive vice president of Development and Acquisitions.

In 2006, Ivanka filled in for Carolyn Kepcher on five episodes of her father's hit television program *The Apprentice 5*, first appearing to help judge the Gillette task in week two. She replaced Kepcher as a primary boardroom judge during the sixth season of *The Apprentice* and its follow-up iteration, *Celebrity Apprentice*.

In 2005, Donald Trump and his daughter Ivanka met with Roger Khafif, a Panamanian real estate developer, at Trump Tower New York to discuss licensing the Trump name to a development project in Panama. It would be one of the first major projects Ivanka would be lead manager on. In a Reuters interview, Khafif said that Trump wanted the Panama project for Ivanka, who had just joined the Trump Organization, to gain experience in the business. Donald was fresh off a bankruptcy, so the plan was for Newland International Properties Corp, run by Khafif, to finance construction with a bond underwritten by Bear Stearns. After Bear Stearns collapsed in 2008, the bond was acquired by J.P.Morgan. To sell the bond, the developer needed to prove it could sell the apartments. This is where Alexandre Ventura Nogueira came in. The Brazilian had arrived in Panama in the mid-2000s from Spain, where he had worked as a car salesman, but in fact the Spanish economy ministry said it had opened proceedings to fine Nogueira for an alleged "serious violation" of money-laundering laws. The proceedings were terminated about nine months later after officials could not determine Nogueira's whereabouts. Nogueira said it was a trivial incident, caused by him taking too much of his own cash through an airport.

In 2006, and on reportedly numerous other occasions, Ivanka met with Nogueira at Trump Tower New York. Ivanka was impressed by Nogueira and helped him to become the leading broker for the project. Nogueira accounted for one-third to one-half of the advance sales in the project. He said he discussed promotion and sales with Ivanka in Panama, Miami, and New York. He promised a return on investment many times over the initial purchase price per apartment. Where he acquired his money to buy the units was never asked by Ivanka or Donald. What is known was that Nogueira joined a group that traveled with Ivanka on a private chartered jet to look at a potential site for another Trump project in Cartagena, Colombia.

A Reuters investigation into the financing of the Trump Ocean Club, in conjunction with the American broadcaster NBC News, found that Nogueira "did business with a Colombian who was later convicted of money laundering and is now in detention in the United States; a Russian investor in the Trump project who was jailed in Israel in the 1990s for kidnap and threats to kill; and a Ukrainian investor who was arrested for alleged people smuggling while working with Nogueira and later convicted by a Kiev court."[1] Three years after getting involved in the Trump Ocean Club, Nogueira was arrested by Panamanian authorities on unrelated charges of fraud and forgery. Released on $1.4 million bail, he fled the country. There are at least four outstanding criminal cases related to the Trump Ocean Club.

Princess of the Trump Towers

In February 2006, Ivanka and Donald Jr. visited Moscow to develop business relationships. A year later, Ivanka formed a partnership with Dynamic Diamond Corp., a company of Moshe Lax, to create Ivanka Trump Fine Jewelry, a line sold at her flagship retail store in Manhattan. In November 2011, her store moved from Madison Avenue to 109 Mercer Street, a larger space in Soho. On October 2, 2015, it was reported that "Ivanka Trump's flagship store on Mercer Street appear[s] to be closed" and noted that the shop had been "stripped clean."[2]

Ivanka, like her father, has great difficulty with the truth. Numerous times she was found to have lied in areas of great significance. The most noteworthy was when she said she knew "literally almost nothing" about the Trump Organization's plans to build a hotel, office, and residential building in Russia while her father was running for office.[3] But the subsequent investigation would show she was copied in on numerous emails in 2015 about the project. She herself suggested an architect for the Trump Tower Moscow project. Ivanka claims it wasn't an "advanced project" and that there was a binding contract to build the project, a sly dodge that would fall apart when the Michael Cohen documents and testimony revealed the project has a memorandum of understanding signed by Trump himself.

Another shady deal made by the Trumps and spearheaded by Ivanka was partnering with Azerbaijanis in a new building in the oil-rich Caspian Sea capital of Baku. Trump Tower Baku was funded by close relatives of Ziya Mammadov, the transportation minister and one of the country's wealthiest and most powerful oligarchs. According to the Transparency International Corruption Perceptions Index, Azerbaijan is among the most corrupt nations in the world. The country's president, Ilham Aliyev, the son of the former president Heydar Aliyev, recently appointed his wife to be vice president. Mammadov became the transportation minister in 2002, around the time that the regime began receiving enormous profits from government-owned oil reserves in the Caspian Sea. At the time of the hotel deal, Mammadov, a career government official, was a well-documented billionaire—but at the time he was a bureaucrat with a salary of about $12,000 per year! Because of the Mammadov family's obvious mafia ties, they were given the nickname "the Corleones of the Caspian." In 2008, the Mammadovs partnered with the Trump Organization to build luxury apartments.

Trump Tower Baku originally had a construction budget of $195 million, but it went through multiple revisions, and the cost ended up being much higher. The tower was designed by a local architect, and in its original incarnation it had an ungainly roof that suggested the spikes of a crown. A London-based architecture firm, Mixity, redesigned the building, softening its edges and eliminating the ornamental roof. By the time the Trump team officially joined the project, in May 2012, many condominium residences had already been completed; at the insistence of Trump Organization staffers, most of the building's interior was gutted and rebuilt, and several elevators were added.[4] Apparently, this was supposed to be another golden ticket for Ivanka. The project was spearheaded by her; she attended most of the planning meetings and was the key decision maker. In November 2014, she posted a photo of herself on Instagram wearing a white helmet and looking out a window in the tower, with the comment, "I love a room with a view. Here I am in the incredible city of Baku, Azerbaijan, checking out the construction progress of our new Trump International Hotel & Tower, which will open in 2015. See more on my project on IvankaTrump.com." On that website, it explained her role: "Ivanka has overseen the development of Trump International Hotel & Tower Baku since its inception, and she recently returned from a trip to the fascinating city in Azerbaijan to check in on the project's progress."[5]

The Mammadov family also had embarrassing ties that would later emerge: Mammadov's projects with Trump had links to an Iranian family Mammadov did business with. The problem? This family was tied to the Iranian Revolutionary Guard Corps, an organization that, a few years later, Donald Trump would designate as an international terrorist group. The tower project allowed the Mammadovs to move money out of Iran, which was under sanctions, and launder it through Trump's agreement. In 2014 the building remained unoccupied when it was announced that it would be converted into a luxury hotel. Surprisingly, like many money-laundering projects, the hotel to this day has never earned back one dollar of profit.

Ivanka and Donald Trump Jr. had a major role in Trump SoHo, which soon became embroiled in controversy. They were in charge of sales at the development. Fraud was alleged in the way the building was marketed. Prospective buyers were led to believe that most of the units were sold when in fact only about 16 percent of them had sold. Most of the buyers were Russian and Latin American. In 2012, investigators were on the verge of indicting the Trump children on fraud charges.

Two years earlier, in April 2010, Trump SoHo buyers had sued the Trump Organization, citing an "ongoing pattern of fraudulent misrepresentations and deceptive sales practices" and alleging that Donald Trump Jr. and Ivanka Trump made misleading statements regarding the percentage of units sold. Manhattan attorney Adam Bailey, who represented the buyers, sent evidence of possible criminal issues to

Manhattan district attorney Cyrus Vance Jr. Trump settled the lawsuit in 2012, refunding 90 percent of the money and paying legal fees while not admitting any wrongdoing. Vance dropped the criminal case. Some of Vance's prosecutors wanted to proceed with the case but were blocked. News reports indicated Trump attorney Marc Kasowitz had made two five-figure donations to Vance's campaign for district attorney of New York County in 2012. Both were received and soon returned before the case was dropped; another one Vance received and also returned after the case was already dropped. In 2013, Donald Trump told the BBC his only involvement in the project was via a licensing deal—but he had announced the project in 2006 on *The Apprentice*.

The morning after the RNC convention in July 2016, where Ivanka made a speech and introduced her father, Ivanka's official Twitter account tweeted, "Shop Ivanka's look from her #RNC speech," with a link to a Macy's page that featured the dress she wore. After her father's election, Ivanka wore a bracelet during a family appearance on *60 Minutes*. Her company then used an email blast to promote the bracelet. After cries of "monetization" from critics, the company quickly apologized.

Other Trump properties, which Ivanka was involved with, would come under deep scrutiny. In March 2019 the FBI was looking into the negotiations and financing surrounding Trump International Hotel and Tower in Vancouver, Canada. Ivanka Trump reportedly negotiated the deal with the developer, Joo Kim Tiah, who is from one of Malaysia's wealthiest families. Though the Trump Organization doesn't own the building, it receives licensing and marketing fees from the Canadian development company, Holborn Group, run by Tiah. According to President Trump's June financial disclosure form, the Trump Organization made more than $5 million in royalties and $21,500 in management fees from the Vancouver property. The $360 million project opened just after Trump took office and quickly became a magnet for foreign buyers. Holborn is backed financially by Tony Tiah Thee Kian, chairman of TA Enterprise, which controls several other businesses. Tony Tiah has a business history that includes securities laws violations and false statements to the Kuala Lumpur stock exchange, according to Malaysia's Securities Commission.

China Trademarks

After the presidential victory, Ivanka Trump and her husband announced plans to establish a family home in the Kalorama neighborhood of Washington, DC. Federal filings revealed that, in 2017, Ivanka and Kushner had upward of $740 million in assets. She resigned from her position at the Trump Organization; the organization removed images of Ivanka and her father from its websites, in accordance with official advice on federal ethics rules. That's about where ethical compliance ended for her. Ivanka soon began serving in her father's presidential administration, where she became the special assistant to the president, an unpaid position. When ethics concerns were raised about her having access to classified material for which she had no need to know, Ivanka said in a statement:

> I have heard the concerns some have with my advising the President in my personal capacity while voluntarily complying with all ethics rules and I will instead serve as an unpaid employee in the White House, subject to all of the same rules as other Federal employees. Throughout this process, I have been working closely and in good faith with the White House Counsel and my personal counsel to address the unprecedented nature of my role.[6]

Like many parts of her public commentary, this one was found to be untrue.

Within three months, whether designed to either reward Ivanka for her financial fidelity or a calculated move to place her in a difficult ethics position, China made moves to make her even richer. In early April 2017, the government of China extended trademarks to Ivanka Trump's businesses. On that same day, Donald Trump hosted Chinese president Xi Jinping at Mar-a-Lago. Ivanka and Jared Kushner sat next to the Chinese leader and his wife, Peng Liyuan, at the state dinner.[7] Also during the visit, the Kushner's five-year-old daughter Arabella "sang a traditional Chinese song, in Mandarin [for Xi]." Tencent QQ, the Chinese state media, played the video clip over 2.2 million times.[8]

The Ivanka Trump brand was criticized for allegedly copying designs by other designers and by animal rights groups for the use of rabbit fur. In 2016, the US Consumer Product Safety Commission recalled Ivanka Trump–branded scarves because they did not meet federal flammability standards. It was also discovered that most of her fashion line was produced outside the United States.

While in the White House Ivanka Trump's fashion brand received preliminary approval on five trademarks in China as President Trump was in trade negotiations with the Chinese government. Ivanka's trademark applications were filed in 2016 and 2017, according to the Associated Press. One trademark for brokerage, charitable fundraising, and art valuation services was approved on January 6, 2019, and finalized in March 2019.[9] Eighteen trademarks were granted to companies linked to President Donald Trump and his daughter Ivanka in November 2018, and another sixteen trademarks granted in October 2018, according to China's trademark office's online database.[10] Critics argue that asking for foreign trademarks opens the administration up to pressure during foreign negotiations and sets the Trumps up to profit from their work in the White House.

According to White House officials, Ivanka was selected to assist the treasury secretary, Steven Mnuchin, and acting White House chief of staff Mick Mulvaney to select the head of the World Bank. Ivanka's involvement with the World Bank was questioned in 2018, when Senator Benjamin L. Cardin, Democrat of Maryland, sent a letter to Mnuchin raising questions about Ivanka's role with the fund, given her clothing and accessories brand reported manufacturing issues in China.[11]

In July 2018, Ivanka announced she would be shutting down her clothing and accessories line, though she still retains the copyrights and intellectual property associated with her brand and continues to seek trademarks. This news came amid a marked decline in sales, with retailers dropping her line as consumers protested the brand, in part because of where the items were manufactured. Ivanka claimed the shutdown was to avoid conflicts with her work in Washington.[12] By mid-2019 her line of "luxury" clothing would be knocked down to one dollar at Marshalls department stores.

Women Entrepreneurs Fund

As one can plainly see, the backstory of this Trump scion has been filled with complicity in corruption, but she has mostly been immune from press scrutiny, based solely on her beautiful face and expensive tastes. Her questionable business activities continued into the presidency. Just two days into President Trump's first foreign trip to Saudi Arabia, May 20–22, 2017, Ivanka Trump's proposed Women Entrepreneurs Fund was promised a combined $100 million by Saudi Arabia and the United Arab Emirates (UAE), specifically to help women in the Middle East.[13]

The fund, run by the World Bank and not Ivanka, was to provide female entrepreneurs with financial support in the form of capital and access to networking and financial markets. This is somewhat of a conflict with Saudi culture and laws in the UAE governing women and money, which state that a woman can't legally have money if she is married, no matter the window dressing.

In February 2019, the White House launched the Women's Global Development and Prosperity Initiative, a government-wide project led by Ivanka. The initiative involves the State Department, the National Security Council, and other agencies to coordinate current programs and develop new ones to assist women in job training, financial support, and legal or regulatory reform, among other things.[14] The US Agency for International Development (USAID) will initially set up a $50 million fund, using already budgeted dollars. Public and private resources will also be used, and PepsiCo and UPS announced their partnerships. The Trump administration's 2020 budget allocated $100 million to Ivanka's pet initiative at the same time President Trump twice tried to slash USAID's budget by a third. He was ultimately not successful.

Jared Kushner

In 2005 Ivanka began dating real estate developer Jared Kushner, whom she met through mutual friends. The couple broke up briefly in 2008 over the objections of his parents, who were Jewish. Ivanka later resumed dating Kushner. Once it became serious and the engagement was announced, she converted to Orthodox Judaism in July 2009, before marrying Kushner. The couple eventually had three children.

Born January 10, 1981, in Livingston, New Jersey, Kushner is the oldest son of former real-estate developer Charles Kushner, who, himself, is the son of Jewish immigrants from the USSR. Kushner attended Harvard University from 1999 to 2003. He graduated with a bachelor of arts degree in government. It was reported that Charles pledged $2.5 million to Harvard, to be paid in annual installments of $250,000, and two US senators helped to get Jared into Harvard, despite his low GPA and SAT scores. The senators included New Jersey senator Frank Lautenberg, to whom Charles and his family gave nearly $100,000 from 1992 to 2002, and Massachusetts senator Edward Kennedy, a Harvard alumnus whose family had been associated with Harvard for three generations. Kennedy reportedly called the admissions dean on Jared's behalf.[15] Jared Kushner graduated from New York University in 2007 with dual JD and MBA degrees.[16]

While attending Harvard, Jared Kushner bought and sold real estate in Somerville, Massachusetts, as a vice president of Somerville Building Associates (a division of Kushner Companies). Its other vice president was his maternal uncle, Richard Stadtmauer, then vice chairman of Kushner Companies. The venture was dissolved in 2005 after earning a profit of $20 million.

In the summer of 2004, Charles Kushner was fined $508,900 by the Federal Election Commission for contributing to Democratic political campaigns. In 2005, a plea deal was negotiated between US Attorney Chris Christie and Charles Kushner. In exchange for pleading guilty to filing false tax returns, eighteen counts of illegal campaign contributions, and witness tampering—for assaulting his sister's husband, William Schulder, who was cooperating with the feds—Charles would spend two years in prison. As a result of his conviction, Charles was disbarred and prohibited from practicing law in New Jersey, New York, and Pennsylvania. Jared took over management of Kushner Companies.[17]

Jared cofounded, along with his brother, and was part owner of Cadre, an online real-estate investment crowd-funding platform that allowed investors to pool money to buy stakes in large real estate projects. Launched in 2014, its CEO was Ryan Williams, who left Blackstone Group to work alongside the Kushners. Cadre raised $65 million in 2017. It was reportedly an $800 million valuation. According to a federal disclosure form, Jared owned a Cadre stake valued at $5 million to $25 million.

Cadre also had a $250 million partnership with Goldman Sachs, which pledged to allow its wealth management clients to use the Cadre platform. Kushner played a pivotal role in persuading Trump to appoint Goldman Sachs's president Gary D. Cohn as his chief economic adviser. Goldman Sachs had also loaned money to the Kushner Companies.

Another financial entanglement was with Africa Israel Investments Ltd. (AFI Group) involving chairman Uzbek-born Israeli citizen Lev Leviev, who owned the former *New York Times* building. As noted before Leviev is known as the "King of Diamonds" for his extensive holdings in Africa, Israel, and Russia, and is one of the world's wealthiest men. He claims to be a "true friend" of Russian president Vladimir Putin through his work with an influential Jewish organization in the former Soviet Union. In 2008, a year after purchasing the building, Leviev invited Donald Trump to his Madison Avenue store. Leviev hoped to work with Trump on Moscow real estate deals. Six years later, Leviev's company was having financial difficulties and sold the building's office portion for $160 million, not including four retail floors. Leviev's daughter, Chagit, attempted to find a buyer for the retail space. The company said it would entertain offers no lower than $300 million. Kushner's company offered $265 million, which was rejected. Kushner himself negotiated with Chagit Leviev and eventually succeeded with a $296 million offer.

On May 4, 2015, at an after-party for a Metropolitan Museum of Art gala, Jared and Ivanka ran into Chagit—an encounter that was memorialized on Instagram by Chagit. The deal was signed a week later and closed in October 2015. The Leviev company said in a statement to the *Washington Post* that Kushner simply made the highest offer and "there was no political element to the transaction."[18]

Kushner Companies bought three apartment buildings in Queens in 2015, with most of the tenants protected by special rules that prevent developers from pushing them out and raising rents. But Kushner Companies did that with unprecedented speed. Two years later, it sold all three buildings for $60 million, nearly 50 percent more than the company had paid for the buildings.

Kushner Companies routinely filed false paperwork declaring it had zero rent-controlled tenants in dozens of buildings it owned across New York City when, in fact, it had hundreds.[19] Housing Rights Initiative, a tenants' rights watchdog, compiled work permit application documents and shared them with the Associated Press. Kushner Companies filed at least eighty applications for construction permits in thirty-four buildings across New York City from 2013 to 2016, all of them falsely indicating there were no rent-regulated tenants. Tax documents show there were more than three hundred rent-regulated units. Nearly all the permit applications were signed by a Kushner employee, including sometimes the chief operating officer. Submitting false documents for construction permits is a misdemeanor, which can carry fines of up to $25,000. But real estate experts say the laws are often ignored by developers with little or no consequences. Landlords often get off with no more than a demand from the city, sometimes a year or more later, to file an amended form with the correct numbers. Housing Rights Initiative discovered Kushner Companies filed dozens of amended forms for the buildings mentioned in the documents, most of them one to two years later.

Current and former tenants of the Queens buildings told the AP that they were subjected to extensive construction—banging, drilling, work area messes, and leaking water—that they believe were targeted harassments to get them to leave.[20] Kushner retained stakes in many of these properties after he joined Trump's administration.

Cadre announced that it would target "opportunity zones" for investments. These zones are benefitting from the Trump administration's tax overhaul, which provides deferments and tax breaks for developers investing in designated low-income neighborhoods. Qualified investments in an opportunity zone can defer capital gains taxes from an unrelated investment, and any gains on an investment in the zone are tax exempt as long as they're held for ten years. The Kushner Companies had at least ten properties in opportunity zones.[21]

Javanka and the Bears

Kushner started working with the Center for the National Interest (CFTNI), a foreign policy organization, and Dimitri Simes, the Russian-born CEO, after attending an event with former secretary of state Henry Kissinger in 2016. CFTNI was established by former president Richard Nixon. Over the years, reports have linked the center to several Russian-government-funded initiatives—which CFTNI denies—and it was alleged to be linked to Maria Butina, a Russian who pled guilty to conspiracy. As I mentioned, Butina used the NRA to infiltrate Republican political circles on behalf of Moscow.

The center also reportedly helped Alexander Torshin, Butina's mentor and the deputy head of the Russian central bank, to organize meetings with US officials. Torshin was a close ally of Vladimir Putin. The center claimed that Butina attended one event with Torshin only as his translator. Kushner also met Russian ambassador Sergey Kislyak at an event at the center.[22]

Kushner was interacting with Simes about Russian matters during the campaign. On March 14, 2016, Simes and Kushner both attended the CFTNI luncheon in New York City. The purpose of the meeting was for CFTNI to recruit new board members, and Kushner told the special counsel he intended to seek Simes's help in finding foreign policy professionals for the campaign.[23]

On March 24, 2016, Simes and Kushner spoke again following the public announcement of a new foreign policy team. A week later, they met again in Kushner's office. Simes told special counsel investigators the reason for the meeting was to discuss the recruiting of policy advisers who could help form Trump's foreign policy. In both these meetings, they planned the foreign policy speech that Trump would give at the Mayflower Hotel. Simes worked with Stephen Miller to create the speech with Paul Saunders and Richard Burt of CFTNI. It was Simes who invited Kislyak with a promise of an opportunity to meet Trump. On April 27, 2016, Simes introduced Kislyak to Kushner and Trump.

Kushner and Simes continued conversations about Trump's foreign policy team. They met again during the 2016 general election on August

17, 2016. Before the meeting, Simes emailed Kushner with details on Trump's reaction to a "Russia Policy Memo." The meeting turned into a discussion of an alleged tape the Russians made of Bill Clinton. Simes told investigators that Kushner did not show interest in the "old news."

Yuri Milner, a Russian investor, gave $850,000 to the Kushner brothers' firm Cadre in 2016.[24] Milner created Digital Sky Technologies (DST) in 2005. Milner's DST Global was started in 2009 with help from Russian oligarch Alisher Usmanov.[25] Milner was involved in investments in Twitter and Facebook. The investments were done in cooperation with the Russian bank VTB. DST Global invested $400 million in Twitter beginning in 2011. Both dropped their investments in Twitter in 2014. The release of the Panama Papers in 2015 gave insight into the dealings of Milner and VTB. Milner cofounded Mail.ru Group Ltd. DST Global investments included over thirty companies, including Airbnb, Alibaba, Spotify Ltd., Groupon Inc., and Zynga Inc.[26]

Milner's investment in Facebook came at the request of Mark Zuckerberg.[27] These transactions were revealed in part by the release of the Paradise Papers, leaked documents from a firm working for superwealthy companies and individuals to avoid tax laws. Though Milner denies working with the Russian government, Gazprom figured prominently in the funding of DST. Gazprom transferred nearly a billion dollars into Kanton Services, a company based in the British Virgin Islands. Then Kanton invested in DST USA II in 2011.[28] After DST USA II invested in fifty million shares of Facebook, its ownership was assumed by Usmanov, who subsequently sold it in 2012.

But Gazprom was not the only investor in Milner businesses. Russian bank VTB transferred approximately $191 million into DST Investments 3, who then invested in Twitter in 2011.[29] VTB and Gazprom are directly controlled by the Kremlin. Milner met with Kushner in Aspen, Colorado, in autumn 2016.[30]

Kushner received a "proposal for reconciliation between the United States and Russia" from his hedge fund manager friend Rick Gerson from Putin associate Kirill Dmitriev. During the transition, Dmitriev remained intent on being in contact with Kushner and Donald Jr. and repeatedly sought contact with them through George Nader. Many areas of the interaction are redacted from volume 1 of the Mueller report (see the

Prince, Nader, and Flynn sections). Through Gerson, Kushner received a two-page document with five points of US-Russia reconciliation. In turn, Kushner sent the document to Steve Bannon and Rex Tillerson.[31]

A week after the election on November 8, 2016, Sergey Kislyak, the Russian ambassador to the United States, reached out to meet with Kushner. They arranged to meet on November 30, 2016, at Trump Tower, and were joined by Michael Flynn at Kushner's request. The meeting was known for its discussion of the creation of a "secure communications line" between Trump's transition team and the Kremlin. Kushner said Kislyak asked if there was a secure line to convey information about Syria that was coming from his "generals." Kushner asked if they could use the secure facilities at the Russian embassy, a massive security red flag. Kushner said he wanted to use Russian diplomatic facilities to shield preinauguration discussions from monitoring by the NSA or the CIA. Kislyak quickly rejected that idea. In a later statement, Kushner denied reports that said he asked for a secret backchannel for communications. Kislyak reported to his superiors in Moscow that Kushner made the proposal during a meeting on December 1 or 2 at Trump Tower.[32]

The Russian embassy pushed for more meetings. It contacted Kushner's assistant to press for another meeting with Kislyak. After wrangling over whether Kislyak was important enough to represent communications with Russia, Kushner agreed to meet with Sergey Gorkov, the chief of VEB, the state-owned bank in Russia. They met December 13, 2016, in Manhattan at the Colony Capital building. The special counsel reported the "accounts from Kushner and Gorkov differ as to whether the meeting was diplomatic or business in nature." On Kushner's account of events, he claimed to meet Gorkov in a diplomatic role, and VEB claimed the two met to discuss business. Though the special counsel did not resolve the conflicting accounts, it pointed out that there was a corresponding decrease in contact between Gorkov (VEB) and Kushner as the Mueller investigation increased its scrutiny.[33]

Kushner was awash in contacts with Russian diplomats during the campaign and after. Between April and November 2016, Kushner had at least two phone calls with Russian ambassador Kislyak.[34] There were four meetings according to Kushner's disclosures.[35] On April 26, 2016, he met Kislyak at the Mayflower Hotel for a reception before presidential candidate Trump delivered a foreign policy speech. Kislyak was one of four ambassadors greeted.

As noted above, on December 13, 2016, Kushner said he was asked by Kislyak to attend a meeting with Sergey Gorkov. Kushner said Gorkov introduced himself and gave him two gifts: a piece of artwork and a bag of dirt from the Belarus village Kushner's grandparents were from. He said Gorkov discussed his bank and the Russian economy and described himself as friendly with Russian president Vladimir Putin. Kushner insisted that the meeting had nothing to do with his work at Kushner Companies. In 2010, VEB assisted the struggling Trump International Hotel and Tower project in Toronto. Since 2014, VEB had been subject to US sanctions over Russia's annexation of Crimea and meddling in Ukraine. Kushner's meeting was not known by the public until March 2017, when the *New York Times* broke the story. The White House refused to disclose the date of the meeting, and then later called it a routine diplomatic encounter that went nowhere. VEB said it was part of its ongoing business strategy.[36] On June 1, 2017, the *Washington Post* reported, based on its own investigation, that on December 13, 2016, a private plane associated with VEB flew from Moscow to Newark, New Jersey, Airport. The following day, the plane flew to Japan, where Vladimir Putin met with Japan's prime minister Shinzo Abe on December 15.[37]

Kushner and Deutsche Bank

One month before election day, Kushner Companies finalized a $285 million loan from Deutsche Bank. Jared Kushner along with his brother, Joshua, made personal guarantees on the loan. They were part of a "nonrecourse carve-out" guarantee. Jared did not reveal this on his financial disclosure form with the Office of Government Ethics. The loan was a refinancing deal for four mostly empty retail floors of the former New York Times Building, a purchase made in 2015 from Lev Leviev. The loan gave Kushner Companies $74 million more than it paid for the property. Separately, Jared Kushner did disclose that he and his mother have a personal line of credit with Deutsche Bank worth up to $25 million.

Just before finalizing this $285 million loan, Deutsche Bank was negotiating a settlement on a federal mortgage fraud case and charges from New York state regulators that it aided a possible Russian money-laundering scheme. Deutsche Bank was also tied to the ongoing investigation into Russian meddling in the 2016 presidential election.[38]

The hedge fund firm Platinum Partners borrowed money in the days leading up to the June arrest of one of its cofounders. Some of the money borrowed included $4.1 million from Marisa Stadtmauer and $6.4 million from Richard Stadtmauer. The Stadtmauers were Kushner's aunt and uncle: Richard was Jared Kushner's mother's brother and a former vice chairman of Kushner Companies.[39]

The Trump Whisperers

In 2017, Joshua Harris, a founder of Apollo Global Management, was advising the Trump administration on infrastructure policy. He met with Jared Kushner multiple times, during which they discussed, among other things, a possible White House position for Harris, though the job did not materialize. In November 2017, Apollo Global Management lent the Kushner Companies $184 million to refinance the mortgage of a Chicago skyscraper. One month after Apollo made the loan, the US Securities and Exchange Commission dropped a pending inquiry into Apollo. Apollo was one of the world's largest private equity firms. The loan to Kushner Companies was triple the size of the average property loan made by Apollo's real estate lending arm, according to securities filings by Apollo. The loan was also one of the largest loans Kushner Companies received.[40]

Kushner Companies got an even larger loan from Citigroup. In the spring of 2017, Citigroup gave Kushner Companies and one of its partners $325 million to finance office buildings in Brooklyn. This loan was made shortly after Citigroup's chief executive Michael L. Corbat met with Kushner at the White House.[41]

The Watchtower, a noticeable complex of buildings on a bluff in Brooklyn Heights and at one time the world headquarters of the

Jehovah's Witnesses, was sold to developers in August 2016, shortly after Donald Trump accepted the Republican nomination for president. The buyer was Jared Kushner and CIM Group, a private equity firm based in Los Angeles. The $340 million purchase was one of the biggest real estate transactions in Brooklyn history.[42]

Documents show that CIM had done at least seven real estate deals that benefited Trump and others in his circle, including Kushner. One of the CIM deals was the Trump SoHo project. That deal, in December 2010, was worth a reported $85 million and literally saved the project before the banks foreclosed. That same month, CIM spent more than a half-billion dollars bailing out the SoHo project's codeveloper, Tamir Sapir, on two other properties he owned: 11 Madison Avenue and the William Beaver House in Lower Manhattan.

At the same time, CIM Group pursued an array of lucrative government contracts, pension investments, lobbying interests, and a global infrastructure fund, all of which were set to benefit from Trump's presidency. CIM was founded in 1994 by Israeli businessmen Shaul Kuba and Avi Shemesh and American Richard Ressler. Ressler's brother Tony Ressler cofounded Apollo Global Management with his brother-in-law Leon Black. Apollo has made large loans to Kushner Companies.

In May 2017, Kushner accompanied Trump on the pair's first diplomatic trip to Israel. This was part of Kushner's White House assignment (his stated goal was to achieve peace in the Middle East). Shortly before this trip, Kushner Companies received a $30 million investment from Menora Mivtachim, one of Israel's largest financial firms. The deal was not made public and added significant equity to ten Maryland apartment complexes controlled by Kushner Companies. Kushner divested some of his business holdings when he joined the Trump administration, but he still has stakes in most of the family holdings—including those apartment buildings.

Kushner's Israel connections run deep and include:[43]

- The Kushners teamed up with Beny Steinmetz (one of Israel's wealthy elite) to buy $200 million of Manhattan apartment buildings and build a luxury rental tower in New Jersey. Beny Steinmetz was the subject of a Justice Department bribery investigation, though he denied wrongdoing.

- Kushner Companies took at least four loans from Bank Hapoalim, Israel's largest bank. The bank was the subject of a Justice Department investigation for allegedly helping wealthy Americans evade taxes.
- The Kushner family's foundation donates money to an Israeli settlement group in the West Bank.

During the last days of the Obama administration, former national security adviser Michael Flynn was instructed to contact foreign ambassadors and foreign ministers of countries on the UN Security Council, in advance of a vote condemning Israeli settlements. Flynn was told to get them to delay the vote until after Barack Obama left office or oppose the resolution altogether. To assist in this effort, *Bloomberg News* reported that intelligence was shared between envoys working for Benjamin Netanyahu and the Trump team.[44]

When the special counsel came into being, it was apparent that Kushner would need a lawyer—a good one. His entire world would come under scrutiny and his criminal liability was increasing. Kushner was represented by Jamie S. Gorelick, a former deputy attorney general. The departure of Bob Mueller from WilmerHale law firm to become special counsel prompted Kushner to seek independent legal advice on whether to continue with his current counsel. After speaking with Abbe Lowell, a prominent criminal defense and trial lawyer, Kushner added him to his legal team. Lowell represents both Republicans and Democrats in high-profile cases.[45]

CHAPTER 7

The Five Dangles

The children of Trump were proving to be accessible though financial ties. Trump himself was now primed to benefit from Russia's moves. Now the network was ready to be brought into Moscow's sphere. This would require inducements and rewards that would be dangled in front of the greedy Americans. Of course, they all would grasp at the gold ring that the ex-KGB officer placed before their eyes.

On June 15, 2015, Donald J. Trump announced his candidacy for president of the United States. Almost at the exact same time, hackers in military intelligence and the FSB's clandestine service would infect the computer servers of the Democratic National Committee with malware suites cybersecurity experts nicknamed Cozy Bear and Fancy Bear. The stolen materials would materialize one month before Trump would win the nomination for the Republican Party. But by that time, Trump was taking no chances and kept up his connections to Moscow to get his golden tower. Neither was Moscow taking chances. They knew that most American assets were only motivated by greed. Threatening men this financially rapacious did nothing. For this operation a special brand of *kompromat* would be needed. For Team Trump the Russians would use a "carrot and carrot" approach. There were five specific approaches identified whose success depended on their target's specific desire for power, money, or recognition. Putin would use his government to "dangle" rewards before these men, and the Americans were eager to snatch at them.

Dangle #1: Trump Tower Moscow 2.0

In January 2016, Trump's personal attorney Michael Cohen reached out to Putin's press secretary Dmitri Peskov but spoke with an assistant in a twenty-minute call.[1] For the first six months of 2016, Felix Sater and Cohen continued their discussions about the visit to Moscow to meet with high-level officials. As noted before, Cohen at one point sent all the pages of his passport with the agreement to send Trump's personal travel documents once a date was scheduled. The conversation turned into an invitation to the St. Petersburg Economic Forum. According to Sater's text messages, Putin's press secretary issued the invite. Sater also promised a meeting with Putin or Dmitri Medvedev at the forum and an official invitation was sent to Michael Cohen as well.[2] Sater would later email: "Let's make this happen and build a Trump Moscow . . . and possibly fix relations between the countries by showing everyone that commerce and business are much better and more practical than politics. That should be a message as well, and we will help him agree on that message. Help world peace and make a lot of money, I would say that's a great lifetime goal for us to go after."[3]

He would continue: "I know how to play it and we will get this done. Buddy our boy can become President of the USA and we can engineer it. I will get all of Putin's team to buy in on this," Sater told Cohen in that email. "I will get Putin on this program and we will get Donald elected."[4]

Trump-Moscow talks continued through the fall of June 2016. In October 2015, Sater wrote Cohen that he was in Moscow meeting with Andrei Molchanov on a potential Trump Tower Moscow. Molchanov is a Russian politician and former owner of LSR Group, a real estate development, construction, and building materials company, which he founded in 1993. Sater wrote that Molchanov's stepfather was governor of St. Petersburg and Putin once worked for him.[5] Andrei Molchanov is the adopted son of Yuri Molchanov. Yuri Molchanov was Putin's boss when Yuri was the deputy director of Leningrad University in the early 1990s and Putin assisted him in a joint venture between the university and Proctor & Gamble.[6] The elder Molchanov is now senior vice president of VTB Capital, one of the three strategic arms of VTB Group. Numerous bankers from Deutsche Bank's office in Moscow were hired to establish VTB Capital. VTB Bank was involved in discussions of Trump Tower Moscow's financing. According to the final Mueller report, Cohen's efforts to have a Trump Tower Moscow built and meetings with Putin would continue well into the 2016 election.

Dangle #2: George Papadopoulos and Dirt on Clinton

The Trump Tower Moscow negotiations were easily the longest dangle of all Trump activities, technically having begun in 1987, but other individuals were being sussed out as multiple backup plans were executed to not only get to Trump but to his key advisers, such as George Papadopoulos.

George Papadopoulos came from a political family in Chicago. After earning a degree in security studies, he went to serve as an intern at the Hudson Institute, then worked for Energy Stream, focusing on energy sector consultation. In December 2015 he joined the Ben Carson campaign.

Papadopoulos reached out to Corey Lewandowski via LinkedIn in the summer of 2015 to ask for help staffing the campaign. Lewandowski said he would keep in touch. "There was something in me that just thought Donald Trump was going to be elected the President of the United States," Papadopoulos told the Joint Judiciary and Reform Committee.[7]

Around March 6, 2016, Papadopoulos learned he would work for the Trump campaign, and Sam Clovis, a longtime Republican operative who has connections to the Kremlin, was the one who brought Papadopoulos onboard.[8] At the time Papadopoulos was twenty-eight years old and had limited experience as a research analyst, beyond his work as an unpaid intern at the Hudson Institute. He was a target ready to be exploited. Evidence suggests that it was Joseph Mifsud, a pro-Kremlin professor from Malta, who had that role. Mifsud approached Papadopoulos around March 14, 2016, while they were both in Italy. In January and February 2016, the Mueller report revealed that while in London Mifsud had contact with one Russian operative connected to the Internet Research

Agency, and they discussed meeting in Russia. In spring 2016, around the exact same time, Mifsud learned about the release of the Clinton emails. Mifsud also communicated with a Russian Ministry of Defense employee who had common contacts with DC Leaks operatives.[9]

Ten days later, Mifsud met with Papadopoulos in London and introduced him at the swank Holborn Hotel to Olga Polonskaya, who claimed she was the daughter of a high-level Russian diplomat and Putin's niece or the "Russian President's niece." Papadopoulos said of the meeting: "She really didn't leave that big of an impression on me except that she was very beautiful." This is a classic espionage technique, dangling a sexual capital to lure in the fish. An agent who uses sex appeal is technically referred to as a "honeypot." Mifsud indicated in an interview with an Italian newspaper that Papadopoulos had a romantic interest in Polonskaya, which is intriguing considering the Mueller report would later indicate Mifsud referred to her as "baby," and he "may have been involved in a personal relationship with her too."[10] All of this speaks to an intelligence activity using sex as a potential lure.

Polonskaya did not speak much English, Papadopoulos said, but following the meeting, Mifsud communicated with a woman who Mifsud claimed was Putin's niece—but she spoke near fluent English. This woman had numerous questions about sanctions.[11] Polonskaya subsequently deleted all of her social media accounts when identified in November 2017.[12] The Mueller report confirmed that Papadopoulos was indeed speaking with Polonskaya at the time.[13]

On March 31, 2016, Papadopoulos attended a meeting of Trump's foreign policy advisory team, which included Trump and other campaign officials, at a Trump hotel. At the meeting, he claimed he could arrange a meeting between Trump and Putin.[14]

A little later Mifsud introduced Papadopoulos to someone he claimed was the Russian ambassador to the United Kingdom, Alexander Yakovenko. Mifsud had a photo taken with the ambassador in 2014 after they met to discuss Russia-UK cooperation.[15] Papadopoulos claimed the man was not Yakovenko—implying he knew what Yakovenko looked like. He instead worked with Ivan Timofeev, from the Russia International Affairs Council. "This misunderstanding that I actually met that person, because I lied to the campaign about it, where I told them I just met the Russian ambassador, my good friend Mifsud—I never met the Russian ambassador, just to be clear," Papadopoulos told a joint House Judiciary and Government Reform and Oversight Committee on October 25, 2018. This was just a month before he went to prison for lying to the FBI, so he was certainly minimizing and lying in the testimony. Later, the Republican-run committee released the transcript of the interview to a known conservative news outlet to spin and minimize what Papadopoulos did. Papadopoulos also claims Mifsud never followed through with any of the Russian contacts he said he had and indicated the attention to Mifsud was misplaced and overblown; however, Mifsud has proven access to Russian diplomats and foreign policy think tanks, which often operate as Russian intelligence fronts.[16]

On April 26, 2016, Mifsud, who had just returned from Moscow, told Papadopoulos at the Andaz Hotel in London that he learned the Russians had "thousands of emails" related to Hillary Clinton. "He was giddy, you know like he had something he wanted to get off his chest," Papadopoulos said. He later emailed Stephen Miller about the meeting with Mifsud and received "interesting messages" from Miller, though he would later back away from this comment.[17]

Note that Papadopoulos's clandestine activities happened nearly two months before the news about the DNC hack broke, which reveals Russia's multilayered intelligence approach. Papadopoulos met with Mifsud over the next several months to set up meetings with Russian government officials, notably Putin, and the Trump campaign. During this time, FBI-obtained emails show he exchanged emails with and Skyped numerous unnamed people from the Russian Ministry of Foreign Affairs (MFA), which contradicts his testimony that he never communicated with any high-level Russians. In the end, the Trump-Putin meeting never occurred, but the effort on Papadopoulos's part was enormous.[18]

My analysis would be validated by more evidence found in the Mueller report. Using Papadopoulos's LinkedIn messages, FBI investigators showed he contacted three MFA contacts during the course of the 2016 campaign. On April 25, 2016, he contacted the first secretary of the Russian embassy in Ireland; in July 2016, he communicated with the spokesman for the Russian embassy in Washington, DC; and on September 16, 2016, he contacted Sergei Nalobin, the deputy press secretary for the

MFA. The Mueller report did not address what Papadopoulos discussed with them.[19]

On May 10, 2016, Papadopoulos told the Australian ambassador to the UK, Alexander Downer, that Russia had "dirt" on Clinton. The Australians reported this to the FBI in July 2016, after the WikiLeaks dump of documents.[20] Papadopoulos also said he spoke with Greek foreign minister Nikos Kotzias about this at the end of May 2016. Kotzias apparently looked surprised and said this was not something Papadopoulos should be talking about.[21]

On June 19, 2016, the last day of Lewandowski on the campaign, Papadopoulos noted to campaign officials that he could meet with Russian MFA contacts. Papadopoulos, according to intercepts included in the Mueller report, wrote he was "willing to make the trip off the record if it's in the interest of Mr. Trump and the campaign to meet with specific people." When Lewandowski left, Papadopoulos continued with this "off the record" idea.[22]

On July 15, 2016, Sergei Millian, a Belarussian American citizen, reached out to Papadopoulos via LinkedIn, and they met up in New York City. The Mueller report noted Papadopoulos asked Timofeev if he knew who Millian was, and Timofeev said he did not.[23] Millian said he could help the Trump campaign with Russian outreach. On August 23, 2016, Millian sent a Facebook message to Papadopoulos that he "share with [him] a disruptive technology that might be instrumental in [his] political work for the campaign."[24]

In October or November 2016, Papadopoulos considered leaving the campaign and working for Millian doing public relations work. Millian was going to pay him $30,000 a month—a kingly sum that was virtually unheard of for that kind of work. Papadopoulos pulled out because he felt Millian was "shady" and "working for someone else," potentially an unnamed former Russian minister. "I would not be working with any sanctioned individuals, and I would be working as George Papadopoulos, private citizen, with another private American citizen."[25] Good instincts, George: Millian was a source in the Steele dossier and worked with Michael Cohen to sell real estate in Florida.[26]

Handwritten notes Papadopoulos provided to Mueller's Office of Special Counsel indicated that he and two other foreign policy advisers were considering meeting with Putin in September 2016, potentially in London. He noted "it is a lot of risk" and "we are a campaign." There also would be no "official" letter or word from Trump.[27]

In mid-September 2016, Papadopoulos met with Stefan Halper and a woman who claimed her name was Azra Turk; he assumed it was a fake name because it means "pure Turk" in Turkish. He called her beautiful and "flirtatious" and indicated that she hinted if he helped her out, she would sleep with him. Halper paid Papadopoulos $3,000 to come to London for the meetings. He met the two at a hotel called the Traveler's Club and then met with Halper alone at Sofitel. Turk asked him pointed questions about Russia and hacking that took Papadopoulos aback, and he did not answer. Later in the month, he met with Halper again, who was sweating profusely and shoved a phone in his face. He also asked questions about the Trump campaign's relations with Russia and hacking. Papadopoulos said he knew nothing about hacking. "What you are talking about is something along the lines of treason," Papadopoulos said.[28] Halper is an American foreign policy scholar at Cambridge University and was an FBI source also known as "the Walrus."[29]

In the end, all that Papadopoulos would get from these efforts was prison, a wife, and an insane Twitter following. The wife is a young Italian woman named Simona Mangiante, who also met the mysterious professor Joseph Mifsud around 2012, when she was introduced to him by an Italian parliamentarian. In September 2016, Papadopoulos sent her a message via LinkedIn and wrote that he "liked her picture."[30] However, she claims Mifsud said Papadopoulos would see her around her office at the London Legal Centre. Mifsud even acted as their matchmaker. He encouraged her to meet Papadopoulos and told her she should say she liked Trump.[31] An equally mysterious grooming for a comely young lady. A reporter who visited the "centre" in October 2017 noted the office was "an undecorated backroom" with four people who would not talk to him.[32] Mangiante said she left London Legal Centre in November 2016 because Mifsud did not pay her as promised, but she did leave with a future husband.

Mangiante and Papadopoulos met in New York City in March 2017 and later married in Chicago in March 2018. Mangiante wanted to pursue a career in film after coming to America with Papadopoulos and was cast in the starring role of Brigitte Bardot in *Affairs on Capri*, a still unfinished film directed by Paul Wiffen. Wiffen is the former chairman of the UK Independence Party, contributes to RT, and once attended a party with Russian spy Anna Chapman.[33] The intersection among Mifsud, Mangiante, and Papadopoulos leads to the obvious question: Was she working with Mifsud for Russia? She has strongly denied, in many interviews, being a Russian spy. To explain why "her accent does not sound very Italian," Mangiante noted, in one interview, that she speaks five languages. "I find it funny, this Russian theory," she said.[34] In Papadopoulos's life, she is a perfect partner. She maintains strong Eurosceptic conservative views. She supported Brexit, loves France's Marine Le Pen, and is an Islamophobe who hawks conspiracy theories that her husband was set up by the CIA.

After the Democratic National Committee sued the Russian Federation in September 2018, it was learned that Mifsud was missing or presumed dead. Speculation on his disappearance became its own storyline; however, a close associate, Stephan Roh, later claimed he was living with a new identity. Robert Mueller and the FBI could never track him down. The Maltese powerbroker turned yenta had disappeared.

Dangle #3:
Dirt on Hillary and the Trump Jr. Meeting

On June 9, 2016, the Russians continued to flood the zone, and this time went after a Trump family member directly. The previous effort using the NRA to reach Donald Trump Jr. was successful, and the Russians realized he was a reliable conduit. The Russians used personal relationships between billionaire oligarchs and the Trump family to send a delegation to New York to meet with Trump's campaign manager Paul Manafort, Donald Trump Jr., and Jared Kushner to offer "dirt" on Hillary Clinton. They spelled it out in precise words that this was an effort by the government of Russia to directly support Trump's presidential bid. The meeting was arranged by Emin Agalarov's publicist and Trump acquaintance Rob Goldstone, who was in attendance along with Russian lawyer Natalya Veselnitskaya, Soviet-born American businessman Irakly "Ike"

Kaveladze, and lobbyist and former Russian counterintelligence officer Rinat Akhmetshin.

The meeting was months in the making after Aras Agalarov, Trump's associate for the 2013 Miss Universe Pageant held in Russia, met with Prosecutor General Yuri Chaika, who had promised damaging information on Clinton. Chaika had a history of being behind *kompromat* campaigns in the past, including using it against Yuri Shuratov, the previous prosecutor general.[35] Under orders from Putin, Chaika's serious interest in the American election appears to have begun in April 2016, approximately the same time that the direct Russian intelligence hackings started. That same month, Chaika's office gave then representative Dana Rohrabacher (R-CA) a film against American sanctions and a confidential letter aimed at delegitimizing American entrepreneur Bill Browder, who had led the global effort to sanction Russia using the Magnitsky Act, a piece of legislation that led to steep financial sanctions (I'll get to this later). The effort was aimed to produce a congressional hearing against Browder.[36] While in Moscow, Congressman Rohrabacher also met with Natalya Veselnitskaya, a suspected agent of Chaika's.

The Participants

Emin Agalarov is the son of Aras Agalarov, mentioned previously. He was a "singer" who featured Donald Trump doing a takeoff of his *Apprentice* role. Emin was also vice president of Crocus Group. Rob Goldstone was his agent. In the song, Emin daydreams singing about being surrounded by beautiful women. At the end of the video, Trump says, "You're fired!" Like his father, Aras, Emin attended all discussions for the 2013 Miss Universe pageant. In 2013, Emin Agalarov was also the singer for an exclusive party for a mafia leader from Solntsevskaya Bratva, Sergei "Mikhas" Mikhailov, where allegedly two unidentified Americans attended and discussed the construction of Trump Towers in Moscow and Kazakhstan.[37]

Aras and Emin both remained in contact with the Trump family throughout 2014 and 2015. They even hosted Ivanka Trump in Moscow in February 2014 and traveled to the states to see Trump and Ivanka that year.[38] A sign of the two families' closeness is exhibited when he met with Trump along with Rob Goldstone at Trump Tower in May 2015 and discussed Trump's then secret candidacy for president, which was announced the following month. It was Emin who helped arrange the June 2016 Trump Tower meeting using Goldstone as the messenger to finalize details.

Goldstone was the British publicist who worked for Emin Agalarov. He met Emin at the end of 2011, and they became close. He, too, attended the Miss Universe planning meeting in Las Vegas with Trump, as well as the pageant and the Nobu restaurant dinner arranged by Agalarov for the Russian oligarchy.

In July 2015 Goldstone emailed Rhona Graff, Trump's executive assistant, to invite Trump to Moscow and arrange a meeting with Putin. It should be noted this was the fifth time where people close to the Trump campaign were offering Trump a personal meeting with Putin (others included Michael Cohen, George Papadopoulos, Felix Sater, Marina Butina, and Alexander Torshin). The offer to meet Putin was "dangled," as if this meeting was the ultimate bait. Virtually everyone seemed to know Trump would salivate at the prospect. That in itself was suspicious, very suspicious. Graff replied politely to the email's invitation but declined due to the campaign. Goldstone replied, "I totally understand re: Moscow, unless maybe he would welcome meeting with President Putin, which Emin would set up."[39]

However, the most significant event was in June 2016 when Goldstone requested a private meeting with Trump Jr. on behalf of Emin. "Emin just called and asked me to contact you with something very interesting." He continued:

> The Crown prosecutor of Russia met with his father Aras this morning and in their meeting **offered to provide the Trump campaign with some official documents and information that would incriminate Hillary [Clinton] and her dealings with** Russia and would be very useful to your father. . . . This is obviously very high level and sensitive information but is **part of Russia and its government's support for Mr. Trump**—helped along by Aras and Emin.

Goldstone then asks how it would be best to get it to Trump. He continued, "I can also send this info to your father via Rhona, but it is ultra-sensitive so wanted to send to you first."[40]

Trump Jr. responded to Goldstone "Thanks Rob I appreciate that. I am on the road at the moment but perhaps I just speak to Emin first. Seems we have some time and if it's what you say I love it especially later in the summer. Could we do a call first thing next week when I am back?"

On June 6, 2016, Goldstone responded to Trump Jr.:

> Let me know when you are free to talk with Emin by phone about this Hillary info—you had mentioned early this week so wanted to try to schedule a time and day. Best to you and your family.

Trump Jr. responded immediately and asked to speak to Emin on his private cell; however, Emin was unavailable. The next day Goldstone wrote back to Trump Jr. that he had scheduled a meeting with "you and the Russian government attorney who is flying over from Moscow for this Thursday. I believe you are aware of the meeting." They agreed to meet at Trump Jr.'s office, and he would bring Paul Manafort and Jared Kushner with him.

The star of the meeting was a Russian woman named Natalya Veselnitskaya. She was an employee of Pyotr Katsyv, a former Russian transport minister and vice governor of Moscow Oblast.[41] Denis Katsyv, Pyotr's son, was involved in a tax fraud scheme worth around $230 million via his company Prevezon Holdings Ltd., based in Cyprus, which was discovered by lawyer Sergei Magnitsky.[42] Denis Katsyv was being investigated by US attorney Preet Bharara in the Southern District of New York before being fired by President Trump in 2017.

Veselnitskaya was sent to help manage the Prevezon case and hire lawyers for Denis Katsyv. She was also involved in a Swiss corruption case for trying to recruit a law enforcement official as an agent for Russia.[43]

By her own admission, she served as an "informant" for a senior Kremlin official, Russian prosecutor general Yuri Chaika.[44] In 2006, Chaika became Russia's prosecutor general, a position equivalent to the American attorney general but without the independence. He is a direct underling of Vladimir Putin and uses the law to execute Putin's wishes. As noted earlier, in April 2016, Chaika gave a letter to Congressman Rohrabacher, expressing Russia's displeasure with Bill Browder, one of the authors of the Magnitsky Act. The letter mirrored Veselnitskaya's talking points at the meeting with Donald Trump Jr.[45]

Another attendee on the Russian side, also noted earlier, was Irakly Kaveladze. He was born in what was then the Georgian Soviet Socialist Republic, now Georgia. He emigrated to the United States in 1991 and set up International Business Creations (IBC). Kaveladze created more than two thousand corporations and opened bank accounts to launder money into the United States. He started working for Crocus in 1989 and then had a few years' lapse. He rejoined in 2003 and became vice president of the Agalarov's Crocus International in 2004.

In June 2013, Kaveladze attended the meeting in Las Vegas with Trump to help organize the Miss Universe pageant along with Michael Cohen, Aras Agalarov, Emin Agalarov, and promoter Rob Goldstone. During the pageant, Kaveladze attended the events and after-party, so he was very well known to Trump. Kaveladze claims to have met Veselnitskaya when she represented Crocus Group on a real estate matter days before the June 2016 Trump Tower meeting. He was instructed by Aras Agalarov to fly to New York for the meeting with Donald Jr. and communicated with Goldstone via text and calls regarding it.[46]

The most interesting member of the Russian team was Rinat Akhmetshin. He was a former Soviet Russian born in Kazan, Tatarstan. When younger he served as an intelligence officer in the Soviet Army in a unit that offered support to Osoby Otdel (Special Department) or counterintelligence.[47]

Akhmetshin moved to the United States in 1994 and opened a lobbying company in 1998 in DC. Akhmetshin was involved in two hacking scandals for two Russian billionaires close to Putin accused of hacking their adversaries during legal battles. One was a smear campaign against former Russian Duma deputy Ashot Egiazaryan when he sought political asylum in America. The second was against a mining company where documents were stolen and leaked to the press. He confirmed in testimony that he worked as a consultant for the law firm BakerHostetler who was representing Prevezon. Akhmetshin dealt with Konstantine Kilimnik, another Russian with an intelligence background, in Ukraine around 2010 but says he met Kilimnik only once in 2014. Interestingly, Akhmetshin also attended a meeting with Veselnitskaya and Dana Rohrabacher on June 14, 2016, to discuss the Magnitsky Act.

Sergei Magnitsky was a Russian lawyer who died in a Russian prison, which caused the West to sanction Russia with the Magnitsky Act. Russian lawyer Nikolai Gorokhov was a witness for the United States and a lawyer for the Magnitsky family. He was thrown out a window in Moscow, March 2017, a few months before the Prevezon trial.[48]

The Magnitsky Act, passed in 2012 in response to the death of Magnitsky,[49] imposed sanctions and travel restrictions on eighteen Russian officials believed to be responsible for Magnitsky's death. It was signed into law by Barack Obama in December 2012. It was later expanded to the Global Magnitsky Act and used to sanction dozens of foreign officials found responsible for violating human rights.[50]

The purpose of the meeting was to pass on to Trump Jr. unspecified dirt about Hillary Clinton. Instead of calling the FBI and reporting this obvious Russian operation, they listened and left since the dirt was not obvious and compelling. When questioned they would later lie with the cover story that the meeting was about "adoptions"—a code word for lifting sanctions because Russia had suspended adoptions in retaliation for US economic punishments.

The Mueller report would later affirm that Kaveladze's lawyer (the redacted name was Scott Balber) learned that the true purpose of the meeting was for Veselnitskaya to pass "negative information on Hillary Clinton" to the Trump team, and they were ready and willing to benefit from it.[51]

Dangle #4: The Saga of Poor Carter Page

Carter Page was a young Trump campaign adviser with a very sketchy history. He served in the US Navy for five years from 1993 to 1998. He once held part-time or collateral duties as an "intelligence officer" during a reserve deployment to Western Sahara. Unlike most Navy officers, he presented several security clearance "red flags": a colleague noted that he "spent lavishly" and drove a black Mercedes.[52] He was a Trident Scholar in the Naval Academy and served as an assistant for Les Aspin before Aspin became Clinton's secretary of defense. Carter served multiple deployments to Europe and the Middle East as a surface warfare officer and went to the Pentagon to work nonproliferation.[53] After leaving service, Page went into finance and became an investment banker. Between 2004 and 2007, he worked in the Moscow branch of Merrill Lynch. In 2008, he opened Global Energy Capital in a coworking space at 590 Madison Avenue, 21st floor. Felix Sater, a partner at Bayrock, LLC, opened up a business at the same address and floor in 2010.

His murky story started to crystallize on June 9, 2008. A US State Department diplomatic cable from the US embassy in Turkmenistan noted Page had met with embassy staff to talk about an oil deal with the Turkmen deputy prime minister and needed to assemble a $1 billion deal. Page made an overwrought claim that it was he who took Gazprom, the global giant in energy, from a state-owned company to "super major status" internationally.[54] It was clear Page saw himself in a light that could be called exaggerated.

In 2013, Russian intelligence tried to recruit Page as a spy. He met with at least one Russian clandestine service (SVR) agent, Viktor Podobnyy. Podobnyy was posing as an attaché at the Russian mission to the UN along with two other agents involved in the spy ring, Evgeny Buryakov and Igor Sporishev. The UN mission is a traditional placement for Russian spies going back nearly seventy years. In a report back to Moscow, Page was not seen as a great asset. The indictment of Podobnyy revealed their opinion of Page as a potential recruit. In it, Page was referred to as "Male-1."[55]

> [Male-1] wrote that he is sorry, he went to Moscow and forgot to check his inbox, but he wants to meet when he gets back. I think he is an idiot and forgot who I am. . . . He got hooked on Gazprom thinking that if they have a project, he could rise up. . . . I also promised him a lot . . . this is intelligence method to cheat, how else to work with foreigners? You promise a favor for a favor. You get the documents from him and tell him to go fuck himself.[56]

The Mueller report later expanded and confirmed how deep Page's connections to Russian intelligence officers went. The report noted he had voluntarily and knowingly met with Russian intelligence from 2008 through 2013, and Moscow took a deeper interest in him once he became the Russia policy coordinator for the campaign. In 2008, Page met with Alexander Bulatov, a known Russian intelligence officer working out of the Russian embassy in New York City, and, as noted earlier, with Podobnyy in 2013. Page said he discussed energy policy with Podobnyy and knew he worked for the intelligence services. Podobnyy meanwhile claimed he gave Page "empty promises" and that he ran assets by promising favors for them until he could get relevant information, then discarding the person. Page explained his dealings with Russian intelligence officers, to FBI investigators, like this: "the more immaterial non-public information I give them, the better it is for this country."[57]

In June 2013, the FBI interviewed Page about his Russian contacts. They noted Russian intelligence officers likely recruited him using business deals in Russia as leverage.[58] Though it was never revealed publicly, Page may have been turned into an FBI double agent or at least a cooperating informant. Podobnyy was gathering information on sanctions and US alternative energy development. As part of the case against them, both Podobnyy and Sporishev were removed from the United States, and Buryakov pled guilty to conspiring to act as a foreign agent.[59]

An August 25, 2013, letter from Page indicated he was "an informal adviser to the staff of the Kremlin in preparation for their Presidency of the G-20." An editor who reviewed a manuscript page sent about Russia–Central Asia relations said it looked "more positively at Russia's economic reforms and Russia's relationship with Central Asia. I didn't think it was so weird, it was just contradictory to most mainstream Russian specialist's views." He added, "I just came to see him as a kook."[60]

Carter Page's pro-Russia views may have seemed strange, but they were not an act. In March 2016, Trump said that he had chosen Page as a member of his foreign policy team because Page had founded Global Energy Capital and had years of experience investing in Russia. Julia Ioffe, an American journalist born in Russia, went to Western business leaders she knew in Russia, and none of them had ever heard of Page or worked with him. This was in September 2016, when Page had become radioactive. Russian business leaders, however, including the head of Rosneft, a Russian energy giant, spoke highly of Page. "He's an extremely well-informed, authoritative expert on Russia," said Mikhail Leontiev, a spokesman for Rosneft. It is noteworthy, however, how Russian oil executives with connections to Putin would come to extol Page as an asset and how Page, in turn, would parrot their talking points.[61]

By June he was representing Trump at an event of influential foreign policy experts, with the prime minister of India present praising Putin as stronger and more reliable than Obama.[62] He also planned a trip to Moscow to speak at an event. He received approval from Corey Lewandowski and J. D. Gordon. Jeff Sessions was made aware of the trip.[63]

The ultra-right-wing anti-NATO Katehon think tank promoted Alexander Dugin's July 7, 2016, speech to the New Economic School at the Moscow World Trade Center. Katehon is an Infowars-type platform in Russia. Its president, Konstantin Malofeev, is an Orthodox Russian businessman and ultra-nationalist. Malofeev's television channel features Alex Jones and Dugin, a controversial Russian fascist known for promoting reorientation of the world with Russia at its center. He openly associates with alt-right leaders in Europe like Marine Le Pen.[64]

The Katehon promotion of Dugin's speech noted "Carter Page is one of the youngest advisors of Donald Trump" and that he had lived in Moscow for three years during which time he advised energy behemoth Gazprom. It also noted he was "one of the few American experts" who wanted people to understand why Russia annexed Crimea. He also has spoken out against NATO expansion. There Page thrilled them with his anti-American and globalist rhetoric. He said America prefers regime change and altering internal dynamics and policies in post-Soviet countries, a Kremlin talking point. Page called for "mutual understanding . . . non-interference and respect for mutual interest" with Russia. He went on about the "failure" of American analysts and leaders to understand any of this. Page stood onstage in Moscow and praised and minimized the repression of Central Asian nations for economic gain and criticized Western nations for focusing on "perceived" shortfalls on democracy and their own corruption.[65]

The Mueller report would add that at the July 2016 Republican National Convention, Page met with Kislyak and told the campaign Kislyak "was worried about candidate Clinton's world views." Shortly after that time, the Mueller team noted the campaign pushed Page aside when his close proximity to Russian officials reached the media. Despite this, on November 14, 2016, Page reached out to the transition team and requested a job in the new administration. He wrote that he had met with world leaders and "effectively responded to diplomatic outreach efforts." No one from the transition team responded to his request.[66]

According to a rumor in the Steele dossier, a Russian close to Trump claimed that in July 2016, Manafort used Page as an intermediary with the Russian government. Another source close to Rosneft claimed Page met with the Rosneft president and close associate to Putin about energy policy and lifting Ukraine-related sanctions.

The Steele dossier was a corporate intelligence report first contracted by a Republican associated with the Ted Cruz campaign but which would later be adopted by the Clinton campaign. It provided thirty-six pages of what is best known as RUMINT or rumor intelligence. RUMINT is information collected in the diplomatic and intelligence services by agents hanging out in bars and attending parties or by having informants pass along what they have heard on the streets. Carter Page is mentioned in the thirty-six-page report no less than three times. The Steele dossier would prove accurate on some of the rumors heard about Page.

Page was also alleged to have met with Igor Diveykin, a member of Russia's presidential administration, a former Russian security official, and deputy chief for Internal Policy. During later testimony before the House Intelligence Committee, Page admitted to meeting with Russian deputy prime minister Arkady Dvorkovich (on the board of VEB Bank) and Andrey Baranov, Rosneft's head of investor relations and a senior aide to Rosneft CEO Igor Sechin.[67]

On September 26, 2016, Page stepped away from the campaign due to accusations of high-level involvement with Russia. At the time, he denied all of them, though all were later proven.[68] After he was fired, the Trump campaign minimized Page's role on the Trump team, even downgrading him to an "informal adviser" akin to a coffee boy. The Justice Department wasn't so sure. It obtained a FISA warrant to allow the FBI to surveil Page's personal communications.

The report concluded "the investigation did not establish that Page coordinated with the Russian government in its efforts to interfere with the 2016 election," but investigators also noted that some of Page's activities in Russia "were not fully explained."[69]

Dangle #5: The Ukraine "Peace" Deal

There were numerous peace plans during the 2016 election relating to Ukraine that were all pro-Russia. The Mariupol Plan was pitched by Manafort's longtime aide Kilimnik. It sought to replace the current Minsk agreement and start a dialogue between Ukraine and the leaders of the separatist-held areas. Kilimnik also envisioned Manafort's former boss Viktor Yanukovych representing Donbas, a region in eastern Ukraine. Yanukovych has since been found guilty of treason.

The Artemenko peace plan involved Ukrainian lawmaker Andrii Artemenko, Alex Oronov, Trump's longtime lawyer Michael Cohen, and business associate Felix Sater and was believed to have been delivered to then national security adviser Michael Flynn. Oronov, a family member and business partner of Cohen, passed away shortly after the plan was revealed. The proposal came after a phone conversation between Flynn and Russian ambassador Kislyak in which the dropping of sanctions was discussed. The *New York Times,* which broke the story, cited Artemenko as saying that it was approved by top aides to Putin. The plan called for a "compromise" and floated holding a national referendum of leasing Crimea to Russia in exchange for the Kremlin withdrawing its troops from eastern Ukraine. The lease was expected to run for a period between fifty and one hundred years. After the annexation of Crimea, Russia was hit with US and international sanctions. Russia supported Trump during the election with the lifting of sanctions and the future of Ukraine in mind.

CHAPTER 8

Team Dirty Tricks

In early March 2016, the Russian GRU cyberintelligence group named Unit 26165 launched an operation to steal thousands of emails and documents from the DNC and DCCC (Democratic Congressional Campaign Committee); subsequently a second GRU team (Unit 74455) launched their cutout operations DCLeaks (June 8, 2016) and Guccifer 2.0 (June 15, 2016), named after the Romanian hacker. The hacking of the DNC was detected and surveilled in real time by Crowdstrike, who released its report on the DNC hack to the public on June 15, 2016. The same day, Unit 74455 launched its Guccifer 2.0 cutout.

The released documents purported to be from the DNC were published by the GRU on the WordPress blog of Guccifer 2.0 beginning on June 15, 2016, and continued for the next few months. For instance, on June 18, 2016, appeared a post titled "New Docs from DNC Network: Lots of Financial Reports and Donors' Personal Data,"[1] then two days later came an announcement of a dossier on Hillary Clinton, with "Dossier on Hillary Clinton from DNC" followed by that release on June 20, 2016.[2]

Following those posts, on June 22, 2016, WikiLeaks sent a private message to GRU officers operating Guccifer 2.0: "send any new material here for us to review and it will have a much higher impact than what you are doing."[3] Along with WikiLeaks, the GRU was in contact with others, including an American reporter with an offer of stolen emails from "Hillary Clinton's staff." The GRU sent access information to DCLeaks.com to the reporter to retrieve emails stolen from a DCCC employee (Victim 1) in March 2016.[4]

WikiLeaks fired off posts aimed at attacking Hillary Clinton on June 28, 2018, with, "Full text of Benghazi Report released" and "Hillary Clinton emails."[5] By mid-July, the GRU sought to use WikiLeaks as a part of its cutout plan. They sent a message to WikiLeaks on July 14, 2016, with a downloadable archive of the hacked files from the DNC.[6] A few days later, on July 18, 2016, WikiLeaks confirmed to the GRU officers (Guccifer 2.0) that it had downloaded the stolen DNC documents and would release them within a week.[7] In preparation for the Democratic National Convention, July 25 to 28, 2016, WikiLeaks released twenty thousand emails three days before they were stolen by the GRU Unit 26165. The window of email time stamps matched the time frame of the GRU hacking of the DNC Microsoft Exchange Server.[8]

After Trump's comments on July 27, 2016 ("Russia if you're listening"), which called the foreign hostile opponent to get emails from Hillary Clinton ("The press will reward you mightily"), Russian hackers worked to infiltrate Democratic Party targets, including phishing and targeting seventy-six emails of the HRC campaign.[9]

Team Roger Stone and Jerome Corsi

We discussed how Roger Stone worked constantly to get the dirt he thought he could find on Hillary Clinton, through any means necessary. Though he officially quit the Trump campaign in August 2015, he bragged repeatedly that he was in contact with the campaign as he sought to damage the Democratic nominee, Hillary Clinton. After the big document dump by WikiLeaks, Stone sent an email on July 25, 2016, to his friend Jerome Corsi looking for any dirt on Clinton. Corsi was another merry dirty trickster who wrote books about Clinton that vilified her every move. He was at the center of the communications between Roger Stone and WikiLeaks. According to the draft indictment against Corsi that was discovered by NBC, on July 25, 2016, days after the first release of the twenty-two thousand emails stolen by the GRU and given to WikiLeaks, Stone sent the email to Corsi requesting him to "Get to [Julian Assange] [a]t Ecuadorian Embassy in London and get the pending [WikiLeaks] emails . . . they deal with Foundation, allegedly." Corsi then sent that to his friend Ted Malloch, another controversial conservative author.[10] Corsi sought out Malloch with the request that he contact associates of Nigel Farage to reach Assange. Malloch would later tell the special counsel that he didn't put Corsi in touch with Assange.[11]

Then on July 31, 2016, Stone emailed again, "Call me MON," and suggested that Malloch "see Assange." On August 2, 2016, Corsi emailed Stone letting him know he was in Europe until mid-August. He told Stone, "Word is friend in embassy plans 2 more dumps. One shortly after I'm back. 2nd in Oct. Impact planned to be very damaging. . . . Time to let more than Podesta be exposed as in bed w enemy if they are not ready to drop HRC. That appears to be the game hackers are now about. Would not hurt to start suggesting HRC old, memory bad, has stroke—neither he nor she well. I expect that much of the next dump focus, setting stage for Foundation debacle."

Repeatedly, Stone went on Alex Jones's show, Infowars, starting on August 4, 2016, saying he knew about upcoming document dumps via WikiLeaks and that he had spoken with Donald Trump on the releases.[12] The next day, Stone published an article on Brietbart.com claiming the hacking of the DNC wasn't done by Russians but by "a hacker who goes by the name Guccifer 2.0," later revealed to be the GRU Unit 74455.[13] Subsequently, in an interview on Infowars, he acknowledged knowing the WikiLeaks data dump in July came from Guccifer 2.0. He continued to broadcast releases and connections to WikiLeaks afterward, including on August 8, 2016, when Stone bragged to the Southwest Broward Republican Organization that he had been communicating with Julian Assange.[14] Stone said, "I actually have communicated with Assange. I believe the next tranche of his documents pertain to the Clinton Foundation, but there's no telling what the October surprise may be."[15] Stone said during an Infowars interview on August 12, 2016, that he had a "back-channel communication with WikiLeaks and Julian Assange" and that all the Hillary Clinton emails from her server were in the possession of WikiLeaks. He continued, claiming foreknowledge of releases and saying, "this is devastating information from WikiLeaks, which I expect to continue." He claimed there was an effort to "discredit Assange because they know he has the goods."[16] Days later again on Infowars he said, "It became known on this program that I have had some back-channel communication with WikiLeaks and Assange." On the same day, he said, again, that he had "communicated with Assange" and had a "mutual acquaintance who is a fine gentleman."[17] Days later on August 18, 2016, Stone said he had communicated with WikiLeaks through an "intermediary, somebody who is a mutual friend."[18]

WikiLeaks continued to release the stolen documents in August. On August 12, 2016, WikiLeaks tweeted: "'Guccifer 2.0' tweets that they have released some files from the Democratic Congressional Campaign Committee #DCCC" with a link to a tweet from GRU's Guccifer 2.0 account.[19] That day, the Guccifer 2.0 account sent a tweet to Roger Stone: "thanks that u believe in the real #Guccifer2." The GRU Unit 74455 officers posted via the Guccifer 2.0 WordPress blog: "Guccifer 2.0 Hacked DCCC."[20] As a result, Twitter suspended the Guccifer account. This caused both WikiLeaks and Stone to react. On August 13, WikiLeaks tweeted: "'Guccifer_2' has account completely censored by Twitter after publishing some files from Democratic campaign #DCCC."[21] WikiLeaks also tweeted: "Washington DC newspaper The Hill is publishing some documents it says are from '@GUCCIFER_2' whose account Twitter just censored completely."[22] Stone replied that the banning of the Guccifer 2.0 account was "outrageous."

On August 14, Twitter reinstated the Guccifer 2.0 account, and then Stone sent a Twitter direct message to the GRU cutout: "Delighted you are reinstated. Fuck the State and their MSM lackeys. R."[23] The next day the GRU Unit 74455 officers responded via direct message (DM) to Stone via the Guccifer_2 account: "wow, thank u for writing back, and thank u for an article about me!!" and "do u find anything interesting in the docs i posted?"[24] A day later, Stone responded to GRU officers from 74455 via DM to @GUCCIFER_2: "PLZ RT: How the election can be rigged against Donald Trump" with a link to an article from the *Hill*.[25] On August 17, the GRU responded to Stone via DM from @GUCCIFER_2: "done . . . i read u'd been hacked" and later "i'm pleased to say that u r great man and i think i gonna read ur books . . . please tell me if i can help u anyhow . . . it would be a great pleasure to me."[26]

Stone wasn't the only Republican who was interested in the releases. On August 15, a post appeared on the Guccifer 2.0 blog titled "DCCC Internal Docs on Primaries in Florida."[27] Officers wrote on the GRU cutout that a US congressional candidate from Florida had requested and received documents.[28] A week later, on August 22, GRU hackers sent 2.5

gigabytes of data stolen from DCCC to Florida state lobbyist Aaron Nevins,[29] including donor records and personal information on two thousand Democratic donors. Additionally, in the indictment against these Russian officers, the special counsel noted that they sent stolen information from the DNC servers regarding Black Lives Matter to a reporter who offered to publicize the information and coordinated its release.[30]

Stone claimed that radio show host Randy Credico brought the WikiLeaks dump of emails to his attention.[31] By late August 2016, Stone was interacting with Credico to get dirt on Clinton. Stone and Credico had known each other since the early 2000s. They repeatedly texted about being in contact with Julian Assange and anticipating the pending releases by WikiLeaks. On August 19, Credico texts Stone, "I'm going to have Assange on my show next Thursday."[32] Then two days later, Credico texts Stone, "I have Assange on Thursday so I'm completely tied up on that day."[33] A couple of days later, Credico asked Stone during a radio interview on August 23, "You've been in touch indirectly with Assange. . . . Can you give us any kind of insight? Is there an October surprise happening?" Stone replied, "Well, first of all, I don't want to intimate in any way that I control or have influence with Assange because I do not. . . . We have a mutual friend, somebody we both trust, therefore I am a recipient of pretty good information."[34] Two days later, Assange was a guest on Credico's radio show.[35] The next day Credico sent a text to Stone, "Assange talked about you last night." Stone asked what Assange said. Credico replied, "He didn't say anything bad we were talking about how the Press is trying to make it look like you and he are in cahoots."[36]

In one of his most important comments leading up to the election, on August 21, 2016, Stone sent a tweet forecasting the Podesta leaks with "Trust me, it will soon be Podesta's time in the barrel. #CrookedHillary."[37]

At the end of August, Credico texted Stone: "We are working on a Julian Assange radio show," with Credico in charge of the show. Later, Credico states, "Assange has kryptonite on Hillary."[38]

On September 9, GRU Unit 74455 officers via @GUCCIFER_2 sent a DM to Roger Stone with a link to Aaron Nevins's page: "hi what do u think of the info on the turnout model for the democrats entire presidential campaign?" Stone replied in the DM: "Pretty standard."[39]

On September 18, Stone texted Credico: "I am e-mailing u a request to pass on to Assange." Credico responded, "Ok," and "just remember do not name me as your connection to Assange you and one before that you referred to."[40] The same day, Stone emailed Credico an anti–Hillary Clinton article with "Please ask Assange for any State or HRC e-mail from August 10 to August 30—particularly on August 20, 2011, that mention [subject of article] or confirm this narrative."[41] The next day Stone texted Credico, "Pass my message . . . to Assange." Credico replied, "I did."[42] The next day Credico forwarded Stone's request to WikiLeaks's lawyer Margaret Ratner Kunstler with Stone in email bcc.[43]

At the end of September 2016, Credico texted a photo of himself standing outside the Ecuadorian embassy in London to Roger Stone.[44] A day later Credico texted Stone "big news Wednesday—now pretend you don't know me." Stone replied, "U died 5 years ago." Credico replied "great" and "Hillary's campaign will die this week."[45] The next day, Stone emailed Credico with "WTF?" with an article link stating WikiLeaks was going to cancel its upcoming big announcement. Credico replied to Stone, "head fake." Stone texted Credico: "Did Assange back off."[46] On the Alex Jones show, Stone revealed to host David Knight more about his knowledge of the upcoming Podesta emails: "An intermediary met with him in London recently who is a friend of mine and a friend of his, a believer in freedom. I am assured that the mother lode is coming Wednesday."[47]

Stone tweeted "Wednesday @HillaryClinton is done. #Wikileaks" on October 2.[48]

On October 3, Credico texted to Stone, "I can't talk about it," and "I think its [sic] on for tomorrow," and "Off the Record Hillary and her people are doing a full-court press they keep Assange from making the next dump. That's all I can tell you on this line. Please leave my name out of it."[49]

The same day, Stone wrote to a Trump supporter, "Spoke to my friend in London last night. The payload is still coming." Stone received an email from Matthew Boyle of Breitbart News asking, "Assange—What's he got? I hope it's good." Stone replied, "It is. I'd tell Bannon but he doesn't call me back."[50] Boyle emailed Steve Bannon: "You should call Roger. See below. You didn't get from me."[51] Stone tweeted that more was coming from WikiLeaks: "I have total confidence that @wikileaks and my hero Julian Assange will educate the American people soon. #LockHerUp"[52] The next day, Bannon and Stone exchanged emails about the Assange conference. Bannon said, "What was that this morning??" Stone replied, "Fear. Serious security concern. He thinks they are going to kill him and the London police are standing done [sic]. However—a load every week going forward." Bannon replied, "He didn't cut deal w/Clintons???"[53]

October 5, 2016, Stone posted a tweet, "Libs thinking Assange will stand down are wishful thinking. Payload coming #Lockthemup."

A week later, on October 12, Stone bragged about having a back channel to WikiLeaks and Assange to NBC.[54] The next day WikiLeaks, on Twitter, denied being in contact with Stone: "Editorial: WikiLeaks has never communicated with Roger Stone as we have previously stated."[55] Stone sent a DM to WikiLeaks, "Since I was all over national TV, cable and print defending Wikileaks and Assange against the claim that you are Russian agents and debunking the false charges of sexual assault as trumped up bs you may want to reexamine the strategy of attacking me-cordially R." WikiLeaks fired back at Stone, "false claims of association are being used by the democrats to undermine the impact of our publications. Don't go there if you don't want us to correct you."[56] Two days later, Stone responded to the WikiLeaks DM: "Ha! The more you 'correct' me the more people think you're lying. Your operation leaks like a sieve. You need to figure out who your friends are."[57]

The Mueller report would reveal that after Manafort left the campaign, he maintained contact with people in the Trump campaign, giving them advice on policy, including Jared Kushner. On October 21, 2016, he emailed Kushner, encouraging him to use WikiLeaks releases to portray HRC as "the failed and corrupt champion of the establishment." He sent another on November 5, 2016, saying he was "really feeling good about our prospects on Tuesday and focusing on preserving the victory" and that the Clinton campaign would seek to "discredit the victory and claim voter fraud and cyber-fraud, including the claim that the Russians have hacked into the voting machines and tampered with the results."[58]

Then on November 9, the day after Donald Trump was declared the winner of the election, WikiLeaks sent a DM to Roger Stone, "Happy? We are now more free to communicate."[59]

Mission accomplished.

Team Peter Smith and Barbara Ledeen

Soon after securing the nomination in July 2016, Republican candidate Trump deployed his staff to find the deleted Clinton emails. This resulted in Michael Flynn reaching out to multiple people including Barbara Ledeen, wife of author Michael Ledeen and ultraconservative leader of the Independent Women's Forum, and Peter Smith. Peter Smith spent sixty years as a Republican public affairs operative. He touted his work for former House Speaker Newt Gingrich, investigating and publishing details about Troopergate, a GOP-led investigation into former president Bill Clinton allegedly using the Arkansas Highway Patrol to cover up his extramarital affairs. As with most Republican investigations, it yielded nothing at all but served its purpose to smear the Clintons.[60] Coincidently, Russian hackers in 2015 stole Smith's emails from the Illinois Republican Party and leaked them on the GRU cutout, DCLeaks.[61]

An initial effort had begun in December 2015 when Ledeen sent an email to longtime Republican operative Smith, saying, "Here is the proposal I briefly mentioned to you. The person I described to you would be happy to talk with you either in person or over the phone. The person can get the emails which 1. Were classified and 2. Were purloined by our enemies. That would demonstrate what needs to be demonstrated."[62]

Along with the email was an attachment proposing searching for Clinton's personal emails via "open-source," which were intelligence sources Ledeen claimed to have. She also said that "Chinese, Russian and Iranian intelligence services could have 're-assembled' the server's email content." She postulated that the recovery of even one email from a foreign source would be damning to Clinton.[63] At first, Smith turned Ledeen down, but he later relented in late July 2016, after Trump made a public call to find Clinton's missing emails.

Smith became fully invested in finding the emails. He built a company, KLS Research LLC, to raise funds to locate the emails and staffed up. He reached out to several people with a recruiting letter clearly proclaiming his close ties to Sam Clovis, Michael Flynn, Steve Bannon, and Kellyanne Conway.[64] Among the key people he picked to work with was right-wing extremist Charles Johnson, who had worked for Breitbart News and was the operator of the right-wing site GotNews. The relationship with Johnson dated back to 2013.[65] It was Johnson who promoted the idea that Smith should reach out to neo-Nazi Andrew Auernheimer. In addition to Johnson, Smith reached out to others, including Royal O'Brien, who taught him how to use encryption. Smith was not known to have technical skills himself and relied on others for their computer experience and advice.[66]

On July 27, 2016, the day Trump publicly called on Russia to find Clinton's emails, Smith contacted Matt Tait, a former information security specialist for the British GCHQ (Government Communications Headquarters), and began looking into the potential release of stolen DNC documents. Tait had been investigating the DNC hacking. Smith told Tait he believed Clinton's private server had been hacked, and someone from the "dark web" had those emails and was offering them to him. Smith wanted Tait's assistance to verify the authenticity of the emails if they should eventually fall into his hands. Tait warned Smith to be wary of the person and that this may have been a Russian operation to filter false information into the United States.[67] Tait wrote in a Lawfare blog post:

> Smith, however, didn't seem to care. From his perspective, it didn't matter who had taken the emails, or their motives for doing so. He never expressed to me any discomfort with the possibility that the emails he was seeking were potentially from a Russian front, a likelihood he was happy to acknowledge. If they were genuine, they would hurt Clinton's chances, and therefore help Trump.[68]

Furthermore, Smith told Tait he was a longtime Republican Party operative, also noting his connections to the top of the Trump campaign, namely General Michael Flynn. Smith emailed wealthy donors to obtain at least $100,000 to pay for the purported Clinton emails. He referred to the funding with cover names like "Clinton Email Reconnaissance Initiative" and "Washington Scholarship Fund for the Russian Students."[69] He said in the email, "The students are very pleased with the email releases they have seen and are thrilled with their educational advancement opportunities."

Emails obtained by the *Wall Street Journal* showed that Smith reached out to the Flynn Intel Group in 2016 during his quest for the purported hacked Clinton server emails. Smith died ten days after his interview with the newspaper but told reporters he began his search for the emails in September 2016. However, the Mueller report showed Smith's efforts started in July 2016. Smith said he hired technology experts, lawyers, and a Russian-speaking investigator to locate the emails. He minimized his connections to Flynn, but other people interviewed said Smith's effort was tied to Flynn and his son.[70]

Smith's team determined there were five groups of hackers who had the alleged emails and at least two were Russian. "We knew the people who had these were probably around the Russian government," he said. After he was unable to verify the authenticity of any of the emails he received, he told the groups to give them to WikiLeaks.[71]

In late August 2016, in an email that was sent to several people including Sam Clovis, Smith claimed to know hackers had breached Clinton's "home-based, unprotected server."[72] In his effort to draw support via his company KLS Research LLC, he claimed to be working with the Trump campaign. The special counsel confirmed Smith remained in contact with Flynn and Clovis.[73]

Soon Smith and Ledeen revisited the original plan. She asked in an email to Smith: "Wondering if you had some more detailed reports or memos or other data you could share because we have come a long way in our efforts since we last visited. We would need as much technical discussion as possible so we could marry it against the new data we have found and then could share it back to you 'your eyes only.'" Additionally, Ledeen, too, claimed she had secured a "trove of emails" from Clinton from the dark web. Erik Prince funded the effort to acquire and validate them but in the end claimed the emails were fake.[74]

The special counsel found Podesta documents on Smith's computer that corresponded with the WikiLeaks email dumps after October 2,

2016. Smith apparently held out hope that WikiLeaks would eventually dump the supposed stolen emails from Clinton's private server, but by election day, nothing came.[75] Repeatedly, Smith claimed to be in contact with Russian hackers, including Guccifer 2.0. This included claims in August 2016 to be in contact with hackers who had "ties and affiliations to Russia." The special counsel could find no evidence that this was true, nor could others who were close to his efforts affirm the legitimacy of his claim.

His quest to be a major dirty tricks player like Roger Stone ended when he killed himself in an Aspen Suites hotel room in Rochester, Minnesota, on May 14, 2017. He left behind a note that said: "No foul play whatsoever—all self inflicted."[76]

Team Trump Brainwashes America's Mind

When Russian intelligence *active measures* meet the insidious strength of computational influence and propaganda warfare, they are a formidable weapon. They do not destroy physical structure, but they hijack the reality of the victim and form an alternative world of fake news and misperceived information. It's crafted to deceive and lead the victim to act as a drone for socially disseminating false information to his loved ones or peers. Executed with precision, this form of personal self-brainwashing can change the perceptions of the populations of entire nations. It was extremely successful in 2016 and could be argued that as much as 37 percent of voters believed false news over the reality they could see with their own eyes.

However, having the skill to change the mind-set of an entire population cannot be achieved unless the attacker understands the target population in fine detail. Knowledge about political activities, issues, and demographic trends at the street level is critical. If that data is in sync with the local political framework, then any foreign narratives or personalities one wished to support, or destroy, are now in a controllable environment. So long as the attacking nation has access to the victim country's social media, then anything and everything can be entered into the psyche of the victim population.

For example, inciting a separatist movement in the central highlands of Papua New Guinea would be a waste of money and manpower if one did not know the precise tribal structure down to the individual village level, such as the critical importance of *wantok* or the concept of tribal obligation. One would also need to know almost every issue that impacted the tribe in real time so that any agitation or grievance could be harnessed and turned into viable propaganda products. This kind of local data gathering is called microtargeting. Without key local knowledge from the ground perspective, one would be unable to control narratives or outcomes and time spent trying to influence people would be wasted.

Microtargeting uses data mining, which sifts through and analyzes small amounts of specific data about millions of people. The goal, for a political campaign, is to segment and focus advertising materials so that they directly reach individuals or groups with peculiar traits.

A larger scale model is called psychographics, when a company collects large quantities of data about the personalities of individuals and creates political profiles based on their psychological preferences to better influence them through extensive microtargeting. A detailed model of a person, identifying his or her preferences for a particular type of government or for specific characteristics of a leader—all with the intent of influencing that person based on his or her psychological preferences—is called a psychographic profile.

The Trump campaign would make extensive use of microtargeting through the services of digital consultant Brad Parscale and his firm Giles-Parscale.

Project Alamo

Brad Parscale served as the digital media director for Trump's 2016 campaign. In 2011, he started work for the Trump organization on the design and development of websites and the creative management of media strategies on the digital side. In 2015 Trump hired Giles-Parscale, which created the Trump campaign's official presidential website. In 2016 Parscale was named its official media director, overseeing digital strategy as well as fundraising.

At the heart of Pascale's efforts was Project Alamo,[77] which allowed highly targeted advertisements on social media platforms, particularly Facebook.[78] During the campaign, Parscale used Facebook as an efficient way to reach large audiences directly, capitalizing on its advertising platform as a means of delivery. This included testing more than fifty thousand ad variations each day in an attempt to microtarget voters.[79] He used this strategy to directly target individual voters in swing states. The term *target audience* is commonly used in advertising, but it is also a crucial component of political and psychological warfare. It involves a careful look at particular segments of the population, usually at a microscopic level. It accounts and factors how the people in each microsector feels, how they think, what their primary and secondary concerns are, and what medium is best suited to reach them. A target audience analysis looks at how a nefarious digital media company will try to influence that particular sliver of people. The purpose—whether it is buying clothes or pool supplies, or selecting a president—is to effect a behavior change by showing viewers advertisements that appeal to them personally. Many advertisements are finely tailored to one miniscule sector.

Parscale once said that he was able to target very specific audiences who felt abandoned by the Republican or Democratic establishment and were tired of being fed the same political noise and people who cared about infrastructure. This would help him advance Trump's narrative about making America great again. He said: "I started making ads that showed the bridge crumbling . . . I can find the 1,500 people in one town that care about infrastructure. Now, that might be a voter that normally votes Democrat."[80] These voters would be bombarded with tailored advertising about the decline of America, crumbling infrastructure, and political elites. Then they would show Trump as the opposite of that. When asked why he identified Facebook as the ideal medium to deliver Trump's message, he said, "Low-cost CPM [cost per thousand impressions], large numbers of conservative voters, ability to broadcast all day, multiple times to the same audience, and the numbers were showing in the consumer side that people were spending more and more hours of their day consuming Facebook content and aggregated news feed." (Aggregated news content refers to aggregating content together on Facebook, so people see more of it.)[81]

He also explained in this interview how he utilized a "shock and awe" tactic and flooded specific states with content: "It's the shock of: here is a considerable amount of content to just continue to show directly from the president or Donald Trump. I think shock and awe just in the military sense of 'Let's just go and flood the zone.' Unlike microtargeting that took place in the general election, that capability wasn't available. You would need an unlimited amount of money to do that nationally, but for a single state like Iowa, the ability to flood the zone is much more capable at a much lower budget."[82]

In an interview with *60 Minutes*, Parscale also said, "I understood early that Facebook was how Donald Trump was going to win. Twitter is how he talked to the people. Facebook was going to be how he won. . . . I think Donald Trump won, but I think Facebook was the method—it was the highway in which his car drove on."[83]

Cambridge Analytica

Christopher Wylie was a young hipster who described himself as the person who "made Steve Bannon's psychological warfare tool."[84] At age twenty-four, while working toward a PhD in fashion trend forecasting, he came up with an idea that laid the foundation for a company that would be called Cambridge Analytica (CA). He would also become one of their first hires. CA was a data analytics firm and political consultancy. Their principal investor was the American conservative hedge fund billionaire Robert Mercer. Not surprisingly, its leadership team was headed by the cream of Trump's election team, Steve Bannon and Jared Kushner.

Bannon and Wylie helped bring about the idea of taking a well-established military methodology called "information warfare operations" and applying it to politics in the exact same way Russian intelligence used it against Eastern European states. Simply put, they would take military cyberwarfare techniques and turn them on the American public through advertising designed to shape the opinions of voters almost without them knowing it. CA would target the US electorate to change the mind-set of large swaths of people to think the way Bannon wanted them to think. Bannon had experience with this before when he made his millions harnessing the passion of teen video gamers, eventually turning them into political piranhas now known as the alt-right.[85]

What was proposed was essentially evil condensed into a Twitter or Facebook message.

Wylie revealed how CA had spent millions to acquire the data stripped from people's Facebook profiles. Unbeknownst to its users, Facebook was selling their personal data to companies like these that wanted to better target them for commercial advertisements. CA harvested fifty million Facebook user profiles for this wider project and then stole the information from the friends and family of the original profiles they legally purchased.[86] Their aim was to build a system that could profile individual US voters in order to target each person with political advertisements in a very personalized way.[87] With this data, CA could identify and target first-time voters and those who felt left out of the political process. They would craft the ads that would motivate more people to come to the polls and vote for Trump.[88] Their ads reached over 150 million American voters.

With authorization from Trump, Bannon, and Kushner, the Mercer family funded Cambridge Analytica's computational propaganda mission. The goal was exactly as Konstantine Rykov had confessed. They were to build a massive personality database to exploit the psychological vulnerabilities of the American voter. It determined who you were, where you lived, what your likes and dislikes were, and where you fell on the spectrum of political opinion. For example, married white, Christian middle-aged men from Wisconsin with incomes of less than $50,000 who worked a low-wage job, owned one firearm, and regularly voted would be given a specific psychographic profile. Ads would be crafted to microtarget him: guns were being taken away by liberals, white women were being raped by Mexican immigrants who were also taking American jobs and bringing in drugs like heroin that ravished the white youth. These were the psychographic profiles crafted by what Wylie called "Steve Bannon's psychological warfare mindfuck tool." The Trump data analytics team under Parscale had access to this data.

The CEO of Cambridge, Alexander Nix, also repropagated Russian Internet Research Agency propaganda, which was also using psychographic profiles. Ads were not formed just to turn out the vote; a portion was designed to make sure minorities did not vote at all.

Three major voter suppression operations were waged by CA against African Americans by hyping the myth that Hillary Clinton saw blacks as superpredators. To black emigrants from the Caribbean, they pushed a lie that she and her husband, Bill Clinton, were stealing donations from Haiti. To split the liberal wing of the party, they supported her opponent in the primary, Bernie Sanders. They targeted young, white progressive women and reminded them of Bill Clinton's affair with Monica Lewinsky. Each group was targeted to support or suppress efforts, but they all had one goal—the election of Donald Trump.

After the victory of Trump, CA moved globally to sell their special brand of cheating and mind bending. In 2018 CA would be caught when a secret video team, posing as Sri Lankan politicians, were told by the company's political division chief Mark Turnbull how they'd use fake organizations to spread fake messages: "Sometimes you can use proxy organizations who are already there. You feed them. They are civil society organizations. . . . Charities or activist groups, and we use them—feed them the material and they do the work."[89]

Turnbull would also explain how they poison opinion and shape the mind-set of the public using false news propagation almost identical to the Russian intelligence agencies: "We just put information into the bloodstream, to the internet, and then watch it grow, give it a little push every now and again over time to watch it take shape. And so this stuff infiltrates the online community and expands but with no branding—so it's unattributable, untrackable."[90]

Alexander Nix explained how their dirty tricks were virtually untrackable because they used a form of disappearing propaganda:

> No one knows we have it, and secondly we set our . . . emails with a self-destruct timer . . . So you send them and after they've been read, two hours later, they disappear. There's no evidence, there's no paper trail, there's nothing.[91]

CA bragged how they carried out these duties for the Trump campaign even though they were not American citizens. CA would skirt US election laws by using these techniques to erase evidence and claiming their staffers were US citizens. Nix gushed how his British company was carrying out all of the data dirty tricks for Trump. He said, "We did all the research, all the data, all the analytics, all the targeting, we ran all the digital campaign, the television campaign and our data-informed all the strategy."[92]

He went further by explaining that the candidate was immune because he had no reason to be informed of what was going on. Nix said, "They don't understand because the candidate never, is never involved. He's told what to do by the campaign team." The reporter realized what he meant and asked: "So the candidate is the puppet?" Nix responded, "Always."

This video scandal would lead to Nix's dismissal and the dissolution of Cambridge as a company—the horse was out of the barn. Digital dirty tricks that operated on the razor's edge of legality were now a weapon to be used to attack the American electoral system itself. No matter, there was money to be made in selling off the bricks of the foundation of democracy.

The word on the street was that Team Trump was fully invested in dirty tricks and that it had the financial backers to make people rich off their efforts. Companies were coming out of the woodwork to make their pitch for Trump money.

PsyGroup

Around March 2016, that pivotal month where dirty tricks would be the ground game for Team Trump, campaign official Rick Gates asked the Israeli private intelligence firm PsyGroup to create a $3.7 million social media manipulation scheme to defame Hillary Clinton.[93]

Similar to what the Russians were doing for Trump, PsyGroup proposed a project, code-named Project Rome, to target Hillary Clinton and ten of her closest aides, from May through November 2016, "to achieve the desired outcome in the 2016 presidential campaign." In other words, to cheat for Trump. PsyGroup noted in a memo to the campaign that it would target "minority communities, suburban female voters, and swing voters in battleground states." Using mainly veteran Israeli intelligence officers, PsyGroup would create online avatars, a name for fake people, to promote Trump and highlight Clinton's weaknesses. PsyGroup would also provide the campaign with "intelligence dossiers" on Clinton and her staff, along with unspecified "actionable intelligence."[94]

PsyGroup said that a separate project, code-named Project Lion and pitched in April 2016, would conduct a similar operation against Senator Ted Cruz, then a front-running challenger for the GOP nomination. PsyGroup would identify five thousand targets and sort them based on their allegiance to Cruz and Trump. Employees would identify the split between the candidates and then conduct "intensive influence activities and campaigns" to sway potential voters to abandon Cruz and vote for Trump. PsyGroup wanted the operation to appear as if the voters were authentic Americans and not part of the Trump campaign.[95]

The Russians had already dominated the space by generating fake Facebook and Twitter influencers, so they did not appeal to Rick Gates, the decision maker on this project.[96] PsyGroup leadership subsequently met with other campaign officials at Trump Tower, including Donald Trump Jr., around August 2016. Trump Jr.'s attorney told reporters his client had no interest in the PsyGroup plan, but like all of Trump's dirty tricks teams, they were not stopping for lack of interest.[97]

The tableau was now set. Multiple Russian agencies were supporting Trump with stolen data. Dirty tricks teams were in place and fishing for more material about Clinton. All that was left was for the great game of stealing the election to begin. They stole it, and they won.

SECTION II

The Mischief Begins

CHAPTER 9

The Worst Presidency in History

In the postelection transition of the Trump team, disbelief over the victory gave way to a slick machine that needed to consolidate quickly and adapt its newfound power to help Trump keep the promises he made publicly, as well as his other commitments—the secret deals and activities done under the table. Many people would have to be rewarded, but more important, the strategic plan was to change the course of America, and the world, without the shackles of decency, human rights, and all the sappy goody two-shoes pomp that previous presidents had demanded. This America would be run like Trump Inc. The world was changing away from democracy and toward strong men who were going to link arms and create a new world order. Putin of Russia, Erdogan of Turkey, al-Sisi of Egypt, Bin Salman of Saudi Arabia, Duterte of the Philippines, Orban of Hungary, Le Pen in France, and the unbelievable choice of Boris Johnson to bring about Brexit—these and future autocrats imagine themselves the leaders of a Russian-led new world. It would be an axis of autocracies.

Almost immediately after the election, Trump acted as though he was already in power; he and his emissaries seemed to believe they were the masters of the universe. This attitude led to a series of actions during the transition that undermined or, worse, ignored the basic norms of American democracy. Additionally, during this period, as people initially resisted their actions and became cognizant of Russia's influence, the first calls for investigations started.

Through WikiLeaks, Russian intelligence was now linked to Team Trump. Both Trump and Moscow apparently worked with the specific intent to elect him. Trump may have hidden his direct ties, but he benefitted immensely. The transition of the Trump administration was a hasty affair. In fact, most of them were shocked by the win, including the new commander in chief.

The day after the election the Republican Party was ebullient: they had managed to hold onto the House and flip the Senate. Republicans took power in all branches of government and would soon change the Supreme Court. The American celebrations were loud, but not as loud as they were in Moscow. The usually staid Russian officials in the Duma celebrated openly. Within hours of Trump's election, politicians in the Kremlin started to brag that they had pulled off an amazing victory. The editor in chief of the Russian talk radio channel Echo, Alexei Venediktov, said, "They're drinking in the Kremlin now . . . [but] we'll see what happens later."[1]

While the hashtag #RussiaChoosesTrump trended on Twitter, pro-Kremlin satirist Mikhail Zadornov told the *Washington Post*, "Judging by the hysterics in [the] West, Vladimir Putin has won the U.S. elections." He would not be wrong. Within days, confessions from officials in Moscow about their ability to swing the election started to emerge. Russian deputy foreign minister Sergei Ryabkov said Russian officials had indeed been in contact with Trump campaign officials.[2] Ryabkov told the Interfax news agency, "There were contacts. . . . We are doing this and have been doing this during the election campaign." He also promised the contacts would continue.

On November 14, Putin and Trump spoke for the first time as elected leaders of their nations. Both promised a stronger relationship.[3] By the end of November, Trump met with a panel from the *New York Times*. When asked if there would be a Trump "reset" with Moscow, he said.

> I wouldn't use that term after what happened, you know, previously. I think—I would love to be able to get along with Russia and I think they'd like to be able to get along with us. It's in our mutual interest. And I don't go in with any preconceived notion, but I will tell you, I would say—when they used to say, during the campaign, Donald Trump loves Putin, Putin loves Donald Trump, I said, 'huh, wouldn't it be nice.' I'd say this in front of thousands of people, wouldn't it be nice to actually report what they said, wouldn't it be nice if we actually

> got along with Russia, wouldn't it be nice if we went after ISIS together, which is, by the way, aside from being dangerous, it's very expensive, and ISIS shouldn't have been even allowed to form, and the people will stand up and give me a massive hand. You know they thought it was bad that I was getting along with Putin or that I believe strongly if we can get along with Russia that's a positive thing. It is a great thing that we can get along with not only Russia but that we get along with other countries.[4]

Like clockwork, exactly one week after this interview, Putin came out and endorsed Trump's belief. In an address to the Russian people, Putin said that he was ready for more cooperation with the United States now that Trump was president.

> We are ready for cooperation with the new American administration. . . . It's important to normalize and develop our bilateral ties on an equal and mutually beneficial basis. We share responsibility for ensuring global security and stability and strengthening the non-proliferation regime.[5]

Then the *Washington Post* reported the CIA had assessed that Russia influenced the 2016 election to help Trump win.[6] The next day, Trump responded to news reports of the CIA assessment that "this is the same agency that noted Saddam had weapons of mass destruction."[7] Trump had just maligned the national intelligence apparatus to the benefit of a foreign power. It would be just the first of many attempts to undermine the legitimacy of both the CIA and FBI. He also said that Russian meddling was just an excuse to explain his election victory.[8]

Not to outdo himself, he then took to Twitter and tripled down on his undermining the CIA's assessment: "Can You Imagine If the Election Results Were Opposite and WE Tried to Play the Russia/CIA Card. It Would Be a Conspiracy Theory."[9] To Trump, it surely was a conspiracy theory, but only because the conspiracy had yet to be discovered. However, the fascinating dissembling he did on Moscow's behalf was troubling. Although Obama was still president, Trump took active steps to interfere with anything that had to do with showing animosity toward the Kremlin.

President Obama soon announced that the United States would respond to the Russian attack on the election process with sanctions and unspecified cyberwarfare actions at a place and time of his choosing. Trump tweeted that the Obama White House only complained about hacking after Clinton lost. This was a classic case of Trump gaslighting. In his mind, Obama had only *just* now spoken about it, but Obama had addressed it first in spring 2016, the same day more DNC leaks came out.[10] On numerous occasions Trump would go on to directly address Obama's assertions about Russian interference.

In a stunning example of expert-level trolling, Putin sent FBI and CIA investigators an obscene gesture in the form of a comment. Putin claimed at his annual news conference that no one believed Trump would win—except for the Kremlin.[11] On Christmas Eve, Trump responded to Putin by acknowledging the Democrats were sore losers in the election: "Democrats are losing on every front and looking for people to blame everywhere. They need to learn to lose with dignity."[12] Trump quickly followed up by praising and supporting Putin's assessment of his fellow Americans, "Vladimir Putin said today about Hillary and Dems: 'In my opinion, it is humiliating. One must be able to lose with dignity.' So true!"

But Russia was not the only foreign power coming to bow to Donald Trump. Diplomatic teams and private visits to Trump Tower started flooding in. Within a short time, the representative of the Austrian government, one whose political party, the Freedom Party of Austria (FPO), was formed by two former Nazi SS officers in 1952 and was now contractually aligned with Putin's United Russia, sent a delegation to New York.

Trump's team opened communications and coordination with the Kremlin, Saudi Arabia, the United Arab Emirates (UAE), and others. Making these contacts could appear to be violating the Logan Act, a law ratified in 1799 that prohibited US citizens from carrying out unauthorized negotiations with foreign powers. The Obama administration was still in power, and technically, until January 20, 2017, they were the only ones that could officially communicate with other nations. However, to Trump, Obama was not a consideration. Trump had objectives and allies to consolidate. The word hit the global street that Obama was to be ignored and Trump was the new man in town. All who needed his friendship would have to come to kiss his ring. And they did.

The most enigmatic of all the genuflections to Trump was the secret visit by Sheikh Mohammed bin Zayed al-Nahyan, the crown prince of the Emirate of Abu Dhabi and defacto ruler of the UAE. Sheikh Mohammed did not inform the Obama administration before coming to the United States, which led National Security Adviser Susan Rice to request the US intelligence community to conduct collection on his trip. A report that a UAE Royal flight aircraft was approaching US airspace and had filed a flight plan to land at JFK Airport was the first the Obama administration knew that someone of importance was arriving from the UAE. Clearly, this was a state-level personage who had completely ignored protocol and was trying to "secretly" fly into the United States to meet with Trump. The meeting was a thumb in the eye of the outgoing administration, indicating that this foreign power did not care what the administration thought or even sought its permission to enter the United States. To the UAE, Trump was the power in America now.

Sheikh Mohammed, Flynn, Kushner, and Bannon attended the meeting in Trump Tower. Details are scarce about what happened. The meeting lasted three hours, and the attendees claimed they discussed Middle East issues, specifically about Israel and Iran.[13] In the lead-up to the meeting, Sheikh Mohammed had pressed for closer ties between Abu Dhabi and Moscow. It is also believed that Sheikh Mohammed wanted to discuss with Trump officials removing sanctions against Russia as a trade-off to encourage Putin to be less involved in Iran and pressure Iran to remove its military assets in Syria.[14] Coupled with Erik Prince's secret meeting in the Seychelles with a high-level Russian oligarch, this was a sign that both Putin and Trump were secretly staking out multiple avenues to get Moscow's sanctions lifted. These sanctions also hurt the UAE, as they lessened the flow of Russian money to the UAE. So, Sheikh Mohammed had a vested interest in helping a rich guy like Trump make other rich men richer.

What to Do with a General Like Michael?

In December 2016, weeks before the Trump inauguration, Flynn allegedly met with Turkish officials to discuss ways to extradite an Iranian Turkish businessman in a US prison who Ankara suspected may have helped Iran evade sanctions.[15] Also during that meeting, Flynn and his son discussed having Fethullah Gülen extradited to Turkey in exchange for millions of dollars. The meeting allegedly took place at the 21 Club in New York City, which is a Trump favorite because of its mafia past.[16]

Dealing under the table to sell Gülen was not the only favor Flynn was doing for Turkish cash. Shortly before Trump took office, Flynn overturned an Obama administration plan to equip the Kurdish YPG guerrillas for an operation against ISIS in Raqqa, Syria. YPG, which stands for Yekineyen Parastine Gel in Kurdish, or People's Protection Units, is a militia aligned with the Syrian Democratic Forces. The Turkish government loathed the YPG and considered them a regional enemy. America was working with the YPG guerrillas because they were the most successful and effective combat forces carrying out direct combat against ISIS in Iraq and Syria. There was no way to beat ISIS without them. Flynn, who in the past was an intelligence architect for elite special operations forces like those operating in Syria, would have known that. Instead, he betrayed the mission and intervened to stop the anti-ISIS mission while under the pay of both Ankara and Moscow.[17]

During this same period, Kushner and Flynn met with Kislyak to set up a back channel, secret communications link with Flynn and an unnamed senior Russian military officer. Ostensibly the back channel was for Syria discussion, but one assumes there was far more to it than that since it was off the books and cloudy.[18]

The Kislyak Phone Calls

On December 29, President Obama made an announcement that he was taking the Russian attack on American democracy very seriously and that his administration was going to act.[19] Obama's beliefs about the Russian hacking were unambiguous and well informed. He had seen how Dutch, Australian, and CIA intelligence collecting revealed a suspicious pattern of activity, with the Trump team soliciting from and possibly conspiring with Moscow before the election. In August 2016 he had ordered James Clapper, then director of National Intelligence, and

CIA director John Brennan to contact the Russians directly, but Russia persisted and released stolen data right up to Election Day. Obama had personally told Vladimir Putin to his face at a September conference in China to stop what he was doing.[20] Russia had already completed the hacks and did not appear to meddle in hacking the vote tallies. Obama was going to make sure Russia paid a price. The one thing the Russians hated was sanctions. Their money could not flow around the world freely, which made the rubles only good in Russia. Obama hit them again, and in a White House speech, he specifically identified Russian intelligence as the reason for the additional sanctions:

> Today, I have ordered a number of actions in response to the Russian government's aggressive harassment of US officials and cyber operations aimed at the US election. These actions follow repeated private and public warnings that we have issued to the Russian government, and are a necessary and appropriate response to efforts to harm US interests in violation of established international norms of behavior.[21]

Obama ordered personal sanctions against nine members of Russian FSB and GRU intelligence agencies and identified four specific GRU officers involved in the plot, as well as three companies working as subcontractors for the GRU. He closed two Russian "recreation centers" in Maryland and in Long Island, New York. Finally, he declared thirty-five Russian spies operating out of these facilities personae non grata and ordered them immediately expelled from the United States. In a conventional world, such sanctions would have been considered blistering, but Russia had selected a new president, and they were sure that whatever the black president did, Trump, who hated Obama, would undo. Trump said it remained unclear who did what in the hacking, and people should move on from it and drop the idea of sanctions.[22]

On the same day after Obama announced his sanctions, Lt. General Michael Flynn, now the front runner for national security adviser, called the Russian ambassador Sergey Kislyak. Flynn was not just giving condolences for an assassinated Russian ambassador and a plane crash of a Russian army band, as he told the news media, he was also conducting secret negotiations with Moscow in violation of the Logan Act. Flynn and Kislyak had met face-to-face in mid-December to discuss the crippling sanctions Obama had placed on Russia after its illegal invasion of Crimea in 2014.[23]

FBI surveillance logs found that this was actually the second set of calls. On December 22, Flynn had seemed to be talking to the Russians to get them to not vote on or delay a vote on a UN resolution against Israel.

The Mueller report would later verify General Flynn was the point man for the campaign's contact with Kislyak, even though Jared Kushner did not believe Kislyak had any power to shape Kremlin policies.

> Mr. Flynn also has acknowledged lying to the agents about his conversations with Mr. Kislyak involving Russia's impending vote in the United Nations on an Egyptian-sponsored resolution to condemn Israeli settlements in the West Bank. He has admitted that he asked that Russia either delay or oppose the resolution.[24]

Russia now knew how power in the new Trump team would flow. Matters related to Israel started with Jared Kushner, went to Trump through intermediaries, and then were passed on by Flynn. This information was good intelligence that could be exploited in the future. No matter what Kushner wanted, Russia later voted for the resolution, which went against Israel.[25]

Not surprisingly, listening in on the December 29 Flynn-Kislyak call were the surveillance teams of the FBI's National Security Branch. Telephone communications with foreign diplomats, particularly from Russia, were monitored for counterespionage purposes. Everyone in the government was briefed that official communications were monitored in what were called OFM or Own Force Monitoring. Almost all calls were benign, but this one had raised the eyebrows of the monitoring teams. The FBI found that Flynn was in communications with the Trump transition team and was asking Kislyak not to escalate the situation as it would change under Trump.

Flynn made five calls to Kislyak and after that he talked with Hope Hicks, who was in Mar-a-Lago with Trump. Flynn's discussion with Kislyak centered around not having a "tit-for-tat" exchange with Moscow and assuring Russia that Obama's sanctions would not be implemented if they moderated their response to Obama's tough actions.[26]

Nance's Law was hovering over the news the next day when Vladimir Putin stated he would not implement countersanctions on the United States in good faith that Trump would resolve the issue as president.[27]

Unfortunately for Flynn and Russia, they were not the only ones who knew the contents of those phone calls. Thanks to the surveillance teams, the US Department of Justice knew what was said. The acting attorney general at the time, Sally Yates, a career prosecutor, felt compelled to warn the White House. That would be her mistake.

Russia saw these secret negotiations as a tipping point. Shortly after winning the election, unnamed Russian officials, using government email addresses, reached out to Hicks for information about the incoming administration, and FBI agents warned her "they were not who they claimed to be."[28]

The Obama team had a briefing ready for the president-elect, but Trump remained noncommittal about believing the intelligence community's assessment on Russian interference. He said he would receive the Obama team's briefing and listen to the "facts" but wanted to move on from the issue.[29]

As the new year dawned and the Trump team was soon to take office, one last part of the Russian cyberwarfare operation played itself out. The Guccifer 2.0 entity posted its last post insulting US intelligence agencies and cybersecurity companies, writing:

> The U.S. intelligence agencies have published several reports of late claiming I have ties with Russia. I'd like to make it clear enough that these accusations are unfounded. I have totally no relation to the Russian government. . . . The technical evidence contained in the reports doesn't stand up to scrutiny. This is a crude fake.[30]

And with that bit of flourish, Guccifer 2.0 set the narrative that every Republican would come to mimic over the life of the Trump-Russia investigation: "It's obvious that the intelligence agencies are deliberately falsifying evidence. In my opinion, they're playing into the hands of the Democrats who are trying to blame foreign actors for their failure."[31]

Not surprisingly, now that Trump was in government, Guccifer 2.0—the officers of GRU cyberintelligence Unit 74455 and the source of the hacked emails to the world's news media—suddenly disappeared from the Internet. With their mission accomplished, it was time for a well-deserved vacation.

CHAPTER 10

Masters of Fake News

On January 6, 2017, the intelligence community principals briefed Trump on the details of the Intelligence Community Assessment, formerly known as *Background to "Assessing Russian Activities and Intentions in Recent US Elections": The Analytic Process and Cyber Incident Attribution*. The report outlined all the information the community had acquired that led up to the DNC hacking. It also included precisely *why* the intelligence community was convinced it was Russian operatives who were working under the direct orders of Vladimir Putin. Clapper and Brennan assured Trump that the CIA had at least a number of these accusations verified by independent intelligence. They also explained that it was the least reliable form of intelligence—rumor intelligence or RUMINT. It had come from the mouths of Russians who seemed to have had a keen base of knowledge about Trump's activities and who liked to tell stories.

The briefing lasted almost two hours, and when it was over, the director of the FBI, James Comey, gave Trump a private overview of the more sensational allegations in the Steele dossier.[1] To most new presidents, a side briefing would have been seen as prudent, understanding that the bureau and its law enforcement professionals were protecting the rear of the man who would lead the free world within two weeks. But Donald Trump was not that kind of man. Having cut his teeth using personal and even sexual blackmail against his enemies, he saw the backgrounder as a personal threat. Trump assumed Comey was trying to intimidate him. To him there was nothing innocent about receiving bad news. The problem was, though Comey was being sincere, it was Trump who knew his complicity in some of these activities was true. The Mafioso-like Trump surfaced quickly. In Trump's estimation, they had to be making a play to uncover his secrets because apparently some of them were no longer secret. Trump was being pushed into a corner by facts he could not control. He took the Steele briefing as a direct threat to his presidency. He decided within days that Comey had to be fired.

James Comey graduated from the University of Chicago Law School in 1985. In 1987, he was assistant US attorney for the Southern District of New York under Rudy Giuliani and was tasked with leading the prosecution of notorious mob boss John Gambino. In 1996, Comey was designated deputy special counsel for the Clinton Whitewater real estate investigation. In 2002, he was confirmed as US attorney for the Southern District of New York and became deputy attorney general in 2003. He was later confirmed as FBI director on July 29, 2013. He has served under presidents Bill Clinton, George W. Bush, Barack Obama, and, for less than five months, under Donald Trump. The FBI director usually holds that position for a ten-year term to maintain continuity and to prevent removal for political considerations. Again, Trump was not the kind of man to maintain any continuity. He wanted a corrupt cop who would do his bidding. Comey was clearly not that kind of cop.

Using his trademark way of lying by reversing the truth, Trump came out of the briefing and told the press an alternate version of his "constructive" meeting with Clapper, Brennan, and Comey. Then he surprisingly added China to the list of actors who attempted to influence the US election, claiming it was also trying to break into the US cybersphere. He then said the DNC was attacked, but the Republican computer servers were strong, and no intrusion was detected. He insisted that *nothing* had impacted his election results.[2]

News about what actually happened when Trump received the intelligence community's assessment quickly made the headlines. When it was revealed that the Steele dossier was briefed and that the CIA was confident some of it was true, Trump attacked. His short temper exploded, and he immediately coined a new phrase that would take on its own life: "fake news." He compared the US spies and investigators to the Nazis: "Intelligence agencies should never have allowed this fake news to 'leak' into the public. One last shot at me. Are we living in Nazi Germany?"[3]

Trump dived back into his strategy to cover for Russia and to keep the goodwill flowing to Putin. Initially, he tweeted that a better relationship with Russia is a good thing and only "fools" and "stupid people" would say otherwise. At his press conference, Trump reversed himself and suddenly agreed Russia influenced the election, "I think it was Russia . . . [Putin] should not be doing it. He won't be doing it. Russia will have much greater respect for our country when I am leading it than when other people have led it." He immediately followed with tweets that encouraged cooperation between the coming Trump administration and Putin's Kremlin. He vowed to improve relations with Russia despite some Republican opposition and said he did not know if he would or would not get along with Putin but insisted, "Do you honestly believe Hillary would be tougher on Putin than me?" In a press conference where he was forced to accuse Putin of malfeasance, speaking about a Trump-Russia future, he could not avoid insulting Hillary Clinton.[4]

The next day the Kremlin did its part to support Trump. Putin claimed that the dossier was a "fantasy" and affirmed "officially" that Russia had no damaging information to hold over Trump. But the few smoldering stories about the Christopher Steele dossier were about erupt into a new firestorm. Up to this point, the Steele dossier had been something ethereal, a political legend. Parts were originally published by investigative journalist David Corn, but the entirety of the report with the details of its salty allegations was not yet a political world story. That was about to end.

As the Trump administration arrived in Washington, BuzzFeed News released the memos in full.[5] The allegations were more than explosive; they were outrageously salacious. The most noteworthy allegation was the story about the hookers. The story went that Trump had stayed at a hotel in Moscow and asked for prostitutes to come up and urinate on the bed Barack and Michelle Obama had slept in when he was president and staying in Moscow. It did not matter if Trump denied it, a new meme about him was created that broke his metanarrative: the idea that the Russians had videotaped this perverted activity and were holding the possession of that tape over his head. The "pee pee tape" was now used to mock and ridicule Trump. Even the NBC comedy show *Saturday Night Live* used a bare-chested actor playing Putin to appear in news conferences holding a VHS tape marked "pee pee tape." The caricature of Trump, played by Alec Baldwin, would now frame whatever Trump had to say about the dossier or any other matter. Although amusing on comedy shows, Trump's conciliatory public statements about Putin seemed to suggest that he was being blackmailed. Veteran journalist Robert Woodward claimed that the CIA had six sources verifying the Steele dossier, but only two were considered solid contacts that supported some elements.

Tapes of urinating prostitutes aside, Trump continued his adoption of Russian behaviors and foreign policy. The day before he was to take over the Oval Office, Trump reiterated to German newspapers that NATO is "obsolete" and that as president he wanted to get rid of sanctions against Russia.[6] Such revelations only reinforced the notion that the sex tapes were real and Putin was holding them over Trump to influence him.

It did not help Trump when word started to leak from the FBI that an investigation into his campaign had existed for months. The *New York Times* followed up by identifying an FBI counterintelligence investigation into Trump and his business ties—which meant the FBI suspected someone, or Trump himself, was working or cooperating with foreign assets or spies.[7]

The Inaugural Address—Khrushchev Style

Trump believed that Russia was behind him, but the maelstrom was just starting. His relationship with Putin was suspicious, but his reputation as a fledgling autocrat was not yet completely developed. Three key events all occurring within twenty-four hours of his taking power would shape Trump's way of moving America away from democratic sharing of power and toward autocratic governance: his inaugural speech, his first press conference, and his visit to the CIA.

President Trump delivered his inaugural address on January 20, 2017. The shock of his election hadn't worn off the nation, and the suspicious activities of the transition team made the inauguration a highly anticipated event. Questions concerning Russia were set aside for a day. Trump would be given an opportunity to bring the nation back together and perhaps put aside some of the misgivings about the unusual events that occurred during the election. But that was not to be.

During the campaign, Trump's stump speeches usually had a dark foreboding tone. He presented a world in which America was a destroyed country; he referred to Americans as a broken people, ripped off by the establishment. He presented himself as someone uniquely equipped, above all others, to personally intervene and save the country. It was a dramatic way of speaking, near Hitlerian in its delivery.

Having won, one would assume that his inauguration speech would be different. Now as elected president, Trump was expected to back away from the brink of authoritarianism and white ethnonationalism that he had courted during the campaign. The inaugural speech was supposed to rally America. That was not to be.

Trump began with a seemingly inclusive message where he promised to "rebuild our country and restore its promise for all of our people." He continued the theme of people power, which had won over many who had voted for him. He sounded a Tea Party–like populist chord: "Today's ceremony . . . has very special meaning. Because today we are not merely transferring power from one Administration to another . . . we are transferring power from Washington, D.C. and giving it back to you, the American people."[8] This customary tone of the speech's start was something one would expect any president to deliver.

But after the perfunctory glad-handing and call to give political power back to the people, his tone shifted abruptly. Within minutes it was clear that Trump had little intention of keeping up the pretense of being an inclusive president who would govern for all the American people. He reverted to his campaign stump speech and ran down a list of grievances of a downtrodden American people and attacked those who had caused their pain.

"Washington flourished, but the people did not share in its wealth. Politicians prospered but the jobs left, and factories closed. The establishment protected itself, but not the citizens of our country." People looked at one another askance as the speech got gloomier, much gloomier. Trump did not describe a nation of immigrants who brought all to this point in history. No, he decided that there was another America, an alternate America that only he and his base could see.

> But for too many of our citizens a different reality exists; mothers and children trapped in poverty in our inner cities; rusted out factories scattered like tombstones across the landscape of our nation; an education system flush with cash but which leaves our young and beautiful students deprived of knowledge; and the crimes and gangs and drugs that have stolen too many lives and robbed our country of so much unrealized potential. . . . This American carnage stops right here and stops right now!

That last line had an explosive impact to an audience well beyond those present. Virtually everyone who was not of Trump's base, particularly the near sixty-five million Americans who had voted for his opponent Hillary Clinton, thought either aloud or to themselves, *What the hell is he talking about?* All that was missing was for him to take off his shoe and beat it on the dais Khrushchev-style to make his point.

Somehow he perceived and described Americans as people closer to Depression-era workers than twenty-first-century tech users each with a mobile communication and news media device in his or her pocket. No, Donald Trump was projecting onto America the dark brutalist architecture of an old enemy: the Soviet Union. He was using terms the way the Russians had described America for almost a century. To political and psychological warfare experts, he wasn't just agreeing with the Russian image of the United States, he was using their exact terms, copying Russian media like RT and Sputnik. Many in the US intelligence community, including myself, wondered, *Where had he picked that up?* and *Why had he picked that up?*

The rest of the speech was standard Trump triumphalism. He complained about other countries being made rich at the expense of the American middle class. He railed about how Americans are victims of weak leadership and an establishment enriching itself on the backs of ordinary Americans. He complained about how globalization, the very trade system created by America after World War II, was the source of economic loss: "The wealth of our middle class has been ripped from their homes and then redistributed across the entire world." Far be it from him to mention that the American middle class wanted those goods and would flood a Walmart daily to get them. And he ended with his campaign motto, stolen from Ronald Reagan: "And, yes, together, we will make America great again."

In the classic comedy movie *The Producers* by Mel Brooks, there is a scene where dozens of glitter-clad Nazis sing a joyous song called "Springtime for Hitler." At the end of the song, the opening night audience, adorned in black tie and gala dresses, are stunned into a deafening silence with mouths literally stuck open. That was the effect of Trump's speech. His followers *loved* it.

When their senses came back to them, it was the consensus of the Washington punditocracy that this was the darkest inaugural speech given in American history. It would simply be referred to as the "American carnage" speech. Republican Michael Green told *Foreign Policy* magazine: "Where friends and allies around the world look to new presidents' inaugural addresses in hopes of seeing Aragorn, they heard from Trump only Gollum."[9]

Former president George W. Bush was overheard to mutter, "That was some weird shit."[10]

This Party Is Funded by Moscow

At the inauguration and the many after-parties, almost all of Trump's Russian billionaire investors would materialize and look wondrously as their former associate got sworn in to become the most powerful man in the world. There were many, but the top four are detailed here: Viktor Vekselberg, Simon Kukes, Roman Abramovich, and Alexander Shustorovich.

Viktor Vekselberg is a Russian oligarch who studied in the 1970s in the same school in Russia with Len Blavatnik. Vekselberg and Blavatnik established a joint venture called Renova in the 1990s. He is one of the Russian oligarchs behind the consortium Alfa-Access-Renova (AAR), along with Blavatnik, Mikhail Fridman, Alexy Kuzmichev, and German Khan.[11] He became a multibillionaire when AAR sold a 50 percent stake in the Russian oil company Rosneft. Blavatnik and Khan gained a huge fortune with the Rosneft deal. *Bloomberg News* reported Vekselberg's personal wealth was around $18 billion when he held the position as the fortieth richest man in the world. While earning these riches he was accused of money laundering, fraud, and other finance-related charges. In 2014, Vekselberg was present at a private fundraiser in Moscow that Ivanka Trump, Jared Kushner, and Roman Abramovich and his then wife also attended.[12]

In 2015, Vladimir Strzhalkovskiy, a close personal friend of Vladimir Putin and a former KGB officer, was the vice chairman of the Bank of Cyprus. When he resigned his position and handed it off to Wilbur Ross, the man who would become Trump's US commerce secretary, he sold part of his stake to Vekselberg.[13]

Vekselberg attended the same RT tenth anniversary gala, along with Michael Flynn, Jill Stein, and the father of Julian Assange.[14] In October 2016, Trump's adviser Michael Cohen established Essential Consultants. This was the account used to pay and silence former porn star Stormy Daniels before the election. Two months later, monthly payments of $83,333 started flowing in from Columbus Nova LLC, an investment management firm controlled by Renova. These payments would last for eight months and total $583,332. Trump's relationship with this oligarch grew even closer. On January 9, 2017, Cohen attended a meeting with Vekselberg and his cousin.[15]

Vekselberg then was invited to attend Trump's inauguration as a guest of his cousin Andrew Intrater, who was seated next to Cohen. Intrater donated over $250,000 to Trump's inaugural committee. A year later Vekselberg was stopped and interviewed by federal agents in a New York airport as part of the Mueller probe.[16] One month after that he was hit with sanctions, levied personally and on all of his businesses.[17]

Simon Kukes was born in Soviet Russia and immigrated to the United States in the late '70s. Kukes was an early Trump buyer when, in 2000, he purchased property at Trump Parc in New York City. In 2003 Kukes was appointed by Putin to head Yukos Oil after the outspoken businessman Mikhail Khodorkovsky was jailed and his assets stripped from him. According to the *Moscow Times*, the CIA spied on Kukes after he was appointed to Yukos.[18] They found him involved in a massive racketeering scheme, money laundering, wire fraud, and mafia-like behavior in business practices that led to a lawsuit filed by Norex in 2002. During the decades that Kukes lived in the United States, he never made any political contributions until Trump ran for president in 2016. Interestingly, around two weeks after Trump Jr.'s controversial meeting with Natalya Veselnitskaya, Kukes made a $100,000 donation to the Trump Victory Commmittee and then two more contributions to the fundraising committee, altogether totaling $273,000.[19] Soon after the 2016 election, Kukes also made small contributions to various Republican state committees around the country, and he was in constant contact with Trump's lawyer Rudy Giuliani.[20] Luke Harding, writing for the *Guardian,* noted:

> Simon Kukes said he was helping Trump with "strategy development" and shared photos of his 29-year-old Russian girlfriend posing with the future president.
>
> Kukes made the claims to Vyacheslav Pavlovsky, a career Kremlin official and former ambassador to Norway. Pavlovsky is currently vice-president of Russian Railways.
>
> During this period he was in regular contact with Pavlovsky. In one email written in July 2016, Kukes wrote in Russian: "I am actively involved in Trump's election campaign, and am part of the group on strategy development."[21]

Roman Abramovich, the Russian Israeli billionaire born in Lithuania, is the owner of Evraz and Millhouse Capital. Abramovich was a principal supporter of Yeltsin's move to install Putin. Abramovich is said to have contracts to provide up to 40 percent of the steel from his company Evraz for the Keystone XL pipeline, which originates from Canada and crosses down into the United States. After his election, Trump signed an executive order to advance the Keystone XL pipeline, which had been canceled by the Obama administration.

Finally, Alexander Shustorovich, another inauguration attendee, is a music mogul who donated $1 million to the Trump inaugural committee. During the George W. Bush campaign, he tried to donate $250,000. That donation was rejected because of his ties to the Kremlin.[22]

The inauguration was a who's who of Russian oligarchs and foreign money. They did not come to just drink to Donald's health: they expected to be under his roof—his *krysha*. But first there was money to be made off US citizens.

Ivanka Trump stepped up and personally negotiated the rates for hotel rooms, meals, and rented space for the Trump hotel in advance of the Trump inauguration. Committee leader Stephanie Winston Wolkoff emailed Ivanka, while she was still an executive with the Trump Organization, to complain that the hotel was attempting to charge $175,000 per day for use of a ballroom and other meeting rooms, according to internal communications.[23] Wolkoff said the maximum rate should have been $85,000 a day, noting the events were for the president-elect and one event was for family and close friends. Someone was pocketing $95,000 in profit. That was the least of the grift. Federal investigators started an inquiry into the possible abuse of more than $100 million in donations and violations of tax law.

The Women's March

On January 21, 2017, the day after Donald Trump's Russian-filled inauguration, a visceral and tangible reaction to his presidency manifested itself. Women took to activism and organized a protest march to signify their distaste that a man who exuded sexist, racist, and elitist attitudes toward women and minorities had been elected president. The morning of the march, Washington, DC, was awash with hundreds of thousands of protesters. By the end of the day, as many as four million people took to the streets around the United States and worldwide. By the end of the weekend, over 673 protests, predominantly women, took place in virtually every city in the country. Internationally, everywhere from Nairobi to Berlin to Kuala Lumpur to Manila, marches organized by women took place. There was even a small one in Antarctica.[24]

Women and men descended onto the capital from all over the country. As a symbol of solidarity, women hand-knit and wore pink "pussy hats," which symbolized their disgust of Trump's comments when he bragged how he could grab a woman "by the pussy." A sea of opposition, they carried signs for a wide variety of causes but with one spoken theme: Trump was not their president.

The First Press Conference and Visit to the CIA

Forty-eight hours after the inauguration, the new press secretary, Sean Spicer, opened the first press briefing of the Trump administration for the White House correspondents. He began by thanking the press for coming to the White House. Everyone expected a simple briefing, short and without substance, as the administration had just begun that same morning. Usually, the press secretary would announce the president's schedule and a few policy objectives, after which a few questions would be taken. But like the inaugural address, the press briefing was not normal at all.

Right out of the box, Spicer took a hostile, combative stance and started berating the news media. He launched into a litany of complaints about the press coverage of the inauguration the previous day. Without missing a mark, he accused the press of being "engaged in deliberately false reporting." What he found most upsetting, he said, was the purposeful effort by the media to undermine the success of the new president. He claimed the press had falsely reported that the president ordered the removal of a bust of Martin Luther King Jr. from the Oval Office. Even though the story had been corrected, he charged that the story was "irresponsible and reckless."

He tore into a point-by-point defense of the crowd size at the inauguration—because the media had reported it was smaller than that of Barack Obama's in 2009. He pointed out details of the ground coverings and fencing, which, he said, gave the impression of a smaller crowd. He complained about photographic tweets from the National Park Service that clearly illustrated the poor showing. As evidence, he pointed out the large number of people who had filled areas from Fourth Street to the media tent and that 420,000 people had used the Washington Metro, the US Capitol's underground public transit. It was clear to him that Trump's inauguration had to have been much larger than Obama's second inauguration because only 317,000 used the Washington Metro that day. He could not fathom that some people riding the Metro, maybe one hundred thousand others, were there to protest the next day (which they did). Finally, as the official spokesman of the president of the United States, he proclaimed, Trump-like, what may be the single most eye-popping lie told by a press secretary: "This was the largest audience to ever witness an inauguration—period—both in person and around the globe."[25]

It was the administration's incredible attempt to exert dominance. Clearly, somewhere, Trump had learned that if you are going to deal with the news media as a national leader then treat them like vermin. Most importantly, his bile-filled contempt for the news was now a formal White House policy. Spicer was not done. He warned darkly that President Trump would hold the "press accountable" and that the "American people deserved better." These veiled threats can easily be found in speeches given by Russian autocrat Vladimir Putin. It's an old dictator's trick to make the news media the "enemy of the people." Only a few months into his presidency, Trump would use those exact words about the news media, taken from the lips of communist Joseph Stalin, who sent millions to their deaths with those very words.

Trump wanted to start his administration off with a conciliatory visit to the US intelligence community, to calm the waters. Having had their reputation savaged by Trump—who refused to believe any assertion that Russia had anything to do with his improbable victory—members of the intelligence community were feeling hurt and disrespected. So, on January 21, 2017, he stood in the lobby of the headquarters building at the Central Intelligence Agency in Langley, Virginia, to address the community.

In the Hall of Honor stands a statue of William "Wild Bill" Donovan. Donovan was the founder of the World War II–era Office of Strategic Services, the famed OSS, precursor to the CIA. The statue is next to the OSS memorial, which consists of a single black star on the south wall above a book of remembrance to the OSS dead. On the opposite side, the north wall, is the Memorial Wall, consisting of 133 stars carved into marble, each representing a man or woman of the CIA who died in the nation's most secret service. It is a place of the deepest reverence for members of the agency. Lowered voices and quiet reflection are expected for all who pass through or visit.

Presidential visits to the agency generally include a visit to the Hall of Honor. Presidents are expected to start their administration by offering both words of admiration and condolence to the fallen and their families. Every president who visits notes that many of the names remain secret and are not listed in the ledger. Their heroism is a national secret. My own visit with my wife led me to such deep reverence for those honored in the hall that I whispered the names of my dead friends, now stars on the wall, as if in a chapel—which it is.

Of course, the small hallway, filled with a few rows of career officers, was the perfect venue for Trump to express high regard for the intelligence community. But to the horror of all who watched, he did not come to recognize the sacrifice of the honored dead; he came to the Hall of Honor to praise himself.

Standing in front of the Memorial Wall, Trump first claimed everyone in the room probably voted for him, and then went on to advise them of the size of his crowd at the inauguration and how his numerous features on the cover of *Time* magazine exceeded that of quarterback Tom Brady. At the end of the hallway, past the security checkpoint, there is an intersecting corridor where receptions are often held. It appeared that Trump had placed a cheering section there and in the second two rows of the memorial hallway. These supporters burst into raucous applause for every statement the president made. The CIA officers standing in front of him were astounded and looked askance at the people on their left who were literally screaming in the Hall of Honor. Trump then went on to attack the US news media: "I have a running war with the media, they are among the most dishonest human beings on Earth—they sort of made it sound like I had a feud with the intelligence community. The reason you are the number one stop is exactly the opposite."[26] Trump's cheering squad squealed with delight at this statement. Such behavior in the hall was sacrilege.

The response from senior career intelligence officers was swift and brutal. Outgoing director of the CIA John Brennan, through Nick Shapiro his longtime aide, enunciated the intelligence community's collective distaste at this apparent desecration of the holiest of holies in American intelligence.[27] He said, "Former CIA Director Brennan is deeply saddened and angered at Donald Trump's despicable display of self-aggrandizement in front of CIA's Memorial Wall of Agency heroes . . . [Trump] should be ashamed of himself."[28] Another unidentified CIA officer told David Ignatius at the *Washington Post:* "Overall, the self-obsession and campaign-style language was not appropriate in that place. . . . It should not be all about you, at a place that memorializes people for whom it was about others and about mission."[29] The same day Spicer flew into a litany of statements about the CIA visit that ranged from delusional to outright bald-faced lies.

Spicer described the visit to the CIA as a "raucous overflow crowd of 400 plus CIA employees. There were over 1,000 requests to attend. . . . The employees were ecstatic. . . . He told them [Trump] has their back, and they were grateful for that." Bizarrely, he claimed that there was a five-minute standing ovation, in a hallway that could barely fit a few dozen when standing, and that the CIA staff had done it as a "display of their patriotism and enthusiasm for his presidency."[30] The veracity of that statement would be challenged every day as intelligence evidence mounted that Russia and members of the Trump administration were behaving in ways that would have had virtually any other government employee cashiered from service and investigated for possible espionage.

In his usual way, Trump attacked Brennan directly on Twitter. He blamed Brennan for Syria, Russia's invasion of Crimea in Ukraine, and a buildup of Russian nuclear weapons. However, he elected to project another conspiracy theory on an already beleaguered CIA, "Was this the leaker of Fake News?"[31]

If Trump had decided to cover up any investigation of his crimes, he apparently decided to do everything he could to get caught. He acted as though *All the President's Men*—Bob Woodward's and Carl Bernstein's history of how Richard Nixon was disgraced out of office—was his how-to manual for how to ruin the presidency. All that was left to do was issue orders and not be found out as a Russian-funded criminal enterprise. He'd start by getting rid of that freakishly tall, pesky FBI director, James Comey.

CHAPTER 11

The Good Guys

> We're in unchartered territory here. . . . I don't think we have pondered it as deeply as we need to—the level of corruption. This is unprecedented in the modern history of the country.
>
> —Steve Schmidt

Over a few days in late March 2017, Trump pressured then director of National Intelligence Dan Coats to speak with FBI director Comey to end the Russia investigation. An ODNI (Office of the Director of National Intelligence) staffer told Mueller and his investigators that Trump seemed to be "musing about hating the investigation" and wanting Coats "to do something to stop it."

On March 26, 2017, Trump called then NSA director Admiral Michael Rogers to voice frustrations with the Russia investigation and asked what Rogers could do to help him. Rogers's deputy was present for the call and called it the strangest thing he had seen in government in nearly four decades. Both men prepared memorandums of the call and put it in a locked safe.

In late March through mid-April 2017, the president called Comey to ask him to end the investigation. He said he was not personally involved, though he left open the possibility that people in his campaign may have been. He urged Comey to ensure that Americans knew Trump was not personally involved and was not under investigation. Comey refused—politely. That refusal became the reason Trump fired him in May 2017.

Trump then began encouraging then attorney general Jeff Sessions to reverse his recusal from oversight of the Russia investigation. This would expose Sessions to liability if he suddenly threw himself back into the investigation. Trump wanted him back so he could control it. Sessions refused and wrote a resignation letter on May 18, 2017. This was dangerous stuff. Even Trump knew that the Sessions resignation would reveal his plan to stop the FBI. So Trump kept the letter for several days before returning it to Sessions and refusing the resignation. Chief of Staff Reince Priebus referred to Trump keeping the letter as holding a "shock collar" on Sessions. If he stepped out of line, Trump would fire him by accepting his resignation. Priebus also believed that by keeping the letter, Trump had the "DOJ by the throat." He eventually asked Trump to return it to Sessions. Not being a fool, Sessions kept it in his pocket whenever he went to the White House right up to the moment he left in January 2018.

These events portray a White House hell-bent on controlling its agencies, distorting their ability to function as Trump tried to cover up his crimes and actions conducted during the 2016 campaign. Like a mafia boss, he expected them to pledge *omertà* (silence) and show allegiance to him over their constitutional duties. As America's enemies made maneuvers against it, the president instead demanded the leaders of our intelligence and law enforcement agencies spend time protecting him from the sins of his campaign, not the country.

Peter Strzok: The Russian Spy Hunter

One of those who was protecting the country was Georgetown-educated, army veteran Peter Strzok. He became an FBI intelligence research specialist in 1996 and actually had a spell of minor fame back in 2010 when he was a lead agent in an FBI counterintelligence mission called Operation Ghost Stories. Strzok, as a Cold War–trained counterintelligence officer, had a deeper understanding than most about how strategic, patient, and far-reaching Russian clandestine infiltration can be. FBI videos and documents of Operation Ghost Stories detail the lengths to which the SVR, the Russian Federation's intelligence unit, will go to steal state secrets from the United States and bury long-running "illegals"—the name they used for deep cover spies—within their target nations.

In the 1980s the KGB sent a young Russian couple, Andrey Bezrukov and Yelena Vavilova, to live in Canada under false identities—the names of two deceased citizens, Donald Heathfield and Tracey Lee Ann Foley. The Russian spies' use of identities of dead people, who were, therefore, technically *ghosts*, was the origin of the mission's name, Operation Ghost Stories. The Russian agents had two sons and remained in Canada nearly twenty years under the control of both the KGB and its successor, the SVR. They used their Canadian citizenship to allow "Heathfield" to move to France to attend graduate school. Having proved he could travel and work freely in the West, Bezrukov, as Heathfield, then moved to the United States, seeking another degree at Harvard. Tipped off by Canada and France, the FBI counterintelligence division had placed them under surveillance and were aware that they were deep cover spies. They were arrested in the United States ten years after entering the country. Their indictment revealed the couple had been assigned to "infiltrate US policy-making circles" with a "focus on obtaining foreign policy . . . [and] gather[ing] information regarding US policy with regard to the use of the internet by terrorists," as well as information regarding "US policies in Central Asia . . . problems with US military policy . . . turnover of the head of the CIA in 2006," and the 2008 presidential election.[1]

The indictments revealed a decade's worth of contacts the couple had made in the United States for Russian intelligence, which included a former legislative counsel to Congress, an economics professor, a former high-ranking government national security official, and even a nuclear weapons researcher. Historically, Russians have attempted to infiltrate academic institutions "to co-opt people they encountered in the academic environment who might one day hold positions of power and influence."[2]

In 2010, the FBI revealed that a nationwide network of Russian spies had been arrested. Of course, there would be an exchange; Russia had spies we wanted back for debriefing. Ultimately, the United States returned Bezrukov and Vavilova to Russia in a spy swap. Their story was so compelling that it became an Emmy Award–winning FX television series

The Americans.[3] The lead FBI counterintelligence agent in this victory? Peter Strzok. He had years of street-level experience with how insidious and dangerous Russian operations can be. He earned his mastery in Russian intelligence operations. Strzok's core involvement with Operation Ghost Stories is the critical lens from which to view his very alarming texts about Team Trump's contact with the Russians. Once Trump knew this, he set about to attack and neutralize Strzok as a witness. He accused him of treason and plotting a coup d'état.

Strzok became section chief of the counterespionage section of the FBI's Counterintelligence Division in 2015. In 2017, Strzok led a team of FBI investigators, including Assistant General Counsel Lisa Page, regarding the security of Hillary Clinton's email server inquiry. He was reported to have been the one to change the language of the report and Comey's public statement from "grossly negligent" to "extremely careless," which may have saved Clinton from criminal implications.[4] However, while the Republicans were accusing Strzok of favoring Clinton by using the softer language of "careless," Strzok was also reported to have written the first draft of the letter Comey wrote to Congress on October 28, 2016, announcing his decision to reopen the Clinton email investigation, only days before the election. Strzok's lawyer stated:

> Not every FBI investigation is of equal importance to US national security. There's simply no equivalence between an investigation of the possible mishandling of classified information a relatively commonplace occurrence in the FBI's Washington field office and credible evidence suggesting that the presidential campaign of a major party candidate was actively colluding with a hostile foreign power in a way that could undermine the integrity of an American presidential election. To require senior national security officials to profess fealty to this false equivalence is short-sighted and dangerous.[5]

When the inspector general investigation into the FBI came out, it reported discovering numerous personal emails between Strzok and Page. In their private exchanges, it was found that they especially detested Trump, whom they called an "utter idiot." Most noteworthy was one in which Strozk wrote: "Trump is a disaster. I had no idea how destabilizing his Presidency would be." The Trump team would seize upon this email to push forward a new conspiracy theory—that the FBI had plotted to overthrow Trump in an illegal coup if he was victorious in his election bid. Trump would hammer this theme for almost two years in tweets such as: "Biggest outrage yet in the long, winding and highly conflicted Mueller witch hunt is the fact that 19,000 demanded text messages between Peter Strzok and his FBI lover, Lisa Page, were purposely & illegally deleted. Would have explained whole Hoax, which is now under protest!"

PolitiFact, a political fact-checking website, countered by pointing out that his tweet was not factual. The report noted that the inspector general discovered a five-month gap in the thousands of text messages between Strzok and Page, which the IG reviewed to find the one that prompted Trump's tweet. The watchdog's findings suggested the most likely reason those texts weren't captured had to do with technical flaws in the FBI's data-collection process, not deliberate wrongdoing. The FBI inspector general's forensic investigation revealed no efforts by Strzok or Page to conceal any of their communications. They were simply expressing their personal opinions in private communications.[6]

For Trump, none of that would matter. He saw a grand conspiracy by the "deep state," and he would prove it—by obstructing justice.

In what would be called Operation Crossfire Hurricane, the FBI inquiry into Russian operations in the 2016 campaign expanded beyond Papadopoulos to include an investigation into Carter Page, Michael Flynn, Paul Manafort, and Roger Stone.[7] Page, in particular, had been especially scrutinized because of the events of the 2013 spy case when Victor Podobnyy, Igor Sporishev, and Evgeny Buryakov tried to recruit him.

Christopher Steele started work on an opposition research dossier for Fusion GPS. It began as a contract for a Republican donor who supported Ted Cruz and who wanted to take down Trump. The report was shared with the FBI as early as July 2016, but it took over two months before it got any attention. It did get the attention of Senator John McCain, and he encouraged the bureau to investigate.

Steele finally met with FBI agents in October 2016, only one month before the election. As a result of the delayed response by the FBI, he had let some journalists know about his findings. Though all of these parties were aware of the accusations and evidence of the Russian and Trump campaign efforts, all but one, David Corn, refrained from publishing the dossier until January 2017, when BuzzFeed released it in full. On the last day of October 2016, just over a week from election day, *Mother Jones* published an article by Corn called "A Veteran Spy Has Given the FBI Information Alleging a Russian Operation to Cultivate Donald Trump." It was too little too late.[8]

The Weird Shit Begins

As noted earlier, on January 6, 2017, Trump was briefed by the FBI on the actions of Russia to get him elected, and Comey also briefed him about the Steele dossier.[9] On January 27, 2017, just seven days after the inauguration, Trump invited Comey to dinner. Trump asked Comey a second time if he wanted to remain the FBI director. Comey reported, and the Mueller report found corroboration, that Trump told Comey, "I need loyalty, I expect loyalty," and nearly demanded Comey prove Russian collusion didn't happen.[10] Comey made real-time written records of these requests because he was concerned Trump was making an effort to suborn him into what was suspicious and illegal behavior. Also, swearing loyalty to the president was not the job of the FBI director. Four months later Trump would fire Comey.

Another person who would get punished for finding potential wrongdoing was Sally Q. Yates, a twenty-seven-year veteran of the Department of Justice, who was filling the role of acting attorney general. Little did she know that Trump was executing a plan to create a Justice Department that was his to control. On January 26, 2017, acting on intelligence provided by the FBI, Yates contacted White House counsel Donald F. McGahn II, requesting a face-to-face meeting regarding a "very sensitive matter" pertaining to Trump's newly appointed national security adviser, General Michael T. Flynn.[11] A suspicious series of phone calls between Flynn and Sergey Kislyak, the Russian ambassador, were a clear example of an American citizen coordinating with Russia to effect a policy change. It was her obligation to inform the executive branch. But that's not how things work in Trump world. She pointed out a potentially grave crime and a blackmailable situation. Trump saw her as an Obama-era busybody who was snooping into his internal business with Putin. So, he fired her.

On January 30, 2017, four days after meeting with McGahn, the White House put out a statement saying Yates "had betrayed the Department of Justice by refusing to enforce a legal order designed to protect the citizens of the United States."[12] In other words, she refused to violate the Constitution. That day, she penned a letter to the *New York Times* defending her position against Trump's immigration ban because she was "not convinced it was lawful" and it "targeted Muslims."[13] It was a convenient excuse that allowed Trump to start his project of purging the constitutional loyalists from the Justice Department and turning it into a private law firm to protect himself from criminal investigation.

Meanwhile, despite Trump's efforts to deflect attention from Flynn, the story about Flynn was bound to come out, and on February 13, 2017, just eighteen days after Yates's initial warning to McGahn, and upon Trump's chief strategist Steve Bannon's request, Michael T. Flynn resigned as national security adviser. Flynn issued a statement that read "unfortunately, because of the fast pace of events, I inadvertently briefed the vice president-elect and others with incomplete information regarding my phone calls with the Russian ambassador."[14]

Flynn allegedly misled Pence by stating that his conversation with Russian ambassador Kislyak was "limited to small talk and holiday pleasantries," but according to the *New York Times*, the transcript of the wiretap between Kislyak and Flynn noted a conversation regarding recent sanctions imposed on Russia by President Obama due to the intelligence assessment of Russian interference in the election.[15]

When Caught, Make Counteraccusations

On March 4, 2017, Trump fired out one of four tweets that would rock the media for a few weeks. Trump tweeted that he "just found out that Obama had my 'wires tapped' in Trump Tower just before the victory. Nothing found. This is McCarthyism!"[16] He then compared the event to

Nixon and the Watergate, questioned the legality of Obama's actions, and contended that "a good lawyer could make a great case out of the fact that President Obama was taping my phone in October, just prior to the Election!"

That same month Jeff Sessions recused himself from overseeing the investigations of Russian interference and the Trump campaign because of his meetings with Ambassador Kislyak and the prominent role he played in the Trump campaign. This would remain a source of angst for Trump for over a year as he waited to fire Sessions. In his stead, newly promoted Deputy Attorney General Rod Rosenstein would assume authority over the investigations. That same month Comey confirmed to Congress that indeed the FBI was investigating the ties between Trump and Russia.[17] He testified along with Admiral Michael Rogers on Russian interference in the 2016 election. He said the FBI was looking at "whether there was any coordination between the campaign and Russia's efforts."[18]

None of this was taken well by Trump. First, he tweeted that "the NSA and FBI tell Congress that Russia did not influence the electoral process" during the hearing itself, which was read back to Comey by Representative Jim Hines of Connecticut. Comey responded, "It wasn't our intention to say that today because we don't have any information on that subject."[19] Comey's fate was already decided. Trump would use his newly appointed attorney general and deputy attorney general to carry out the firing of the FBI director.

In the meantime, despite Obama's protest statement that said "neither Barack Obama nor any White House official under Obama ever ordered surveillance of any U.S. citizen" using a wiretapping, despite then FBI director James Comey's request that the Justice Department deny the allegations publicly, and despite former director of National Intelligence James Clapper's confirmation that "he was not aware of any foreign-intelligence court order authorizing a wiretap," Trump and his surrogates held the line for weeks about it, though they were never able to provide supporting evidence.

The White House called for House and Senate congressional intelligence committees to accuse the Obama White House of abusing its powers and starting illegal surveillance without any evidence. Trump and his minions kept pushing the idea that there was "no question something happened. The question is, is it surveillance, is it a wiretap, or whatever?"[20] It was a perfect example of floating a nonsense accusation and then associating legitimate court-ordered surveillance with illegal espionage. That was the exact purpose of their evasions—fog the air and claim almost anything.

By March 13, 2017, Sean Spicer was trying to backpedal Trump's initial tweet, citing semantics and punctuation to try and put a new spin on Trump's words. "If you look at the president's tweet, he said very clearly, quote, wiretapping, end quote," he said. "The president used the word *wiretap* in quotes to mean broadly surveillanced and other activities."

On the same day, however, House Intelligence Committee chairman Devin Nunes (R-CA) announced that the committee had no evidence that Trump Tower was ever wiretapped by Obama, adding, "We don't have any evidence that that took place . . . I don't think there was an actual tap of Trump Tower." Nunes still tried to come to Trump's defense, asking if his tweets necessarily needed to be taken literally. "And if you are, then clearly the president is wrong," he said, adding "but if you're not going to take the tweets literally, and if there's a concern that the president has about other people, other surveillance activities looking at him or his associates, either appropriately or inappropriately, we want to find out."

This was followed by a statement from the Senate Intelligence Committee: "Based on the information available to us, we see no indication that Trump Tower was the subject of surveillance by any element of the United States government either before or after Election Day 2016."

Scrambling to justify allegations based on total fabrication and unable to pin the deed on the American intelligence services, Sean Spicer, citing Fox News commentator Andrew Napolitano (who himself based his allegations on unnamed sources), suggested that Obama used the British Intelligence Agency GCHQ, through which "he was able to get it and there's no American fingerprints on this." This prompted Fox News to distance itself from Napolitano's claims, with anchor Shepard Smith claiming that "Fox News knows of no evidence of any kind that the now president of the United States was surveilled at any time, in any way. Full stop."

The rebuttal came from the GCHQ itself the very next day, calling Spicer's comment "utterly ridiculous" and "nonsense." In addition, British prime minister Theresa May said through a spokesman "that the British government received assurance from the White House that these allegations would not be repeated." Still, the same day, Trump continued to assert he had been wiretapped during a joint press conference with German chancellor Angela Merkel on a visit to Washington. "As far as wiretapping, I guess, by this past administration, at least we have something in common," he joked. Later that day, Spicer even told the press they "don't regret anything" and that "he had just been citing media reports."

More refutations came from Comey and NSA director Mike Rogers during a House Intelligence Committee hearing held on March 20. "With respect to the president's tweets about alleged wiretapping directed at him by the prior administration, I have no information that supports those tweets and we have looked carefully inside the FBI," Comey said. "The Department of Justice has asked me to share with you that the answer is the same for the Department of Justice and all its components. The department has no information that supports those tweets."[21]

PolitiFact reported that "Rogers denied that he ever requested that the British intelligence service GCHQ wiretap Trump. He said that would be 'expressively against the construct of the Five Eyes agreement,' an intelligence agreement between Australia, New Zealand, Canada, the United Kingdom, and the United States." But back to Nunes, whose focus was now shifting from the wiretapping of Trump Tower to the "incidental" surveillance of Trump or his associates.

On March 21, Nunes went to the White House to meet "with his source (. . .) in order to have proximity to a secure location where he could view the information provided by the source. The chairman is extremely concerned by the possible improper unmasking of names of U.S. citizens, and he began looking into this issue even before that Trump Tower had been wiretapped."[22] Although Nunes would not disclose his source, he maintained that the surveillance was "conducted legally under a FISA warrant." He then proceeded to hold a press conference before even briefing the committee's ranking member, Rep. Adam Schiff (D-CA), which angered Schiff, who called the chairman's actions "inappropriate."

Seemingly reversing course the very next day, Nunes was now asserting that he did not know "for sure" whether Trump or his associates actually took part in the intercepted communications, which he said were "incidental" and "legally conducted."[23]

Nunes's actions led a coalition of Democrats to ask for his recusal from the Russia probe—despite the fact that Nunes asserted that he had not discussed Russia while visiting the White House or from his position as chairman of the House Intelligence Committee. Calls to Speaker of the House Paul Ryan from Senate minority leader Chuck Schumer (D-NY) remained unanswered. Nunes refused to step down and held his position for a week until complaints to the Office of Congressional Ethics forced him to recuse himself from the investigation. "The charges are entirely false and politically motivated," he said, adding that "he's requested to speak to the Ethics Committee as soon as possible to expedite the dismissal of these false claims."

Interestingly, Nunes's behind-the-scenes machinations with the White House put a lid on Trump's allegation that Obama ever wiretapped his tower.

The question it left in the minds of most observers was obvious: Was Devin Nunes actively using his position as House Intelligence Committee chair to cover up the president's own ties to Russia to hide evidence that he himself may be personally involved? This remained to be seen.

Obstruction in Plain Sight

On February 14, 2017, after a scheduled counterterrorism briefing with the president and the intel community, Trump asked others to clear the room so he could speak with Comey in private. Once alone, Trump began with, "I want to talk about Mike Flynn . . . I hope you can see your way clear to letting this go, to letting Flynn go. He is a good guy. I hope you can let this go."[24] Comey demurred and returned to the FBI, where he briefed subordinates and made an exact memo of what was said in the meeting. A few weeks later Comey testified before the House Intelligence Committee confirming that there was indeed an investigation into the Trump campaign. Trump called Comey on March 30, 2017, to ask him to "lift the cloud" on the investigation.[25]

On April 11, 2017, in an exchange with Comey, Trump "asked what I had done about his request that I 'get out' that he is not personally under investigation. I replied that I had passed his request to the Acting Deputy Attorney General, but I had not heard back. He replied that 'the cloud' was getting in the way of his ability to do his job.... He said he would do that and added, 'Because I have been very loyal to you, very loyal; we had that thing you know.' I did not reply or ask him what he meant by 'that thing.' I said only that the way to handle it was to have the White House Counsel call the Acting Deputy Attorney General. He said that was what he would do and the call ended."[26]

That was enough for Donald. At Trump's insistence, Deputy Attorney General Rod Rosenstein penned a letter recommending Comey's removal. Almost laughably the excuse was that Comey's July 2016 press conference regarding Clinton's email investigation was the wrong one. Rosenstein cynically noted that his decisions were "a textbook example of what federal prosecutors and agents are taught not to do." He indicated that Comey should have followed Justice Department protocol regarding the sensitivity of releasing information close to an election.[27]

On May 9, 2017, he received a termination letter from Trump, brought to FBI headquarters by his personal bagman, Keith Schiller, a former NYPD cop. It read:

> I have received the attached letters from the Attorney General and Deputy Attorney General of the United States recommending your dismissal as the Director of the Federal Bureau of Investigation. I have accepted their recommendation and you are hereby terminated and removed from office, effective immediately.[28]

Trump included the following in his firing letter, "While I greatly appreciate you informing me, on three separate occasions, that I am not under investigation, I nevertheless concur with the judgment of the Department of Justice that you are not able to effectively lead the bureau."[29] Trump was making it clear he needed a loyalist to be put in the FBI, who would get rid of any ability for law enforcement to meddle in his business.

Comey was in Los Angeles speaking to FBI agents when it was announced on cable news that he was fired. Acting Director Andrew McCabe stepped in and brought Comey back on the bureau's executive jet. Trump contacted him almost immediately and insisted on knowing why Comey was allowed to fly on a government plane and not put on a commercial flight.[30] This event shows the depth of Trump's personal pettiness. He calculated that Comey would be humiliated and would have to fund his own flight back in coach class. The thought of humiliating Comey had somehow brought him glee, and now denied his schadenfreude, he was furious.

Comey was discovered to be a secret political pugilist. He gave back as good as he got. He soon released copies of his memos taken the day Trump tried to get him to stop investigating Flynn. In response, Trump again tried to obstruct the investigation with a conspiracy theory. He falsely implied on Twitter that he had video or audio of the meeting as proof of Comey's wrongdoing. The media went wild asking if the White House had a secret taping system. Comey called Trump's bluff when he responded, "Lordy, I hope there are tapes!" Days later the White House backed down on the claim, but the damage had been done. Surprisingly that same day, in an interview with NBC's Lester Holt, Trump admitted that he fired Comey because of the Russian investigation. Apparently, he had forgotten that he had Rosenstein write a bogus letter because he told Holt, "When I decided to just do it I said to myself, 'You know, this Russia thing with Trump and Russia is a made-up story.'"[31]

Within twenty-four hours, Trump would have Russian foreign minister Sergey Lavrov and former Russian ambassador Sergey Kislyak in the Oval Office for a meeting that only included Russian press. There he said told them he had fired Comey to stop the Russia investigation. Trump bragged, "I just fired the head of the F.B.I. He was crazy, a real nut job. I faced great pressure because of Russia. That's taken off. . . . I'm not under investigation."

Andrew McCabe, the acting director, had cut his teeth taking on the Russian mafia in New York City. His first case involved him taking down a small-time criminal network. He said that "the central idea of Russian organized crime is *vory v zakone* [thieves in law]."[32] The same day McCabe was appointed, he was called to the White House. In his initial interview, Trump asked McCabe if he knew "Comey had told him three times that he himself was not under investigation."[33] McCabe said he did not. Trump did manage to send him off with a warning. At the end of the meeting, McCabe recalled that he asked about his wife, who had run for office as a Democrat and had lost. Trump said, "Ask her what it was like to lose. It must be tough to be a loser." Of course, Trump denied it in a tweet, but it would be just one of ten thousand lies.

On May 17, 2017, eight days after James Comey was fired and seven weeks after he had testified before the House Permanent Select Committee on Intelligence (HPSCI), Acting Attorney General Rod Rosenstein appointed Special Counsel Robert Mueller to complete Comey's counterintelligence investigation. The investigation into Russian involvement would examine all potential activities that may be criminal and any other matter derived from his investigation, including obstruction of justice.

Mueller would later report the drama around his appointment. Trump was apoplectic. He was dismayed that the attorney general was not actively working to cover his crimes. Mueller wrote "Sessions told the President that a Special Counsel had been appointed, the President slumped back in his chair and said, 'Oh my God. This is terrible. This is the end of my Presidency. I'm fucked.'"[34]

Witnesses, who also provided written notes, told Mueller's office that when Sessions notified Trump about Rosenstein's appointment of the special counsel Trump stated, "This is the end of my presidency." According to Mueller, the president was angry and lambasted the attorney general for his decision to recuse himself from the investigation, stating, "How could you let this happen, Jeff?"[35]

Minions under Pressure

Trump's minions were having less success in covering up the communications and dirty tricks they had participated in during the election period. Trump was under enormous public pressure related to his suspicious associations with Russia, and some tried to clean up after him. A letter sent to the House Intelligence Committee by an unnamed person noted that foreign policy adviser George Papadopoulos had continued Russian outreach after Trump's November 2016 election. It claimed to identify a deal between Russia and the United States that would create "large financial gains for himself [Papadopoulos] and Trump." In late 2016, Papadopoulos noted Greek Orthodox leaders and Russian Orthodox leaders were "playing an important role" in helping link Russians and Americans.[36]

On January 27, 2017, the FBI interviewed Papadopoulos, and he denied everything the bureau had learned through the emails from him to senior campaign officials. He refused to wear a wire to entrap the suspected Russian asset Joseph Mifsud. He came to believe that this is when the FBI decided to punish him for not cooperating. Two weeks later, Papadopoulos deleted his Facebook account, which had numerous entries about his communications with Mifsud and an unnamed Russian Ministry of Foreign Affairs official.

Now with a special counsel investigating, Mueller became aware of these activities and took immediate and forceful action. On July 27, 2017, Papadopoulos was returning to the United States from overseas. After leaving the aircraft, he was arrested by the FBI for lying to federal agents.[37] The FBI pressured Papadopoulos to cooperate and help clarify the activities related to Mifsud and Russia's involvement in the election. But Papadopoulos believed Trump would eventually pardon him, and initially he refused to cooperate. Eventually he did. It's noteworthy that soon after Papadopoulos was taken into federal custody, the mysterious Professor Joseph Mifsud disappeared and has not been heard from since.[38]

Taking down Papadopoulos was relatively easy compared to the travails the special counsel would have with Paul Manafort. Rather than try to eat a criminal whale in one bite, Mueller wisely had subordinate cases of wrongdoing passed on to the Southern District of New York to be prosecuted. There was prima facie evidence that Manafort carried out a raft of crimes extending back to his days in Ukraine working for Opposition Bloc, a pro-Moscow anti-European political party. The boldest claims were his money-laundering profits and evading taxes on his illicit gains. It would later emerge that Manafort had been under investigation by the FBI for years before joining the Trump campaign, beginning in

2014, because of his reputation as a successful dirty trickster.[39] Manafort had a rare FISA warrant drawn up by the FBI to surveil Manafort, since he was suspected of being a foreign asset at the time. The surveillance effort was dropped due to lack of evidence. However, in light of his role in the Trump camp, the FBI obtained a second warrant in 2016. This one would stick.

Manafort's partner in crime, from working for a Ukrainian pro-Putin political party to becoming deputy campaign manager of the Republican Party, was Rick Gates. Both Manafort and Gates were eventually indicted for money laundering, conspiracy, failure to register as foreign lobbying agents, and lying to investigators. Gates pleaded guilty, but Manafort went to trial and was found guilty. Before his second trial on related charges, Manafort pleaded guilty and promised to work with investigators. However, he repeatedly broke the arrangements in the plea deal. Manafort was also charged for conspiring with Gates and Kilimnik as an "unregistered agent" from 2006 to 2015 working for Viktor Yanukovych, the Party of Regions, the Opposition Bloc party, and the government of Ukraine.[40]

IRA and GRU Indictments

By the end of 2018, the special counsel would indict Michael Flynn for charges of lying to a federal agent about his telephone calls with the Russian ambassador. Soon afterward, Mueller started squeezing others, including indicting Papadopoulos, Gates, Cohen, Roger Stone, Richard Pinedo, who was caught on identity theft charges for unwittingly providing US identities to Russian spies, and Alex van der Zwaan, who had lied about his contacts in Ukraine.

However, that wasn't enough for Mueller. He needed to go after Moscow itself so that anyone found to have been in communication with the Russians would be associated with wanted criminals. On February 16, 2018, he struck hard and exposed Russian intelligence's labyrinthian cyberwarfare network. A US Federal Grand Jury indicted "Putin's chef," businessman Yevgeny Prigozhin, for orchestrating and funding the IRA, a Kremlin troll farm. The entire senior management and operatives who attacked the United States were indicted as well. Though the IRA was no longer active, tax filings show that the former heads of the IRA had shifted to another clandestine organization and were operating out of the same St. Petersburg location under the name Glavset.[41] Along with the IRA, the actual intelligence officers of the Russian military intelligence agency GRU were also indicted. These officers were the men and women manning GRU cyberintelligence Unit 26165 and Unit 74455.

According to the indictments against them, they also stole the identities of US citizens and fooled Americans into thinking they were carrying out protest acts and political activities for living, breathing Americans. They were just Russians hiding behind keyboards, manipulating the easily misled into thinking what they were reading was truthful. A US Senate investigation and the Robert Mueller report would later reveal that 126 million Americans, or one out of every two voters, saw the content created by Russia during the election. Over 470 false Facebook accounts run by the IRA allowed them to make eighty thousand posts. Twitter found that Moscow had created 3,814 accounts, garnering over 1.4 million followers. Instagram and Tumblr had smaller but equally significant numbers.

Working in concert, Russia, Cambridge Analytica, Project Alamo, and their cheerleaders amplified the message of the Trump team. The investigation also discovered that Russia provided support for Green Party leader Jill Stein and socialist Bernie Sanders in an effort to split the vote on the left and anger mainstream conservatives on the right, galvanizing them to vote for Trump. Simply put, anyone but Hillary Clinton was given positive coverage. Clinton was framed as an evil witch who could not be trusted.

CHAPTER 12

All the (Russian) President's Men

If we are to have a contest in the near future of our national existence. I predict that the dividing line will not be Mason and Dixon's but between patriotism and intelligence on one side and superstition, ambition and ignorance on the other.

—General Ulysses S. Grant

In Al Capp's apocryphal cartoon strip *Li'l Abner* was a fictional creature called a shmoo. It was a small two-legged, armless, mustachioed beast that inhabited the Kentucky backwoods around Dogpatch, the Depression-era home of the Yokum family. The shmoos were a food source for the Yokums because their greatest desire was to be eaten by people. Nothing gave a shmoo greater pleasure than to be caught, fried, boiled, diced, sautéed, and made into a meal for anyone. When a shmoo was looked at with hunger, it would instantly turn into whatever the observer desired at that moment, usually a bottle of milk, a dozen grade A eggs, or a ham steak. Shmoos conformed to the dreams of the person that wanted to eat them.

By the time Donald Trump finished his first year in office, the Republican Party had transformed into a shmoo for both Donald Trump and Moscow. From a party staunchly opposed to Russia and communism and dedicated to the national defense of America, it flipped, in less than a decade, into a subservient amalgamation of Trump lickspittles and bootlicks. Nearly instantaneously, the party became overtly pro-Moscow and considered the Russian attack on America as liberal propaganda.

In fact, by 2016, polls of Republican voters showed a massive flip in their support of Vladimir Putin once Donald Trump entered the race and explained why Russia should be considered America's friend.

Russia had quite a bit of experience in changing the political mind-set of smaller nations. State-run television, radio, and online media spent years unraveling Moscow's opponents in Ukraine, Georgia, Montenegro, Hungary, Germany, France, Austria, Latvia, Lithuania, and Spain. They even managed to help convince Great Britain's citizens that membership in the European Union was bad for them, even though the UK might end up losing Northern Ireland and Scotland. That same state espionage apparatus barely had to invest in their active measure strategy to help American conservatives destroy their own government. Republicans were already taking a sledgehammer to any effort that would help take care of all its citizens. Moscow's efforts were a sideshow compared to the work done by the Republican Congress under Obama.

Convincing the Republicans in Congress to become allies with the Trump-Putin world would be a watershed moment, heralding a new Russian century. The alliance could weaken, even kill, NATO and the EU. American Republicans as allies could put an end to the transatlantic alliance once and for all. They could even be convinced that doing this was a great act of patriotism—all while ending the crippling economic sanctions against the Russian oligarchs. Enter the Republican shmoos of the Kremlin.

The founding fathers could never have conceived that their legacy—based on considered enlightenment truths, girded by science and tempered by thoughtful discourse—would be squandered by Congress, that legislators would lose their way and willingly abdicate their role as a coequal branch of government. Presidents and Congresses fight all the time. That was to be expected. This friction is deliberate to incite debate and discovery, to compromise and advance legislation, to use the power of democracy to make the nation always great.

Of course, the framers also assumed nation-states such as the great powers of Europe would attempt machinations, but the very size of the body of representation and the coequal branches would put a check on that. Congress's ability to investigate chicanery stood that test even during the Civil War. But no one—not Jefferson, Franklin, Madison, Adams, Hamilton, or Washington—ever considered a situation in which most of the US Congress and its sustaining political party would come under the thrall of a president as corrupt and unethical as Trump. It can be assured that the founders would also never consider it possible that Americans would be comfortable publicly bowing down to a European adversary. George Washington would be especially appalled since he ran numerous spy rings.

Under Article I of the Constitution, the House of Representatives and the Senate are supposed to be the people's check on any president's abuse of Article II powers to exercise authoritarian rule. Yet under Trump, the Republican Congress, initially both the House and the Senate, willfully abdicated that job. They have simply become Trump's Soviet-style politburo. If this were the Republican Party of old and such a level of intrigue occurred under a Democratic president, there would have been 24/7 treason trials broadcast from the US Capitol, followed by a full-scale auto-da-fe of Democrats on the national mall around the base of the Washington Monument.

The republic was not designed to endure this type of event. It was designed to work in defense of the Constitution, not to subvert it by a combined assault from two of three branches. Undermining democracy using all branches of the government and then engineering the usurpation of the courts has never occurred before—no one dared betray the foundations of democracy. But it has happened, with the result that an entire party has become loyal to one man and not to the Constitution. These are not normal times.

This surrender did not go unnoticed. On MSNBC, the former press secretary for Republican president George W. Bush, Nicolle Wallace, put it this way: "[T]he Republican Party has become the pro-Russia, anti-FBI party." Under Trump, the Republicans have been in mortal fear of their base. Trump holds the leash of Cerberus, the middle-aged white male voter, with its snarling, drooling triple heads of racism, ignorance, and xenophobia. Republican politicians at first feared this power. They would do and say just about anything to be seen as part of the Trump team. Eventually it became clear to them they, too, loved this form of government. Political philosopher and anticommunist thought leader George Kennan once described the mind-set of the leadership of the Supreme Soviet in the Cold War as "impervious to logic of reason, highly sensitive to logic of force." This is an accurate description of the Republican shmoos in the Trump era.

Russia-love fever exploded among the Republican political elite in Washington soon after Trump took power, but one follower who joined in the strategic flip-flop early was Trump's first supporter in the US Senate, Senator Jeff Sessions. Throughout the campaign, Sessions would find himself within the Russian bubble of influence as Trump's biggest cheerleader. And like all Trump's flunkies, he would come to conveniently not remember or lie about his contacts with Russian diplomats. Even after becoming Trump's attorney general in 2017, reports surfaced during his confirmation hearing that he failed to disclose two meetings with Russian ambassador Kislyak and a third much later.[1] The Mueller report felt that the meetings were incidental, but in the whirlwind of finding out about the Trump team's contacts with Moscow, why dissemble? Because of these contacts Sessions subsequently recused himself from the Department of Justice investigation into Russian interference.

Team Trump at one point even went so far as to accuse the Obama administration of treason for not defending the nation when in fact Team Trump had subverted all attempts to stop Russia. As it turns out it would be Republicans who would slowly become Trump's most loyal followers and would block all attempts to find and document how Russia had aided Trump.

Becoming Moscow's Men in Washington

In late August 2016, then CIA director John Brennan was directed by President Obama, under the supervision of James Clapper, the director of National Intelligence, to brief the "gang of eight"—the top eight officials in the House of Representatives and the Senate who hold the same security clearance as the president. These eight represent the top decision makers in the legislative branch on matters of intelligence as well. Obama felt they needed to be aware that Russia was carrying out nefarious activities around the election. Not all of them could be found in the same place at one time, so some were given the briefing via telephone using secure communications. Others were given face-to-face briefings. The eight who were briefed were Senate majority leader Mitch McConnell (R-KY), Senate minority leader Harry Reid (D-NV), Speaker of the House Paul Ryan (R-WI), then House minority leader Nancy Pelosi (D-CA) (now the House majority leader), head of the Senate Select Committee on Intelligence Senator John McCain (R-AZ), Senator Dianne Feinstein (D-CA), House permanent Select Committee on Intelligence chairman Devon Nunez (R-CA), and Representative Adam Schiff (D-CA).

In response, the Obama team drafted a joint letter to warn state election officials about computer intrusion threats by Russia. However, it would be McConnell who refused to put the name Russia in the letter. Because of McConnell's obstinacy, the letter was changed to softer language, making it a generic caution, and not the three-alarm fire that it truly was.

It should be noted that these same members were briefed about the underlying intelligence revealing that Russia was trying to co-opt the Trump campaign and had conducted the hacking of the DNC to support the Republican candidate. Former FBI deputy director Andrew McCabe wrote in his book *The Threat* that none of them objected when they were informed by Director James Comey that the FBI had opened a counterintelligence investigation on Trump: "No one objected. Not on legal grounds, not on constitutional grounds and not based on the facts." Senator Harry Reid, who was set to retire, tried to send out warnings, through hints that Trump should be checked more closely, without breaking the sanctity of the classified information they were exposed to.

The four Republican senators, briefed about every aspect of the initial Trump and Russian scandal, would take that information and repeatedly lie about what they knew and when they knew it. Each one of them would also lie to the American public when they signed on to Trump's mischaracterization that it was a "hoax" made up by "18 angry Democrats."

Next to Mitch McConnell, it would be Lindsey Graham who would prove to be the most two-faced of the Republicans. When Senator John

McCain was alive, he was a bomb thrower into Trump's careful plan. Before the election Graham reviled Trump and called him a "kook," a "race-baiting bigot," and "the most flawed nominee in the history of the Republican Party" and said, "I think Donald Trump is a con man." This is the same Graham who once tweeted "If we nominate Trump we will get destroyed . . . and we will deserve it." For example, in early January 2017, a week before Trump's inauguration, Graham criticized the Obama administration for "throwing a pebble" at Russia when he said, "I'm ready to throw a rock."[2] In March 2017, Graham and close friend Senator John McCain spoke at George Washington University and said that while Trump understood many threats around the world he did not understand the threat Russia presented to America. "Vladimir Putin is not a friend to democracy. He is a crook. I wish our president, who I want to help, would stand up to Putin and say, 'an attack on one party is an attack on all of us.'"[3] In 2016, Graham had acknowledged Russian hackers had penetrated his campaign accounts.[4]

Then in August 2018, McCain died of incurable brain cancer. His funeral was a state affair, which infuriated Donald Trump. But the casket was barely in the ground when Graham's language changed to full-throated support of both Trump and Russia. A few weeks later Trump invited Graham to golf with him, and by the end of eighteen holes they were close friends. In March 2019, Graham acknowledged he had received the Steele dossier, along with John McCain, just before the election. He had encouraged McCain to send it to the FBI, even though Graham called it potentially "garbage." His whole demeanor changed after that golf outing. Graham would take back every negative thing he ever said about Trump. He would become Trump's closest ally and would completely lose his old hawk rhetoric against Moscow. "I want President Trump to be successful," he said. "He's been very good to me in the sense he's let me into his world."[5]

At nearly the same time, Len Blavatnik, a Soviet immigrant and dual US-UK citizen close to Putin and the oligarchy, moved over $6 million to support GOP campaigns in the 2018 election cycle, among them Graham's.[6]

If Graham was the most blatantly two-faced, then the most publicly devoted to Moscow was "Putin's favorite congressman": California

Republican congressman Dana Rohrabacher. Once chairman of a House Foreign Affairs subcommittee with purview over Russia, Rohrabacher was universally hailed as Moscow's man in Washington.[7] He claimed to have fought the Soviets in 1988 in Afghanistan when he traveled there and met Ahmed Shah Masoud, the Lion of Panjshir. He then later joined the Reagan administration as a speechwriter. He told a local radio station the fantastical story that after the fall of the Soviet Union, he met Putin in Washington, DC, around 1991. According to him they got drunk after playing a game of touch football. At an Irish pub, Rohrabacher claimed to have challenged Putin to an arm-wrestling match to prove who really won the Cold War. "He put me down in a millisecond," Rohrabacher said. "He is tough. His muscles are just unbelievable."[8]

In April 2015, Rohrabacher met in Moscow with sanctioned officials close to Putin. During the trip, Russian officials prodded Rohrabacher to cancel sanctions or at least remove the name Magnitsky from them, which became an amendment he later sponsored but never passed. Other congressmen noted he had concerning closeness to Moscow.[9]

Even though the FBI warned him in 2012 it believed Moscow's intelligence agencies were attempting to turn him into an asset, Rohrabacher continued to travel to Moscow, and noted Russian intelligence officers were likely in meetings he attended. In August 2015, he met in Russia with Russian agent Maria Butina and Alexander Torshin, a Putin associate and central banker, to discuss natural resources and "strategic issues."[10]

I had a personal encounter with Rohrabacher at the 2017 Politicon event in Pasadena, California. His behavior would typify why everyone in Washington thinks he works for Putin and not the US Congress. On a panel with Congressman Ted Liu and commentator Anna Navarro-Cardenas and hosted by the International Spy Museum's historian Vince Houghton, Rohrabacher waxed eloquent about how wonderful Russia and its people were. He would tolerate almost no criticism of Russia. He extolled the virtues of the people and the land. It was much akin to hearing communist propaganda from the 1950s. The women were beautiful! The land was plentiful! The men were God fearing and strong! His response to criticism was simple: "Have you ever been to Russia?" The consensus was he was thoroughly enamored with Putin and Russia.

Rohrabacher's deep personal relations with Russia became an issue during his 2016 reelection effort. What we did not know was that on his 2016 trip to Moscow he had met with none other than Natalya Veselnitskaya, the Kremlin-backed lawyer who would become notorious for claiming she had dirt on Hillary Clinton to Donald Trump Jr. one year later. The FBI had informed Rohrabacher that Russian spies may have been trying to target him. He dismissed it. But having met him, I could see it was too late: if he was a target of Moscow then they had already gotten to him. Rohrabacher ultimately lost reelection in 2018. His undying affinity for Moscow was thought to be a primary reason.[11]

Rorahbach was bad, but no one jumped onto the Trump-Moscow bandwagon faster than the farmer-turned-congressman Devin Nunes of California. He put Graham to shame for sycophancy. When the Trump-Russia scandal broke, Nunes immediately and without prompting used his position as chairman of the HPSCI to manipulate information, release data, and outright lie to the American public to cover up Trump's actions. As I mentioned before, when Trump tweeted the false claim that Obama had wiretapped him, Nunes was the first to come out and try to validate it. He breathlessly held a press conference at the White House where he supposedly had been informed by a "whistleblower" in the "intelligence community" that Obama's White House had done illegal surveillance by unmasking the real names of Trump campaign staff involved with Moscow.

In fact, the so-called whistleblower was a low-level national security staffer who had done a search on the classified internet database (SIPRNET) and discovered that the Obama team had legitimately been allowed to see the real names of American citizens who may have been involved with foreign spies. Of course they did—it was their job.

Somehow Nunes and the Trump team turned this into a scandal that fizzled out the instant it was revealed the secret source was a White House staffer and Nunes was just reading out White House propaganda literally handed to him. Nunes then tried to release information to attack the FBI investigation in a memo drafted for the HPSCI that contained sensitive intelligence. For weeks Republicans demanded that Trump "Release the memo!" Trump gleefully acquiesced, but it quickly revealed that Nunes had nothing. Worse for Nunes, declassifying it inadvertently revealed that the FBI was carrying out a serious counterintelligence investigation against Team Trump.

In February 2017, Nunes told the *Washington Post* that the entire Trump-Russia scandal amounted to nothing: "It's all a dead trail that leads me to believe no contact, not even pizza-delivery-guy contact." At the time, he was fully aware that Trump was under investigation and that serious contacts with Moscow were being hunted down. Ryan Evans, best known for playing the role of American icon Captain America, tweeted about Nunes: "This guy is an arsonist trying to hold a match to the framework of our republic."[12]

Several events occurred that hinted at the softening of the Republican Party on Russian matters, at the insistence of Trump, and provided a withering spectacle of Trump-supporting Republicans in bed with Moscow. In 2018, a group of Republican senators decided that the best thing for the United States would be to visit Russia, meet Putin's most loyal acolytes, spend the Fourth of July holiday in Moscow, and introduce Russians to a Texas barbecue. The group included Steve Daines (R-MT), Kay Granger (R-TX), John Hoeven (R-ND), John N. Kennedy (R-LA), Jerry Moran (R-KS), Sen. Richard Shelby (R-AL), and John Thune (R-SD). After the nine-day trip, questions arose as to exactly how tough they were during a series of talks at the Kremlin. Not very tough.

When Republican senator Ron Johnson returned from the trip, he suggested that US sanctions against Russia were not working and maybe they should just be done away with. The other senators disputed with Johnson about the effectiveness of sanctions. To many, Johnson also appeared to downplay the Kremlin's election interference, saying it was "not the greatest threat to our democracy" and "we've blown it way out of proportion."[13] However, the senators present with him at the series of long meetings with Russian officials also disputed his account of what went on behind closed doors in Moscow. Senator Shelby, who led the congressional delegation, stated that he, along with his colleagues, told their Russian counterparts that "the worst thing you can do is try to meddle in our elections."

Another senator who rapidly changed positions was Rand Paul of Kentucky. Senator Paul's position on both Trump and Russia morphed from calling Trump "a delusional narcissist" and calls to isolate Russia during the Obama era to acting as Trump's key liaison between Trump and Putin. Additionally, his policy advocacy became increasingly pro-Kremlin. He voted against sanctions on Russia in June 2017. He pushed against Montenegro joining NATO, causing the late senator John McCain to accuse him of "working for Vladimir Putin."[14] He pushed to have Trump lift Russian sanctions to allow Russian officials to visit the United States.[15] His position on Syria was paraded by Russian media after he applauded Trump for withdrawing from Syria. In an interview with Wolf Blitzer, host of *The Situation Room*, Paul said he doubted that President Bashar al-Assad had carried out chemical weapons attacks against his own people—a frequent Russian talking point.[16] Paul alone fought against his fellow senators on HR 1677, the Caesar Syria Civilian Protection Act of 2018, which would have imposed sanctions on anyone contributing to the Syrian massacres.[17]

After Trump's public presser with Vladimir Putin, it was revealed that Paul, on a visit to Russia, brought a letter from Trump to Putin. Instead of meeting with Putin, however, Paul was only able to submit the letter to Putin's staff. It was noted by Hogan Gidley, White House deputy press secretary, that it was Paul who asked Trump to send a "letter of introduction."[18] Paul had been seeking more interaction between Trump and Putin as he prepared for his visit to Russia. The trip was supposedly not a diplomatic visit, but Paul met with Sergey Kislyak.[19] Paul also suggested this visit would result in a delegation of lawmakers from Russia visiting the United States. Not surprising, his father Ron Paul took to RT (Russia Today) television to praise the infamous Helsinki meeting between Trump and Putin as "the best step ever."[20]

The newly minted pro-Russia members of Team Trump were also teetering on being rabidly anti-NATO. A bloc of them embraced a platform that made America anti-NATO. In January 2019, the House of Representatives voted 357 to 22 to prevent Donald Trump from withdrawing from NATO. Trump had been suggesting the alliance was obsolete, which forced Congress to act. Cosponsored by Tom Malinowski and Jimmy Panetta, the bill matched a Senate effort that forced Trump to get two-thirds approval of the Senate before he could withdraw the United States from the alliance. However, twenty-two Republicans in the House Freedom Caucus, a hardline pro-Trump block, voted against the effort.[21]

In essence, they voted for Trump's desire to break up NATO. After a firestorm of opposition, they claimed they voted against it because they saw the effort as partisan. The twenty-two representatives who voted against the measure were: Rick Allen (GA), Justin Amash (MI—then a Republican, now an Independent), Andy Biggs (AZ), Tim Burchett (TN), Ben Cline (VA), Scott DesJarlais (TN), Russ Fulcher (ID), Matt Gaetz (FL), Louis Gohmert (TX), Paul Gosar (AZ), Morgan Griffith (VA), Andy Harris (MD), Jody Hice (GA), Jim Jordan (OH), Thomas Massie (KY), Tom McClintock (CA), Mark Meadows (NC), Scott Perry (PA), John Rose (TN), Chip Roy (TX), Gregory Steube (FL), and Randy Webe (TX).[22]

By early 2019, the takeover of the party by pro-Moscow fever was complete. By Trump's second year, pro-Moscow commentary would become a requirement to be a Republican, as were pro-fascist statements and admiration of authoritarianism. For example, Senator John Cornyn would quote Italian dictator Benito Mussolini in a positive manner on Twitter when he wrote about white Western Christendom: "We were the first to assert that the more complicated the forms assumed by civilization, the more restricted the freedom of the individual must become." The Internet is an unforgiving mistress, however, and the backlash against Cornyn was staggering. One Twitter user scolded: "Almost 119,200 young American servicemen were killed in the often-brutal Italian campaign in WW2. A galling 36,000 American boys were killed, injured or MIA after the bruising battle of Anzio, alone. You just quoted the leader of the forces that killed those Americans."

The Imperius Curse

In a 1788 missive from George Washington to the Marquis de Lafayette, he wrote about the separation of powers under the Constitution: "The general Government is arranged, that it can never be in danger of degenerating into a monarchy, an Oligarchy, an Aristocracy, or any other despotic or oppressive form so long as there shall remain any virtue in the body of the People."[23]

Washington was correct in his assessment, as the virtue of the people held off oligarchy, autocracy, and other disreputable forms of government for 232 years. The inherent goodness and honor remained embodied in the American people, and with occasion stumbles, the darker passions were suppressed. Unfortunately, that would end at noon on January 21, 2008, with the inauguration of Barack Obama. From the moment the first black man ascended to the presidency, the dark hatreds of unwashed America were unleashed. The virtue of the nation, which Washington waxed eloquently upon, was systematically dismantled in service of vilifying the most modest, thoughtful, and serious man to sit in the Oval Office in the modern era. A compassionate family man, with a Harvard-educated constitutional scholar wife and two intelligent, well-behaved children, was instantly transformed into a monkey, his wife referred to regularly as an ape, and his children as pickaninnies. Those were the least of the comments made about him. They so vilified him that by 2016 Republicans openly preferred Putin over Obama. Polls showed they preferred the ex-KGB officer at 35 to 9 percent to Obama, who had committed the crime of providing twenty-five million Americans with health care.

Along with tossing their virtue, Republicans threw their capacity for decency and compassion overboard. Trump's brand of unhinged conservativism found common cause to demonize any form of decorum and decency. In their estimation, decency and dignity of the office is a form of weakness and compromise. To many Trump voters, compromise meant discussion with the most hated of all people—liberals, progressives, and never-Trump Republicans. The ability to work together on modest proposals had already been completely eliminated from a Republican-controlled Congress when Barack Obama was reelected in 2012. During the 2016 campaign, the Republicans successfully argued to their base that compromise with Obama and liberals had caused their losses. To them, the triumph of Trump was the victory of the philosophy of "never, ever." Never, ever means never, ever working with or allowing one's political enemies to be comfortable or to trust good intentions. With Trump's ascension and the attention that has come with it, they feel vindicated. To Trump supporters, their deeply felt rancor against others is their superpower. They literally hate 60 percent of America for wanting to maintain the norms of the past 244 years. Decency or dignity is reserved for members of their tribe. To Trump's voters, being nice to political opposites is a weakness that must be ignored and ridiculed, but when questioned by the media, few will actually say these words out loud.

Trump's brand of "populist" extremism is anything but popular. A horribly unpopular person, Trump has never broken 46 percent approval and has often hovered between 37 and 44 percent for virtually all of his presidency. Still, he has successfully parlayed the inner hatred of his followers on many subjects, particularly his anti-immigrant theme in which he claims to speak for what he calls the "silent majority's" expressions of unhappiness with the "other." Instead of celebrating America's strength through assimilation and cultural diversity, he has embodied a public loathing of immigrants. He first equated white neo-Nazis, white nationalists, and Ku Klux Klansmen with legitimate protesters in 2017, at the Unite the Right rally in Charlottesville, Virginia, and then in 2019 he doubled down and claimed they were actually innocent of the violence.

Former John McCain presidential campaign manager Steve Schmidt made a disturbing claim that the people around Trump shield him and hide his incapacities, in effect infantilizing him, while at the same time they are bullied by him to do whatever he says, including lie. Mark Slater wrote on Twitter "The party of Reagan is as dead as the Whigs. The House GOP killed it. It's now an association of frat boys, grifters, self-dealers, racists and cowards."[24]

By 2019 evidence of Trump's corruption has become so widespread after the Michael Cohen hearing that, on February 26, 2019, the conservative *Wall Street Journal* editorial board threw up its collective hands and wrote that the party was now in the thrall of its ultimate destroyer, Donald J. Trump: "The day was a reminder that Americans elected a President in 2016 who had spent decades in the sleazier corners of New York business and tabloid life. He surrounded himself with political rogues. Now he and the GOP will pay a political price."[25]

Like a dark wizard in the Harry Potter saga, Trump seems to have cast an Imperius Curse—an incantation that makes people do things against their will—on his supporters. They otherwise appear as normal working Joes, but while attending a Trump rally, they transform into an angry, racist mob, taunting the press and demanding, still, to lock up Hillary Clinton.

CHAPTER 13

The Trump Doctrine: Buying This American, Buys America

Twentieth-century Republican president Theodore Roosevelt anchored his foreign policy in the ability to predict crises and respond thoughtfully. Roosevelt believed that "the exercise of intelligent forethought and of decisive action sufficiently far in advance of any likely crisis" should be the guiding principle. His use of American power was conceptualized in the phrase "speak softly and carry a big stick."[1]

MSNBC commentator Joe Scarborough once asked, "Why has US foreign policy gone off the rails after three-quarters of a century?" If you want to understand Trump's foreign policy, you have to assume, based on his actions and lack of documentation, that the world order as it has existed since the end of World War II cannot serve his family. To understand Trump foreign policy, one need only follow the money. That would be the money that he intended to flow to him, his family, and his personal associates by dint of his achieving the Oval Office.

He expected the money to come from three avenues: First, he expected to enrich himself and the Trump organization businesses at the expense of the American people. He knew well that by occupying the highest office in the nation, the Trump brand would gain in stature, but being president would also mean that people would want to kiss his ring and slip him money, business, and gifts directly and under the table. The second leg of his foreign relations—such as moving the American embassy to Jerusalem, ceding the Golan Heights to Israel, surrendering Syria to Russia, or lifting sanctions on a specific Russian oligarch—was just political payoffs. Those who funded or supported his campaign—such as Israeli prime minister Benjamin Netanyahu, major donor Sheldon Adelson, Vladimir Putin, and oligarch Oleg Deripaska—had to be given a reward for loyalty. In the third category were those who knew Trump would do their bidding because they had insane quantities of money, which they spent on American defense, automobiles, and products. This category is almost exclusively comprised of the Gulf oil sheikhs and princes of Saudi Arabia, the United Arab Emirates, and, once Trump was properly educated about how rich it was, Qatar.

Trump's personality is attuned and attracted to the direct action and absolute power of dictators; he desires to work with and appease people he sees as his authoritarian "peers." He has set his sights on creating friction with China because he believes he needs to confront China, arguably the United States' closest economic competitor, to gain concessions on trade. In Trump's world, there are only three options: making money, ripping off a competitor by playing the bully, or being ripped off. He needs to demonstrate his strength and dominance but trying to bully China and Chinese president Xi Jinping, an autocrat he admires for having declared himself president for life. Trump loudly espouses his opinion that the "weaker" Obama and Bush presidencies gave away American economic power to China in exchange for global influence in the Middle East and by raising the ire of Russia.

Insults litter his vocabulary when discussing China, but what it may really reflect is his own unease that he has gladly used Chinese labor, who were paid a pittance while he was contracting with them, and materials, including Chinese steel for his projects—not to mention the Chinese silk for his line of made-in-China neckties. His ethno-nationalist view is that the Chinese are fundamentally inferior but have managed to out-hustle America in the international marketplace because previous administrations allowed them to. Trump expressed the same contempt for the Japanese in the 1970s and '80s when he complained bitterly about their labor practices, which at the time were showing a greater efficiency in car manufacturing than America. Granted much of this is rooted in personal bigotry against Asians. What he refers to as "economic nationalism" is simply a way of saying that his money won't be spent on peoples he views as inferior. His xenophobia regarding Latin America and

China may have informed his decisions to start trade wars with Mexico and China.

Trump also eschews globalism—the inexorable trend of internationally weaving together economies, so that people, products, and capital can be accessible anywhere at any time in an increasingly computer-networked world. He views any interconnectivity and interoperability of the world as the domain of his hated liberal rivals and European do-gooders. Despite the fact that the United States essentially created globalism after World War II, along with modern computer technology, Trump views it as a weakness that prohibits his bullying nationalism. By mid-2019 the American farmers who relied on sales to China were finding that their support of Trump literally took their profits and burned them. He may also have burned their ability to return to the Chinese markets. Time will tell if America has permanently lost a global commodity market that American farmers dominated just weeks before Trump's election.

However, despite the fact that he sought to ban an entire class of people based on their Islamic religion in his first month in office, he has shown a loving affinity to the kings and princes of the Arabian oil sheikhdoms. Jared Kushner coordinated the first foreign visit of Trump's presidency to Saudi Arabia to impress upon Trump the need for this critical financial relationship, which the American defense establishment relies upon. It's also a relationship that promised to be profitable for both Trump and Kushner.

The *Washington Post* published a report that at least four countries (Mexico, Israel, China, and the United Arab Emirates) had discussed how to exploit Kushner by using his lack of experience, financial troubles, and business deals. It was not clear if these countries acted on any of the conversations.[2]

Kushner's involvement of foreign policy in his personal financial dealings went public when he met with Wu Xiaohui, the chairman of Anbang Insurance Group. Anbang is a Chinese financial giant with an estimated $285 billion in global assets. The two were negotiating a deal to redevelop 666 Fifth Avenue just after Trump clinched the Republican nomination. However, the amateurs in the White House committed a major faux pas.

Not caring about diplomacy or traditions to maintain balances of power, Trump arranged ahead of time to speak with the president of Taiwan, Tsai Ing-wen, who reached out to him via a phone call. China exploded at the breach of protocol. In early December 2016 the Chinese ambassador to the United States called the White House to express China's "deep displeasure" at president-elect Trump's break with a long-standing diplomatic tradition of maintaining the nominal diplomatic break with Taiwan, in place since 1979. China lodged a diplomatic complaint, but more importantly, they sent Trump's family a message: we can hurt you or help you—you decide. Likely at the direction of the Chinese government, Anbang backed out of the deal with Kushner ninety days later.[3]

Jared Kushner didn't allow Anbang's withdrawal to impact his desperation to get his building refinanced. He was now being called the Trump administration's wunderkind, and he apparently took advantage of that. Kushner paid a record-setting $1.8 billion for the building in 2007 and spent more than two years searching for new partners. He reportedly looked for offers from investors in the United States, the Middle East, and China. Charles Kushner and his son Jared pitched a deal to demolish the building and build a $7.5 billion luxury super tower in its place. They got close to a deal with Qatari billionaire Hamad Jassim Al-Thani, the country's former prime minister, Korean Investment Corporation, and with Anbang.[4] Financially, things looked grim for Trump's boy wonder.

Who Bailed Out 666 Fifth Ave?

In December 2016, Richard Gerson, hedge fund manager and longtime friend of Jared Kushner, met with a Lebanese American businessman with close ties to the UAE named George Nader, Kushner, Mike Flynn, Steve Bannon, and UAE ambassador to the United States Yousef Otaiba. The guest of honor was Sheikh Mohammed bin Zayed al-Nahyan—the real power behind the UAE. As noted earlier, Sheikh Mohammed made an undisclosed visit to New York without informing the Obama administration. Nader later claimed he did not attend the three-hour meeting but greeted Emirati officials as they left.[5]

Further to their December meeting, Sheikh Mohammed was said to have arranged a secret meeting just days before Trump's inauguration between Blackwater founder Erik Prince and a close associate of Vladimir Putin. Prince was a perennial favorite among the Emiratis, admired for his daring and almost pirate-like work. He had no scruples, dreamt big, and did what he wanted. That meeting took place in the Seychelles, a remote archipelago in the Indian Ocean. Prince later told Congress that he just happened to be there and just happened to run into some Russian and had a beer. It was fantastical, but Prince told Congress it was just kismet:

> After the meeting, they mentioned a guy I should meet who was also in town to see them, a Kirill Dmitriev from Russia, who ran some sort of hedge fund. I met him in the hotel bar, and we chatted on topics ranging from oil and commodity prices to how much his country wishes for a resumption of normal trade relations with the—relationship with the USA. I remember telling him that if Franklin Roosevelt could work with Josef Stalin to defeat Nazi fascism, then certainly Donald Trump could work with Vladimir Putin to defeat Islamic fascism.[6]

Weeks after Trump's May 2017 trip to Riyadh, Saudi Arabia and the UAE began a cyberblockade of key Qatari companies and businesses. Trump responded that he supported their efforts, as they were curtailing terrorist financing. Coincidentally, Kushner had not received an expected $500 million bailout on a property he owned in New York, the funds to come from a Qatari firm, connected to the royal family—which may have played a role in Trump's anger against the Gulf state.[7] A year later, in August 2018, a Canadian firm funded by a Qatari investment firm bought the 666 Fifth Avenue property and paid off around $1 billion of the mortgage on the building. Kushner's father, who managed the building, rid himself of major debts in the deal.[8]

It looked like Kushner was just lucky. But applying Nance's Law we can see a golden thread that reveals more. Around the time of the blockade, someone, in a bizarre move, had apparently determined that Al-Jazeera television, owned by Qatar, was a supporter of terrorists because the television network had access to some of their spokesmen. The

Qatari royal family were also a major detractor of the Saudi government and acted as middlemen for America's negotiations with the Taliban. Apparently, the Saudis informed the Trump administration, likely through Jared Kushner, that they would be instituting the blockade and were assured Trump supported their efforts, claiming it was an effort to curtail terrorist financing. That was an insane proposition, as several Saudis, including one man named Osama bin Laden, have been funding the global Salafist terror movement since before 1985.

However, speculation grew rampant that this was payback for Kushner. As noted earlier, Kushner had failed to receive a $500 million bailout from the Qatari firm. The Saudi blockade split the Qataris from regional cooperation agreements; in response Qatar further developed its relationship with Turkey. Then in April 2018, almost a year later, Trump suddenly announced that Qatar no longer funded terrorism as he alleged, and just 120 days after that, the Canadian company conveniently bought 666 Fifth.

According to analysts, 666 Fifth Avenue had about a 30 percent vacancy rate and only generated about half of its annual mortgage. It was rumored that the largest tenant was planning to move out. A Canadian company named Brookfield Property Partners took a ninety-nine-year lease on 666 Fifth Avenue. Brookfield paid the rent for the entire century-long lease, upfront, which amounted to about $1.1 billion—removing Kushner's biggest financial headache (a $1.4 billion mortgage on the office portion of the tower due in February 2019). Brookfield got its financing for this deal from a $750 million mortgage from ING Group, a Dutch multinational and financial services corporation, and a $300 million mezzanine loan from Apollo Global Management.[9] However, the Qatar Investment Authority, the government-run agency that made decisions about the nations' financial investments, bought a $1.8 billion stake in Brookfield Property Partners. As the second largest shareholder, they had a lot to say about what should be purchased; in this instance, they apparently used Brookfield to bail out 666 Fifth Ave. This investment was a godsend to Kushner, who was now out of debt just as Qatar was suddenly no longer blockaded by Mohammad bin Salman bin Abdulaziz Al Saud, crown prince of Saudi Arabia (known colloquially as MBS), and his allies.[10]

In the Gulf states, officials joke two men control Saudi-US policies: MBS and Trump's "clown prince," Jared Kushner. The two became very close after Kushner became Trump's top adviser and solutions man. MBS and Kushner communicated regularly on WhatsApp, a secure messaging app. MBS often boasted he had Kushner "in his pocket."[11] Proof of that would come quickly.

Early into the Trump administration, Kushner took an interest in detailed US intelligence reports about the Middle East. He frequently requested specific information about Saudi politics and people opposed to MBS. Following Kushner's October 2017 trip to Riyadh, the Saudi royal family cracked down on the extremely rich Saudi families. Using internal security forces and the royal guard, dozens of rich Saudi citizens were arrested, moved to the Ritz-Carlton Hotel, and placed under a luxurious house arrest. The way out was simple: turn over cash assets to the royal family and you could go free with the balance. It was simply a mafia-style shakedown. Four of the ten richest men in the world were pulled off that list when they lost their assets to the Saudi government.

MBS boasted to friends that Kushner had shared some of the names from American intelligence with him during those October conversations. Among the people arrested were those mentioned in presidential daily briefs Kushner had read before going to Riyadh. Trump subsequently tweeted that he had "great confidence" in the Saudi leaders who conducted the crackdown and had arrested and tortured the many people who had "been 'milking' their country for years!"[12] The names Kushner supplied to MBS also constituted a debt that MBS now owed Kushner, and he would likely pay it off in kind.

Kushner's wife, Ivanka, was no stranger to paying to play in overseas markets. I have discussed her being the point woman for Trump properties in Central Asia. According to a *Washington Post* investigation, Ivanka's clothing and accessories relied exclusively on foreign factories in India, Bangladesh, Vietnam, Indonesia, and China. The *Post* researched shipping and import records to track down the origins of her products. Her reliance on foreign labor was in direct conflict with President Trump's "Buy American, Hire American" policy. But why bother questioning her since Trump did the same thing with his products? The bottom line is always money, not morals.

At the same time, Kushner's sister Nicole Kushner Meyer was in China apparently selling access to the Trump White House for investments by Chinese businessmen. Her PowerPoint was designed to gain $150 million in funding for a Kushner project in Jersey City by showing the chain of command from Trump to acquiring a visa. She asserted that E5-B visas for investors who pony up $500,000 could be acquired from this project, while coolly mentioning her brother and Trump.[13]

These few examples show that the finances of the Trump family are now inexplicably tied to the foreign policy of the United States. If the policy does not enrich Donald Trump personally or enhance his personal prestige, then it is not considered seriously. One could call it the New Money World Order. The State Department was gutted of professionals: diplomats were fired, and ambassadors were never replaced. By 2019 it was clear that this was done so that communications to global interests would come directly from Trump's mouth with virtually no records. These orders would be passed on via Secretary of State Mike Pompeo, acting as bagman for the Don.

The Murder of Jamal Khashoggi

Trump's first foreign trip as president was to Saudi Arabia on May 20, 2017, and it denoted the strong relationship he wanted to build with the oil-rich nation. The Saudis hailed it as a chance to "reset" a relationship with the United States, which had wavered under Obama, and specifically noted Trump would take a much harder line with Iran.[14] Trump spoke out against terrorism and Iran in a speech before Gulf leaders and signed an arms deal with the Saudis during his two days in the country.[15]

There was no media specifically declaring US intel agencies had anything to do with targeting critics; actually, the CIA worked with foreign liaisons in Canada and Norway to let Saudi dissidents know they were targeted. One article mentions an Israeli private intel firm helping Saudi services install spyware on a phone of a specific dissident, but nothing ties that to the United States.

On October 2, 2018, a *Washington Post* reporter and Saudi dissident named Jamal Khashoggi entered the Saudi embassy in Istanbul, Turkey.

The purpose of his visit was to obtain a visa for his future wife. While his fiancée, a Turkish citizen named Hatice Cengiz, waited outside, Khashoggi entered the embassy and never came out. Four hours later his fiancé called Turkish police and told them what she knew. Saudi diplomats initially claimed Khashoggi had left the embassy: they had security footage to prove it. He was captured on video by Turkish authorities, which showed a man dressed similar to Khashoggi leaving the embassy from the rear in the company of a young, powerful-looking man.

A man did leave the embassy by the back door. That man was discovered to be a Saudi Arabian member of the Royal Guard wearing the clothes of the now-dead Khashoggi acting as a body double. He was in the company of an intelligence officer, executing a preplanned ruse that the Turks caught on camera. In fact, nearly every camera in downtown Istanbul recorded the pair, with one pretending to be Khashoggi. The pair entered the restroom of the legendary Blue Mosque and changed back into regular clothing. In a dumpster near the mosque, they dumped a bag of Khashoggi's clothing, which Turkish plainclothes police recovered.

The Saudis continued to insist he had left the embassy. Then the Turks produced audio confirmation of the murder. Khashoggi had worried that there might be unpleasantness inside the embassy, so he streamed audio from his Apple Watch to an iPhone his fiancé had retained. While he was being interrogated and dissected, the actual audio of it was being recorded and broadcast. Turkish intelligence acquired the audio, and President Erdogan sent copies to other governments and the Saudis. CIA Director Gina Haspel confirmed the audio for the United States.

After interrogating him, they tortured and then strangled him. To dispose of the body, Saudi Arabia's highly regarded forensic pathologist and autopsy expert, Salah Muhammad al-Tubaigy, was sent to make Khashoggi go away forever. Using a bone saw while listening to music on his iPhone (he told the others in the room that music makes bloody dissections easier), al-Tubaigy dismembered Khashoggi's body and placed the pieces in a vat of acid. Their mission, as the Turkish prosecutor general stated, was "to leave no trace behind."[16] A local Turkish man then poured the dissolved remains in a remote forest. To the rest of the world, they wanted to make it appear he had vanished. It was, literally, true.

What had happened to Khashoggi in the embassy was worse than death. It was a macabre, gruesome, and unspeakable murder. The CIA and Turkish intelligence assessed that a fifteen-person Saudi hit squad had been dispatched by MBS to kill him and make him disappear. US intelligence agencies also quickly determined that Saudi royalty had sponsored Khashoggi's death. Khashoggi was a permanent US resident. Although the Saudis denied it, Saudi Arabia had been caught murdering a US resident, which would normally make this an international incident. The situation was grave.

Except to Donald Trump. Trump decided that his position was to be pardoner-in-chief for MBS. He sent Jared Kushner to Saudi Arabia. There Kushner had repeated meetings, often one-on-one, with MBS, regarding how to "weather the storm." Some of these meetings included King Salman of Saudi Arabia.[17]

Trump tried to adopt the shifting Saudi position that "rogue" vigilantes went to talk to Khashoggi and then "accidentally" killed him. Trump said from the Oval Office that "they had a very bad original concept; it was carried out poorly and the cover-up was the worst in the history of cover-ups. Whoever thought of that idea, I think is in big trouble. And they should be in big trouble."[18] Former CIA director John Brennan was the station chief in Riyadh during the Bush-Obama era before he was chosen to lead the agency. He said on MSNBC, "It also seems now we're in this surreal and morally horrific situation in which the White House and the Saudis seem to be trying to sort of figure out what story they can come up with that they can both have plausibility for Mohammad bin Salman."

When demands came for MBS to take responsibility and leave power, Trump supported him. "In fact, if anything, I've heard that he's very strongly in power."[19] In the end, Trump did what he always did—he accepted the word of the Saudis without question and attacked his own intelligence agencies. Trump stated that "whether he did or whether he didn't, he denies it vehemently. His father denies it, the king, vehemently. The CIA doesn't say they did it, they do point out certain things, and in pointing out those things you can conclude that maybe he did or maybe he didn't."

Trump's intention to absolve MBS of the entire matter is based on money—because the Saudis buy American weapons. "We have a very strong ally in Saudi Arabia . . . an ally that said at the very top level, the crown prince, they did not commit this atrocity, and it's an atrocity, it's a terrible thing. I dislike it more than you do. But the fact is they've been a very strong ally, they create tremendous wealth in their purchases, but more importantly, they keep the oil price down." When asked who should be held accountable for Khashoggi's death if not the Saudis, Trump said, "Maybe the world should be held accountable because the world's a very, very vicious place."[20]

The Saudi relationship with Trump et al. has a backstory that is more worrying than the murder of Khashoggi. It involved shortcutting the acquisition of nuclear reactors for Saudi Arabia. To be sure, Trump's go-to man, General Michael Flynn, was going to make sure he got a cut by using his position to ensure that a deal went through. The problem was his deal worked both sides.

The Trump/Putin Mideast Marshall Plan—for Nuclear Power

After his firing by the Obama administration, Michael Flynn went to Israel and Egypt at the behest of a defense contractor called X-Co Dynamics/Iron Bridge Group. The trip was funded by a nuclear power plant consultancy, ACU Strategic Partners. Flynn's job was to promote a plan providing Russian nuclear power plants to Gulf states, funded by Saudi Arabia. At the time, the Obama administration was trying to limit nuclear proliferation in both Iran and the oil states. To get them onboard the nuclear deal required stopping Saudi acquisition of nuclear power, so they took a very dim view of Flynn's efforts.

Soon afterward Flynn became a principal in the Trump campaign. As I discussed earlier, he'd already been called out for taking money he did not report to the US government, including $42,000 from RT for a speech and $600,000 in illegal lobbying money from Turkish lobbyist Ekim Alptekin and his Russian partner Dmitri "David" Zaikin. Do not forget the Turkish government also offered Flynn up to $15 million for something more nefarious—the abduction and rendition of Fethullah Gülen to Turkey.

As the incoming head of the National Security Council, he had a say in whether to approve a nuclear deal with Saudi Arabia. In his mind, Trump's win sealed the deal. During the inauguration, photographers caught Flynn texting the owner of a company that would benefit from the deal indicating that the power plant's operation was "good to go."

A week later, as national security adviser, Flynn introduced the plan to build forty nuclear plants in the kingdom. Trump and the Saudi king would discuss it in their first meeting. A financial backer to the plan said it was informally called the Trump/Putin M.E. [Middle East] Marshall Plan.[21] The CEO of ACU Strategic Partners, Alex Copson, said, "Donald Trump's election as president is a game changer because Trump's highest foreign policy priority is to stabilize U.S. relations with Russia which are now at a historical low-point."[22]

The only problem with this grand plan was that Russia was under sanctions for the invasion of Crimea, among other nefarious acts. For this deal to change the nuclear dynamic in the Middle East, Flynn would have to convince Trump to lift Russian sanctions. NSC staff told him the proposal circumvented its legal requirements and that Flynn, as national security adviser, simply could not order it to happen.

Flynn wanted Trump's personal friend Tom Barrack to be part of the deal; that way he could inform Trump that Barrack supported the deal. NSC staffers told ethics officials Flynn's former business partners would benefit from this deal and that it was ethically dubious.

In February 2017, Barrack noted his firm, too, would be able to profit off the administration and that the deal had the support of Gulf dignitaries who had close ties to Flynn. It was a circular financial pat on the back for everybody. All the cognoscenti would be involved, from Trump to Putin and everyone in between. Everyone would personally profit from the sale of the reactors and the transfer of technology.

On February 13, 2017, Trump fired Flynn supposedly for lying to the FBI and Vice President Mike Pence. That did not stop the power plants deal. Two weeks after he left the White House, an NSC staffer working the Saudi deal told a coworker, "I speak with Michael Flynn every night." Flynn still had his foot in the game, pariah or not. Even though NSC attorneys directed the work on the deal to stop in early March 2017, corporate clients and NSC staffers close to Flynn continued to promote the plan. They just did not want any of it mentioned in Presidential memos and briefings.

In early March 2018, Israeli prime minister Benjamin Netanyahu asked Trump to not complete the deal with the Saudis. Netanyahu asked that if the Americans had to go through with it then the deal should ensure the kingdom could not enrich uranium so they could not start a clandestine nuclear weapons program.[23] At the end of March, Trump rejected Netanyahu's request because "if the US does not sell the Saudis nuclear reactors, other countries like Russia or France will."[24]

The plot was not helped when MBS announced later that month that the Saudis would develop nuclear weapons if the Iranians started back down that path. This happened in the backdrop of Trump withdrawing from the Iranian nuclear deal brokered by the Obama administration and the Europeans. The Iranians were seriously considering whether to restart in the face of Trump's backsliding. That deal was all that kept Iran from developing nuclear weapons. At the time it was signed, Iran had the ability to develop a bomb within a year. Obama pushed that back to fifteen years and removed virtually all the fissile material needed from the country.[25] Trump wanted to go back on the deal half the world had signed off on. In theory, Iran could go back to making the bomb because Trump nixed the deal.

Russia was not waiting for rapprochement with the United States. They could see that Trump's chaotic White House was creating numerous financial opportunities worldwide, and they were going to scoop them up. On December 5, 2018, the Middle East and North Africa representative for the Russian state atomic energy company Rosatom went to Riyadh to meet with MBS. Its representative, Alexander Voronkov, said Russia would supply Generation 3+ VVER-1220 reactors for the kingdom, which he said were the most advanced ones Russia offered.[26]

It's worth noting here that in 1994 Russia built the first nuclear reactor in Iran, also a VVER model. The reactors in Bushehr nuclear station were to be the same VVER-1220 as those Russia promised to Saudi Arabia.[27] Even more interesting, Russian arms exporter Rosobornexport, a sanctioned arms company, sold S-300 air defense systems to Iran to protect Iran's reactors, and one could imagine this could be part of the package to Saudi Arabia as well.[28] The Russians were brilliantly offering regional parity and stability to both Iran and Saudi Arabia if the reactors were bought. It came with a tacit guarantee neither side could attack the other since they would have the same air defense system.

On January 22, 2019, the International Atomic Energy Agency (IAEA) delivered a report on what Saudi Arabia needed to do to stay within international norms if it pursued a nuclear power program. Mikhail Chudakov, a former head of Russian nuclear programs and IAEA deputy director, delivered the report that gave the kingdom the green light to move forward.[29] The following day, the kingdom received offers from five nations for construction of the project: the United States, Russia, France, South Korea, and China.[30] The Saudis originally wanted sixteen reactors but have scaled that back to two as part of a larger effort to diversify its energy grid.[31]

The "tilt" seems to be toward the Russians, with the Russian IAEA official paving the way and the Rosatom folks working over the royal family. Like their arms sales, the Russians promised a fairly cheap but stable deal that comes with massive long-term costs. But it was Team Trump that started this game, trying to cheat, abuse ethics, and lie its way into potentially gaining billions of Arab sheikdom money under the guise of a major foreign policy initiative. In the end, they got played by Russia, who knew corruption at a master-class level. Trump was a piker. And Russia ate America's lunch . . . again.

CHAPTER 14

Hydra 2.0—Destroying America's Security from Within

The dangers that the United States has endured during the Trump era are incredible for the amount of damage that he has done in so short a period of time. By the end of the second year, the commitments of the United States to its fundamental security relationships around the world would all be called into question. Worse, the basic security of the nation would also be knocked askance. Like Benedict Arnold, who removed the defenses of West Point under the guise of building them up, Trump has seemed hell-bent on destroying the pillars of national security while acting as if he was increasing them. Russia was so pleased at Trump's work that Alexander Dugin, Vladimir Putin's extremist philosopher, claimed that "the peak of American dominance is behind us."[1] It would appear that Trump sought to ensure that this was made a reality.

Trump has openly and loudly embraced his relationship with dictators and mass murderers. His disdain for our closest allies, long-standing security cooperation, and historic alliances has been equally public. Despite his toy soldier affection for the armed forces, hiring generals and admirals by the bushel, Trump has been like a book reviewer who proclaims his never-ending love of literature but who regrets he must burn all the books he disagrees with—and then publicly calls to raze libraries. Former senator Chuck Hagel, who sat on the Foreign Relations Committee, came out of retirement to warn of the risks to America's standing in the world: "[Trump] is doing great damage to our country internationally." Trump is "'intentionally dividing the country and the world by pulling out of alliances and trade deals such as the Trans-Pacific Partnership."[2]

A critical component of America's defense is the North Atlantic Treaty Organization, best known by the acronym NATO. Established in 1949 by the United States and eleven other countries who signed the treaty, NATO is not only part of American defense, it is the heart of the defense of democracy worldwide. It now totals twenty-nine nations, mainly in Europe. The heart of the treaty is Article 5, the ability of any of its members to request mutual defense. Should a NATO member be invaded, the other members would come to its aid. In its fifty-year history, Article 5 has been invoked only once. On September 12, 2001, one day after the devastating Al Qaeda terror attacks in New York and Washington, the other NATO nations, without any prompting from the United States, invoked Article 5. They called for the alliance to stand together and defend the United States from Al Qaeda. This allied commitment led to NATO fighting side by side with US forces in Afghanistan for more than a decade. Until the election of Donald Trump, American commitment to NATO was unwavering.

Trump first started expressing doubts about NATO just before his trip to the Soviet Union in 1988. He harbored the then Soviet, now Russian Federation view that NATO was ripping off the United States. Not only was America paying more than its fair share of NATO, the entire organization was suspect. It had come into existence because of an ideological standoff between America and Russia, provoked by the dictator Joseph Stalin in 1945. To both Trump and the ex-communist Putin, it was an old-school outdated organization from the Cold War era. Clearly, Trump kept this point of view, which was enhanced after that secretive two-hour meeting in 2014 with Putin's richest allies at the Nobu restaurant in Moscow. Afterward, Trump started to publicly express Moscow's opinion that NATO is obsolete and that it encroached on Russia's borders. After the 2014 Russian invasion of Crimea, he tweeted and commented that Russia was just exercising its rights to defend the ethnically Russian minority. These were literally Kremlin talking points used to justify its actions.

Soon after his election, Trump started to publicly question the necessity of NATO. On May 25, 2017, four months after taking power, Trump shocked our allies and delighted our enemies by declining to commit the United States to defend all NATO members. Ironically, Trump refused to do this while standing next to a memorial at NATO headquarters dedicated to the victims of 9/11, made from pieces of twisted steel.

At the NATO summit, Trump delighted Putin when he bullied his way through the scrum of leaders—grabbing the arm of Montenegro's Prime Minister Dusko Markovic and shoving him aside so that Trump could pose, front and center, for the cameras. I believe, at that moment, Trump was just being the bully he is. But was Trump aware of Moscow's attempt to kill the entire Montenegro government and topple this newest member of NATO just a few weeks after Trump was elected? Markovic was the target of a Russian-planned attempt to assassinate him and stage a coup de'état. It was broken up by NATO counterintelligence. Perhaps he was not, but to ex-KGB officer Putin, Trump's brusqueness and arrogance toward NATO leaders indicated that Trump would continue to damage the Atlantic alliance on the dangled promises of a grand bargain with Russia. Admiral Bill McMullin, former chairman of the Joint Chiefs of Staff, was skeptical of Trump's intentions when he said, "Those who have been our friends for many years ask questions about our commitments to them . . . and our enemies, those that would do us ill, seem to be able to take advantage of the uncertainty."[3]

For many, suspicions that Trump was in the thrall of Putin were now confirmed. NATO had to consider the United States an inside threat.

The evidence that Trump would hold the line for Moscow over our allies was strongly felt. But without allies, his America first policy would mean America alone. Many counseled to give Trump time, suggesting he would learn. When, one year later, leaders from NATO nations assembled in Brussels for the 2018 NATO conference, the key question was: Would President Donald J. Trump be representing the United States of America or Vladimir Putin?

NATO was forged in the furnace of the most destructive war the world has ever seen. It was a shield tempered in the blood of the millions who suffered through it. Historic events severely tested the alliance over its seven decades, as four hundred thousand Americans stationed in Germany faced off against the Russian-allied Warsaw Pact, a military amalgam of Soviet puppet governments with almost a million men under arms, poised to invade Western Europe from behind the Iron Curtain.

That alliance held strong through the chaotic collapse of the Soviet Union. In the post-Soviet era, its membership has swelled after many of the former communist countries have sought the political and economic freedom that their new democratic allies in America and Europe already enjoyed.

That year was apparently wasted. Trump's contentious belief that NATO was either like a country club with dues-paying members or a protection racket, forcing countries, as businesses, to pony up protection money, continued. He is not the first Western politician to take a shot at NATO, wittingly or not promoting the interests of Moscow, but he is the first American to do so. In France, the Putin- and Trump-backed conservative candidate for the 2017 French elections was Marine Le Pen. During her campaign, she declared that if she won the French election, her first two acts would be to start the breakup of the European Union and then withdraw France from NATO. Although French voters soundly defeated Le Pen and her absurd policy prescriptions, Trump appeared to take up the mantle.

At the summit, Trump also made equally destructive geopolitical calculations based on his bizarre interpersonal amities or animosity toward European leaders. His dislike of Angela Merkel translated to a perception of German vulnerability, so he dispatched his newly appointed American ambassador, Richard Grenell, to undermine German democracy. In an interview with far-right news site Breitbart in June 2018, Grenell said, "I absolutely want to empower other conservatives throughout Europe" and appeared to openly advocate regime change in Germany.[4] This led to public calls by German politicians to revoke Grenell's credentials and expel him for interfering in an ally's internal politics. This was exceedingly rare and almost always reserved for ambassadors from communist nations.

Trump also upset the alliance when he proposed the removal of thirty-five thousand US troops from Germany, despite the fact that nearly the entirety of US command-and-control, logistical, and medical support for the African, Middle East, and South Asian theaters is forward-deployed from Germany, as it has been since 1949. If this came to pass, combat action in and military operation support for the Eastern

Hemisphere would come at an enormous cost or become impossible. Another assessment was that Trump has quietly signaled a possible move of US logistical support to nations that are ideologically aligned with his conservative views, such as Poland, in a form of economic patronage for political fellow travelers. But Poland is geographically much, much closer to Russia. By proposing moving American bases that much closer to the East, the speculation rose that Trump's meeting would occasion much kowtowing, supplication, and pleading during his special audience with Putin in Helsinki in 2018.

At the time I had speculated on national TV that if Trump had a contentious meeting in Brussels, it would be just one more indicator that he was deeply under the sway of a foreign power and indifferent to the damage he would do to the national security of the United States, Europe, and the cause of freedom and democracy.

What was not known before the NATO summit was that Trump and Putin had engaged in a series of secret telephone communications, in the process developing a close relationship of mentor and confidant. In early 2018, Trump apparently requested that Putin send his top spies to Washington to meet and discuss terrorism issues. Meetings between intelligence peers, both with adversaries and allies, occur with some frequency, usually in a location that is neutral, such as Vienna or Helsinki. Attending this late January 2018 meeting were the top three Russian spies, two of whom—Sergey Naryshkin of the SVR and Alexander Bortnikov, director of the FSB—were under sanction for the armed invasion of Crimea. The director of the GRU came as well. This meeting took place with the personal approval of both Trump and Putin.

Trump's private conversations with Putin and other private meetings have had a corrosive effect on the United States and among its allies. Trump's insistence on their clandestine nature, and Moscow's perpetual embarrassing him by revealing them, indicates that their substance may be deeply unpopular or deeply disturbing.

Trump's words, and now his actions, have tripped a series of warning alarms for American and European intelligence professionals. Did an insidious asymmetric cyberattack result in the nominal conquest of our political system of government? It appeared that it had. Russia's information warfare campaign, with Trump as the vector of ten thousand lies, has given Russia a strategic geopolitical victory—without firing a shot.

In summation, the 2018 Brussels conference was more than contentious—it was insulting. Imagine if Vladimir Putin had arrived and decided to lecture NATO on how much he viewed the organization as a threat. That about sums up Trump's visit. His behavior at NATO headquarters was nothing short of scandalous. There was no way he could ever exceed the disgrace he accrued. It was unbeatable.

Now imagine that Trump decided that this display was merely an hors d'oeuvres in a buffet of unpleasantness. When Trump arrived in Helsinki to meet Vladimir Putin, little did I know that my worst nightmares were about to unfold. Trump was not just beaming in the company of Putin, he was clearly in love. In any other circumstance, one would have thought it was his wedding day.

Helsinki: Bizarre Love Triangle

On July 16, 2018, Donald Trump and Vladimir Putin held a strategic summit in Helsinki, Finland. The two leaders had met before in Hamburg, Germany, but this would be the first time Trump would be in a one-on-one meeting with Putin for the sole purpose of discussing US-Russian relations. Trump's disastrous NATO meeting in Brussels had set the expectation that he would behave a bit more conventionally with Putin. Those expectations were quickly dispelled. Suspicions that Trump was in thrall with the Russian dictator only grew when he met privately in Hamburg and excluded all press and staff and destroyed the notes of the American translator. It quickly became apparent that Trump wanted no record of his discussions with Putin.[5]

In Helsinki, Trump engaged in the same behavior. He forbade the presence of any staff and once again met Putin for two hours privately with only their interpreters present.[6] Again, the notes of the interpreter were taken by Trump, and she was forbidden to reveal what was discussed. A perplexed world watched what seemed like a strange series of ominous events. All that was missing was some sign that Putin had sway over Trump. Pens at the ready, the global press corps expected a relatively dull joint press conference full of pleasantries and diplomatic niceties. What they did not expect was the surrender of the United States to Moscow.

The forty-five-minute presser sent a clear message: Vladimir Putin was in charge of this relationship. Putin opened the event, describing their "negotiation" as "business-like" and stating that it elevated the relationship of the United States and Russia to "key issues of the global agenda."[7] He then dismissed the Russian hacking and information warfare campaign against the United States to elect Trump, saying "those impediments, the current tension, the tense atmosphere essentially have no solid reason behind it."[8]

Regarding the most important topic on the table, Putin then said they discussed the Russian interference in the 2016 election and beyond. Putin flatly denied that Russia has ever interfered in American affairs, a claim completely at odds with any historical record. He then said the United States and Russia could work together on cybersecurity.[9] It was classic Putin. He established dominance at the press conference, and all it took was for Trump to prove it by groveling. And grovel he did.

There was almost no time to gasp because Trump was only getting started. When he addressed the Russian interference campaign, Trump says he delivered a message to Putin in person and spent a "great deal of time talking about it" but at no time said he confronted him about the attack on democracy. Instead, Trump deferred to Putin.[10] The real show was when the questions started. It would not disappoint.

Jeff Mason of Reuters asked Trump if he held Russia accountable for "anything in particular," and if so, "what would you consider that they were responsible for?" Trump immediately blamed "both countries," first by bashing the United States as "foolish," and said, "we're all to blame." He claimed to be taking steps to deal with nuclear proliferation, when, in fact, both countries would leave the long-standing treaty, INF, within less than a year. He said that "both sides made some mistakes" before claiming the Mueller investigation was a "disaster for our country." He then made a strange remark, "They will have to try really hard to find something that did relate to the campaign." He crowed, "I beat

Hillary Clinton easily and, frankly we beat her." Last, Trump said he and Putin discussed "zero collusion."[11]

Then turning to Putin, Mason asked, "Why should Americans and why should President Trump believe your statement that Russia did not intervene with the 2016 election given the evidence that US intelligence agencies have provided? Will you consider extraditing the twelve Russian (GRU) officials that were indicted last week by the US grand jury?"

Instead of hearing from Putin, Trump took over and claimed victory in the 2016 election again, noting the electoral college count, not the popular vote count, and repeated "no collusion." He continued in a stream-of-consciousness ramble that "every time you hear all of these twelve and fourteen, it's stuff that has nothing to do, and frankly, they admit, these people are not people involved in the campaign." Then he continued, "Even the people involved, some perhaps told mis-stories. One case the FBI said there was no lie. There was no lie. Somebody else said there was. We ran a brilliant campaign and that's why I'm president, thank you."[12]

Putin followed up with even more cryptic talk, "As to who is to be believed, who is not to be believed: you can trust no one. Where did you get this idea that President Trump trusts me or I trust him?" Then defending Trump, he said, "He defends the interests of the United States of America, and I do defend the interests of the Russian Federation. We do have interests that are common."[13]

Putin continued with, "Can you name a single fact that would definitely prove the collusion?" He then added that, of course, Russia would "be sympathetic towards" a candidate who would seek to "restore the Russia/US relationship." He then said, "There is no evidence when it comes to the facts."

In one of the key exchanges during the press conference, Putin veered into investigating the twelve GRU officers. He said that Russian interrogators "are perfectly able to do this questioning [of the twelve officers] and send the appropriate materials to the United States" and that the special counsel could be present. But he did not say Mueller's team could participate in the questioning. Then Putin said the Russians, in exchange, wanted to interrogate Bill Browder, claiming that Browder had left the Russian Federation with $1.5 billion without paying taxes and had sent $400 million to the Hillary Clinton campaign. This lie was so big PolitiFact gave Putin a "pants on fire" rating.[14]

Later, Jonathan Lemire of the Associated Press said to Trump: "Putin denied having anything to do with the election interference in 2016. Every US intelligence agency has concluded that Russia did." Lemire then asked, "My first question for you, sir, is who do you believe? My second question is would you now with the whole world watching tell President Putin, would you denounce what happened in 2016 and would you warn him to never do it again?"[15]

Trump deflected blame away from Russia immediately by attacking the FBI. He continued, "My people came to me, Dan Coats came to me and some others and they think it's Russia." To Trump, Putin's answer was sufficient: "I have President Putin. He just said it's not Russia. I will say this; I don't see any reason why it would be."

As if this denial wasn't enough, Trump continued about the DNC server (which is actually a cloud of 140 servers)[16] and rambled about Hillary Clinton's emails before saying, "I think in Russia they wouldn't be gone so easily," and "I have great confidence in my intelligence people, but I will tell you that President Putin was extremely strong and powerful in his denial today."[17]

The reaction to the press conference was one of near universal revulsion in the United States, with Trump being seen as weak and out of his league with Putin. On the Internet and Twitter, the words *treason* and *traitor* started to trend. Many thought Trump's slavish devotion to Putin was the ultimate surrender to the Russians. Trump was roundly scorned by political officials, including right-wing pundits on Fox News, for his response to Russian interference. A month before his death, Senator John McCain, Trump's chief Republican critic, blasted Trump, calling the conference "one of the most disgraceful performances by an American president,"[18] and conservative pundit Douglas Schoen of Fox News said, "Putin eats Trump's lunch in Helsinki. This is no way to win against Russia."[19]

All that lacked in this surrender was the raising of a white flag. But Trump walked away feeling like it was the greatest moment of his presidency. When he returned to Washington, he was stunned by the scorn. He couldn't see what the problem was.

To add insult to injury, in a June 2018 meeting with Swedish prime minister Stefan Lofven, Trump was fascinated to learn about Sweden's unusual relationship with NATO. Lofven explained to Trump that Sweden was not a member but would occasionally cooperate with NATO when it suited Sweden's goals. Trump stated that perhaps the United States should proceed this way. Some in the administration took it as a joke, but Trump's words and actions indicated that he was not joking.[20]

Kim Possible: The North Korea Romance

Nowhere is Trump's adoration of dictators more evident than in North Korea, even though Trump began his presidency by creating conflict between the two nations. The love affair began in July 2017 when Kim launched two intercontinental ballistic missiles that had the potential to reach Alaska.[21] A month later he threatened to target American bases in Guam with ballistic missiles.[22] Apparently, this challenge titillated Trump.

In September 2017 an explosion in North Korea indicated that the North Koreans had successfully tested a hydrogen bomb. Early on Trump issued a series of threats that politically destabilized the Korean Peninsula and placed dictator Kim Jong Un on notice. He announced at the United Nations that the United States might have to destroy the isolated nation. He referred to the diminutive Kim as "little rocket man."[23] Kim responded by calling Trump a "dotard."[24] Then Trump's true feelings about the Korean dictator slowly materialized. In November 2017, Trump tweeted, "Oh well, I try so hard to be his friend—and maybe someday that will happen!"[25]

Following Trump's willingness to soften his language, Kim personally oversaw, at the end of November 2017, the launch of more intercontinental ballistic missiles capable of hitting the United States. North Korea announced, "Now we have finally realized the great historic cause of completing the state nuclear force, the cause of building a rocket power."[26] Earlier that year, the Defense Intelligence Agency assessed that the North Koreans had achieved the ability to miniaturize their nuclear weapons and could place them in the types of missiles its military forces were testing.[27] By December, media reports noted the Pentagon had begun drawing up plans to target a North Korean launch site or weapon stockpile.[28]

In his first State of the Union address at the end of January 2018, Trump addressed the Joint Session of Congress, while the parents of Otto Warmbier, an American student who had died shortly after being released from North Korean custody, watched. “We need only look at the depraved character of the North Korean regime to understand the nature of the nuclear threat it could pose to America and our allies,” he said.[29] However, by early March 2018, Trump began to backpedal on his tough talk against Kim and noted relations were heading in the opposite direction. Trump agreed to meet with Kim in early summer 2018 for a historic summit between the leaders.[30] The issue, to all who were outside his bubble, was that Trump felt an affinity for the strongman; he admired Kim’s strength. He felt that Kim could be enticed into a deal with the offer of future riches and developments in North Korea. So, he decided to use a real estate agent’s trick, overwhelm him with honors and luxury. Kim Jong Un was given equal stature with the president of the United States; its flag flying on an equal level with the US flag.

Trump stepped back from his saber-rattling rhetoric after their initial meeting in June 2018.[31] Trump’s adoration reached its peak later in 2018 when he told an American audience that he and Kim “fell in love.”[32] He “fell in love” with a dictator, with a man who poisoned his half brother with nerve gas in Malaysia[33] and executed other family members with a large caliber anti-aircraft gun. When issues of Kim’s murder of his half brother and killings of his staff were discussed, Trump dismissed them: “They’re not taking orders from anybody. He’s a very strong guy, and they’re able to do things that are pretty amazing.”

In 2019, Trump’s praise of Kim continued when, in his State of the Union address, he said of Kim, “We have great fantastic chemistry” and then later called him “a great leader.”[34] Worse than this rhetoric were the actions behind it. Trump was so completely seduced and enmeshed in his belief that his personal chemistry with Kim was successful, he unilaterally declared the Korean Peninsula nuclear-free. It was a level of delusion few could grasp. He repeated this claim numerous times. In his mind, once he got a verbal agreement, the subject disappeared from his psyche.

Kim understood how to handle a man like Trump. At every turn, North Korea sent flattering letters to the White House, and Trump would gush and beam over them on camera. He was thoroughly played by the little dictator in a manner that virtually every other petty tyrant had learned—Trump's ego and wallet were the way to his heart.

On February 28, 2019, Kim and Trump met again in Hanoi, Vietnam. The second summit ended with no progress on further curtailment of the North Korean nuclear program in exchange for sanctions relief. In fact, North Korea was rumored to have executed the entire negotiation team who had contact with Trump's team—just to make a point. They wouldn't be bullied.

President Trump, to keep the compliments flowing from Kim, sought to absolve him from blame at almost every turn. When asked about Kim's responsibility for Otto Warmbier's death, Trump explained: "A lot of people, big country" and "[Kim Jong Un] tells me that he didn't know about it, and I'll take him at his word." Warmbier was ruthlessly beaten until he lapsed into a vegetative state. He died within days of his return to America. It later emerged that Trump approved a $2 million compensation package demanded by Kim in exchange for the release of Warmbier. North Korea estimated that was the cost of detaining (and torturing) him to death. Later Trump would claim he stiffed them and didn't pay up. This is highly unlikely considering the level of admiration Trump has for Kim's ruthlessness.

Signs of a rare Russia–North Korean dictator bromance surfaced in a surprising story recounted by Andrew McCabe. The CIA and DIA had assessed that North Korea's missile, known as Rodong-1 or Nodong-1, was an ICBM capable of striking the continental United States. Former FBI director McCabe revealed that when the CIA briefed Trump about this threat to the American homeland, he refused to believe it. Trump exclaimed that Kim Jong Un had no such weapons, and he called it a "hoax" because "Vladimir Putin had told him so."[35]

On May 4, 2019, North Korea launched a volley of short-range ballistic missiles from its east coast, for the first time since November 2017. The missiles signaled North Korea's willingness to show it still had the capability to target South Korean forces and US forces in South Korea. It also suggested North Korea was willing to abandon talks with Trump and return to its status quo as world pariah. Still, Trump adored the strength and steadfastness of Kim in the face of adversity. He waved all of his foibles away as just some fake news. The love was never returned.

Giving and Taking Security Clearances

When Jared Kushner became senior adviser to his father-in-law, he had some issues acquiring a Top Secret/Sensitive Compartmented Information security clearance. There was a reason for that. Kushner's financial and personal relationships were more than worrisome. The suspicion was he would likely start trading America's secrets with his friends in the business world. Then news emerged that several of Trump's advisers such as Sebastian Gorka, a former Hungarian citizen with a questionable PhD and no appreciable experience in counterterrorism (and who was a Fox News talking head), could not even make the basic secret level clearance. Kushner's clearability was even more difficult. No matter, according to the *New York Times*: President Trump overruled objections from White House senior staff and intelligence officials to grant Jared Kushner top-secret security clearance. The president may have "ordered" then chief of staff John Kelly to grant him clearance one day after the White House Counsel's Office urged against it. Trump's decision reportedly troubled senior officials. Kelly was so upset he wrote an internal memo about being "ordered" to give Kushner top-secret clearance. The White House counsel at the time, Donald F. McGahn II, also wrote an internal memo recommending that Kushner not be given top-secret clearance and cited concerns that had been raised about Kushner, including those by the CIA.

The White House previously reported that Kushner's security clearance was handled "in the regular process." The president reiterated these claims in an Oval Office interview, responding directly to a question by the *New York Times* on January 31, 2019. Trump said that he did not tell officials to overrule security officials for Kushner's clearance, stating that he didn't think he had the authority to override security officials, and he wouldn't do that. Trump said, "I was never involved with his security," but he added that he knew there were some issues for several people, but he didn't want to get involved.

The FBI and the CIA had concerns over Kushner's foreign and business contacts, including those related to Israel, the United Arab Emirates, and Russia. Other officials reportedly raised questions about Kushner's and his family's real estate ties to foreign governments and investors and about unreported contacts Kushner had with foreigners.[36]

In February 2018, Chief of Staff John Kelly downgraded Kushner's top-secret security clearance in an effort to clear the scandal over whether top administration players are qualified to access the sensitive intelligence. [37]

These revelations came after National Security Adviser H. R. McMaster ordered intelligence reports on conversations where foreign leaders discussed interactions with senior Trump officials, including Kushner. The order came after McMaster learned that Kushner had contacts with foreign officials without coordinating with the National Security Council. This news came out after CNN reported that Robert Mueller had expanded his probe beyond Kushner's contacts with Russia to include Kushner's efforts to secure financing for his company from foreign investors during the presidential transition.[38]

Kushner had several omissions on his security clearance application, including his December 2016 meetings with Russian ambassador Sergey Kislyak, Sergey Gorkov, chief of the Russian bank VEB, and Russian lawyer Natalya Veselnitskaya—who had met with Kushner, Donald Trump Jr., and Paul Manafort on June 9, 2016.[39] Later amendments to Kushner's form added more than one hundred names. Kushner's attorney, Jamie Gorelick, claimed that an incomplete draft copy of the form had been accidentally submitted.[40]

Russia's illicit money was under direct pressure from US law enforcment. The DOJ settled a civil Russian money-laundering case three days before the scheduled start of the Prevezon Holdings trial. The Justice Department approved a settlement for less than $6 million. Allegedly, the action involved more than $230 million in a fraud scheme. When the complaint was announced in 2013, then US attorney Preet Bharara said, "As alleged, a Russian criminal enterprise sought to launder some of its billions in ill-gotten rubles through the purchase of pricey Manhattan real estate."[41]

Kushner sold only 10 percent of his holdings before joining Trump's administration. The companies, properties, and other assets that Kushner still owned were worth between $167.5 million and $569.5 million. Kushner's fifty-four-page financial disclosure revealed little information and was revised multiple times. There were multiple omissions. Some of the divested assets were sold to family members or put into a trust run by his mother. It was not clear whether Kushner's personal business interests would have benefited from his position in the White House.[42]

Kushner was not the only one with security clearance problems. On March 23, 2019, Tricia Newbold, the adjudicator manager in the White House Personnel Security Office, told a Congressional Oversight Committee that her supervisor and senior White House staff—which included the White House counsel—had overruled her denials of twenty-five staff members' security clearances. The denials stemmed from the employees and contractors having contacts with foreigners and conflicts of interest. Some also posed concerns over personal and criminal conduct and drug use and had financial problems. She acknowledged the president could overrule her and other officials' decisions, but still observed his staff was not following proper protocols.

Newbold had worked for the office for nearly two decades, under both Republican and Democratic presidents. "I would not be doing a service to myself, my country, or my children if I sat back knowing that the issues that we have could impact national security," she told the committee.

She noted outside agencies had expressed "serious concerns" about some of the officials who had received clearance. She also noted many staffers around the president had access to highly classified material, despite only having an interim clearance, which would normally prohibit them from some special accesses. Some of these staffers were later denied full clearance.

She was suspended without pay for two weeks on January 30, 2019. When she returned, someone else had replaced her, which Newbold claimed was retaliation for bringing up these issues. Her supervisor had begun taunting her a year earlier: Newbold, a small woman, was unable to reach items she needed because her supervisor would deliberately place them out of her reach. "Some of my staff have left," she told the committee. "They shared the same concerns as well. And they raised those concerns, but they didn't go anywhere."[43]

In November 2018, Deborah Roberts of ABC News interviewed Ivanka Trump. Roberts asked Ivanka about her use of a personal email account to conduct White House business in 2017, noting the similarities between her actions and those of Hillary Clinton. Ivanka defended her actions by saying no emails related to White House business were deleted. After her father's presidential campaign, Ivanka stated that she didn't think the rules on email applied to her.[44] As the princess of the Oval Office, none ever did. But her emails were the least of the Trump administration's worries in the White House.

The War on Intelligence

Giving clearance to family members was bad enough: it was clear nepotism. But in mid-August 2018, Trump decided to attack his enemies by using the same accusations they had leveled against his family. He ordered his critics, who had lifelong security clearances, stripped of access to secret information, particularly former CIA director John Brennan. But it didn't stop with Brennan. White House press secretary Sarah Huckabee Sanders named several other former officials who were to be targeted for removal from security clearance, including James Clapper, Andrew McCabe, Peter Strzok, Lisa Page, Michael Hayden, Bruce Ohr, and, of course, Trump's nemesis from the beginning, James Comey.[45]

In one of the most important rebukes of Trump's dictatorial moves, Admiral William McRaven, the retired Navy SEAL admiral who oversaw the operation to take out Osama bin Laden, fired back in a scathing op-ed in the *Washington Post* titled, "Revoke my security clearance, too, Mr. President."[46] A top-ranking SEAL, McRaven, known as the "Bull Frog(man)," didn't hold back: "I would consider it an honor if you would revoke my security clearance as well, so I can add my name to the list of men and women who have spoken up against your presidency." But that wasn't all he said. In a direct hard hit on Trump's character, the admiral said:

> A good leader tries to embody the best qualities of his or her organization. A good leader sets the example for others to follow. A good leader always puts the welfare of others before himself or herself. Your leadership, however, has shown little of these qualities. Through your actions, you have embarrassed us in the eyes of our children, humiliated us on the world stage and, worst of all, divided us as a nation.

SECTION III

Obstruction of Justice

CHAPTER 15

The Asteroid of Awfulness

A Republic . . . if you can keep it.

—Benjamin Franklin

On July 4, 2017, National Public Radio aired a reading of the Declaration of Independence, which included the articles of grievances listed against King George III, as they do every year. In one article in the declaration was the phrase: "A Prince whose character is thus marked by every act which may define a Tyrant, is unfit to be the ruler of a free people."[1]

After extensively researching and studying the wrongdoings of Donald Trump for four years and chronicling him in three books, I unequivocally assert that Trump is unfit to be a ruler of the just people of the United States precisely as stated in the Declaration of Independence. He meets every definition of a tyrant as presented to the first Continental Congress. He is a rogue. A self-appointed "king" who used the election to the highest office to redefine the American presidency and America itself. Trump may not have "plundered our seas, ravaged our coasts, burnt our towns, and destroyed the lives of our people," but he has destroyed and damaged the Constitution and the rights of a free people in so many ways. Most of this book has listed many examples of his corruption. Let us enumerate the sins of our modern American tyrant:

Trump wantonly violates the oath of office. Not a day goes by without Trump proving over and over again that he does not defend the nation.

He has never upheld the oath of office to protect and defend the Constitution: our laws, our values, our cultural legacy as the lighthouse of democracy worldwide. Trump, instead, holds truck with white supremacists and neo-Nazis, working to facilitate a plan that would end the American experience.

He abandoned human rights as a part of America's global legacy. Secretary of State Mike Pompeo's State Department's annual US report on human rights wrote in its preface that "the policy of this administration is to engage with other governments, regardless of their record, if doing so will further US interests." The phrases *defense of democracy* and *adherence to human rights* were removed: they would no longer be a consideration for doing business with the United States. The entire legacy of America's fight in the world, particularly after the liberation of Europe from the Nazis, was holding high the lamp for democracy around the world. Under Trump's orders, this legacy of honor has been abandoned.

Trump is the tyrant prince whose character led to a direct frontal attack on legal immigration into the United States, even though his grandfather's mother and his two wives and their parents have all benefited from it. He has tried to dismantle the constitutional right to birthright citizenship. His terrible attack on ethics has been so successful that the mere mention of an ethical review by his administration gets laughed at. It was reported that when they took power, one of their first acts was to have the transition team cancel all ethics training. The reason given was that the transition team's goals had shifted with leadership changes and the program no longer met the requirements given to the training company.[2] This was technically correct—since the administration has never had an ethical requirement to this day.

Trump's entire multiyear legacy was one of abandoning American values to side with dictators, warlords, and the traditional enemies of America. He admires them for their strength and ability to carry out assassination and mass murder. These are not the values of a true American president; for this his anti-American legacy should justifiably be excoriated.

He disarmed the country against foreign threats. Trump's abandoning the policies and organizations that defend us against the Russian cyberthreat to the United States elections is unbelievable. He has left America defenseless in the face of a new enemy because of his own narcissism. A congressional report on the Russian operation to attack the United States stated bluntly that "never before in American history has so clear a threat to national security been so clearly ignored by a US president."[3]

He initiated the attack on freedom of the press. A former US Ambassador to Russia responded to Trump's tweet "Fake News coming out of NBC and the Networks, at what point is it appropriate to challenge their licenses?" by noting that this was precisely how dictators start and "exactly what Putin did in Russia in 2000."[4] Vladimir Putin attacked his news media detractors directly. He used the FSB and his state media agencies to turn his anger against the few independent news organizations. Trump stole a phrase used by Russian dictator Joseph Stalin and applied it to those who were reporting on Trump's crimes and misdeeds. Hundreds of times he has called the followers of the First Amendment "enemies of the people." During his rallies, he has stoked the audience until they are screaming and threatening nearby journalists, with the result that his supporters label anyone in the media as part of the "opposition."

Despite the fact that Bannon was editor in chief of Breitbart News, which he described as the voice of the alt-right, he, too, constantly proclaimed his disdain and disgust at the news media. In an interview with the *New York Times,* Bannon said, "The media should be embarrassed and humiliated and keep its mouth shut and just listen for a while." He added, "The media here is the opposition party. They don't understand this country. They still do not understand why Donald Trump is the president of the United States.... The media has zero integrity, zero intelligence, and no hard work."[5] Trump himself adopted the term *fake news* to degrade any news he did not personally approve of. Ironically, Bannon lost his White House job by giving on-the-record criticisms of Trump and Jared Kushner to journalist Michael Wolff, for his book *Fire and Fury*. In fact, he was so excoriated by Trump, personally, and by the alt-right that he was removed from Breitbart News.

Taking the fight further, Trump has also publicly attacked individual journalists and exposed them to threats of death. He has used the bully pulpit of the presidency to intimidate media companies into getting rid of critics. He has successfully gotten a good number of journalists fired for publishing truths or opinions he found unpalatable, including Katie McHugh, Terry Frei, Bart Hubbuch, and Julia Ioffe. Each was fired for posting negative comments about Trump on Twitter. Several other journalists were forced to apologize to Trump for their comments, though they were factual.[6] This is the behavior of a tyrant, not a president of the United States.

Common journalistic errors have given him the opportunity to pounce on and demagogue against the journalists and their parent companies. On December 9, 2017, Trump demanded that Dave Wiegel, a reporter for the *Washington Post,* be fired over a photo of an arena, which appeared to be partially empty. In fact, the crowd couldn't be seen well due to the angle of the camera. Weigel posted it on his Twitter account and made a comment about the small crowd size. Several of his followers saw it and immediately told him he was inaccurate. Twenty minutes later, the photo and comment were deleted, but Team Trump had seen it and went on the attack. Trump tweeted saying he wanted an apology from Weigel, who responded saying that he was sorry. Instead of dismissing it, Trump said that Weigel should be fired.

When CBS's Leslie Stahl asked Trump why he did that, he responded: "You know why I do it? I do it to discredit you all and demean you all so that when you write negative stories about me no one will believe you."[7]

Trump will continue his effort to bring the news media under his control. It is imperative that his allies continue to buy, gut, and reorient what he calls the fake news media. Trump is very aware that a free and fair press will shine such an intense light of scrutiny on him that there will be no hiding his criminality from the public.

He attacked the legitimacy of the independent judiciary. As the president of the United States, Trump appears to have little idea what the courts do—except he believes they are supposed to act in his interests. The numerous statements he made about one of his Supreme Court picks, Brett Kavanaugh, indicate he expects court cases to go his way—not according to the law but because he put Kavanaugh on the bench. He also believes that the lifetime appointments for federal judges is one way he can rig the system and law to support his anti-American vision and keep him out of trouble. When cases do not go his way, he argues that the judiciary is at fault and that cases should go to the Supreme Court where he believes he will be treated favorably.

He championed white supremacy and xenophobia. One of Trump's first acts as a candidate was to conduct a racist attack against all people of Mexican descent. He called them "rapists"; he called out American judge Gonzalo Curiel as "a hater of Donald Trump" because the judge ruled on a fraud case brought against Trump's fraudulent Trump University. Trump and his team stated multiple times that the judge could not be fair because he was a Mexican. Trump has said all Haitians have AIDS and that African countries are "shithole[s]." He called black NFL players who took a knee to protest black shootings by police "sons of bitches" and called neo-Nazis, the KKK, and white supremacists "fine people."

He is the autocrat in chief. Trump co-opts blue-collar law enforcement to question the laws they uphold. Numerous times he has called on police to abuse suspects and even told the Customs and Border Patrol to ignore judicial warnings. He lamented that the military he dispatched to the border "can't act like a military would act. Because if they got a little rough, everybody would go crazy."[8] He seemed to be referring to the military in Israel or some ex-Communist countries that shot anyone who crossed a border.

He nurses and enunciates the authoritarian's desire to casually threaten to jail opponents, citizens and foreign visitors alike. Checks and balances, free press, free speech, right to redress, free and fair elections to select a truly representative government—these must all be ignored, discredited, or dismantled to achieve the goals of what former Bush speechwriter David Frum calls the Trumpocracy. Kicking over the Lego castle construct of American democracy and reshuffling the most valuable pieces into a new internal order is a goal he has bragged about since he started his campaign.

None of it ever was nor ever will be normal. As *New York Times* bestselling author and a historian on the White House Paul Brandus once said, "Whatever past disagreements we had with past presidents, we didn't wake up each day wondering what cringeworthy embarrassment awaited us. We never worried about Harry Truman acting like a buffoon, or Ronald Reagan crying like a child."[9]

He is a pathological liar. The hallmark of a true autocrat is the ability to harness the potency of a lie and use it to alter the citizens' perception of what the truth is. I could write a multivolume encyclopedia documenting Trump's lies, but a good example of this was Trump's fantastical series of years-long lies about Obamacare. In his effort to dismantle the Affordable Care Act, popularly known as Obamacare, Trump has lied, first saying Obamacare no longer exists and then reversing himself and saying Obamacare was under attack by the Democratic Party itself and that he was saving it! The range of lying by Trump is breathtaking in his ability to claim all sides as his own and then attack those same sides. He is quantifiably the greatest liar in American history.

In response to a statistic that 44 percent of Republicans believe Obamacare has been repealed, Ezra Klein, Vox editor at large, said, "Basically all democratic theory is based around the idea people have a roughly accurate and shared view of what's going on. What if they don't?"[10]

Donald Trump is a master at using the shock value of lies, spin, and disinformation to challenge the very existence of observable reality. He would openly attack people such as immigrants to capture his voters' emotions and weave his own presidential tapestry of what was right and wrong, through a withering litany of lies. Former FBI director Andrew McCabe said Trump was "someone who will say whatever he pleases to get whatever he wishes."[11]

When McCabe also affirmed that "the President exposes himself as a deliberate liar" without taking any action to defend the Constitution and expose the truth, that's where we have a problem.[12] The problem is that an FBI director has given him a pass and deference by merely acknowledging that a thin sliver of the American public voted for a liar. Instead of confronting Trump on the spot and resigning, McCabe held a press conference, calling on the public to not believe what Trump says. McCabe put his nose to the grindstone and worked, supporting the FBI within that hailstorm of lies without saying a word, until he wrote his autobiography two years later.

Lying and reengineering the meaning of truth is the power that autocrats and dictators love to exercise. It is a critical part of their sociopathy. Their construct reveals the pleasure of finding out they have the power to change the meaning of truth, lies, history, and even the existence of human beings. This was proven true by Stalin, Hitler, Kim Jong Un, Mummar al-Qaddafi, and Saddam Hussein. Our ability to process and expose lies is overwhelmed in the Trump era, and this is by design. The *Washington Post* documented that Trump told over ten thousand fact-checkable lies in the first two years of his presidency. This isn't just astounding; it is the single most dangerous aspect of his presidency—a man who will lie on matters great (claiming Iran is making nuclear weapons) and small (how imaginary people say how great he is). His lying is extremely transactional. His weapons are those of political warfare. He feels that he has to win each battle to win the war. He has almost no concern at all when he makes statements in which he lies at the beginning of the sentence and by the end has observed how the audience will receive it.

Trump employs another technique when he lies called the "fog of unknowability." Trump adopts all sides of an argument when speaking, sometimes doing so within the same sentence. He claims he is listening to others and that their opinions must be considered while at the same time indicating he feels strongly the other way—but he might change his mind. This tactic gives the listener the impression Trump is not accountable for what he might do: he might do what he claims to do or another action. What he does or may do is unknowable. When asked about Kim Jong Un's amassing additional missiles and nuclear materials following his first summit, Trump said, "Well, some people, David, are saying that, and some people are denying that. They have shots from above, way above. And some people are saying that, and some people aren't." In other words, who knows? But whatever is happening, Trump is not responsible, and whatever happens may be wrong or it may be right. Who is to know?

Another leader who uses this technique is Trump's most admired man, Vladimir Putin. Putintologists Fiona Hill and Richard Gaddy assessed Putin's ability to confound and lie this way: "The end result of Putin's misinformation and contradictory information is to create the image that he is unknowable and unpredictable and therefore even dangerous. It is part of his play in the domestic and international political game—to keep everyone guessing and, in some cases, in fear of how he might react."[13] Donald Trump plays the game of keeping one guessing to maintain the unknowability factor. But it's so transparent when he walks by journalists and says: "I don't know. We will see." It is taken at face value that he knows, and whatever happens next is designed to be a reality-show surprise.

Russian dissident chess master Garry Kasparov wrote about this special brand of autocrat: "'The truth doesn't matter because only what I say matters.' And autocrats enjoy watching their subjects twist in knots avoiding calling obvious lies what they are."[14]

As we saw in the Central Park Five incident, Trump's greatest desire is to be at the pinnacle of notoriety in almost every aspect of his life. He has achieved that but perhaps in ways he did not calculate. To him, the news media is just a venue for dispersing disinformation. His lies take the shape of truth simply because when those apocryphal barrels of ink are spilled his name is on them. The adage "any press is good press" is his watch-phrase.

The issue with Trump is that his lying is not just an efficient way to manipulate people, it has also become apparent to all but his most ardent supporters that his lying is pathological. Trump does not seem to know where his own fake news ends or begins. He seems incapable of knowing what the truth ultimately is. The great comedian Carl Reiner tweeted about Trump's perpetual lying about Russian involvement in our election: "Was Trump aware of it, and if not, when did he become aware and when did he start lying about never being aware and when [did] he stop lying?"[15]

The dictator's playbook says stop investigations that get close to the truth. Putin has done it. Erdogan immediately fired his corruption investigators when he consolidated power. The first rule of the dictator's playbook is to create the impression of campaigning as an anticorruption crusader and then get rid of the investigator. Removing checks and balances makes the dictator stronger.

Threats are often referred to as multidisciplinary because of the numerous collection techniques that can be applied to gain information, analyze it, and then use it to exploit victims. Computer technology has increased the ability to collect, exploit, and disseminate lies on a scale that eclipses the reach of the twentieth century's great dictators, who only had wireless radio and newsprint at their disposal. In the past, readers had time to ponder what was being said. In today's hyperspeed news processing, information must be consumed in a split second before the next allotment comes along. This information overload shapes opinions faster and, more insidiously, deeper into the psyche.

Our greatest founding father, George Washington, was humble at all times when reflecting upon himself. Until this era, he set the standard for how chief executives should comport themselves when he wrote:

> If I had ever assumed the character of a military genius, and the officer of experience; if, under these false colors, I had solicited the command I was honored with; or if, after my appointment, I had driven on, under the sole guidance of my own judgment, and self-will; and misfortunes, the result of obstinacy and misconduct, not of necessity, had followed, I should have thought myself a proper subject for the lash.[16]

Was Washington not the full measure of a man and the best of all presidents?

It was the UK Labour Party's spokeswoman on foreign affairs Emily Thornberry who would have merited a low bow and kiss of the hand from the ghost of Washington when she said of Trump, "He is an asteroid of awfulness that has fallen on this world. . . . I think that he is a danger and I think that he is a racist."[17]

CHAPTER 16

"The End of My Presidency..."

I'm fucked.

—President Donald J. Trump

Practically from the beginning of his term as the attorney general of the United States, Jeff Sessions was constantly under attack by President Trump for his recusal from the Russian investigation. Trump berated Sessions as stupid, mocked his southern accent, and threatened to fire him—which Trump finally did after the Republican Party suffered sweeping defeats in the 2018 midterm elections. Trump appointed a critic of the Russia investigation named Matthew Whitaker to oversee the Department of Justice. Whitaker repeatedly criticized and scoffed at the Mueller investigation, including in an early August 2017 op-ed he penned for CNN where he said it was "going too far."[1] Unlike Sessions, Whitaker refused to step aside from overseeing the Russia probe despite many conflicts of interest, including his op-ed and numerous prejudicial comments about the investigation. He was also friends with one of the subjects of the inquiry, Trump campaign cochair Sam Clovis.[2] As questions arose about Whitaker's suitability for the job and his sketchy source of income, another man was nominated for and eventually became the eighty-fifth attorney general, William "Bill" Barr.

If Barr was unknown to the nation, he was not to the Washington, DC, swamp. He had been a Washington legal player since the 1970s, with a propensity for covering up crimes. In 1976, while working as an analyst at the CIA, he wrote a memo to promote then CIA director George H. W. Bush's letter in favor of destroying CIA documents, despite specific requests by the Senate Select Committee on Intelligence to retain them.[3] After a series of jobs working in the judicial and executive branches of the government, including for the Reagan administration, Barr eventually became deputy attorney general under George H. W. Bush in 1990, and, one year later, he was promoted to the position of attorney general of the United States.

While working in the Bush Sr. administration, Barr pushed to pardon those who had been involved in the Iran-Contra scandal under Ronald Reagan, including Oliver North, Caspar Weinberger, and Elliott Abrams. After Congress forbid sending money to the Contra rebels in Nicaragua because of civilian massacres, the Reagan administration illegally and secretly sold advanced weapons to the Ayatollah Khomeini in revolutionary Iran and then funneled those funds to the Contra rebels. The incident rocked Washington, and an investigation was launched and led by independent prosecutor Lawrence Walsh. Walsh sought to prove that Reagan was more involved than had been publicly disclosed. People went to prison for the illegal scheme. Enter Bill Barr.

Barr suggested the players involved be pardoned, without consulting the pardon office, and claimed that he had turned to others in the DOJ to arrive at this conclusion. Bush issued the pardons in the final days of his only term, and in doing so, the criminal actions of the Reagan administration were effectively erased.[4] After George H. W. Bush lost the presidency to Bill Clinton in 1992, Barr went into the public sector and ended up at the law firm of Kirkland & Ellis in 2009 and again in 2017.[5] While there, the firm worked for Russia's Alfa Bank. Despite this apparent conflict of interest, Barr's former associate Brian Benczkowski was later nominated to the DOJ's criminal division and oversaw the investigation covering Alfa Bank server communications with Trump Tower.[6]

In terms of investments and roles, Barr already had numerous conflicts of interest with the special counsel's investigation into Trump—which he promptly ignored. First, Barr earned dividends from the

Vector Group, the company that worked in the 1990s to develop Trump Tower in Russia. Vector Group president Howard Lorber not only was heavily involved in those arrangements but also was identified as a person in contact with Donald Trump Jr. after the infamous June 9, 2016, meeting with Natalia Veselnitskaya.[7] At a meeting the day before, Veselnitskaya also addressed the Magnitsky Act, which involved Och-Ziff Capital Management, a hedge fund company for which Barr had served on the board directors during the 2016 election.[8] Veselnitskaya testified that her meeting with Trump Jr. discussed the work between Och-Ziff and Bill Browder.[9] As if that was not enough, Barr had assets ranging between $100,000 and $250,000 in Trump-backed Deutsche Bank, while being tasked with the role of investigating Trump's bank records.[10]

Barr made his views on the accusations of Trump's obstruction of justice clear well before he was considered for nomination. Early in the administration, when Trump fired Acting Attorney General Sally Yates for her rejection of the racist Muslim ban struck down by the courts, Barr publicly defended Trump, saying, "Trump was right to fire Sally Yates."[11] Later on, when Trump fired James Comey, Barr again jumped to his defense, saying Trump "made the right call."[12] A few months later, Barr criticized the attorneys on Mueller's team, claiming, "I would like to see him have more balance on this group."[13] Barr was also quoted by the *New York Times* promoting the idea that Hillary Clinton was the more appropriate target for an in-depth investigation. In a November 2017 article, he even pushed the fake story that implied Clinton had sold large quantities of uranium to Russia.[14] None of it was true, but Republicans loved the accusation. He later went back and attempted to clarify his supposed intentions, but the damage was done.[15]

On June 8, 2018, Barr sent a nineteen-page letter to Deputy Attorney General Rod Rosenstein and Assistant Attorney General Steve Engel, criticizing the special counsel's potential case of obstruction of justice against Donald Trump. In the letter, Barr claimed that "Mueller's theory should be rejected for the following reason," and then presented his case—without being privy, at that point, to the special counsel's opinion or conclusion regarding obstruction of justice.[16]

The Barr Memo: "No Conspiracy, No Obstruction"

On March 22, 2019, the Mueller report was delivered to the attorney general.[17] The nation expected a damning report. However, forty-eight hours later, Barr issued a surprising letter dismissing the accusations, essentially saying that nothing was found and no crimes were committed. Two days after that, Barr released a four-page letter addressed to Senator Lindsey Graham, Representative Jerrold Nadler, Senator Dianne Feinstein, and Representative Doug Collins, summarizing the Mueller report's "principal conclusions" with two particular claims:

1. "The investigation did not establish that members of the Trump Campaign conspired or coordinated with the Russian government in its election interference activities."
2. "After making a 'thorough factual investigation' into these matters, the Special Counsel considered whether to evaluate the conduct under Department standards governing prosecution and declination decisions but ultimately determined not to make a traditional prosecutorial judgment. The Special Counsel, therefore, did not draw a conclusion—one way or the other as to whether the conduct constituted obstruction." He then parsed "The Special Counsel states that 'while this report does not conclude that the President committed a crime, it also does not exonerate him.' "[18]

Additionally, Barr wrote: "In making this determination, we noted that the Special Counsel recognized that 'the evidence does not establish that the President was involved in any underlying crime related to Russian election interference.' "

Harvard legal scholar Laurence Tribe summed up well Barr's outlandish memo when he wrote:

> There is mounting reason to ask whether the president and his associates sought to secure his election by conspiring with foreign adversaries and domestic accomplices to defraud the American people. Yet the memos in question would shield him from being held accountable

> precisely because he won that office. There is a maddeningly circular, bootstrap quality to arguing that even a crime committed to putting somebody into a privileged position can't be pursued because, well, it helped put him into that position of privilege.[19]

As noted above, Barr had auditioned for the job of attorney general after he wrote a nineteen-page study specifically claiming that it was impossible for President Trump to obstruct justice *because* he was president. Of course he would stick to that assessment. And so it's not entirely shocking that, just forty-eight hours after seeing the secret Mueller report, he completely absolved Donald Trump of any guilt. The Barr letter was splashed all over the headlines for days, as news outlets, the punditry, and the Trump administration alike loudly declared Trump's innocence.

In the same breath, however, Barr asserted that Robert Mueller found an enormous amount of evidence that Russians made multiple attempts to coordinate with the Trump team. More alarmingly, at no time did anyone in the Trump campaign, including Trump, try to stop Russian activities that were being performed for Trump's benefit. It was an open form of conspiracy in which information was made available and actions were conducted. Trump accepted the benefits, especially from WikiLeaks, and used them in his campaign. This in itself is a conspiracy and evidence of collusion.

The next day, Trump proclaimed his total innocence and immediately declared he would hunt down and destroy his enemies using William Barr. First, he would start with the media. Trump's legal team sent a memorandum to all the major news channels demanding that the critics and politicians who wanted Trump investigated or anyone who had disparaged him be banned from the airwaves. This included almost every major Democratic Party leader, as well as former CIA director John Brennan. Some cable news programs secretly executed that order and even removed critics from the airwaves who were not on Trump's list, including me.

The Barr letter essentially validated the claim that conspiracy with a foreign power was acceptable and that as long as it was done in one's favor without one overtly communicating back, it was justified. In other words, stay one step away from coordination, and it can't be considered conspiracy or collusion or even a crime. Barr had effectively done what Trump put him in office to do.

The resulting report of the entire investigation became news all by itself as time passed. While the news media, elected officials, and the public waited eagerly for the results, for nearly two years Trump's legal team repeatedly professed knowledge that the Mueller investigation was almost complete and would find nothing. His lawyers hinted at inside information on the status of the investigation but never produced evidence of their claims. Those promoting the sure results of treason were also waiting to be validated by the special counsel. But many were still caught off guard on March 22, 2019, when the announcement came that the report had been turned over to the Department of Justice. The public still did not know its contents, scope, or volume.

What was not widely known at the time was that three days after Barr's initial letter, Robert Mueller wrote a scathing reply to Barr that said his four-page memo to Congress, which was also released to the public, failed to "fully capture the context, nature, and substance" of the investigation. He encouraged Barr to release the investigation team's executive summary as prepared by the special counsel. He also called Barr a day later and discussed how the media and public were confused about the findings of the special counsel.

Two days later, Barr sent another longer letter to Congress disavowing the first Mueller letter as a summary and stating that a report of the special counsel's findings would be made available after redactions could take place. Barr also testified on April 9–10, 2019, about his letters and the report, but his responses only created more confusion. He said Mueller's letter was "snitty." He also acknowledged that he didn't know "whether Bob Mueller supported my conclusion."

The Pre-Report Presser: "No Collusion. Trump Did Nothing, Go Away"

On April 18, 2019, nearly a month after the report was turned in to the Office of the Attorney General, the redacted report was released to Congress and the public. To preface the release, Barr held a twenty-minute news conference to announce the results and take questions. He was joined by Deputy AG Rosenstein. Absent was the author of the report, Robert Mueller. When asked later why Mueller didn't attend, Barr dismissed the need for Mueller's presence: "It's a report he did for me as the Attorney General. He is required under the regulation to provide me with a confidential report. I'm here to discuss my response to that report and my decision, entirely discretionary, to make it public since these reports are not supposed to be made public."[20]

In addressing the content of the report, Barr generally followed the material examination of the Russian efforts to interfere in the 2016 election, including the activities of the Internet Research Agency (IRA) and the Russian military intelligence agency (GRU), and isolated the terms of the scope to "Russian government" and "Russian officials," without acknowledging the roles of intermediaries and cutouts working on behalf of the Kremlin. He repeated the claim of "no collusion" while affirming the Russian government's efforts to interfere. Barr also said the report stated that Russia's efforts did not have the cooperation of the Trump administration despite how Roger Stone, Donald Trump Jr., Paul Manafort, and others directly interacted as unwitting assets or direct conspirators with Guccifer 2.0 and WikiLeaks and had face-to-face meetings with various Russian representatives, interlocutors, and cutouts.

Among other things, Barr's presentation directly contradicted his claims of no cooperation pertaining to WikiLeaks. He said the report affirmed the passing of stolen documents from GRU to WikiLeaks "for publication" and then gave a legalistic reading of whether "the Trump campaign illegally participated in the dissemination of the materials" and the claim that it would only be illegal if "the publisher also participated in the underlying hacking conspiracy." Because Stone, Trump Jr., and Trump himself promoted WikiLeaks releases of stolen Russian emails and called directly for hacking his opponent, clearly Barr was attempting to spin the results of the evidence of cooperation (emphasis is mine):

> The Special Counsel found that, after the GRU disseminated some of the stolen materials through its own controlled entities, DCLeaks and Guccifer 2.0, the GRU transferred some of the stolen materials to

> WikiLeaks for publication. WikiLeaks then made a series of document dumps. The Special Counsel also investigated whether any member or affiliate of the Trump campaign encouraged or otherwise played a role in these dissemination efforts. Under applicable law, *publication of these types of materials would not be criminal unless the publisher also participated in the underlying hacking conspiracy*. Here too, the Special Counsel's report did not find that any person associated with the Trump campaign illegally participated in the dissemination of the materials.[21]

Then he reviewed the known contacts of the Trump campaign, claiming that meetings with Russians and in-betweeners like Trump Jr., Kushner, Manafort, Page, Papadopoulos, Sessions, Gordon, and others did "not violate US law."

Barr pivoted to the report's discussion of obstruction of justice using doublespeak spin, arguing about "potential legal theories" on obstruction of justice. Barr said that instead of relying upon the special counsel's legal theories on obstruction he had turned to the Office of Legal Counsel and Attorney General Rosenstein to conclude that Trump had not "committed an obstruction-of-justice offense." He then went off on a rambling off-the-cuff defense of Trump, including claims that he was justifiably "frustrated" and angry about the "unprecedented situation" and that the investigation was "propelled by his political opponents and illegal leaks." In fact, the Mueller investigation was often characterized by many observers as setting a tight antileak standard.

Barr also claimed that Trump had been very cooperative, that investigators had "unfettered access" to him, and that he had never asserted privilege claims or "deprived the Special Counsel of the documents and witnesses necessary to complete the investigation." On the contrary, Trump repeatedly sought to prevent access to his staff and his documents, and even encouraged people to lie to Mueller's team. Barr blatantly ignored the fact that Trump never testified in person, was never deposed, and only submitted answers in writing, which were carefully groomed by his legal staff, and that he frequently claimed to have "no recollection."

The first journalist to question Barr began by acknowledging that none of the press had seen the report and then asked Barr about the comments of Judge Reggie Walton, a George W. Bush appointee, who said, "The attorney general has created an environment that has caused a significant part of the public... to be concerned about whether or not there is full transparency."[22] The reporter continued pressing Barr about clearing Trump of obstruction, noting that Trump was fundraising on Barr's "quite generous" comments from the press conference. Barr responded by claiming these views came from the Mueller report, then turned the question around on the reporter over the use of the word *unprecedented.* A common ploy in the right wing is to argue over definitions of words rather than to address substance, a ploy Barr employed frequently. The last question posed by a reporter was: "Is it an impropriety for you to come out and sort of spin the report before people are able to read it?" Barr responded no and walked away.

The Mueller Report: Full of Collusion, Guilty of Obstruction, Should Be Impeached

Two hours after Barr's press conference, the redacted version of Robert Mueller's report was released—and it contradicted everything Barr had said. It was full of accusations of collusion; furthermore, Mueller listed eleven points where obstruction of justice had likely occurred. Barr had lied to the nation for more than a month. He had massaged the framework around what the media thought was in the report so that it would be seen from his, not Mueller's, perspective. Trump also spent an enormous amount of time claiming that he and his campaign had rejected Russia's advances. Yet the actual Mueller report tells a very different story, a story that shows the campaign's actions were nothing less than treasonous.

Right out of the box, on page one, the Mueller report proved Barr a liar. Although the conclusions were that the special counsel chose not to bring charges, the entire document amounted to 448 pages of evidence of conspiracy and collusion.

An analysis of the special counsel's report reveals that virtually all of the assessments I make about Russia's activities in the chapters of this book and in my previous two books, *The Plot to Hack America* and *The Plot to Destroy Democracy*, were exactly right, with a few exceptions. Here I will summarize the report's most salient parts:

> As set forth in detail in this report, the Special Counsel's investigation established that Russia interfered in the 2016 presidential election principally through two operations. First, a Russian entity carried out a social media campaign that favored presidential candidate Donald J. Trump and disparaged presidential candidate Hillary Clinton. Second, a Russian intelligence service conducted computer-intrusion operations against entities, employees, and volunteers working on the Clinton Campaign, then released stolen documents. The investigation also identified numerous links between the Russian government and the Trump campaign.[23]

Mueller made it clear that the investigation did not even consider the word *collusion* because that word didn't exist in the legal lexicon: The investigation adhered to "the framework of conspiracy law, not the concept of 'collusion.' In so doing, the Office recognized that the word 'collude[e]' was used in communications but that collusion is not a specific offense or theory of liability found in the United States Code, nor is it a term of art in federal criminal law. For those reasons, the Office's focus in analyzing questions of joint criminal liability was on conspiracy as defined in federal law." Mueller had looked at using the term *coordinated*—whether the Trump campaign "coordinated" with the Russian government in the 2016 election. The report specifically noted that this would have required both parties to be "informed by or responsive to other's actions or interests."[24]

This is a logical loophole that only gave Trump an excuse to say they did not "conspire" because they did not have a tactical agreement—that Robert Mueller could find. Even though both parties were working directly in each other's interest, Mueller seemed to define away all of the actions that would have led to the dozens of examples he included as "coordination." There was a reason for that: they covered up a lot of their tracks. Mueller said many people lied to the special counsel, destroyed documents and electronic mail, and/or lived overseas and could not be found. The special counsel noted that the investigation could "not always yield admissible information or testimony, or a complete picture of activities undertaken by subjects of the investigation. Some individuals invoked their Fifth Amendment rights against compelled self-incrimination and were not, in the Office's judgment, appropriate candidates for grants of immunity." Also, the lies told by witnesses created problems: "When individuals testified or agreed to be interviewed, they sometimes provided information that was false or incomplete, leading to some of the false-statement charges described above. And the Office faced practical limits on its ability to access relevant evidence as well—numerous witnesses and subjects lived abroad, and documents were held outside the United States."[25]

The Mueller report was divided into two volumes. Volume 1 addressed the Russian interference campaign as well as Trump team ties and interactions with Russian operatives. Volume 2 addressed the obstruction of justice efforts of Trump and accomplices. The portions that were redacted reportedly included references to pending cases, closed cases, methods of intelligence, and private information. The second volume also included four appendices covering Trump's written answers, the original appointing document from Rod Rosenstein, a list of the individuals and organizations referred to in the report, and a list of the cases resulting from the investigation.

Origins of the Betrayal

The Mueller report was delivered as I was wrapping up the first edition of this book. I had endured three weeks of ridicule and calls for me to be fired by MSNBC by both right-wing extremists like Tucker Carlson and the extreme pro-Moscow left such as Glenn Greenwald and Matt Taibbi because Bill Barr had said nothing was found against the president. However, the actual Mueller report conclusively validated almost all of my assessments in my books and on TV. Trump and Russia had worked together, but because of technicalities, Mueller chose not to charge them with crimes.

The FBI had begun its counterintelligence investigation into Russian interference in July 2016. Peter Strzok, an FBI counterintelligence agent, learned that Australian officials had reported Papadopoulos's activities looking for incriminating information on Hillary Clinton. In a secret visit to London, FBI agents met with Australian ambassador Alexander Downer to learn about the Papadopoulos meetings with Joseph Mifsud.[26] The FBI launched the operation, codenamed Crossfire Hurricane, on July 31, 2016, and it became a multiagency investigation, in cooperation with the CIA and NSA. CIA director John Brennan met with FBI director James Comey to share collected intelligence illustrating Russian involvement in the DNC hacking and influence operations.[27] The overall investigation would eventually involve the Director of National Intelligence (DNI) and the Department of Homeland Security, which were looking at the larger scope of the Russian interference efforts.

Because the investigation was launched in the later stages of a presidential election, the FBI was aware of the perception of political bias and potential damage to its reputation if seen to be working in favor of either candidate. This hindered its ability to directly question the candidates' campaign staff without revealing what the FBI, CIA, and NSA knew about the Russian active measures campaign already in progress. Former deputy attorney general Sally Yates said, "Folks were very careful to make sure that actions that were being taken in connection with that investigation did not become public."[28]

Though the investigation itself remained hidden from public view during the 2016 election and the special counsel period that followed, multiple testimonies acknowledged its existence in July 2016, including those of John Brennan, James Comey, Devin Nunes, and the Office of Inspector General. The Mueller report acknowledged that the investigation was conducted in two phases and in response to Papadopoulos's activities. And Mueller pulled no punches:

> The actions we investigated can be divided into two phases, reflecting a possible shift in the President's motives. The first phase covered the period from the President's first interactions with Comey through the President's firing of Comey. During that time, the President had been repeatedly told he was not personally under investigation. Soon

> after the firing of Comey and the appointment of the Special Counsel, however, the President became aware that his own conduct was being investigated in an obstruction-of-justice inquiry. At that point, the President engaged in the second phase of conduct, involving public attacks on the investigation, non-public efforts to control it, and efforts in both public and private to encourage witnesses not to cooperate with the investigation. Judgments about the nature of the President's motives during each phase would be informed by the totality of the evidence.[29]

Trump Jr. Gets a Pass

The Mueller report set an extremely high bar for conspiracy in the meeting of Donald Trump Jr., Jared Kushner, and Manafort with Russian government representatives. Mueller explained that the trio wanted to find "dirt" on Hillary Clinton from Russia, but under the standard of conspiracy, it appears that Trump Jr. and others did not realize what they were doing was a crime "beyond a reasonable doubt":

> In the declination to charge Donald Trump Jr., the Special Counsel discussed the reasoning in not charging for campaign violations. It concluded: a) "thing of value" could include passing of information, b) the offered information would be hard to resolve whether uncompensated opposition research would be treated under existing judicial decisions, c) the defendant would have to know that the receipt of documents or information would be unlawful beyond a reasonable doubt, d) the evidence was found there was an effort to "prevent the disclosure of the nature of the June 9 meeting" but that the Office could not prove any prior knowledge of illegality, and e) the value of the information would exceed the threshold of criminal violation.[30]

On this, the special counsel noted that Trump Jr., Kushner, and Manafort could feasibly argue that they didn't know they would be violating the law in holding the meeting or receiving the information.

Finally, the special counsel concluded that charging Donald Trump Jr. for receiving the information in the June 9, 2016, meeting would be difficult because of the "high burden to establish a culpable mental state in campaign-finance prosecution and the difficulty in establishing the required valuation."[31]

Some pundits have characterized this pass for Trump Jr. as him getting off because he's too stupid to know the laws, but as many black men in America can tell you—whether imprisoned or shot dead—ignorance of the law is no excuse. Whether Mueller pulled this punch because Trump Jr. was Trump's son or because Rosenstein and Barr were adamant that they would not charge him, Mueller's acquiescence is fodder for another book.

The Eleven Findings Where Trump Obstructed

Mueller then laid out exactly which incidents prompted his office to examine the obstruction of justice inquiry:

> (a) The President's January 27, 2017, dinner with former FBI Director James Comey in which the President reportedly asked for Comey's loyalty, one day after the White House had been briefed by the Department of Justice on contacts between former National Security Advisor Michael Flynn and the Russian Ambassador;
>
> (b) The President's February 14, 2017, meeting with Comey in which the President reportedly asked Comey not to pursue an investigation of Flynn;
>
> (c) The President's private requests to Comey to make public the fact that the President was not the subject of an FBI investigation and to lift what the President regarded as a cloud;
>
> (d) The President's outreach to the Director of National Intelligence and the Directors of the National Security Agency and the Central Intelligence Agency about the FBI's Russia investigation;
>
> (e) The President's stated rationales for terminating Comey on May 9, 2017, including statements that could reasonably be understood as acknowledging that the FBI's Russia investigation was a factor in Comey's termination; and

> (f) The President's reported involvement in issuing a statement about the June 9, 2016, Trump Tower meeting between Russians and senior Trump Campaign officials that said the meeting was about adoption and omitted that the Russians had offered to provide the Trump Campaign with derogatory information about Hillary Clinton.[32]

Mueller continued, "We determined that there was a sufficient factual and legal basis to further investigate potential obstruction-of-justice issues involving the President."[33]

Despite attempts by Attorney General Barr, the Trump Republicans, and the media to drive the narrative that the Mueller report exonerated Trump, all anyone had to do was read the report to see Mueller's indicators of the president's and his allies' obstruction. Therein lies the rub. They fully expected that few journalists and noncitizens would read such a report, so their summary would become the reality no matter what words or accusations were contained within.

1. The campaign's response to reports about Russian support for Trump

On multiple occasions in 2016, Trump and his campaign staff (and Roger Stone) publicly cast doubt on whether Russia was involved in stealing and disseminating documents from the Democratic campaign. At the same time, Trump knew his team was actively pursuing the contents of those emails, including "further WikiLeaks releases." His stories about having no business ties with Russia also were false because he had been pursuing the Trump Tower in Moscow.[34]

2. The president's conduct concerning the investigation of Michael Flynn

After it was revealed that Flynn had lied to investigators about his meetings with Kislyak, the ambassador, and subsequently stepped down, Trump asked Comey to "see your way clear to letting this go, to letting Flynn go. He is a good guy. I hope you can let this go." Trump also sought to have Deputy National Security Advisor K. T. McFarland prepare a denial that he had asked Flynn to speak with Kislyak, but she refused because she didn't know whether that was true.

3. The president's reaction to public confirmation of the FBI's Russia investigation

As the investigations into Russian meddling and Trump cooperation ramped up after he took office, Trump pushed to have Sessions "unrecuse" himself and, furthermore, asked Don McGahn to pressure Sessions into complying. The Mueller report also noted that Trump wanted an attorney general to "protect him." He asked the heads of his intelligence agencies to deny the allegations that he had ties to Russia and repeatedly asked Comey to "lift the cloud" on what was created by the investigation.[35]

4. The events leading up to and surrounding FBI Director Comey's termination

The special counsel noted Trump's admissions about why he fired James Comey in May 2017, namely, to relieve the "great pressure because of Russia," as he later confessed to Lester Holt on NBC and bragged to Sergey Lavrov and Sergey Kislyak in the Oval Office. It was also observed that in Comey's termination letter, Trump emphasized that Comey had assured him that he was not under investigation.[36]

5. The president's efforts to remove the special counsel

Trump was so unhappy about the announcement of the special counsel he declared it was the "end of his presidency." He went on the attack against Mueller through his team, accusing the special counsel of having conflicts of interest. Trump's advisers told him that these claims had already been covered by the Department of Justice and were without merit. Nonetheless, Trump ordered his personal counsel, Don McGahn, to get Rosenstein to remove Mueller over conflicts of interest. McGahn threatened to resign if he was forced to do so.[37]

6. The president's efforts to curtail the special counsel's investigation

Trump asked Corey Lewandowski to have Sessions take over the special counsel, to say that the investigation was "very unfair" to Trump, and to exonerate him of wrongdoing. Lewandowski didn't send this message to Sessions, and after being asked again to do so, he passed it on to Rick Dearborn, who also did not pass the message to Sessions.[38]

7. The president's efforts to prevent disclosure of emails about the June 9, 2016, meeting between Russians and senior campaign officials

Trump directed his aides to hide the emails related to the Donald Trump Jr. meeting with Veselnitskaya and crew, and he was personally involved in crafting the press release that lied about his son's activities. Instead of acknowledging that the meeting was to gather "information helpful to the campaign," the administration said it was about Russian adoptions.[39]

8. The president's further efforts to have the attorney general take over the investigation

After Jeff Sessions recused himself from the investigation, Trump repeatedly pressured him privately and publicly to reverse that decision. Additionally, he asked Sessions to start investigating Hillary Clinton.[40]

9. The president's ordering of McGahn to deny that the president had ordered him to have the special counsel removed

As news circulated that Trump was attempting to fire Mueller, he told McGahn to publicly deny these reports and falsify a record saying he had not been ordered to fire the special counsel. Trump persisted and asked McGahn again to do this. Instead, McGahn testified and brought notes to the special counsel to confirm that these stories were true.[41]

10. The president's shifting conduct toward Flynn, Manafort, and a third person (redacted)

Michael Flynn's legal team cut off cooperation with Trump's legal team. As a result, Trump's behavior toward Flynn shifted from "the president's warm feelings toward Flynn" to the accusation that Flynn's cooperation would be seen as "'hostility' towards the president." Likewise, Trump said Manafort was a good man and was being treated unfairly and that he would never flip. Additionally, the special counsel listed a third person, but the name was redacted. Because it related to an "ongoing matter," it is likely Roger Stone, whom Trump supported while Stone was being investigated and pending his trial.[42]

11. The president's shifting conduct toward Michael Cohen
Trump initially expressed strong support for Michael Cohen after he was raided. He saw Cohen as a loyalist. But when he learned that his former lawyer was cooperating with prosecutors, Trump subsequently turned on him and called him a "rat."[43]

Why Did Trump Attack the FBI and the Special Counsel?

Mueller pointed out the reason for the attacks on the special counsel and FBI. Trump wanted to cover it up, stop it, or control its outcome: "At that point, the President engaged in a second phase of conduct, involving public attacks on the investigation, non-public efforts to control it, and efforts in both public and private to encourage witnesses not to cooperate with the investigation. Judgments about the nature of the President's motives during each phase would be informed by the totality of the evidence."[44]

Despite all the evidence laid out in the Mueller report—which noted over a hundred contacts between Russians and the Trump campaign, in addition to the corroborating evidence of Trump's attempted obstruction—the following was included at the end of it: "At the same time, if we had confidence after a thorough investigation of the facts that the President clearly did not commit obstruction of justice, we would so state. Based on the facts and the applicable legal standards, we are unable to reach that judgment."

More importantly, the report concluded (emphasis is mine): "Accordingly, while this report does not conclude that the President committed a crime, *it also does not exonerate him.*"[45]

Mueller ended by punting the charges to Congress. In what was clearly intended to spur impeachment charges to bring Trump to account, he wrote (emphasis is again mine):

> With respect to whether the president can be found to have obstructed justice by exercising his powers under Article II of the Constitution, we concluded that Congress has authority to prohibit a president's corrupt

> use of his authority in order to protect the integrity of the administration of justice.... The conclusion that Congress may apply the obstruction laws to the President's corrupt exercise of the powers of office accords with our constitutional system of checks and balances and the principle that *no person is above the law*.[46]

Earlier in the report, Robert Mueller made a note that this report's results were not final. As a last caution, he warned:

> While this report embodies factual and legal determinations that the Office believes to be accurate and complete to the greatest extent possible, given these identified gaps, the Office cannot rule out the possibility that the unavailable information would shed additional light on (or cast in a new light) the events described in the report.[47]

The Barr Star Chamber: Putin's Little Helper

After the report was released in its redacted form, Barr came under criticism for his summary letters and was called to testify to Congress on the rollout of the Mueller report. It was clear that he had lied to the nation and perhaps perjured himself before Congress, but his response to the accusations was bemused and unconcerned.

Representative Jerry Nadler, chair of the House Judiciary Committee, held a vote on April 19, 2019, to subpoena the unredacted Mueller report. The committee held Barr in contempt for failure to appear in a hearing on his release of the report. In response, Barr had Trump invoke executive privilege over the report and related evidence. Then on May 21, the Department of Justice relented on that demand in an attempt to get the House Judiciary Committee to drop its contempt charge.[48]

Because of the comments several people made in the report, subsequent hearings were called for in the US House of Representatives and Senate, including more testimony from Barr and from Robert Mueller and Trump's lawyer Don McGahn. Trump responded by ordering McGahn to resist testifying to Congress, invoking executive privilege.

On May 1, 2019, after weeks of "no collusion" rants by Trump and his followers, it was revealed that Mueller had sent two letters to Barr about his initial summary on March 24 in which Barr falsely claimed that Mueller had cleared Trump of any wrongdoing. On the eve of Barr's appearance before the Senate judiciary, one of those letters (sent on March 27), which referenced an earlier letter sent on March 25, was released. In the March 27 letter, Mueller said Barr's summary released to the public "did not fully capture the context, nature, and substance of this Office's work and conclusions" and that his office had immediately addressed those concerns in the March 25 letter. Mueller's second letter said that the summation led to "public confusion about the critical aspects of the results of our investigation."[49]

That same day Barr testified before the Senate Judiciary Committee and was cornered several times by its Democratic members. Opening the hearing, Senator Lindsay Graham set the conversation in motion by saying "no crime has been committed, so how can there be obstruction" and then worked to spin the investigation as a pro-Clinton partisan venture conducted by bitter FBI agents, including Peter Strzok. He then promised to investigate the origins of the Russia investigation, including FISA warrants, the Steele dossier, and counterintelligence investigations.[50]

During the hearing, senator and former 2020 presidential candidate Kamala Harris asked Barr whether anyone had requested he investigate the investigators of the Russian interference campaign. Barr was elusive in his answer, despite Senator Harris's multiple attempts to rephrase. "Perhaps they 'suggested'?" she asked.

"I wouldn't say suggest," Barr said.

"Hinted?" replied Harris.

"I don't know."

"Inferred?" she persisted. She asked these questions in multiple ways to identify any activity Trump may have used to encourage Barr to attack those who launched the investigation.

Next, Harris homed in on whether Barr had looked at the evidence in the Mueller report when he wrote his memo summarizing and exonerating Trump on March 24. Under her questioning, Barr admitted he had not examined the evidence presented by the Mueller report. Harris asked, "You did not question or look at the underlying evidence that supports the conclusions in the report?"

"No," replied Barr.

"Did Mr. Rosenstein review the evidence that underlines and supports the conclusions in the report, to your knowledge?" asked Harris.

"Not to my knowledge. We accepted the statements in the report and the characterization of the evidence as true."

"Did anyone in your executive office review the evidence supporting the report?" she asked.

"No."[51]

The next day Barr refused to testify before the House Judiciary Committee, objecting to the use of staff attorneys to question him on his role in the Mueller report rollout.

In response to the letter from Mueller, Democratic members of Congress insisted on Mueller testifying. During the Senate Judiciary Committee hearing, Barr claimed he would have no objection to Mueller testifying. Trump, however, objected in a series of tweets, including one that specifically said "Bob Mueller should not testify."[52]

On May 7, Trump invoked executive privilege to keep Barr from testifying.[53] On May 8, then White House press secretary Sarah Huckabee Sanders said it was Barr who asked Trump to invoke executive privilege: "At the Attorney General's request, the President has no other option than to make a protective assertion of executive privilege." Ultimately, Barr was held in contempt by the House Judiciary Committee after a contentious round among the members of both parties, with the Republicans complaining about the vote and the Democratic members holding ground to pass the vote 24–16.[54]

In reaction to the contempt vote, Assistant Attorney General Stephen Boyd sent a letter to Congress saying the remainder of the evidence supporting the Mueller report would not be shared with Congress or the public.[55] In the letter, Boyd directly tied the assertion of executive privilege to the vote of contempt after recognizing that there had been "ongoing negotiations" to release Mueller investigation materials.[56]

On May 9, Trump reversed direction again on Mueller by hiding behind Barr and saying it would be up to Barr to decide whether Mueller could testify to Congress.[57]

Barr launched an internal investigation into the investigation of Russian interference in the 2016 campaign. He appointed US attorney John Durham to conduct the investigation and claimed that the investigation itself would result in changing how counterintelligence operations related to political campaigns.[58] In dramatic hyperbole, Barr declared that "government power was used to spy on American citizens." Then in an interview Barr told Fox News that the claim he had lied to Congress was "laughable" and part of "the unusual political circus."[59]

Hunting the Trump Hunters

For Trump, it wasn't enough to have Bill Barr cover up the damage inflicted by the Mueller report. He wanted revenge, and he sent Barr out to fulfill his vendetta. After the Mueller report was released, Trump ramped up his rhetoric, calling for investigations on everyone. First, he would go after the people involved in opening the investigations into the 2016 election interference. He wanted to punish everyone who had exposed him and Russia.

Back on the campaign trail, Trump had continuously regarded media and anyone with damaging information as his personal enemies. But it was in January 2018 that he started to adopt a conspiracy theory, whispered into his ear by Rudy Giuliani and others, that the FBI's top spy hunter Peter Strzok was forming a coup against him, based on the emails Republicans had uncovered between Strzok and Lisa Page. At this point, Trump decided that anyone who crossed him was committing "treason."

William Barr would then back up any plan to use governmental power to destroy and block those who would investigate Trump, and he set about framing everyone as traitors. After the Mueller report, Barr opened at least two investigations into the FBI. Then Trump gave him the power to declassify sensitive intelligence methods and sources from the intel agencies in order to root out and hunt down the people who had discovered Russia's plot.

Fox News host Greg Jarrett wrote that the Russia investigation and the Mueller report were part of a grand conspiracy Hillary Clinton had developed before the election as an "insurance policy" just in case there was an unlikely Trump victory. The premise was that if Trump won, he would be investigated by a corrupt FBI and "taken out" through impeachment.[60] Trump came to publicly embrace the existence of this conspiracy against him and repeatedly claimed that the FBI, the CIA, and other agencies had organized to conduct what he called a coup d'état and overthrow the sitting government. Most of Trump's remarks come out like the ravings of a mentally ill man on a street corner, but here was the president of the United States claiming the entirety of the US government was conspiring to take away his presidency.

When Robert Mueller finished his remarks at the initial news conference, he clearly pointed the way for Congress to remove Trump. But Mueller, like all institutionalists, wanted it done right and according to the Constitution. Trump, on the other hand, referred to the legitimate investigation into Russian interference as an attempted "coup." He had used the word *coup* before. In February 2019, Trump tweeted of "illegal and treasonous" behavior and an "illegal coup attempt." Soon after he started to hint that multiple FBI investigators and former heads of our agencies may have committed "treason."

And Trump hasn't reserved these charges for the investigators alone. At a May 2019 rally, Trump accused the FBI and Democrats of treason. "We have a great new attorney general who will give it a very fair look,"[61] Trump promised. When asked about a recent court ruling, Trump stated that he was able to ignore rulings from Obama-appointed judges. During the 2018 State of the Union address, Trump called Democrats who refused to stand and applaud "un-American" and "treasonous."[62]

What is more worrying is Trump's willingness to hint toward violence and government forces as a solution to those he perceives to be a threat. In a March 2019 interview with Breitbart, Trump said:

> You know, the left plays a tougher game, it's very funny. I actually think that the people on the right are tougher, but they don't play it tougher. OK? I can tell you I have the support of the police, the support of the military, the support of the Bikers for Trump—I have the tough people, but they don't play it tough—until they go to a certain point, and then it would be very bad, very bad. But the left plays it cuter and tougher. Like with all the nonsense that they do in Congress...with all this

> investigation—that's all they want to do is—you know, they do things that are nasty. Republicans never played this.[63]

At a White House event in May 2019, NBC's Peter Alexander asked Trump to specify whom he was accusing of committing treason: "Sir, the Constitution says treason is punishable by death. You've accused your adversaries of treason. Who specifically are you accusing of treason?" Trump's response was: "A number of people. They have unsuccessfully tried to take down the wrong person." He then gave James Comey, Andrew McCabe, Lisa Page, and Peter Strzok as examples.[64]

The most dangerous part of all is that even though Barr only recently opened these investigations, as of the writing of this book, Trump has already decided the verdict of these farcical investigations, with everyone guilty, committing "treason," and attempting a "coup."

On Fox News, Lewandowski laid out the plan to use Barr and the Department of Justice as a weapon to carry out a vendetta against Trump's enemies and those who dared investigate him. Lewandowski told host Gregg Jarrett:

> The inspector general report is going to come out, and I suspect it is going to be devastating about corruption in the Obama Administration, under his leadership, at the FBI and the Department of Justice.... The person who has gotten a pass on this offer is Joe Biden. Because I believe that the investigation which was launched, came from somewhere inside the White House, to green light Clapper, Comey, and Brennan to start this investigation into Donald Trump for no valid reason.... Joe Biden has not answered what he knew and when he knew it about how this investigation began.[65]

In Trump's world, he lives by King Louis XIV's motto: "The State? It is me!" Purer words of an autocrat have never come from the Oval Office. One MSNBC analyst opined that America was not in a constitutional crisis but characterized it as a nation in a stage of constitutional collapse. One of the three supposedly coequal branches of government was legally requesting subpoenas while the executive branch was essentially saying "we don't care what you want—you won't get it."

It is this lack of tactical correction in an attempt to restore order that brings the United States closer and closer every day to the geopolitical chaos that Vladimir Putin craves. It is not normal to legally go after Christopher Steele for presenting information he had that he felt should be taken to law enforcement. None of this is normal, and yet the longer it persists, the more legitimate this behavior becomes in the eyes of world leaders and future American leaders. The mere act of setting a precedent and then believing in that precedent, no matter how wrong it is, can ensure its longevity.

Misframing the Narrative

It seemed like William Barr and Donald Trump got away with misframing the metanarrative of the Mueller report as "no collusion, no obstruction." Understanding that Robert Mueller was an institutionalist, they knew he would never violate rules and come out against them, which allowed the cover-up to take place in plain sight. However, on May 29, 2019, Mueller held a surprise press conference at the Department of Justice to announce the closing of the Office of Special Counsel and his return to private life, and to respond to the characterizations and opinions in the final report.[66] Though he maintained his institutionalist dignity, he essentially came out and told the nation that Trump should be impeached—just not in so many words.

Mueller reminded listeners that the investigation started by looking into the Russian interference efforts during the 2016 campaign. Without saying "Hillary Clinton," he affirmed that the action was done to "damage a presidential candidate." He then went over the indictments of the Russian operatives in the IRA and GRU. Mueller emphasized that the special counsel, as he saw it, was created because the interference needed to be "investigated and understood." Mueller also pointed out the investigation was to look at not only the "Russian influence of the election" but also the "Trump campaign's response to this activity," and that it concluded there was insufficient evidence to charge (beyond a reasonable doubt) a broader conspiracy.

Mueller seemingly felt compelled to reiterate what was written in volume 2 of the report on the obstruction of justice claims. He issued a forceful reminder that obstruction efforts hindered the government's ability "to find the truth and hold wrongdoers accountable." He said that there was a "reason we investigated efforts to obstruct the investigation" and "the matters we investigated were of paramount importance."

Mueller apparently also decided that the administration's claim of complete innocence needed a correction. He affirmed that "if we had confidence that the president clearly did not commit a crime, we would have said so. We did not, however, make a determination as to whether the president did commit a crime." It was a powerful punch at Trump, but Mueller wasn't quite finished with him yet.

Mueller then emphasized that the reason Trump was not indicted was because "under long-standing department policy, a president cannot be charged with a federal crime while he is in office. That is unconstitutional. Even if the charge is kept under seal and hidden from public view, that, too, is prohibited." Mueller added that the special counsel was part of the DOJ and bound by DOJ rules. "Charging the president with a crime was therefore not an option we could consider," said Mueller. He left hanging in the air the notion that Trump wouldn't always be president and that indictments could be brought up at a later date by another prosecutor.

Mueller broke down two items related to this decision. First, he said that the special counsel was allowed to hold an "investigation of a sitting president because it is important to preserve evidence while memories are fresh and documents available." He added that "evidence could be used if there were co-conspirators who could be charged now"—a reminder that Flynn, Papadopoulos, Manafort, Gates, Stone, and others were charged with lying to investigators. Second, Mueller said, "the Constitution requires a process other than the criminal justice system to formally accuse a sitting president of wrongdoing." This would be the congressional power of impeachment. On the basis of this legal guideline, Mueller said that the result would be an accusation of a crime that would have "no court resolution of the actual charge." Because of this, the special counsel "concluded that we would not reach a determination one way or the other about whether the president committed a crime."

Mueller finished by addressing his possible testimony to Congress: "I hope and expect this is the only time that I will speak to you in this manner." He claimed that nobody told him that he could not testify and that the decision was his own. He said that even if he did testify before Congress, he'd only discuss items already concluded in the report and nothing further. He clarified that this press conference appearance was intended to be his only comment and that he would not take questions. He then thanked those who worked on the case for the professional manner in which they conducted the investigation.

But Mueller's most important message he saved for last, reiterating "the central allegation of our indictments [is] that there were multiple systemic efforts to interfere with our election. And that allegation deserves the attention of every American." And with that final blow, Robert Mueller walked off the public stage.

In response to Mueller's statement, chair of the House Judicial Committee Jerry Nadler said, "All options are on the table."[67] And, "Given that [Mueller] was unable to pursue criminal charges against the president, it falls to Congress to respond to the crimes, lies, and other wrongdoing of President Trump...we will do so."[68] He also stated that Trump welcomed the Russian effort, that Mueller backed up this assertion by not exonerating Trump of obstruction of justice, and that it was up to Congress to act on these offenses to "hold the president accountable for his misconduct." Nadler also said the policy prohibiting the DOJ from taking action against a sitting president was wrong and, furthermore, prevented the special counsel from pursuing justice "to the fullest extent possible." As a result, Nadler noted, the responsibility was on Congress to make sure that "no one, not even the President of the United States, was above the law."

And so the sphinx who was Robert Mueller spoke, and in the same riddle-like way as his report was written, he pointed to what he thought was the path forward: Congress would have to impeach Donald Trump.

What is arguably the single greatest scandal in American history is that a president of the United States attempted to stop not only any investigation of Russian interference in the 2016 election but also any investigation into his campaign or himself. By firing the investigators and covering up what law enforcement could find, he also tried to stop the investigation of a counterespionage operation of a foreign power. And then he went a step further. He tasked Bill Barr with investigating the intelligence sources that identified Trump's cover-up and obstruction in order to exact revenge. The only people who stood to benefit were, and still are, Vladimir Putin and Donald Trump.

In the end, Robert Mueller's single step out of the shadows to make his press statement was a patriot's final duty. But for the president, after being exonerated by Bill Barr, let off the hook by Robert Mueller's conventional rigidity, and essentially issued a "get out of jail free" card by Congress, the lack of consequences of the Mueller investigation seemingly gave Trump a permission slip to do whatever he wanted. And since he had permission, he decided the day after Mueller's testimony that he would cheat in the 2020 election.

The 2020 Scandal: Trump's Mortal Fear of Joe Biden

By getting away with defanging the Mueller report and counterattacking his opponents, Donald Trump, Rudy Giuliani, and Bill Barr started on a path to cheat in the 2020 election. This time, their target was Joe Biden, the man most likely to beat Trump. In Ukraine, Giuliani met with shady characters who assured him they had the goods on Biden. When considering Ukraine, one must remember that two divisive political cultures are at play. One Ukraine is the democratic populist nation that aligns itself with western Europe and desires freedoms similar to those of other liberal democracies. In 2014, this faction spared a people's revolution and pushed many corrupt politicians out of the government.

As discussed earlier, the "other" Ukraine is the pro-Moscow government led by the rich and backed by Putin and his billionaire oligarchs. It supports Russia's goals of bringing the country back into an alliance similar to the old Soviet Union. This is the same corrupt pro-Moscow government that contracted Paul Manafort (who was later sent to prison after being convicted of related money laundering) to shift Ukraine away from Western ideals. Until 2014, this government was led by Viktor Yanukovych, who fled to Moscow after he ordered the police to kill over fifty protesters and citizens. Even after Yanukovych left office, many of his cronies remained. One of these cronies in the new Poroshenko government was the prosecutor general Viktor Shokin, who took the office in February 2015. The entire Western world saw Shokin, whose position is equal to that of our attorney general, as a steady hand who manipulated the law and led selective investigations to maintain internal corruption at the highest levels.

In January 2016, the point man for the global effort to take down Shokin was then vice president Joe Biden. He called attention to Shokin's historic corruption in a meeting with Poroshenko.[69] Shokin resigned on February 16, yet a month later, his return was announced. Subsequently, Shokin was then formally fired after a Ukrainian Parliament vote.[70]

Two years later, in a speech to the Council on Foreign Relations, Biden boasted about the effort to stop corruption in Ukraine. He revealed that he had told Petro Poroshenko that the United States would forfeit $1 billion in loans if Shokin was not fired.[71] Ukraine relented and the money was released.

It is at this point that Trump and his "lawyer" Rudy Giuliani learned from Paul Manafort that Biden's son Hunter was on the board of a company Shokin once investigated called Burisma Holdings. Though nothing was discovered in the investigation and Hunter Biden later resigned from the board, Giuliani saw an opportunity to smear Joe Biden. Working with pro-Moscow Ukrainians, Giuliani secretly met with Shokin and other politicians and started to turn the anticorruption narrative upside down by framing Vice President Biden's attack on Shokin as a concerted effort to protect his son's interest in Burisma. Despite the fact that a global effort was made to get rid of Shokin, the tactic went over well with Trump, who also wanted to push Putin's conspiracy theory about Russia's innocence in the 2016 election affair.

The irony of this misdirection wasn't lost on Trump's adversaries. As noted before, on July 25, 2017, Donald Trump had accused Ukraine of helping Hillary Clinton in the 2016 election. He tweeted, "Ukrainian efforts to sabotage Trump campaign—'quietly working to boost Clinton.' So where is the investigation A.G. @seanhannity."[72] Special Counsel

Robert Mueller cited this tweet in his obstruction of justice claim. But Trump was seemingly determined to spread a conspiracy theory that would absolve Putin of any culpability, despite reams of evidence that pointed to the specific FSB spies involved.

In 2018, two Soviet-born Russian Americans named Lev Parnas and Igor Fruman connected Giuliani to Shokin. Giuliani and Trump met with Parnas and Fruman in private at the annual White House Hanukkah party on December 6, 2018 (though when they got into legal trouble, Trump would deny ever knowing them).[73] Parnas and Fruman had a track record when it came to meddling with US elections. While being investigated for funneling illegal campaign finance money to Texas congressman Pete Sessions, they also bragged that they could get rid of American ambassador Marie Yovanovitch. The name of Parnas and Fruman's company? They called it *Fraud Guarantee*. I kid you not.

A second pro-Trump team was working to introduce the smear against Joe Biden by using journalist John Solomon, who writes for *The Hill* newspaper. Solomon wrote negative articles on Biden using his cover as a journalist and coordinated with Giuliani to spread the rumor of a criminal investigation into Hunter Biden via an interview with then prosecutor general Yuriy Lutsenko in March 2019. Solomon's reporting was broadcast widely on Fox networks (particularly on the *Sean Hannity Show*) and was promoted by Donald Trump.[74] A week later, Solomon published more damning clips from the Lutsenko interview, this time linking a nonprofit tied to the right wing's favorite target, billionaire George Soros.[75] Later on, it was revealed that Solomon sent a preview of the article by email to Lev Parnas and the two celebrity lawyers working for Giuliani (Victoria Toensing and her husband, Joe diGenova) five hours before he published it.[76]

On March 28, Giuliani would quote these two articles, along with comments from Viktor Shokin and Yuriy Lutsenko, in a scathing fifty-page packet presented to Secretary of State Mike Pompeo. Deputy Assistant Secretary of State George Kent later testified that Giuliani's disinformation packet also included claims that the Ukrainians had helped Hillary Clinton by leaking the Paul Manafort black ledger, a document that revealed his millions in illicit payments.[77] It also claimed Ambassador Yovanovitch gave a list to Ukrainian prosecutor Lutsenko of people she did *not* want him to prosecute. However, Lutsenko, who had been fired for corruption the previous October, noted in his deposition that this supposed list, which included a photograph of names with his business card attached, was fake. He verified the business card was his but that the list was a random bunch of misspelled names. He suggested the list was crafted by someone who was actually Czech or Serbian, based on the transliterated names.[78]

Additionally, Serhiy Leshchenko, the Ukrainian citizen who leaked the Manafort ledger, responded with vehement denial in a *Washington Post* op-ed. He explained that "my desire to expose Manafort's doings was motivated by the desire for justice." He added, "Giuliani's entire approach is built on disinformation and the manipulation of facts."[79] Lutsenko also recanted the story trumpeted by Solomon and Giuliani, and said, "Hunter Biden did not violate any Ukrainian laws—at least as of now, we do not see any wrongdoing."[80]

Even after it had been disavowed, this Putin-originated and Trump-approved conspiracy theory planted the seed that it was Ukraine that interfered in the 2016 election against Trump and in favor of Hillary Clinton, and that Russia was innocent.[81] On the same day, Pompeo scheduled calls with Giuliani and Congressman Devin Nunes apparently to further coordinate the plot.[82]

On May 3, 2019, Trump had an extensive call with Putin.[83] Deputy Assistant George Kent's later testimony said this conversation was part of a concentrated effort to influence Trump's view of Ukraine.[84] Soon after this contact, Barr called for his own investigation into the origins of Mueller's Russia investigation in an apparent witch hunt.[85]

In an effort to frame Ukraine, Giuliani launched an offensive against Ukrainian president Volodymyr Zelensky, claiming in a tweet that he was "surrounded" by "enemies of President Trump."[86] Zelensky's office initially rejected a meeting, saying this was an American domestic issue; however, Zelensky was quietly being pressured to do something about Biden and Burisma.

In early May, Trump and Zelensky had their first phone call, which lasted sixteen minutes. They exchanged pleasantries; Trump promised to send someone important to Zelensky's upcoming inauguration

(Energy secretary Rick Perry would attend) and then invited the newly elected president to the White House.

President Zelensky was a comedian who had played being president on a comedy show and then, surprisingly, got elected to the official office. Though he was new to politics, he knew he needed American weapons that the US Congress had funded. As far as he knew, those weapons were on their way, because Trump had already approved the $141 million authorization in February. Instead, Trump decided to extort Zelensky into announcing a formal investigation of former Vice President Biden and his son Hunter. Trump was particularly desperate to attack Biden because March and June 2019 polls showed Joe Biden with an 11 to 13 percentage point advantage over Trump in the upcoming 2020 election. Biden was also appealing to virtually all of Trump's core supporters except for evangelicals. To ensure the scheme would remain undetected, Giuliani directed Trump to fire Ambassador Yovanovich so no one would discover their plan, and they routed all of their secret communications into the hands of the US ambassador Gordon Sondland, who reported to the European Union—an entity Ukraine was not part of.

In June, Trump almost tipped his hand. He publicly criticized FBI director Christopher Wray, who had stated public officials or campaign staff should contact the FBI if they learned foreign actors sought to influence American elections. When asked directly, Trump said he would consider using foreign assistance despite the warning and could not see any reason why not.[87]

On July 25, 2019, the day after the Mueller inquiry concluded, Trump felt emboldened and saw an opportunity to knock down Biden's rise in the polls. In a phone call to supposedly congratulate President Zelensky on his victory, Trump talked to him about Biden. He started the conversation by saying: "I would like you to do us a favor, though."[88] Trump asked Zelensky to start an investigation into Hunter Biden and by extension Joe Biden. It would later be revealed through intermediaries that Trump wanted it announced on CNN by Zelensky himself. Only then would Trump release the military funds he had secretly frozen.

Forty-eight hours after Zelensky called, the director of national intelligence Dan Coates suddenly resigned. Unbeknownst to Congress, on August 12, an individual who was listening to that call filed a whistleblower complaint with Inspector General for the Intelligence Community Michael Atkinson. In the complaint, the person attested that the president had demanded a quid pro quo, something for something, from President Zelensky. In this instance it was to extort the Ukrainian president by exchanging critically needed weapons for an investigation into Biden. A month later, the whistleblower complaint would be published in a *Washington Post* article.[89]

Because House Intelligence Committee chairman Adam Schiff is required by law to be notified of these types of complaints, this set off alarm bells. Schiff recognized clear malfeasance on Trump's part and possibly an impeachable offense. He sent a demand letter to Secretary Pompeo seeking documents on Rudy Giuliani's smear efforts against Biden.[90] In response, State Department staff acknowledged that they had helped arrange meetings between Giuliani and Ukrainian officials subsequent to Trump's July 25 call with Zelensky.[91] Schiff then demanded the full whistleblower complaint be delivered to the House committee. In response, Trump, sensing trouble, fired his national security adviser John Bolton, one of the few who opposed the secret plan.[92] On September 20, the *Wall Street Journal* broke the news to the public.[93] In the face of media pressure, Trump admitted that he had discussed Biden but denied there was anything wrong with it, calling it "beautiful." At this admission, Schiff launched an investigation and the movement to impeach Trump took off.[94]

Impeachment

On September 22, 2019, Adam Schiff formally demanded that President Trump be impeached. Two days later, Speaker of the House Nancy Pelosi announced an impeachment inquiry. The Trump administration went into complete denial and attempted to cover its tracks. Trump released a partial transcript of the second Zelensky call that, contrary to his intentions, actually provided the final straw. The transcript validated everything the whistleblower alleged and even added the missing context. Trump had said this to Zelensky:

> I would like you to do us a favor, though, because our country has been through a lot and Ukraine knows a lot about it. I would like you to find out what happened with this whole situation with Ukraine, they say CrowdStrike.... I guess you have one of your wealthy people... The server, they say Ukraine has it. There are a lot of things that went on, the whole situation. I think you're surrounding yourself with some of the same people. I would like to have the Attorney General call you or your people and I would like you to get to the bottom of it. As you saw yesterday, that whole nonsense ended with a very poor performance by a man named Robert Mueller, an incompetent performance, but they say a lot of it started with Ukraine. Whatever you can do, it's very important that you do it, if that's possible.[95]

But that wasn't the last of Trump's troubles. In a surprising blow, Lev Parnas and Igor Fruman were arrested in early October 2019 at Dulles airport while trying to board a flight to Europe. They were charged with campaign finance fraud, and subsequent investigations tied them closely to Trump. Parnas and Fruman decided to cooperate closely with the House investigations, releasing many documents that revealed the plot against Joe Biden. The House inquiry also saw testimony from ambassadors Bill Kent and George Taylor, Ambassador Yovanovich, and Lt. Col. Alexander Vindeman. Ambassador Gordon Sondland, a campaign donor who worked specifically on this assignment, stated in his written statement:

> Fourth, as I testified previously, Mr. Giuliani's requests were a quid pro quo for arranging a White House visit for President Zelensky. Mr. Giuliani demanded that Ukraine make a public statement announcing investigations of the 2016 election/DNC server and Burisma. Mr. Giuliani was expressing the desires of the President of the United States, and we knew that these investigations were important to the President.... I know that members of this Committee have frequently framed these complicated issues in the form of a simple question: Was there a "quid pro quo"? As I testified previously, with regard to the requested White House call and White House meeting, the answer is yes.

The proceedings to impeach Trump went quickly. On December 12, the House Judiciary Committee drafted two charges against Donald Trump. The committee then voted 23–17 to impeach.[96] On January 15, 2020, the two Articles of Impeachment—one for abuse of power and one for obstruction of Congress—were delivered to the Senate.[97] A week later, on January 22, Adam Schiff and other House members presented the opening arguments.[98] This was followed three days later by Trump's defense.[99] In his powerful closing remarks, Adam Schiff made clear that Trump was unfit to remain in the Oval Office:

> We must say enough—enough! He has betrayed our national security, and he will do so again.... He has compromised our elections, and he will do so again. You will not change him. You cannot constrain him. He is who he is. Truth matters little to him. What's right matters even less, and decency matters not at all.

Alas, it was no use. The Republican-controlled Senate quickly acquitted Trump 52–48 on count one and 53–47 on count two.[100] Trump was off the hook. To celebrate, he started firing everyone who had testified against him. His revenge on America, and against the 60 percent of Americans who supported his removal, was already in motion. He was about to commit mass murder of the American electorate through an unprecedented mix of selfishness, indifference, and sheer incompetence.

CHAPTER 17

Fixing a Fractured Democracy

These are the times that try men's souls.

—Thomas Paine

How do we fix a broken nation? With forty million out of work after the coronavirus pandemic, hundreds of thousands dead, a nation in flames from racial strife, and a white supremacist president who is hated by the majority of Americans, it's no question that the nation is utterly broken. After the Civil War, the wounds were also physical and psychological, but the underlying solution was thought to lie with embracing the Constitution and letting bygones be bygones. Today, the attacks on the Constitution are insidious. Though the Constitution has remained intact, the ideas behind it have morphed into a hideous monstrosity encapsulated in the visage of one man: Donald J. Trump. Trump promises if American voters follow him, all of the American ideals will be theirs—but in the end, the only ones who prosper are white, rich, or both.

We have entered what could be the worst period in American history unless we do something about it. As I close out this three-part book series on Trump's time as president, I want to look at how to move forward in the midst of this wreckage and assure the American people that it can be done—it just requires some reflection.

People of Good Character

As chief executive, the president is more than the most powerful person in the world; the president is caretaker of the largest and most devoted republic. The electoral process is supposed to be a selection and vetting process the people use to choose the first citizen, who is sworn to uphold and defend the Constitution. For 243 years, American elections have also been a character test, wherein the best of all citizens are freely selected to be the leader of 340 million. At its base, the electoral contest has also been a test of a candidate's inherent decency just as much as his or her fortitude.

There are many ways to test the character of a man or woman who would become the president of the United States. The characteristics that best describe the national leader should include compassion, empathy, decisiveness, intellect, and an unwavering desire to defend the principles and rules of the Constitution above all. We believe that the first citizen not only should reflect the best aspects of the national character and embody a personal character that the citizenry can admire and emulate but also, above all things, should understand the American experiment from its founding. The president, as the first citizen, should seek to maintain, defend, and further the success of that experiment.

Additionally, it has always been an unspoken assumption that the person running to represent all Americans should be well versed in, if not a scholar of, the American system of government, the Constitution, and how it all came to be. A certain level of gallantry has always been expected of the president. By *gallantry,* I mean chivalrous honor in form and attitude. Yes, some taking the seat have proved themselves craven and crude, but the head of the first family has usually been a person with a sense of calmness, strength, and refinement. For 243 years, the person occupying the office of the presidency has generally behaved in such a way that it was clear, from the moment they held office, that they feared to let the country down. Even those perennially listed among the worst, like Millard Fillmore, Andrew Johnson, and especially Richard Nixon, worked to advance the nation. The defense of the Constitution is above all else the principal mission of the person behind the Resolute desk. And until 2016, these beliefs held strong and firm across American history.

There can be no better example than our first president, George Washington, who wore the dignity of the office best. For all the stories of his short temper, impatience, and subsequent suffering, Washington always led in both combat and government with the belief that patience, persistence guarded by strong intellect, and reliance upon the intelligence of others around him would lead providence to bless the nation. Yes, Washington kept slaves and occasionally let his temper fly, but he remains, by far, the ultimate example of how America's leaders should comport themselves in the Oval Office.

The United States Constitution was designed to stop authoritarian rule à la George III. It separated powers among Congress, the presidency, and the judiciary to ensure checks and balances on extremism from any branch were in place. It guaranteed the system would maintain the laws enshrined in the Constitution.

Abraham Lincoln is also a cherished example of how balance, consideration, and tweaking the system with a wink and a nod would lead to success not only in war but also legislatively in the midst of a tumult that was literally tearing the nation in two. Through his strong, unwavering belief in the founding principles of the Constitution, he achieved the Herculean task of holding together two opposing philosophies while simultaneously freeing millions from bondage. He did it with such grace, aplomb, and gallantry that it is no surprise he is a martyr to the nation. As is the case with persons of good heart who care more for others than for themselves, they often see not the assassin's bullet.

Theodore Roosevelt was a brash political figure who emerged as a warrior not only in action but in spirit, who recognized the beauty and greatness of the nation. Roosevelt did more for the country than just establishing the national park system; he also volunteered to go into combat. At his own expense, he participated in the Spanish-American War, deploying to Cuba and charging up San Juan Hill. He was the leader and founder of the American environmentalist movement, at a time when the robber barons were stripping the nation of all the resources they could find.

The list goes on. President Franklin D. Roosevelt understood the lessons that had gone unlearned in World War I when he defied Congress and gave aid to Winston Churchill and Great Britain through the lend-lease program. On the cusp of a second world war, he understood that standing with our allies was the greatest defense of our ocean-bound nation. President Harry S. Truman had to make the momentous personal decision to drop not one but two atomic bombs on Japan. Dwight D. Eisenhower, former supreme commander of all forces in the European theater, literally saved the Western world from Hitler's conquering murderers. Yet, when Eisenhower became president, he took on the established powers and warned the nation against falling in love with wars and the profits that stem from them. His warnings were ignored.

Of all the presidents, one of the most dedicated to maintaining the standards, norms, and ceremony of the presidency was the first black president. Barack H. Obama had an almost feverish passion for demonstrating the dignity and grace expected of anyone in the White House. He reflected on the routes many past leaders had taken, particularly those of Washington, Lincoln, and FDR. His graceful manner and fierce intellect are fine examples of the success of the American experiment. At the same time, his intellectual brilliance and dedication, not only to our nation but also to those around the world, helped him stop the collapse of the American and world economy. Obama defended our honor by bringing to justice Osama bin Laden, a man who mass-murdered three thousand of our citizens.

Since we are expounding on leadership, we should note that our armed forces employ a centuries-old method for producing leaders of substance. Their focus on honor is reflected in their mottos: The US Navy: *Courage. Honor. Commitment.* The US Army: *Duty. Honor. Country*. The US Air Force: *Integrity first. Service before self. Excellence in all we do.* The US Marines Corps values are established in the Latin phrase *Semper Fidelis*: "Always Faithful." And the US Coast Guard has its ever-proven *Semper Paratus,* which means "Always Ready." These are the deeply held principles for which tens of thousands of men and women have sacrificed their lives to keep our flag unsullied and to advance the cause of freedom and democracy.

The most important trait of our military servicepeople is that they be men and women of character. When we say *character*, we mean that they must love their country and embody personal integrity. They must maintain a code of honor and be ready and willing to fight and die to uphold these principles. Many presidents had experience serving in war: George Washington, Ulysses S. Grant, Theodore Roosevelt, William McKinley, James Garfield, Rutherford B. Hayes, Richard Nixon, Gerald Ford, John F. Kennedy, and George H. W. Bush. Regardless, the president is also commander in chief and should live by the same honor code as the armed forces.

Dave Richard Palmer is a retired US Army lieutenant general and a military historian. In a discussion of George Washington's travails in dealing with the treachery of General Benedict Arnold, Palmer invokes the name of Colonel Joshua Lawrence Chamberlain, the hero of one of the most decisive battles at Gettysburg.[1] Chamberlain distinguished himself and his small regiment, the 20th Maine, by standing firm in an untenable position at a critical time and juncture when his faltering could have led to the complete collapse of the Union battle lines. Had Chamberlain failed, the Civil War might have quickly ended—and ended badly for the Union. America, as we know it now, might have been rent asunder into competing nations that would have likely gone on to battle each other in other wars.

The Southern army was led by slaveholders and rebels who held out hope that, by destroying the army of the republic, their rebel nation would defeat the heart of the original United States of America. The Northern army was mobilized to restore the great union. Gettysburg would be the forge of either future nation, and Chamberlain's position was the fault line between saving America and splitting it permanently in two. When pressed by Southern forces, which were attacking uphill at Little Round Top, Chamberlain's men could barely hold the Union right flank. If Chamberlain collapsed, America likely would have collapsed with him. Chamberlain was in a desperate situation: his men had almost run out of ammunition, and at his center, men were falling under withering Confederate gunfire. Except for a small group of men protecting the flag, he was losing cohesion of his forces left, right, and center. At the moment when the enemy was about to storm up the hill and wash them away, Chamberlain saw one chance to save it all.

Palmer, a former superintendent of West Point (the same job Robert E. Lee abandoned to lead the Southern armies), wrote that this moment in history, in particular, should come to define the American character. With the entire army in peril, Chamberlain ordered his last companies to organize into lines and fix their bayonets. Without ammunition, they would storm down on the gathering Southerners with only the slightest hope that the surge of steel and charging men would break the Southern assault. They did so, and so it did. In that instant, America was saved by this one act of bravery. A self-effacing man, Chamberlain attributed the measure of his men, who could make such a courageous and risky attack in the face of a tsunami of death, to one trait—character. In his own words:

> The lesson impressed on me as I stand here and my heart and mind traverse your faces, and the years that are gone is that in a great, momentous struggle like this commemorated here, it is character that tells. I do not mean simply or chiefly bravery. Many a man has that, who may become surprised or disconcerted at a sudden change in the posture of affairs. What I mean by character is a firm and seasoned substance of soul. I mean such qualities or acquirements as intelligence, thoughtfulness, conscientiousness, right-mindedness, patience, fortitude, long-suffering and unconquerable resolve.[2]

It bears repeating that Chamberlain, a man tempered in the forge of one of America's greatest battles, saw character as a "firm and seasoned substance of soul." Virtually all of our American presidents have stood firm in their character, taking actions that ensured the nation came first, their generally oversized egos placed in check in relation to their moment in history, their wealth and fortunes set aside for the good of the American republic.

You've seen the evidence I have laid out on America in the era of Donald Trump. *What say ye now?*

Donald Trump's presidency is proof that he has none of the character traits we desire in a leader. The first three years of the Trump White

House not only have shown the world a man who is incapable of the job of president but also have revealed who Donald J. Trump truly is: a man without substance of the soul. Trump's existence is a master class in all of the personality faults one could imagine. He is a human rending of the garments that measure a person's worth in life; a walking, talking alternate universe, where the traits and mottos of our national services are reversed; a national "leader" for whom the values of duty, honor, country, courage, gallantry, commitment, excellence, selflessness, and sacrifice are unacceptable. He leads a world where disgrace, dishonor, and ruthlessness are admired and provide the perfect adhesion for a family-run kleptocracy. Trump is the antithesis of George Washington; he's much more like the Roman emperor and tyrant Caligula. And now, he has killed just as many as Caligula, too.

Author Steven Beschloss reflected on the present state of the presidency brilliantly: "One day, we'll have a president again who's not a demagogue, a fraud, a malignant narcissist and conman bent on exploiting the office to enrich himself and serve his foreign masters. One day we'll have a president again who cares about democracy, improving lives and justice. We will."[3]

Until such time, we must examine what we do know about Donald J. Trump: a man who has lacked courage his entire life. When the nation called, he showed himself a coward by dodging the draft and service in the Vietnam War five times. During that period, more than 16,592 men would die and 87,388 would be wounded. Trump himself joked on the *Howard Stern Show* that he served America by avoiding venereal diseases from prostitutes in New York City as his own personal Vietnam.[4]

Trump lacks the intellect that guides and moderates a truly accomplished man, save his mean-spirited cruel cleverness, that of tricksters, sociopaths, and confidence men who can convince others to relinquish all that they value for promises made of hot air and quick lies. He lacks both patience and thoughtfulness—a litany of memoirs document his volcanic explosions of hate, anger, vindictiveness, and rancor. Trump's lack of self-control is legendary. He exhibits impulsiveness, self-absorption, and a crass quickness to abuse, many times in the form of sexual assault on women—there are currently no less than twenty-five sexual assault accusations against him.

He shows no conscientiousness because he lacks a conscience. He trusts only his "gut" and the lessons of his hate-filled mentor, Roy Cohn, a Trump family lawyer who was famous for steering Senator Joseph McCarthy through one of the most disgraceful moments in American history. Trump's mental fitness is so questionable that acting attorney general Rod Rosenstein thought the Twenty-Fifth Amendment, which removes a president from power due to incapacity, could be enacted if someone were to wear a listening device in a meeting with the president.[5] Of the characteristics Colonel Chamberlain listed, Trump possesses only two: fortitude and long-suffering resolve. However, these are dismissible because they are oriented in the wrong direction: Trump's fortitude is employed only in the destruction of the norms of American society. His pathological lying, cursing, demeaning, insulting, and visceral spitefulness barely allow him the title of human being.

Finally, behold his unconquerable resolve to tear apart America as it has existed since its inception. Trump has proven to the world that he does not love America because he has never known America. To him, America is the privilege of the richest of the rich, and its Stars and Stripes can be traded and sold around the globe by those wealthiest few who share his view that green money has no borders. He has taken some of our great secrets and the products of the daily duty of tens of thousands of American soldiers, sailors, airman, Marines, guardsmen, and intelligence warriors and has traded them away for personal profit. His utter lack of a center, of any palpable soul, belies his one true core value: self-love.

Resolve to never again allow this to happen to America. Ensure that when you utter his name, as happens with the names of Benedict Arnold and Charles Lee, you do so with a Looney Tunes–like spit on the ground.

Deprogram Your Neighbors

As one Twitter follower queried: "How do we un-ring the bell of insidious internal subversion?" The problem is that we cannot. What was done was done. The fabric of the United States has not unwoven; it has been torn along the length of its stripes, for the first time since 1860. The potential for an autocracy is real. The pervasive transition from democracy to autocracy has been so insidious that Nina Khrushcheva, a professor at the New School in New York and granddaughter to Soviet premier Nikita Khrushchev, once said, "As a former Soviet citizen, I am frequently overcome by a horror-movie feeling of fear and disbelief. It's almost as if I don't know where I am. In cosmopolitan New York? Or back in monotonous Moscow, listening to Soviet leaders boasting from the Kremlin about Communism's drummed-up victories and denouncing their illusory enemies?"[6]

This indicates how much American politics has changed and how it is morphing into something unrecognizable. The Trump presidency has come to feel like an unbridled psycho-cyberwar. A wild mélange of psychological warfare that keeps the mind in a swirl of madness at all times but delivers, through careful manipulation, a new reality through cyber systems—our mobile phones, televisions, and computers. Almost 40 percent of Americans act as if they are Russian citizens, loyal to Vladimir Putin. Perhaps a component of the Russian strategy is that over time Americans will come to see Russian influence as a natural companion to their own political worldview in the post-Obama era. One commenter referred to the Republicans' co-option as the "Russian invasion of the body snatchers." Perhaps that's somewhat true. Many loyal Trump followers have been steeped in radical evangelical and orthodox Christianity and white ethnonationalism; they are virulently antiterrorism, anti-Islam, and anti-immigrant. They see themselves as pilgrims on a mission to save global Christendom. To President Putin, the ex-KGB officer and spymaster, they are only easily duped fellow travelers, in spy parlance. He consumes them because, like the shmoo, they want to be eaten.

There remain many, many vulnerabilities that the Russians can exploit in the future. My friend, author Jonathan McCullough, wrote in a letter his exasperation with the trend away from democracy to autocracy: "Probably the worst and most easily-exploited American vulnerability is the greed of our elites. We created the oligarchs and now the Trumps, Mercers, Kochs and Kushners want to have an autocratic society where there are two states—one for billionaires and the other for the rest of us, just like in Russia, where state authority is exercised against the citizenry on behalf of Gazprom and Exxon-Mobil."[7]

President Franklin Delano Roosevelt described the challenges of an America that had come under the sway of a "money first" ideology, which had literally bankrupted the nation and left millions starving. "We had to struggle with the old enemies of peace—business and financial monopoly, speculation, reckless banking, class antagonism, sectionalism, war profiteering. They had begun to consider the Government of the United States as a mere appendage to their own affairs. We know now that Government by organized money is just as dangerous as Government by organized mob."[8]

A bipartisan group of representatives want to meet the Russian challenge, but many in the Republican Party have found common cause with Moscow. Supporting Trump as a person appears to have supplanted their patriotism. Presidential leadership is needed to steer government to identify and meet the challenges of the Russian attack head-on. However, Trump, ostensibly beholden to Putin, is doing the opposite: he is helping a foreign intelligence agency attack his own nation by pushing its discredited false news.

Never before in our history has a president actively worked against an investigation and furthered the goals of a foreign power against the national interests of America—but here we are.

Adopt the Finnish Method

Russian disinformation expert Nina Jankowicz notes that although Russia has been engaging in disinformation and propaganda techniques for decades, its new disinformation tactics no longer focus on pro-Russia propaganda but rather on a strategic approach of sowing discord among Americans by exploiting our nation's vulnerabilities, like stoking racial tensions and other highly charged societal issues like abortion, LGBTQ and gender issues, religion, and immigration. With the advancement of technologies, it is able to use social media to inject its disinformation and amplify its message of distrust using troll farms and ultimately impacting millions of Americans.

In her article "The Disinformation Vaccination," Jankowicz wrote: "What we need is something familiar to many who have worked in foreign assistance: capacity-building. But rather than mounting such an effort abroad, we should pursue it for our own people. It's a harder, longer process, but one that seeks to move beyond band-aids and vaccinate against the virus, prioritizing the citizens who fall victim to disinformation."[9]

The Pew Research Center found only 19 percent of Americans "trusted government" in October 2016, and another study from the 2017 Edelman Trust Barometer claims that "trust is in crisis around the world."[10] Rough estimates suggest that only 20 percent of Americans "place a lot of trust" in national media, while two-thirds, or 66 percent, get some of their news from social media.[11] These numbers are proof we have our work cut out for us.

Decades of psychological research show that attempting to debunk often repeated lies is extremely difficult. Given that Russia has been attacking Western democracies across the globe, as I wrote extensively in *The Plot to Destroy Democracy*, some countries have perfected their defense systems because they've had so much practice. With their proximity to Russia, Finland and Ukraine have experienced these attacks decades longer than the United States has. They have employed citizen-focused solutions to combat this nebulous and dangerous propaganda warfare tactic.

Alice Stollmeyer, Belgian founder of the cyberawareness group Defending Democracy, told the *Washington Post* about the global disinformation network arrayed particularly against democracies. "It's a whole ecosystem.... It's no longer just state-backed, but it's of domestic origin as well.... There's a shift from misleading facts to misleading narratives—and it's not just one article or tweet, but a tapestry that's being woven all year long."[12] Stollmeyer recommends we apply several of the digital literacy solutions that Finland has successfully deployed, including these:

- Equip every citizen with digital skills and educate all in digital literacy.
- Strengthen and support an independent media and fact checkers.
- Adopt electoral laws that are sensitive and adaptable to the digital era.

Jed Willard, director of the FDR Center for Global Engagement at Harvard University, consulted with the government of Finland and recommended that the country focus "on telling the country's story instead of responding directly to Russian lies. The program is now finishing its third year."[13] Willard attributes Finland's success to several of its traits: its decades-long experience with Russia's disinformation campaigns, which gives it an advantage in understanding and preparing a defense; its ability to understand how difficult it is to unpack the lies of the propaganda; and its willingness to trust that a new way of "storytelling" and a concurrent educational program are the country's best defense.

"The Finns have made a concerted effort to educate their military, civilian, and journalistic leadership on the social science behind it," Willard said, which empowers officials to make more strategic decisions and ultimately to produce a more compelling public narrative. "They didn't look for purely technical solutions or quick fixes, as some other states have."[14]

In addition to training their military, civilian, and journalistic leadership, the Finns took it to the classrooms: they established an educational campaign to combat disinformation, starting with children at a very early age. The leadership of Finland has an established belief system that "media and information literacy—which is predicated on critical thinking," is a mandatory "civic competence."[15]

It is imperative that the United States immediately adopt and implement this long-range, sweeping educational campaign in all facets of American life. Without it, the nation's citizens will further descend into unthinking, uncaring drones trapped in their own information bubbles—thoughtless, that is, until fed thoughts by an evil actor.

White Helmets of Democracy

In 2017, Hamilton 68, created by the Alliance for Securing Democracy, was set up to track Russian hashtags and other Russian disinformation activities online. The tool was fine-tuned to monitor approximately six hundred accounts. Analysts such as J. M. Berger joined up with Jonathan Morgan, Andrew Weisburd, and former FBI agent Clint Watts to develop this system to analyze Russian influence operations on social media, notably on Twitter. The site was designed to be a real-time analysis tool for tracking Russian propaganda.

The analysts divided the six hundred accounts into three categories for examination. According to Berger, the first type includes accounts that actively share overt disinformation from sources like RT and Sputnik.[16] The second is any account that has a "professed pro-Russian stance" and that shares tweets reflective of Russian policies. The third kind of account includes potential bots used to amplify the messages of accounts in the other two categories.

Empowering and joining an organization like Hamilton 68 gives us a third-party early warning system of the waves of bot and troll incursions that swell before an attack. Finding the leading edge of disinformation offensives and exposing their methods of interference is a critical component to stopping them.

Last Chance for Democracy

Meanwhile, we are entertained with social distractions, as has always been the case when countries are crept up on unawares. In our fantasy of ourselves as a powerful nation, we believe we are a redoubt—impenetrable. Though our sophisticated intelligence operations worked cooperatively and in unison, in 2016 we were still blindsided—just as we were that fateful day of September 11, 2001—by simple, low-budget terrorism that required nothing more than imagination, a choreographed effort, and an abundance of malice.

In the 1950s, theologian and philosopher Reinhold Niebuhr wrote a stunning warning at the end of his *The Irony of American History* that now seems fresh and applicable in the age of Trump: "If we should perish, the ruthlessness of the foe would be only the secondary cause of the disaster. The primary cause would be that the strength of a giant nation was directed by eyes too blind to see all the hazards of the struggle; and the blindness would be induced not by some accident of nature or history, but by hatred and vainglory."[17]

The only word to use here is *abdication*. So obsequiously has Congress, both House and Senate, abdicated its role as protector of America that it openly does the bidding of foreign agents and assets in its midst. Congress itself has corrupted justice and the American electorate. Congressmen and women publicly vote to disenfranchise Americans from voting in order to save the tyrant they have sworn allegiance to over our beloved Constitution. They toy with treason as casually as with a cup of coffee and are ready to swallow that poison if it can protect their master.

Trump rules as an unpredictable if not highly unstable autocrat-in-training. The highest office has only served to magnify his authoritarian tendencies. At the 2012 Democratic National Convention, First Lady Michelle Obama said, "I have seen firsthand that being president doesn't change who you are—it reveals who you are."[18] When it comes to how the presidency has revealed the character flaws and nature of Trump, MSNBC host Joy-Ann Reid put it succinctly: "I have never observed anyone who is more precisely like his biographers have described him. And Trump's biographers have, to put it mildly, not been kind. He lives inside his own reality, where he is part beloved autocrat/dictator and part main character in a never-ending TV show."[19]

Platitudes

In *Agents of S.H.I.E.L.D.*, the TV show spin-off from the Captain America movies, a band of loyal patriots fights a modern-day derivative of the Nazis that has taken over the US government. They are led by agent Phillip Coulson (the owner of a full set of Captain America trading cards). In the movie *Captain America: The Winter Soldier*, Coulson dies fighting alongside Captain America but is somehow resuscitated. In one crucial episode, Coulson must motivate the American people, who have been brainwashed by the dreaded Hydra administration, to rise up against the fascist government. To do so, he actually uses the phrase "alternative facts," pulled right from the Trump White House. In trying to incite a popular uprising, he chooses the words of Captain America, an old-school patriot cut from the same cloth as those who survived the Depression and World War II: a black-and-white world hero who wears red, white, and blue. To paraphrase Coulson's motivational speech: everyone today has an opportunity to be a patriot. If we all choose to stand up and take a chance to be a part of something bigger, together we can accomplish anything.

The words of Thomas Paine, author of this chapter's epigraph—"These are the times that try men's souls"—inspired me to choose the characters from the Captain America series as examples of true patriots. But the words that follow Paine's famous phrase, written in the freezing winter of 1776, should be our guiding star, allowing each of us to resolve to stand and be part of that bigger picture:

> The summer soldier and the sunshine patriot will, in this crisis, shrink from the service of their country; but he that stands by it now, deserves the love and thanks of man and woman. Tyranny, like hell, is not easily conquered; yet we have this consolation with us, that the harder the conflict, the more glorious the triumph.[20]

We are in the winter of the American republic, and we must make the choice to be the winter soldiers who stand by the nation when the faux sunshine "patriots" seek to sell it out to our ideological enemy.

So now you've been exposed to the truth. "The truth is incontrovertible," Sir Winston Churchill said. "Malice may attack it, ignorance may deride it, but in the end, there it is."

EPILOGUE

Benedict Arnold Vindicated

Instead of me
He promotes Charles Lee
Makes him second-in-command
I'm a general! Wheeee!
—*Hamilton*, the musical

Like everything Trump does, he seeks to eclipse all those who came before him. As he crossed the threshold of making twenty thousand false statements, he became arguably the most documented liar in history.[1] He is assured of winning one more major point: he will likely achieve a greater level of derision than all who come after him.

Judas Iscariot betrayed Jesus Christ, for just thirty pieces of silver.

Donald Trump has clearly made a yeoman's effort to sell the presidency and the hopes and dreams of more than 320 million souls to the greatest enemy of the United States, simply to satisfy his own ego and see his name atop another building. In his mind, he likely thinks he still has time. That the price was not in silver but in citizens' bodies matters not to him. In his estimation, the dead cannot vote.

A man who views himself in superlative terms, Trump apparently decided he would eclipse the treachery of Judas, whose name has come to mean one who betrays another under the guise of friendship, and of General Benedict Arnold, whose name represents the historical definition of betrayal for Americans. No schoolchild would fail to recognize either name. In 1780, Benjamin Franklin noted, "Judas sold one man, [Benedict] Arnold, three million." Perhaps Trump has not considered that he would gallop past both of these renowned scoundrels by exceeding their betrayals.

But here is the part of the story where I must apologize to Trump for believing he exhibited the traits of a traitor like Benedict Arnold because Donald Trump has not betrayed America in the same way Benedict Arnold did. Arnold committed treason by action, inaction, and misdirection. Arnold relished physical danger. He carried out his treason over a period of time. It took cunning and guile and quite a bit of nerve. And when he was found out, he confessed and cleared those below him who didn't know about his treachery. Although earlier in the Revolution Arnold served the nation well, he deserves his inglorious end, sealed in a crypt turned into a kindergarten in St. Mary's Church, Battersea, London. He and Peggy Shippen Arnold share a view of a tropical fish tank and preschool drawings in a well-lit basement.

Trump Is No Benedict Arnold—He Is Charles Lee

Trump has none of the spirt and action of Arnold. After the Mueller report was issued, it became clear that Trump was not the equal of the traitorous General Benedict Arnold. No, he managed to do what many thought he could not: take a poor situation and manipulate those around him to protect his perfidy. Of this trespass, at least, Arnold is clear. Trump's treason, on the other hand, is worse.

Trump, instead, is equal to a lesser-known traitor in American history. His actions and behaviors are closer to those of an ignoble character of the Revolution: Major General Charles Lee.

Major Lee was George Washington's rival for command of the Continental Army. He was also the man the British thought would defect and walk through their door well before they ever imagined Benedict Arnold would. But history would prove their expectations wrong. Lee started his career as a British army major, adventuring around Europe and fighting under General Burgoyne in Portugal. Later he tried to gain a command in the Russian and Polish armies as a mercenary officer. He was commissioned in the Polish army as a major general. After his service there, he traveled to the Americas on half pay as a British army reserve major. Lee bought land in Virginia and became a social force in the colonies. As a major, he took part in Braddock's 1755 incursion against the French and Indians, which led to the decimation of a large British force outside Fort Duquesne in the Battle of the Monongahela. Another colonial officer named Colonel George Washington was present, as well as Lee's neighbor in Virginia, Horatio Gates.

In 1773, he became a cause célèbre in the colonies as an advocate for the Revolution. He proclaimed his military skill and prowess unceasingly and petitioned the Continental Congress nonstop to make him commander in chief over the quiet but focused George Washington. Washington was chosen, and Lee was essentially made his second.

After fighting a running retreat out of New York City, where the British attacked with tens of thousands of men and took the city, Washington had fallen back into New Jersey. Washington ordered Lee to follow but found the major was ignoring his orders and acting as if he were an independent commander. Lee had decided his mission was to do whatever he thought it appropriate to do, to act according to his ego. He removed his forces from the chain of command, thereby acting against Washington's orders.

The effect was to split critical troops away from Washington at a time of crisis. Lee wrote, "We must save the community in spite of the ordinances of the legislature...there are times we must commit treason against the laws of the state for the salvation of the state."[2] He continued in the same letter to explain that he was not disobeying orders so much as ignoring them because his command required "a brave, virtuous kind of treason," necessary to save the Revolution—from General George Washington and the Continental Congress.

While commanding a division under Washington near Jersey Heights, Lee let down his guard and was captured by the notorious British cavalry officer Banastre Tarleton. Lee was taken prisoner and brought to New York and entertained by General Howe. He was allowed to roam the city without guard and seemed to acquiesce to the British, becoming very solicitous of General Howe. He seemed to enjoy his time as captive, even winning $500 in a local lottery, but much later it would come out that he lived in fear that London would brand him a deserter of the British army, which technically he was, and execute him. So he may have become quite compliant indeed.

Lee was eventually returned to the American army in 1777 as part of a prisoner exchange. Washington needed his second in command and gave the man a chance to redeem himself, thinking Lee would be ready to take on the British again. In the summer of 1778, Lee was given the task of engaging British forces near Monmouth Court House in New Jersey. The British troops, led by General Sir Henry Clinton, were attempting to escape to Sandy Hook, where they could be moved offshore by the Royal Navy.

On a broiling summer day, the Americans, with forces equal in size to those of the British, held lines against three British assaults. But the fog of battle and a misunderstood tactical withdrawal by the Marquis de Lafayette made Lee think he should also withdraw. Although it was an orderly operation, Washington rode into the thick of it and found Lee retreating. Washington, in a foul mood, tore into Lee with a hurricane of insults and curses and relieved him of command on the spot. Never has such a momentous firing occurred before or after in American history. Though some say General MacArthur's firing by President Harry Truman is the greatest in our country's history, imagine being fired, in combat, by General George Washington himself.

Lee had the nerve to stammer out: "You know all this was against my advice."

Labeled a "damned poltroon" by Washington, Lee was sent to the rear to await his court-martial. Washington then took charge and brought the battle from the brink of disaster to a stalemate that was eventually called a victory when British General Clinton left the field. Lee was soon court-martialed for (1) disobeying direct orders to attack the British, (2) misbehavior in the face of the enemy for his retreat, and (3) insulting the commander in chief, George Washington. He was found guilty.

In an exchange of letters, Alexander Hamilton wrote to his friend Elias Boudinot about the battle and Lee's behavior:

> We, in all probability should have had, had not the finest opportunity America ever possessed been fooled away by a man, in whom she has placed a large share of the most ill-judged confidence. You will have

> heard enough to know, that I mean General Lee. This man is either a driveler in the business of soldiership or something much worse.[3]

Hamilton had much to say about Lee. He viewed Lee as a man who had tried to dispose of Washington and believed him to be a traitor. He said Lee maintained "a certain preconceived and preposterous notion of his being a very great man. Which always operated in his favor."

Rumors flew about Lee's behavior during his New York captivity the previous year. His subsequent behavior at Monmouth, perhaps not entirely fairly evaluated, made many wonder aloud whether his errors were in fact errors at all. Their concerns were well founded. The whisperings about Major General Charles Lee went on right until his death.

What was not known until 1857, more than half a century later, was that while in captivity Lee had drafted a plan for his captor, General Howe, that could help the British quickly destroy the American Revolution. All Lee wanted in return was for his lands in Virginia to be preserved and to be rewarded should the British win. General Lee's information caused the British to abandon their original plan to take the northeastern colonies and decide instead to effect Lee's plan and take the Chesapeake Bay region, thereby hoping to split the colonies in two.

But fortune favors not only the bold but often those with a just cause. Unfortunately for Lee, George Washington learned that Arnold, already gone over to the other side, would be leading the British expedition to Chesapeake Bay. The pain of Arnold's treachery had cut Washington deeply.

Under Arnold's command, American Loyalist militias had carried out raids in Connecticut against American patriots. They had burned the village of New London and slaughtered eighty of Washington's soldiers at nearby Fort Griswold, even after the troops had surrendered.

Washington ordered a special operation of one thousand select men from the West Point garrison to go south and destroy Arnold's command in the Chesapeake area. He ordered the Marquis de Lafayette to execute Arnold in "the most summary way" if Lafayette should capture him.[4] Washington's burning desire to capture Arnold inadvertently led him to shift his forces to a major campaign that, by sheer fortune, eventually led to Cornwallis's surrender and the end of the war.

So Arnold is vindicated at least on this point: Lee, not Arnold, is a more appropriate role model in treachery for Donald Trump. Lee's villainy was not discovered for seven decades. Perhaps, as in Lee's case, only future historians will discover and record Trump's obvious villainy. Yet there are heroes among us today who are working to shine a light on the man who could arguably be called, just three years into his administration, the worst president in American history. I leave you once again with former CIA director John Brennan:

> When the full extent of your venality, moral turpitude, and political corruption becomes known, you will take your rightful place as a disgraced demagogue in the dustbin of history. You may scapegoat Andy McCabe, but you will not destroy America.... America will triumph over you.

The Players Glossary

Team Trump

Stephen Bannon Former senior adviser to the president and his campaign and Breitbart founder; has ties with European alt-right and Cambridge Analytica.

William Barr Attorney general after Jeff Sessions; summarized the Mueller report after likely pressuring its early conclusion; Trump protector, called the investigation "misconceived" before appointment.

Tom Barrack Real estate investor; close friend of Donald Trump and Paul Manafort; arranged the inauguration events, Russia apologist.

Michael Caputo Trump campaign adviser and Roger Stone acolyte; lived in Russia in the '90s, worked for Gazprom when back in the United States, left the Trump campaign in June 2016.

Sam Clovis Trump campaign adviser; recruited Carter Page, had meetings with George Papadopoulos.

Michael Cohen Donald Trump's lawyer; worked Trump Tower deal in Moscow and arranged hush money payments; denied he met in Prague with Russian intelligence cutouts as alleged in the Steele dossier; pleaded guilty to lying to Congress, campaign finances violations, and tax evasion.

Jerome Corsi Conspiracy theorist, Roger Stone friend, and WikiLeaks contact.

Randy Credico WBAI radio host, Julian Assange friend, and Roger Stone associate.

Rick Dearborn Former chief of staff of Senator Jeff Sessions and White House deputy chief of staff; tried to arrange Trump-Putin meeting in June 2016.

Tad Devine Bernie Sanders's campaign chief; worked with Paul Manafort for Viktor Yanukovych and Party of Regions.

TONY FABRIZIO Pollster, Republican strategist, owner of Multi Media Services, and Paul Manafort colleague.

MICHAEL FLYNN Former national security adviser, former army general, and former head of the Defense Intelligence Agency; involved in back-channel discussions and met with Sergey Kislyak, pleaded guilty to lying to investigators over contacts with Russians.

RICHARD GATES Lobbying partner with Paul Manafort; pleaded guilty of tax evasion and money laundering, then became witness for the special counsel against Paul Manafort.

LAURANCE GAY Head of Rebuilding America Now PAC and Paul Manafort associate.

J. D. GORDON National security and foreign policy adviser to the Trump campaign; arranged the Ukraine Republican National Committee (RNC) platform change; met with Maria Butina prior to campaign and Sergey Kislyak after the RNC.

SEAN HANNITY Fox News personality, Trump ally, and informal adviser.

HOPE HICKS Executive vice president and chief communications officer for Fox News and former White House communications director; Trump talked about the Russia probe with her in the room; Russian officials attempted to contact her after the election.

SARAH HUCKABEE SANDERS Former White House press secretary; confessed to lying repeatedly to American public for Donald Trump.

JARED KUSHNER White House senior adviser and Ivanka Trump's husband; involved in most of the back-channel meetings with Russians.

ED KUTLER Lobbyist for Mercury Group working with Party of Regions and Viktor Yanukovych.

PAUL MANAFORT Donald Trump's former campaign chief; worked for Viktor Yanukovych and Rinat Akhmetov, worked with Konstantine Kilimnik, owed Oleg Deripaska; convicted of failure to report foreign lobbying, tax evasion, and money laundering along with partner Richard Gates.

K. T. MCFARLAND Former deputy national security adviser to Michael Flynn; lied about Flynn-Kislyak meeting, wrote in December 2016 email that Russia had "thrown" the election to Donald Trump.

STEPHEN MILLER White House policy adviser on hardline immigration policy; allegedly spoke with George Papadopoulos about the "interesting messages" from Joseph Mifsud and Moscow.

George Nader Lebanese American businessman and lobbyist; key conduit for back-channel communications; met in Trump Tower in December 2016 with campaign officials in the then UAE with Russian and American officials.

Devin Nunes US House representative and former House Intelligence Committee chair; Trump apologist, visited White House to get information on FISA warrants disclosed to him by Trump staff.

Carter Page American energy analyst in Russia and foreign policy adviser to the Trump campaign; worked for major companies, including Gazprom; targeted by Russian spies in 2013 and served as a key node to Russia in the Steele dossier; left the Trump campaign in September 2016 when his ties became public.

George Papadopoulos Foreign policy adviser to the Trump campaign; learned in April 2016 about Russians having Democratic National Committee emails through Joseph Mifsud; unsuccessfully tried to arrange meeting between Donald Trump and Vladimir Putin; convicted of making false statements to the FBI about his contacts with Russian agents.

Brad Parscale Digital media coordinator for the Trump 2016 campaign and manager for the Trump 2020 campaign; linked with Cambridge Analytica.

Michael Pence Vice president, handpicked by Paul Manafort; claimed no knowledge of any Russian involvement despite having led the transition that saw many Russian interactions.

Richard Pinedo Brokered stolen identities and bank accounts to Russian hackers, convicted by the special counsel of identity theft.

Reince Priebus Former chief of staff; discussed the Russia probe with Donald Trump, called the Trump Tower meeting a "nothingburger."

Erik Prince American businessman, former US Navy SEAL officer, founder and former CEO and chairman of Blackwater, and brother of Betsy DeVos, the secretary of education; worked with George Nader and Kirill Dmitriev, attended the Seychelles meeting to create back channel with Russia.

Anthony Scaramucci Former communications director; met with Kirill Dmitriev in January 2017, then publicly discounted effect of sanctions.

Jeff Sessions Former attorney general and former US senator; Donald Trump's first national political supporter, involved in national security and foreign policy for campaign, repeatedly denied meeting Kislyak, recused himself from Russia probe due to his ties to Russian officials.

Sean Spicer Former White House press secretary; sought out by Robert Mueller to discuss why he lied about Michael Flynn and Donald Trump's dealings with Russian officials.

Roger Stone Political consultant, lobbyist, and strategist; Paul Manafort and Donald Trump ally; interacted with WikiLeaks and the GRU looking for DNC and Clinton emails; corresponded frequently with Randy Credico and Jerome Corsi about WikiLeaks releases; charged with lying to House Intelligence Committee and obstruction of justice.

Rex Tillerson Former secretary of state; worked with Sechin for Exxon deal, received the Order of Friendship from Russia.

Donald Trump Jr. Executive vice president of the Trump Organization and eldest son of Donald Trump and first wife, Ivana Trump; involved in numerous extracurricular meetings with Russian intelligence officers and oligarchs, communicated with WikiLeaks about its stolen releases.

Eric Trump Executive vice president of development and acquisitions of the Trump Organization and third oldest child of Donald Trump and first wife, Ivana Trump; no seeming exposure to any of the Trump-Russia meets and deals.

Ivanka Trump White House adviser and daughter and second oldest child of Donald Trump and first wife, Ivana Trump; involved in Azerbaijan hotel deal.

Alex van der Zwaan Belgian-born Dutch attorney, formerly with Skadden, Arps, Slate, Meagher & Flom law firm; helped Paul Manafort on Ukraine, pleaded guilty to lying to FBI agents about work with Manafort.

Allen Weisselberg Chief financial officer of Trump Organization and Donald Trump's money man; likely moved the money around for the hush payments.

American Officials

Preet Bharara Attorney for the Southern District of New York; fired by Donald Trump on March 11, 2017, for refusing to resign.

James Comey Former FBI director; fired by Donald Trump.

Andrew McCabe Former FBI agent; became acting director of FBI after James Comey firing, fired by Donald Trump.

Robert Mueller Former FBI director, appointed special counsel.

Rod Rosenstein Deputy attorney general, authorized creation of the special counsel.

Peter Strzok Former FBI counterintelligence agent working for the special counsel; removed over appearance of conflict of interest, fired by FBI deputy director David Bowdich.

Sally Yates Former acting attorney general; fired by Donald Trump for not defending Trump's "Muslim ban" in court.

The Russians

Aras Agalarov Russian billionaire and president of Crocus Group; close to Vladimir Putin; partnered with Donald Trump for Miss Universe in Moscow in 2013; involved in planning the June 2016 Trump Tower meeting where Russian operatives offered "dirt" on Hillary Clinton.

Emin Agalarov Singer, vice president of Crocus Group, and son of Aras Agalarov; involved in the 2013 Miss Universe pageant in Moscow and in setting up June 2016 Trump Tower meeting; Donald Trump made a cameo appearance in Emin's music video; was made aware, along with Rob Goldstone, of Trump plans to run for president at luncheon in Trump Tower in May 2015.

Roman Abramovich Russian billionaire, owner of Millhouse Capital, and part owner of Evraz; originally recommended Vladimir Putin as a successor to Boris Yeltsin; Ivanka Trump and Jared Kushner are friends with his former wife Dasha Zhukova.

Rinat Akhmetshin Russian American lobbyist and former Soviet counterintelligence officer; lobbied against the Magnitsky Act, present at the June 2016 Trump Tower meeting.

TEYFIK ARIF Kazakh-born developer and founder of Bayrock Group; partners with Felix Sater on several projects with Donald Trump, had office in Trump Tower.

ANDRII ARTEMENKO Ukrainian politician; met with Michael Cohen and Felix Sater in January 2017 to discuss a pro-Putin Ukrainian "peace plan" and lifting of sanctions against Russia, which Cohen delivered to Michael Flynn in a sealed envelope, a week before Flynn's resignation.

ELENA BARONOFF Vice president of customer relations at Trump Grande in Sunny Isles and "The Russian Hand of Donald Trump"; catered to Eastern European real estate clients.

LEONARD "LEN" BLAVATNIK Soviet-born British American businessman, founder of Access Industries, and business associate of Mikhail Fridman and Viktor Vekselberg; contributed heavily to Republicans (Mitch McConnell, Marco Rubio, Scott Walker, and Lindsey Graham) during 2016 election and $1 million to Donald Trump's inaugural fund.

MARIA BUTINA Russian foreign agent; accused of posing as gun rights activist along with Alexander Torshin to influence the NRA; Butina's boyfriend Paul Erikson tried to arrange a meeting during 2016 election between Butina and Donald Trump in Las Vegas, where she asked Trump his thoughts on Russia; was indicted for trying to establish back channels with American officials on behalf of the Kremlin to influence policies toward Russia and pleaded guilty for conspiring to act as an illegal foreign agent and opted for cooperation.

YURI CHAIKA Prosecutor general of Russia; arranged 2016 Trump Tower meeting through Aras Agalarov and Natalya Veselnitskaya to offer damaging information on Hillary Clinton to the Trump campaign.

OLEG DERIPASKA Russian billionaire, close associate of Vladimir Putin, and founder of Basic Element, Rusal, EN+ Group, and several other sanctioned companies; employed Paul Manafort for over a decade to promote Russian interests in Ukraine, the United States, Georgia, and Kyrgyzstan; Manafort allegedly provided the Trump campaign information to Deripaska during election.

KIRILL DMITRIEV CEO of Russian Direct Investment Fund (RDIF) created by the Russian government; friend of Vladimir Putin's daughter and close Putin ally; in January 2017 met with Blackwater's Erik Prince

(Betsy DeVos's brother) in Seychelles to establish a back channel between Russia and President-elect Trump.

Yuri Dubinin Soviet ambassador in 1980s; met with Donald Trump and arranged Trump's first trip to the Soviet Union in 1987.

Arkady Dvorkovich Russian politician and close confidant of Russian prime minister Medvedev; met with Carter Page during his July 2016 trip to Moscow and expressed strong support for Donald Trump.

Fedor Emilianenko MMA (mixed martial arts) fighter; admired by Vladimir Putin, hired by Donald Trump and Michael Cohen in 2008 for business ventures; questioned by FBI in April 2018.

Dmitry Firtash Ukrainian businessman and head of Group DF board; major backer of pro-Putin Yanukovych, allegedly partnered with Paul Manafort on a real estate project; indicted on racketeering charges and awaiting extradition to the United States in Vienna; Lanny Davis, Michael Cohen's lawyer, worked with Firtash for years.

Mikhail Fridman Cofounder of Alfa Group; in July 2016, a server from Alfa Group was mysteriously found to be communicating with servers in the Trump Organization; was mentioned in the Steele dossier and sued BuzzFeed.

Pavel Fuchs Ukrainian businessman and client of Rudolph Giuliani; close to Vladimir Putin; negotiated Trump Tower Moscow deal in 2006, which never came to fruition, and was present at Trump's inauguration.

Rob Goldstone British publicist; became a Trump acquaintance during the 2013 Miss Universe pageant in Moscow and was present at several meetings; worked closely with Emin Agalarov; met with Agalarov at May 2015 Trump Tower meeting and learned of Donald Trump's plan to run for president; was key in planning the June 2016 Trump Tower meeting with Donald Trump Jr.

Sergey Gorkov Graduate of FSB academy and head of state-run VEB bank during election; close Putin associate; held secret meetings with Jared Kushner during transition period arranged by Russian ambassador Kislyak; involved in attempted recruitment of Carter Page via a Russian spy ring operating in New York City in 2012; VEB bank funded Donald Trump's Toronto project and is suspected of being a front for Russian intel services.

HERMAN GREF CEO of Sberbank, Russia's largest bank, which is under sanctions; met Donald Trump during the 2013 Miss Universe pageant through a dinner arranged by Aras Agalarov.

ANDREW INTRATER Founder of US-based Columbus Nova and Viktor Vekselberg's cousin; donated $250,000 to Trump's inaugural committee, the RNC, and the Trump Victory Committee; attended Trump's inauguration; Columbus Nova funneled over $580,000 to Michael Cohen's company in 2017; Cohen held a Trump Tower meeting with Vekselberg and Intrater in January 2017 to discuss Russia-US relations.

SERGEI IVANOV Former KGB officer and former chief of staff, dismissed in August 2016; longtime Putin ally; according to the Steele dossier, Ivanov was angry at Dmitry Peskov and others for encouraging the attack of US elections, claim not proven.

IRAKLY KAVELADZE Longtime trusted associate of Aras Agalarov; present at most meetings with Trump during the 2013 Miss Universe pageant and present at the June 2016 Trump Tower meeting; was investigated for money-laundering activities via the creation of over two thousand shell companies.

GERMAN KHAN Russian Ukrainian billionaire, former executive director of TNK-BP, and member of Alfa Group Consortium supervisory board; Khan's son-in-law, Alex van der Zwaan, was charged by the special counsel for making false statements about his communications with Rick Gates.

KONSTANTINE KILIMNIK Russian intelligence officer; worked with Paul Manafort and Richard Gates, charged with obstruction of justice and conspiracy to obstruct justice.

SEMYON KISLIN (SAM KISLIN) Ukrainian American businessman; decades of dealings with Trump and Giuliani, suspected of having strong ties to high-level members of Russian organized crime in Russia, Ukraine, and the United States.

SERGEY KISLYAK Russian ambassador to the United States during the 2016 election; held multiple secret meetings and communications with various Trump campaign officials during election and transition period, including easing of sanctions with Michael Flynn and establishing private back-channel communications through Russian facility with Jared Kushner; all the campaign officials who met with

Kislyak lied about their communications; Trump bragged about firing Comey to Kislyak in Oval Office meeting.

DMITRY KLOKOV Former Russian Olympic weightlifter; offered to help get a Trump Tower in Moscow, managed by Ivanka Trump, and introduced Donald Trump to Vladimir Putin during the election.

IGOR KRUTOY Wealthy Ukrainian composer; close Putin ally and friend of Rinat Akhmetov; met with Donald and Ivanka Trump to discuss Trump Tower project in Latvia, which was abandoned after Krutoy was questioned over a criminal investigation by Latvian authorities who asked the FBI to interview Trump in 2014.

SIMON KUKES Russian American businessman; affiliated with Leonard Blavatnik and Viktor Vekselberg; had never made any political donations until two weeks after the June 2016 Trump Tower meeting when he donated $273,000 to Trump and other Republicans in 2016 election and boasted of his "active involvement" in the Trump campaign during the election.

SERHIY LYOVOCHKIN Ukrainian pro-Russian politician and businessman; very influential in the Yanukovych administration; funneled $50,000 to Trump's inaugural fund via Sam Patten; worked with Paul Manafort, who allegedly sent polling data to him via Russian agent Konstantine Kilimnik, although some reports indicate Deripaska.

ALEKSANDER MASHKEVICH Influential businessman with relationships and business holdings in Kazakhstan; known, along with Patokh Chodiev and Alijan Ibragimov, as the Kazakh Trio; was a major backer of Trump Soho via Bayrock Group, Teyfik Arif, and Felix Sater; investigated for associations with influential Russian mafia figures.

VICTOR MEDVEDCHUK Ukrainian politician and oligarch; close to Putin, was in contact with the Trump campaign during election to discuss US-Russia relations.

SERGEI MILLIAN (SIARHEI KUKATS) Belarusian-born American and founder of the Russian American Chamber of Commerce; met Trump in 2007 at the Moscow Millionaires Fair at Crocus Expo (Agalarov's) to discuss attracting Russian investors; met Michael Cohen at Trump Tower and signed an exclusive broker agreement; met and developed a relationship with George Papadopoulos; identified as a source for the Steele dossier.

ANDREI MOLCHANOV Russian politician and businessman and founder of LSR Group; his father was Vladimir Putin's boss in Leningrad University; met with Felix Sater during election to scout sites for Trump Tower Moscow and line up VTB bank financing.

SAM PATTEN Longtime political operative; spent many years in Russia and Ukraine alongside Paul Manafort and Russian intelligence agent Konstantine Kilimnik; has ties to Cambridge Analytica and opened a company with Kilimnik in Washington, DC, in February 2015; pleaded guilty to failure to register as a foreign lobbyist and for steering $50,000 from a pro-Russian Ukrainian oligarch into Trump's inauguration.

DMITRY PESKOV Putin's spokesman since 2000; during 2016 election, Michael Cohen emailed Peskov to discuss Trump Tower Moscow.

VIKTOR PINCHUK Ukrainian businessman and oligarch and founder of investment group EastOne Group; close associate of Rinat Akhmetov; paid Trump $150,000 to appear via a video link to Kiev in September 2015 and paid John Bolton for multiple speaking appearances after the 2016 election.

YEVGENY PRIGOZHIN CEO Russia's Concord Management, Concord Catering, Wagner Mercenary Private Military Contractors Group, "Putin's chef"; intelligence subcontractor to GRU: Internet Research Agency.

VLADIMIR PUTIN President of Russia; former KGB agent, former head of FSB, and former prime minister, appointed by Boris Yeltsin.

ROTEM ROSEN Right-hand man of Lev Leviev, a close Putin associate involved in a real estate deal with Jared Kushner; married Tamir Sapir's daughter at Mar-a-Lago; joined Sapir Organization dealing with Trump Soho; attended the 2013 Miss Universe pageant as an associate of Michael Cohen.

ANDREY ROZOV Developer in Russia and CEO of IC Expert; partnered with Felix Sater and Michael Cohen to develop Trump Tower Moscow, including signing a letter of intent.

SERGEI RYABKOV Counselor at the Russian embassy in DC and deputy minister of foreign affairs; acknowledged Russian contacts with the Trump campaign.

TAMIR SAPIR Georgian businessman; opened electronics store in New York City with Sam Kislin in the late '70s; Sapir and his son Alex Sapir partnered with Trump organization for the Trump Tower Soho project; introduced Trump to Pavel Fuchs, a Ukrainian oligarch close to Putin, to develop a Trump Tower in 2006.

Felix Sater Russian American businessman, former managing director of Bayrock Group, and convicted felon; worked with Trump through Bayrock (including Trump SoHo) and directly for Trump Organization; worked with Michael Cohen, Ivanka Trump, and Donald Trump Jr. to develop Trump Tower Moscow.

Igor Sechin Former KGB agent, former deputy Russian prime minister of Russia, Putin's right-hand man, and executive chairman of state-owned oil company Rosneft; sanctioned for his role in Putin's invasion of Crimea; mentioned in the Steele dossier regarding meeting with Carter Page to seek lifting of sanctions in return for a Page stake in Rosneft; US intelligence officials investigated whether Page and Sechin sought to establish a back channel.

Alexander Shustorovich Russian American millionaire; attempted to donate $250,000 to the 2000 Bush campaign but his money was returned due to his close ties with the Kremlin; donated $1 million to Trump's inaugural committee.

Alexander Torshin Deputy governor of the Central Bank of Russia; worked with Maria Butina to influence the NRA including sponsoring fully paid trips for their influential members to Russia; met with Trump (in 2010 and during election), Trump Jr. (May 2016), Governor Scott Walker, Dana Rohrabacher, and Nathan Sheets, under secretary of the Treasury; was sanctioned for his efforts to influence the 2016 election.

Viktor Vekselberg Ukrainian-born oligarch and owner of holding company Renova Group (largest shareholder in Bank of Cyprus); business associates include Oleg Deripaska, Mikhail Fridman, Len Blavatnik, and German Khan; close to Putin, publicly advocated lifting sanctions against Russia; funneled money with Andrew Intrater to Michael Cohen and then met to discuss Russian relations; present at 2014 fundraiser in Russia attended by Ivanka Trump and Jared Kushner, the RT gala that featured Michael Flynn, and the Trump inauguration.

Natalya Veselnitskaya Russian lawyer; worked for Yuri Chaika, Russia's prosecutor general, and for the Katsyv family to defend Prevezon company on money-laundering case in New York and lobbied against the Magnitsky Act; present at the June 2016 Trump Tower meeting with Donald Trump Jr., Paul Manafort, and Jared Kushner and met with Congressman Rohrabacher during his 2016 trip to Moscow.

DASHA ZHUKOVA Former wife of Roman Abramovich; close friends with Ivanka Trump and the Kushner brothers and seen with them numerous times, along with Wendi Deng, Rupert Murdoch's ex-wife; hosted Ivanka Trump and Jared Kushner on their 2014 Russia trip and attended Trump inauguration.

Notes

Chapter 1—Betraying the Oath . . . in Plain Sight

1. Ashley Parker and David E. Sanger, "Donald Trump Calls on Russia to Find Hillary Clinton's Missing Emails," July 27, 2016, *New York Times*, https://www.nytimes.com/2016/07/28/us/politics/donald-trump-russia-clinton-emails.html.

2. Callum Borchers, "Donald Trump Orders NBC's Katy Tur to 'Be Quiet,'" July 27, 2016, *Washington Post*, https://www.washingtonpost.com/news/the-fix/wp/2016/07/27/donald-trump-orders-nbcs-katy-tur-to-be-quiet/?utm_term=.2bd6d962ae74.

3. US Code, Title 18. Crimes and Criminal Procedure, Part I. Crimes, Chapter 115. Treason, Sedition, and Subversive Activities, Section 2381. Treason, https://www.law.cornell.edu/uscode/text/18/2381.

4. US Constitution, Article 3, Section 3, https://www.usconstitution.net/xconst_A3Sec3.html.

5. US Constitution, Article 3, Section 3, Constitutional Law Reporter, https://constitutionallawreporter.com/article-03-section-03/.

6. Laurence H. Tribe, "Yes, the Constitution Allows Indictment of the President," Lawfare (blog), December 20, 2018, https://www.lawfareblog.com/yes-constitution-allows-indictment-president. "There is mounting reason to ask whether the president and his associates sought to secure his election by conspiring with foreign adversaries and domestic accomplices to defraud the American people. Yet the memos in question would shield him from being held accountable precisely because he won that office. There is a maddeningly circular, bootstrap quality to arguing that even a crime committed to put somebody into a privileged position can't be pursued because, well, it helped put him into that position of privilege."

7. Ibid.

8. R. L. Duffus, "Traitor Caused the Loss of New York: Capture of Fort Washington Followed the Desertion of William Demont, Who Took Its Plans to the British," *New York Times*, November 14, 1926, https://www.nytimes.com/1926/11/14/archives/traitor-caused-the-loss-of-new-york-capture-of-fort-washington.html.

9. Krishadev Calamur, "For American Defectors to Russia, an Unhappy History," NPR, July 25, 2013, https://www.npr.org/sections/parallels/2013/07/24/205121529/for-american-defectors-to-russia-an-unhappy-history.

10. Yochi Dreazen, "Obama's CIA Chief Just Offered a Trump Russia Quote for the Ages," Vox, May 23, 2017, https://www.vox.com/policy-and-politics/2017/5/23/15681508/trump-russia-election-meddling-fbi-mueller-john-brennan.

11. Joe Hoft, "Report: Hillary's Emails Hacked by Russia—Kremlin Deciding Whether to Release 20,000 Stolen Emails," Gateway Pundit, May 10, 2016, https://www.thegatewaypundit.com/2016/05/hillarys-emails-hacked-russia-kremlin-deciding-whether-release-20000-emails-hacked/.

Chapter 2—The Super Villain with a Leash

1. Nathan Hodge, "Russia's Hookers-and-Hidden-Cameras Unit Strikes Again," *Wired*, September 24, 2009, https://www.wired.com/2009/09/of-hookers-and-hidden-cameras-the-dark-art-of-kompromat/.

2. Alexander Dugin, "Dugin's Guideline; American Hegemony; The Dragon Is Wounded," Katehon Think Tank, YouTube video, 8:43, July 22, 2016, https://www.youtube.com/watch?v=KqTqnaB7hRM.

3. Alexandra Ma, "'Traitors Will Kick the Bucket'—Watch Vladimir Putin's Chilling Warning to Spies Who Betray Russia," *Business Insider*, March 7, 2018, https://www.businessinsider.com/putin-threatened-russian-traitors-the-year-sergei-skripal-went-to-uk-2018-3.

4. Vladimir Isachenkov, "Vladimir Putin Warns Enemies of Russia They Will 'Swallow Poison,'" *Independent* (London), March 7, 2018, https://www.independent.ie/world-news/vladimir-putin-warns-enemies-of-russia-they-will-swallow-poison-36680187.html.

5. Valery Gerasimov, "По опыту Сирии" (Based on the experience of Syria), Voyenno-promyshlennyy kur'er, March 9, 2016, http://vpk-news.ru/sites/default/files/pdf/VPK_09_624.pdf (accessed June 22, 2016).

6. Rosalía Sánchez, "La Mentalidad KGB de Putin," *El Mundo* (Madrid), April 14, 2014, https://www.elmundo.es/internacional/2014/04/14/534c1b28ca4741b44f8b4581.html.

7. "United Russia Party Part of Large Team Creating New Russia," Sputnik, December 23, 2017, https://sputniknews.com/russia/201712231060268973-united-russia-party-prime-minister/.

8. Vladimir Putin, "Presidential Address to the Federal Assembly," President of Russia, December 12, 2013, http://en.kremlin.ru/events/president/news/19825.

9. Michael Birnbaum, "Russia's Anti-American Fever Goes beyond the Soviet Era's," *Washington Post*, March 8, 2015, https://www.washingtonpost.com/world/europe/russias-anti-us-sentiment-now-is-even-worse-than-it-was-in-soviet-union/2015/03/08/b7d534c4-c357-11e4-a188-8e4971d37a8d_story.html?utm_term=.4b05a43110d8.

10. Karoun Demirjia, "Russian Cancellation of U.S. Student Exchange Heightens Chilly Relationship," *Washington Post*, October 3, 2014, https://www.washingtonpost.com/world/europe/russian-cancellation-of-us-student-exchange-heightens-chilly-relationship/2014/10/02/e831ce8a-bfd5-4d04-9a27-4ab171ff42e1_story.html?utm_term=.c9a7e63abc73.

11. Birnbaum, "Russia's Anti-American Fever Goes beyond the Soviet Era's."

12. Ibid.

13. Harper Neidig, "Clinton Campaign Hits Trump over Putin Interview," *Hill* (Washington, DC), October 16, 2016, http://thehill.com/blogs/ballot-box/presidential-races/301255-clinton-campaign-hits-trump-over-putin-interview.

14. Ladislav Bittman, *The KGB and Soviet Disinformation: An Insider's View* (Washington, DC: Pergamon-Brassey's International Defense Publishers, 1985), 48.

15. Nicholas Schmindle, "Michael Flynn, General Chaos," *New Yorker*, February 27, 2017, https://www.newyorker.com/magazine/2017/02/27/michael-flynn-general-chaos.

16. Chris Sommerfeldt, "Trump's Ex-national Security Adviser Michael Flynn Had Undisclosed Meet with Russian Ambassador in 2015," *New York Daily News*, April 27, 2018, https://www.nydailynews.com/news/politics/ex-trump-official-michael-flynn-met-russian-ambassador-2015-article-1.3959006.

Chapter 3—Trump: The Dog to Be Walked

1. Jolyon Naegele, "Czech Republic: Secret Police Files Unlocked This Weekend," RadioFreeEurope, May 9, 1997, https://www.rferl.org/a/1084871.html.

2. Luke Harding, "Czechoslovakia Ramped Up Spying on Trump in Late 1980s, Seeking US Intel," *Guardian* (Manchester, UK), October 29, 2018, https://www.theguardian.com/us-news/2018/oct/29/trump-czechoslovakia-communism-spying.

3. Ibid.

4. Agence France-Presse, "Czech Communist Secret Police Had Dossier on Donald Trump: Report," Raw Story, October 30, 2018, https://www.rawstory.com/2018/10/czech-communist-secret-police-dossier-donald-trump-report/.

5. Harding, "Czechoslovakia Ramped Up Spying on Trump in Late 1980s."

6. Hans-Wilhelm Saure, "Tschechen-Stasi spähte die Trumps aus," *Bild* (Berlin), December 14, 2016, https://www.bild.de/news/ausland/donald-trump/tschechen-stasi-spaehte-trumps-aus-49320410,jsRedirectFrom=conversionToLogin.bild.html.

7. Kate Connolly, "Czechoslovakia Spied on Donald and Ivana Trump, Communist-era Files Show," *Guardian* (Manchester, UK), December 15, 2016, https://www.theguardian.com/us-news/2016/dec/15/czechoslovakia-spied-on-donald-trump-ivana-files.

8. Ibid.

9. Saure, "Tschechen-Stasi spähte die Trumps aus."

10. Scott Feinberg, "Donald Trump Angled for Soviet Postings in 1980s, Says Nobel Prize Winner (Exclusive)," *Hollywood Reporter*, May 26, 2017, https://www.hollywoodreporter.com/news/donald-trump-angled-soviet-posting-1980s-says-nobel-prize-winner-1006312.

11. Ibid.

12. William E. Geist, "The Expanding Empire of Donald Trump," *New York Times*, April 8, 1984, https://www.nytimes.com/1984/04/08/magazine/the-expanding-empire-of-donald-trump.html?pagewanted=all.

13. Lois Romano, "Donald Trump, Holding All the Cards: The Tower! The Team! The Money! The Funds!," *Washington Post,* November 15, 1984, https://www.washingtonpost.com/archive/lifestyle/1984/11/15/donald-trump-holding-all-the-cards-the-tower-the-team-the-money-the-future/8be79254-7793-4812-a153-f2b88e81fa54/?utm_term=.43ca933ad323.

14. Ibid.

15. Ilan Ben-Meir, "That Time Trump Spent Nearly $100,000 on an Ad Criticizing U.S. Foreign Policy in 1987," BuzzFeed News, July 10, 2015, https://www.buzzfeednews.com/article/ilanbenmeir/that-time-trump-spent-nearly-100000-on-an-ad-criticizing-us.

16. Maureen Dowd, "The Gorbachev Visit: Manhattan Goes Gorbachev; From Fish to Oreo Cookies," December 7, 1988, *New York Times,* https://www.nytimes.com/1988/12/07/world/the-gorbachev-visit-manhattan-goes-gorbachev-from-fish-to-oreo-cookies.html.

17. Connolly, "Czechoslovakia Spied on Donald and Ivana Trump."

18. "Archivy StB: Trump se chtěl stát prezidentem v roce 1996," *Česká Televize* 24, December 1, 2016, https://ct24.ceskatelevize.cz/domaci/1970461-archivy-stb-trump-se-chtel-stat-prezidentem-v-roce-1996.

19. Saure, "Tschechen-Stasi spähte die Trumps aus."

20. Petr Zidek, "Trump v Česku cestoval letadlem od JZD. Čuba s ním jednal o spolupráci," *Lidovky,* January 23, 2017, https://www.lidovky.cz/domov/byvaly-reditel-jzd-cuba-trump-diky-ivane-jednal-s-jzd-poskytla-nam-plazu.A170122_132117_ln_domov_ele.

21. Luke Harding, "'A Very Different World': Inside the Czech Spying Operation on Trump," *Guardian* (Manchester, UK), October 29, 2018, https://www.theguardian.com/us-news/2018/oct/29/czechoslovakia-spied-on-trump-to-exploit-ties-to-highest-echelons-of-us-power.

22. Arjan den Boer, "The New Travel Land: Intourist Posters from the Soviet Union," Retours, September 26, 2016, https://retours.eu/en/39-intourist-USSR-posters/.

23. John Reed, "Trump and His Buddies Keep Red Flags Flying in the Russia Probe," *Newsweek,* April 1, 2017, https://www.newsweek.com/trump-and-his-buddies-keep-red-flags-flying-russia-probe-576995.

24. Andrew E. Kramer, "Mining Executive Receives Payout of $100 million, Russia's Largest Ever," *New York Times,* December 17, 2012, https://www.nytimes.com/2012/12/18/business/global/norilsk-nickel-pays-strzhalkovsky-100-million-severance.html.

25. Reed, "Trump and His Buddies Keep Red Flags Flying in the Russia Probe."

26. Ibid.

27. Donald J. Trump with Tony Schwartz, *Trump: The Art of the Deal* (New York: Ballantine Books, 2015), 26–27.

28. Ibid., 364.

29. Luke Harding, "The Hidden History of Trump's First Trip to Moscow," *Politico,* November 19, 2017, https://www.politico.com/magazine/story/2017/11/19/trump-first-moscow-trip-215842.

30. Michael Oreskes, "Trump Gives a Vague Hint of Candidacy," *New York Times*, September 2, 1987, https://www.nytimes.com/1987/09/02/nyregion/trump-gives-a-vague-hint-of-candidacy.html.

31. Twohey and Eder, "For Trump, Three Decades of Chasing Deals in Russia."

32. Maggie Haberman, "The Donald Reins in Roger Stone," Politico, February 25, 2011, https://www.politico.com/story/2011/02/the-donald-reins-in-roger-stone-050231.

Chapter 4—Swimming in Rubles

1. Clyde H. Farnsworth, "K.G.B, Runs Commerce Unit, U.S. Says," *New York Times*, October 28, 1987, https://www.nytimes.com/1987/10/28/world/kgb-runs-commerce-unit-us-says.html.

2. Mark Champion, "How a Trump Soho Partner Ended Up with Toxic Mining Riches from Kazkhstan," *Bloomberg News*, January 11, 2018, https://www.bloomberg.com/news/features/2018-01-11/how-a-trump-soho-partner-ended-up-with-toxic-mining-riches-from-kazakhstan.

3. Simon Bell, "First Oligarch Claims His Due," *Guardian* (Manchester, UK), June 2, 2007, https://www.theguardian.com/business/2007/jun/03/russia.

4. Craig Shaw, Zeyneb Sentek, and Stefan Candea, "World Leaders, Mobsters, Smog, and Mirrors," The Black Sea, December 20, 2016, https://theblacksea.eu/stories/football-leaks/the-football-leaks-family-world-leaders-mobsters-smoke-and-mirrors/.

5. Davis International, LLC et al. v. New Start Group Corp et al., No. 1:04-1482-GMS (D.Del. May 31, 2005), https://www.deepcapture.com/wp-content/uploads/Ivankov-Case.pdf.

6. Julia Flynn and Patricia Kranz, "Grabbing a Corner on Russian Aluminum," *Bloomberg News*, September 16, 1996, https://www.bloomberg.com/news/articles/1996-09-15/grabbing-a-corner-on-russian-aluminum-intl-edition.

7. Tom Burgis, "Dirty Money: Trump and the Kazakh Connection," *Financial Times* (London), October 19, 2016, https://www.ft.com/content/33285dfa-9231-11e6-8df8-d3778b55a923.

8. Bozena Rynska, "Counted the Stars," *Izvestni*, June 20, 2005, https://iz.ru/news/303482.

9. James Fanelli, "Donald Trump associate Tevfik Arif charged with running prostitution ring aboard Turkish yacht," *New York Daily News*, October 2, 2010, https://www.nydailynews.com/news/world/trump-associate-charged-running-prostitution-ring-article-1.187634.

10. Charles V. Bagli, "Real Estate Executive with Hand in Trump Projects Rose from Tangled Past," *New York Times*, December 17, 2017, https://www.nytimes.com/2007/12/17/nyregion/17trump.html.

11. Rosalind Helderman and Tom Hamburger, "'We Will Be in Moscow': The Story of Trump's 30-year Quest to Expand His Brand to Russia," *Washington Post*, November 29, 2018, https://www.washingtonpost.com/politics/we-will-be-in-moscow-the-story-of-trumps-30-year-quest-to-expand-his-brand-to-russia

/2018/11/29/91f9f100-f3f4-11e8-aeea-b85fd44449f5_story.html?utm_term=.63a95306a5f6.

12. Allan J. Lichtman, "Here's a Closer Look at Donald Trump's Disturbingly Deep Ties to Russia," *Fortune*, May 17, 2017, http://fortune.com/2017/05/17/donald-trump-russia-2/.

13. Twohey and Eder, "For Trump, Three Decades of Chasing Deals in Russia."

14. ctown legend, "Watch the Trump Vodka Ad Designed for a Russian Audience," YouTube video, 0:59, July 29, 2016, https://www.youtube.com/watch?v=Ysxt66TIL28.

15. "Georgian Businessman's Hollywood Story: From Taxi Driver to Billionaire," *Georgian Journal*, May 13, 2014, https://www.georgianjournal.ge/society/27190-georgian-businessmans-hollywood-story-from-taxi-driver-to-billionaire.html.

16. Ibid.

17. Khalil Aminov, Anna Ryabova, Olga Sichkar, and Evgeniy Khvostik, "Donald Trump Will Sell His Name," *Kommersant*, April 6, 2008, https://www.kommersant.ru/doc/899538.

18. David Goldstein, Kevin G. Hall, and Peter Stone, McClatchy D.C. Bureau, "Birthday Video Call Captures a Telling Moment in Trump's Russia Connections," *Philadelphia Enquirer*, April 9, 2017, https://www.inquirer.com/philly/news/politics/presidential/Donald-Trump-Russia-Tofik-Arifov-Trump-Tower.html.

19. Caleb Melby and Keri Geiger, "Behind Trump's Russia Romance, There's a Tower Full of Oligarchs," *Bloomberg News*, March 16, 2017, https://www.bloomberg.com/news/articles/2017-03-16/behind-trump-s-russia-romance-there-s-a-tower-full-of-oligarchs.

20. Sam Kislin (blog), https://samkislin.weebly.com/.

21. Craig Unger, "Trump's Russian Laundromat," *New Republic*, July 13, 2017, https://newrepublic.com/article/143586/trumps-russian-laundromat-trump-tower-luxury-high-rises-dirty-money-international-crime-syndicate.

22. Robert I. Friedman, *Red Mafiya: How the Russian Mob Has Invaded America* (New York: Warner Books, 2000).

23. Melby and Geiger, "Behind Trump's Russia Romance."

24. Richard Behar, "Trump and the Oligarch 'Trio,'" *Forbes*, October 25, 2016, https://www.forbes.com/sites/richardbehar/2016/10/03/trump-and-the-oligarch-trio/#d879bf15314f.

25. Lily Galili, "A Kazakh Oligarch Trying to Be a Jewish Tycoon," *Hareetz*, October 28, 2002, https://www.haaretz.com/1.5145478.

26. Twohey and Eder, "For Trump, Three Decades of Chasing Deals in Russia."

27. Rucriminal, "Aras Agalarov and Mafia: The Owner of 'Crocus City' and the Singer's Father Emin Builds Business with 'Thieves in Law,'" Russian Criminal, February 7, 2017, https://rucriminal.info/en/material/128.

28. Margarita Papchenkova and Darya Korsunskaya, "Putin Hands Top Post at Ailing VEB Bank to Sberbank Manager," Reuters, February 26, 2016, https://uk.reuters.com/article/uk-russia-veb-idUKKCN0VZ0VH.

29. *Advisor: Trump Has 5 Years' Worth of Media Requests,* CNN video with Brian Stelter, CNN, October 11, 2015, https://www.cnn.com/videos/tv/2015/10/11/trump-has-5-years-worth-of-interview-requests-advisor-says.cnn.

30. Trump Moscow, DocumentCloud, page 202, contributed by Azeen Ghorayshi, BuzzFeed News, https://www.documentcloud.org/documents/5719169-Trump-Moscow.html.

31. Sonam Sheth and Sarah Gray, "Cohen's Sentencing Memo Brings the Spotlight Back to Ivanka Trump's Contacts with a Russian Athlete Who Pitched a Trump-Putin Meeting during the Election," *Business Insider*, December 7, 2018, https://www.businessinsider.com/ivanka-trump-cohen-dmitry-klokov-trump-tower-moscow-2018-6.

32. Trump Moscow, DocumentCloud, page 205, Azeen Ghorayshi, BuzzFeed News, https://www.documentcloud.org/documents/5719169-Trump-Moscow.html.

33. Ibid., 207–208.

Chapter 5—Team Trump

1. Lieutenant General Michael T. Flynn, US Army, June 24, 2012, https://usgif.org/system/uploads/3036/original/Lieutenant_General_Michael_Flynn.pdf?1386016231.

2. Nicholas Schmindle, "Michael Flynn, General Chaos," *New Yorker*, February 18, 2017, https://www.newyorker.com/magazine/2017/02/27/michael-flynn-general-chaos.

3. William Fox, "James Clapper: Fired Trump Adviser Flynn 'An Angry Man,'" NBC News, June 7, 2018, https://www.nbcnews.com/politics/first-read/james-clapper-fired-trump-adviser-flynn-became-angry-man-n880991.

4. Dana Priest, "The Disruptive Career of Michael Flynn, Trump's National Security Adviser," *New Yorker,* November 23, 2016, https://www.newyorker.com/news/news-desk/the-disruptive-career-of-trumps-national-security-adviser.

5. DIA Public Affairs, "Lt. Gen. Flynn Retires from DIA, 33-Year Army Career," Defense Intelligence Agency, Public Affairs, August 7, 2014, http://www.dia.mil/News/Articles/Article-View/Article/567011/lt-gen-flynn-retires-from-dia-33-year-army-career/.

6. Nicholas Schmindle, "Michael Flynn, General Chaos."

7. Tim Hains, "Flashback 2015: Mike Flynn's Much-Discussed Guest Appearance on 'Russia Today,'" Real Clear Politics, May 9, 2017, https://www.realclearpolitics.com/video/2017/05/09/flashback_2015_mike_flynns_much-discussed_guest_appearances_on_russia_today.html.

8. Gloria Berger, Pamela Brown, Jim Sciutto, Marshall Cohen, and Eric Lichtblau, "First on CNN: Russia Officials Bragged They Could Use Flynn to Influence Trump, Sources Say," CNN, May 19, 2017, https://www.cnn.com/2017/05/19/politics/michael-flynn-donald-trump-russia-influence/index.html.

9. "New Files Reveal Flynn Received US$68,000 from Russian Airline, TV Network and Cybersecurity Firm," *National Post* (Toronto), March 16, 2017, https://nationalpost.com/news/world/new-details-reveal-flynn-received-money-from-russian-airline-tv-network-and-cybersecurity-firm.

10. Margaret Hartmann, "Democrats Say Flynn Failed to Disclose Middle East Travel on Russia Nuclear-Plant Deal," *New York Magazine*, June 20, 2017, http://ny

mag.com/intelligencer/2017/06/democrats-say-flynn-failed-to-disclose-middle-east-travel.html?gtm=bottom>m=bottom.

11. Zia Wise, "Turkey's Torrid Love Affair with Michael Flynn," Politico, November 27, 2017, https://www.politico.eu/article/turkeys-torrid-love-affair-with-michael-flynn/.

12. *United States of America v. Bijan Rafiekian and Kamil Ekim Alptekin,* No. 1:18-CR-457 (AJT) (E.D. Va. Dec. 12, 2018) https://www.justice.gov/opa/press-release/file/1120621/download.

13. Ibid.

14. Michael T. Flynn, "Our Ally Turkey Is in Crisis and Needs Our Support," *Hill* (Washington, DC), November 8, 2016, https://thehill.com/blogs/pundits-blog/foreign-policy/305021-our-ally-turkey-is-in-crisis-and-needs-our-support.

15. *United States of America v. Bijan Rafiekian and Kamil Ekim Alptekin.*

16. Ibid.

17. Michael Kruse, "Trump's Long War with Justice," Politico, August 23, 2018, https://www.politico.com/magazine/story/2018/08/23/donald-trump-jeff-sessions-justice-department-war-219592.

18. Jim Geraghty, "Donald Trump's Departed Top Adviser Speaks Out," *National Review,* August 10, 2015, https://www.nationalreview.com/2015/08/donald-trump-roger-stone-interview/.

19. Jason M. Breslow, "The Frontline Roger Stone Interview," *Frontline,* September 27, 2016, https://www.pbs.org/wgbh/frontline/article/the-frontline-interview-roger-stone/.

20. Sophie Gilbert, "*Get Me Roger Stone* Profiles the Man Who Created President Trump," *Atlantic,* May 11, 2017, https://www.theatlantic.com/entertainment/archive/2017/05/get-me-roger-stone-donald-trump-netflix/526296/.

21. Azi Paybarah, "N.Y. Today: Roger Stone's History in New York," *New York Times,* January 28, 2019, https://www.nytimes.com/2019/01/28/nyregion/newyorktoday/new-york-news-roger-stone.html.

22. Anzish Mirza, "10 Things You Didn't Know about Roger Stone," *U.S. News & World Report,* April 25, 2017, https://www.usnews.com/news/national-news/articles/2017-04-25/10-things-you-didnt-know-about-roger-stone.

23. Franklin Foer, "Paul Manafort, American Hustler," *Atlantic,* March 2018, https://www.theatlantic.com/magazine/archive/2018/03/paul-manafort-american-hustler/550925/.

24. Emma Best, "FBI Documents on Roger Stone Reveal Sabotage, Espionage and the Life of a Serial Bagman," Property of the People, September 7, 2018, https:/propertyofthepeople.org/2018/09/07/fbi-documents-on-roger-stone-reveal-sabotage-espionage-and-the-life-of-a-serial-bagman/.

25. Matt Labash, "Roger Stone, Political Animal," *Weekly Standard,* November 5, 2007, https://www.weeklystandard.com/matt-labash/roger-stone-political-animal-15381.

26. Ibid.

27. "Unpaid Dole Adviser Resigns," *Chicago Tribune,* September 12, 1996, https://www.chicagotribune.com/news/ct-xpm-1996-09-12-9609130259-story.html.

28. Carl Golden, "Roger and Me: New Jersey and the Stone Zone," *Insider NJ*, January 28, 2019, https://www.insidernj.com/roger-new-jersey-stone-zone/.

29. "A Political Power Broker," *New York Times*, June 21, 1989, https://www.nytimes.com/1989/06/21/us/a-political-power-broker.html.

30. Tim Padgett, "Mob Scene in Miami," *Time*, November 26, 2000, http://content.time.com/time/nation/article/0,8599,89450,00.html.

31. Carol Lloyd, "The C-word as a Political Tool," Salon, January 25, 2008, https://www.salon.com/2008/01/24/roger_stone/.

32. Jim Geraghty, "Donald Trump's Departed Top Adviser Speaks Out," *National Review*, August 10, 2015, https://www.nationalreview.com/2015/08/donald-trump-roger-stone-interview/

33. Susan Swain, "Trump Presidential Campaign," Interview of Roger Stone, C-SPAN, November 28, 1999, https://www.c-span.org/video/?153873-1/trump-presidential-campaign.

34. Charles V. Bagli, "Trump and Others Accept Fines for Ads in Opposition to Casinos," *New York Times*, October 6, 2000, https://www.nytimes.com/2000/10/06/nyregion/trump-and-others-accept-fines-for-ads-in-opposition-to-casinos.html.

35. Maggie Haberman, "Did Roger Stone Jump, or Was He Pushed from Donald Trump's Campaign?," *New York Times*, August 8, 2015, https://www.nytimes.com/politics/first-draft/2015/08/08/did-roger-stone-jump-or-was-he-pushed-from-trump-campaign/.

36. Ana Radelat, "Their Political Road Began in CT and Led to Mueller," CT Mirror, February 1, 2019, https://ctmirror.org/2019/02/01/their-political-road-began-in-ct-and-led-to-mueller/.

37. Foer, "Paul Manafort, American Hustler."

38. Pamela Brogan, "The Torturers' Lobby: How Human Rights-Abusing Nations Are Represented in Washington," Center for Public Integrity, 1992, https://cloudfront-files-1.publicintegrity.org/legacy_projects/pdf_reports/THETORTURERSLOBBY.pdf.

39. Yashwant Raj, "Trump Aide Lobbied for Group That Was Front for Pakistan's ISI," *Hindustan Times* (New Delhi), April 19, 2016, https://www.hindustantimes.com/world/trump-aide-once-lobbied-for-a-front-for-pakistan-s-isi/story-IL3V4Ue3wNfzs50PCoN7gL.html.

40. Kim Barker and Habiba Nosheen, "The Man behind Pakistani Spy Agency's Plot to Influence Washington," ProPublica, October 3, 2011, https://www.propublica.org/article/the-man-behind-pakistani-spy-agencys-plot-to-influence-washington.

41. Kenneth P. Vogel, "Paul Manafort's Wild and Lucrative Philippine Adventure," *Politico Magazine*, June 10, 2016, https://www.politico.com/magazine/story/2016/06/2016-donald-trump-paul-manafort-ferinand-marcos-philippines-1980s-213952; FARA E Files, 3600-Exhibit-AB-19851101-D-XCT601, Fara E Files, https://efile.fara.gov/docs/3600-Exhibit-AB-19851101-D0XCT601.pdf.

42. FARA E Files, 3600-Exhibit-AB-19851101-D-XCT601.

43. Fara Report, Report of the Attorney General to the Congress of the United States on the Administration of the Foreign Agents Registration Act of 1938, as

amended, for the calendar year, Fara Report, https://www.fara.gov/reports/Archive/1986_FARA.pdf.

44. Foer, "Paul Manafort, American Hustler."

45. Fara Report, Report of the Attorney General to the Congress of the United States on the Administration of the Foreign Agents Registration Act.

46. Patrick Tyler and David Ottaway, "The Selling of Jonas Savimbi: Success and a $600,000 Tab," *Washington Post*, February 9, 1986, https://www.washingtonpost.com/archive/politics/1986/02/09/the-selling-of-jonas-savimbi success-and-a-600000-tab/d9fd8686-8f8d-497b-a3b4-7b636fec9b69/.

47. Ronald Reagan, "Ronald Reagan, State of the Union Address," C-SPAN, February 4, 1986, https://www.c-span.org/video/?125975-1/1986-state-union-address.

48. Jack Anderson and Dale Van Atta, "Mobutu in Search of an Image Boost," *Washington Post*, September 25, 1989, https://www.washingtonpost.com/archive/lifestyle/1989/09/25/mobutu-in-search-of-an-image-boost/d0626644-1a49-4414-82b2-70701894dfae/?utm_term=.32f4825e3ffc.

49. Glenn Thrush, "To Charm Trump, Paul Manafort Sold Himself as an Affordable Outsider," *New York Times*, April 8, 2017, https://www.nytimes.com/2017/04/08/us/to-charm-trump-paul-manafort-sold-himself-as-an-affordable-outsider.html.

50. Matt Apuzzo, Eileen Sullivan, and Sharon LaFraniere, "Paul Manafort Was Deep in Debt: He Saw an Opportunity in Trump," *New York Times*, August 3, 2018, https://www.nytimes.com/2018/08/03/us/politics/paul-manafort-trump-campaign.html.

51. Maggie Haberman, Alexander Burns, and Ashley Parker, "Donald Trump Fires Corey Lewandowski, His Campaign Manager," *New York Times*, June 20, 2016, https://www.nytimes.com/2016/06/21/us/politics/corey-lewandowski-donald-trump.html.

52. Jill Colvin and Steve Peoples, "Trump Fires His Campaign Manager in Dramatic Shake-Up," Associated Press, June 20, 2016, https://apnews.com/f96d270584754b63b44008ce706a1e67.

53. Christina Wilkie, "A Mysterious Payment to Paul Manafort's Lawyer Reveals a Hidden Chapter of Trump's 2016 Presidential Campaign," CNBC, March 10, 2019, https://www.cnbc.com/2019/03/10/paul-manafort-lawyer-mysterious-payment-hidden-chapter-of-trump-2016-campaign.html.

54. Brant Houston and Michele Jacklin, "Senate Candidate's Counsultant Investigated in HUD Scandal," *Hartford Courant*, June 12, 1992, https://www.courant.com/news/connecticut/hc-xpm-1992-06-12-0000200812-story.html.

55. Wilkie, "A Mysterious Payment to Paul Manafort's Lawyer."

56. *United States of America v. Paul J Manafort Jr.*, declaration of support of the government's breach determination and sentencing, January 15, 2019, https://www.documentcloud.org/documents/5684993-Manafort-SPC-Support-of-Breach.html.

57. Josh Rogin, "Trump Campaign Guts GOP's Anti-Russia Stance on Ukraine," *Washington Post*, July 18, 2016, https://www.washingtonpost.com/opinions/global-opinions/trump-campaign-guts-gops-anti-russia-stance-on-ukraine/2016

/07/18/98adb3b0-4cf3-11e6-a7d8-13d06b37f256_story.html?utm_term=.4d1de018a094.

58. Carrie Johnson, "2016 RNC Delegate: Trump Directed Change to Party Platform on Ukraine Support," NPR, December 4, 2017, https://www.npr.org/2017/12/04/568310790/2016-rnc-delegate-trump-directed-change-to-party-platform-on-ukraine-support.

59. Sally Bronston, "Trump Chairman Denies Any Role in Platform Change on Ukraine," NBC News, July 31, 2016, https://www.nbcnews.com/meet-the-press/trump-chairman-denies-any-role-platform-change-ukraine-n620511.

60. Andrew Kramer, Mike McIntire, and Barry Meier, "Secret Ledger in Ukraine Lists Cash for Donald Trump's Campaign Chief," *New York Times*, August 14, 2016, https://www.nytimes.com/2016/08/15/us/politics/paul-manafort-ukraine-donald-trump.html.

Chapter 6—The Dynastic Crime Family

1. Ned Parker, Stephen Grey, Stefanie Eschenbacher, Roman Anin, Brad Brooks, and Christine Murray, "Ivanka and the Fugitive from Panama," Reuters, November 17, 2017, https://www.reuters.com/investigates/special-report/usa-trump-panama/.

2. Laura Gurfein, "Discontinued: Ivanka Trump's Soho Flagship Has Quietly Shuttered," Racked New York, October 2, 2015, https://ny.racked.com/2015/10/2/9440019/ivanka-trump-soho-store-closed.

3. Veronica Stracqualursi, "Ivanka Trump Says She Knew 'Almost Nothing' about Trump Tower Moscow Poject," CNN, February 8, 2019, https://www.cnn.com/2019/02/08/politics/ivanka-trump-russia-investigation/index.html; Associated Press, "Ivanka Trump Says She Knew Little about Moscow Project," February 8, 2019, https://apnews.com/e29b16db08794d1da2b24abbc932e045.

4. Adam Davidson, "Donald Trump's Worst Deal," *New Yorker*, March 5, 2017, https://www.newyorker.com/magazine/2017/03/13/donald-trumps-worst-deal.

5. Martha Ross, "Ivanka Trump Played Key Role in Her father's Failed—and Potentially Corrupt—Azerbaijan Hotel Deal, Report Says," *Mercury News* (San Jose, CA), March 22, 2017, https://www.mercurynews.com/2017/03/10/ivanka-trump-played-key-role-in-her-fathers-failed-and-potentially-corrupt-azerbaijan-hotel-deal-report-says/.

6. Dan Merica, Gloria Borger, Jim Acosta, and Betsy Klein, "Ivanka Trump Is Making Her White House Job Official," CNN, March 30, 2017, https://www.cnn.com/2017/03/29/politics/ivanka-trump-white-house-job/index.html.

7. Brian Bennett and Noah Bierman, "China's President Xi Gets an Awkward Front-Row Seat to U.S. Military Might," *Los Angeles Times*, April 7, 2017, https://www.latimes.com/politics/la-fg-trump-china-20170407-story.html.

8. "Ivanka Trump's Brand Prospers as Politics Mixes with Business," Associated Press, April 18, 2017, https://www.voanews.com/a/ivanka-trump-brand-prospers-politics-business-mix/3815333.html.

9. Renae Reints, "Ivanka Trump's Brand Received Five New Trademarks from China This Month," *Fortune*, January 21, 2019, http://fortune.com/2019/01/21/ivanka-trump-china-trademarks/.

10. "Ivanka Trump Receives 5 Trademarks from China Amid Trade Talks," CBS News, January 21, 2019, https://www.cbsnews.com/news/ivanka-trump-receives-5-trademarks-from-china-amid-trade-talks/.

11. Annie Karni, "Ivanka Trump to Help Choose New World Bank President," *New York Times*, January 14, 2019, https://www.nytimes.com/2019/01/14/us/politics/ivanka-trump-world-bank-president.html.

12. Abha Bhattarai and Drew Harwell, "Ivanka Trump Shuts Down Her Namesake Clothing Brand," *Washington Post*, July 24, 2018, https://www.washingtonpost.com/business/2018/07/24/ivanka-trump-shuts-down-her-namesake-clothing-brand/.

13. Kate Bennett, "Saudis, UAE Pledge $100 million to Ivanka Trump-Proposed Fund," CNN, May 21, 2017, https://www.cnn.com/2017/05/21/politics/saudi-pledge-trump-women/index.html.

14. Catherine Lucey, "Ivanka Trump Unveils White House Global Women Initiative," Associated Press, February 6, 2019, https://apnews.com/82c46b839cdb41ec95e11da8fe932115.

15. Andrew Prokup, "As Trump Takes Aim at Affirmative Action, Let's Remember How Jared Kushner Got into Harvard," Vox, July 6, 2018, https://www.vox.com/policy-and-politics/2017/8/2/16084226/jared-kushner-harvard-affirmative-action.

16. Jeff Pillets and Clinton Riley, "Paying for Power: The Kushner Network," *Record* (Bergen County, NJ), June 16, 2002, 1.

17. "Kushner Companies," TRData, The Real Deal: New York Real Estate News, https://therealdeal.com/new-research/topics/company/kushner-companies/.

18. Michael Kranish, "Kushner Firm's $285 Million Deutsche Bank Loan Came Just Before Election Day," *Washington Post*, June 25, 2017, https://www.washingtonpost.com/national/kushner-firms-285-million-deutsche-bank-loan-came-just-before-election-day/2017/06/25/984f3acc-4f88-11e7-b064-828ba60fbb98_story.html?utm_term=.84573724fdd0.

19. Associated Press, "Kushner Companies Filed False Documents about Rent-Regulated Tenants," WNYC News, New York Public Radio, March 18, 2018, https://www.wnyc.org/story/kushner-companies-filed-false-documents-about-rent-regulated-tenants/

20. Associated Press, "Kushner Cos. Accused of Pushing Out Williamsburg Tenants," WNYC News, New York Public Radio, July 16, 2018, https://www.wnyc.org/story/kushner-cos-accused-pushing-out-williamsburg-tenants/.

21. David Jeans, "Kushner Brothers-Backed Cadre Looks to Cash in on Opportunity Zones," The Real Deal, November 30, 2019, https://therealdeal.com/2018/11/30/kushner-brothers-backed-cadre-looks-to-cash-in-on-opportunity-zones/.

22. Cristina Maza, "Jared Kushner Began Relationship with Russia Expert Following Meeting with Henry Kissinger, Reports Say," *Newsweek*, August 13, 2018, https://www.newsweek.com/jared-kushner-russia-henry-kissinger-center-national-interest-1070675.

23. Robert S. Mueller III, special counsel, *Report on the Investigation into Russian Interference in the 2016 Presidential Election*, vol. 1 (Washington, DC: US Department of Justice, March 2016), 4.

24. David Kocieniewski, Tom Metcalf, and Caleb Melby, "Early Facebook Backer Tied to Russia Bank, Kushner Platform," *Bloomberg News*, November 4, 2017, https://www.bloomberg.com/news/articles/2017-11-04/early-backer-of-facebook-linked-to-russia-bank-kushner-platform.

25. Luke Harding and Jon Swaine, "Russia Funded Facebook and Twitter Investments through Kushner Investor," *Guardian* (Manchester, UK), November 5, 2017, https://www.theguardian.com/news/2017/nov/05/russia-funded-facebook-twitter-investments-kushner-investor.

26. Kocieniewski, Metcalf, and Melby, "Early Facebook Backer Tied to Russia Bank, Kushner Platform"; Harding and Swaine, "Russia Funded Facebook and Twitter Investments through Kushner Investor."

27. Harding and Swaine, "Russia Funded Facebook and Twitter Investments through Kushner Investor."

28. Ibid.

29. Ibid.

30. Ibid.

31. Mueller, *Report on the Investigation into Russian Interference*, vol. 1, 147.

32. Ellen Nakashima, Adam Entous, and Greg Miller, "Russian Ambassador Told Moscow That Kushner Wanted Secret Communications Channel with Kremlin," *Washington Post*, May 26, 2017, https://www.washingtonpost.com/world/national-security/russian-ambassador-told-moscow-that-kushner-wanted-secret-communications-channel-with-kremlin/2017/05/26/520a14b4-422d-11e7-9869-bac8b446820a_story.html.

33. Mueller, *Report on the Investigation into Russian Interference*, vol. 1, 161.

34. Ned Parker, Jonathan Landay, and Warren Strobel, "Exclusive: Trump campaign had at least 18 undisclosed contacts with Russians: Sources," Reuters, May 18, 2017, https://www.reuters.com/article/us-usa-trump-russia-contacts/exclusive-trump-campaign-had-at-least-18-undisclosed-contacts-with-russians-sources-idUSKCN18E106.

35. Ibid.

36. Jo Becker, Matthew Rosenberg, and Maggie Haberman, "Senate Committee to Question Jared Kushner Over Meetings with Russians," *New York Times*, March 27, 2017, https://www.nytimes.com/2017/03/27/us/politics/senate-jared-kushner-russia.html.

37. David Filipov, Amy Brittain, Rosalind S. Helderman, and Tom Hamburger, "Explanations for Kushner's Meeting with Head of Kremlin-Linked Bank Don't Match Up," *Washington Post*, June 1, 2017, https://www.washingtonpost.com/politics/explanations-for-kushners-meeting-with-head-of-kremlin-linked-bank-dont-match-up/2017/06/01/dd1bdbb0-460a-11e7-bcde-624ad94170ab_story.html?utm_term=.edb3758b6dc2.

38. Michael Kranish, "Kushner Firm's $285 Million Deutsche Bank Loan Came Just Before Election Day," *Washington Post*, June 25, 2017, https://www.washingtonpost.com/national/kushner-firms-285-million-deutsche-bank-loan-came-just

-before-election-day/2017/06/25/984f3acc-4f88-11e7-b064-828ba60fbb98_story.html?utm_term=.84573724fdd0.

39. Kaja Whitehouse, "Family of Trump's Son-in-Law Linked to Hedge Fund Probe," *New York Post*, September 12, 2016, http://nypost.com/2016/09/12/family-of-trumps-son-in-law-linked-to-hedge-fund-probe/.

40. Jesse Drucker, Kate Kelly, and Ben Protess, "Kushner's Family Business Received Loans after White House Meetings," *New York Times*, February 28, 2018, https://www.nytimes.com/2018/02/28/business/jared-kushner-apollo-citigroup-loans.html.

41. Stephen Braun, Bernard Condon, and Tami Abdollah, "SEC Dropped Inquiry a Month after Firm Aided Kushner Company," Associated Press, March 2, 2018, https://apnews.com/dcea3eecab2b478aacd70321c6ce9a91.

42. Andrea Bernstein and Ilya Marritz, "Trump and Kushner's Little-Known Business Partner," WNYC News, New York Public Radio, May 25, 2017, https://www.wnyc.org/story/trump-kushner-little-known-business-partner/.

43. Jesse Drucker, "Kushner's Financial Ties to Israel Deepen Even with Mideast Diplomatic Role," *New York Times*, January 7, 2018, https://www.nytimes.com/2018/01/07/business/jared-kushner-israel.html?module=inline.

44. Eli Lake, "Kushner Is Said to Have Ordered Flynn to Contact Russia," *Bloomberg News*, December 1, 2017, https://www.bloomberg.com/opinion/articles/2017-12-01/kushner-is-said-to-have-ordered-flynn-to-contact-russia.

45. Matt Apuzzo, "Kushner Adds Prominent Lawyer Abbe Lowell to Defense Team," *New York Times*, June 26, 2017, https://www.nytimes.com/2017/06/26/us/politics/jared-kushner-abbe-lowell.html.

Chapter 7—The Five Dangles

1. Aaron Rupar, "Michael Cohen's Plea Deal Shows That Russia Did Have Something on Trump," Vox, November 30, 2018, https://www.vox.com/2018/11/30/18119798/cohen-plea-deal-email-lies-cover-up-peskov-kremlin.

2. Trump Moscow, DocumentCloud, pages 209–284, Azeen Ghorayshi, Buzz Feed News, https://www.documentcloud.org/documents/5719169-Trump-Moscow.html.

3. Sonam Sheth, "Lawmakers Grill Trump Associate Felix Sater, Who Was Instrumental in 2 Pivotal Events in the Russia Probe," *Business Insider*, April 4, 2018, https://www.businessinsider.com/felix-sater-senate-intelligence-committee-trump-tower-ukraine-peace-plan-2018-4.

4. Ibid.

5. Trump Moscow, DocumentCloud, page 67.

6. Boris Grozovski and Maxim Trudolyubov, "Capitalism the Kremlin Way," Wilson Center, September 13, 2018, https://www.wilsoncenter.org/blog-post/capitalism-the-kremlin-way; "Yuri Molchanov—Former Vice Governor of St Petersburg," Rusmafiozi (blog), November 3, 2012, http://rusmafiozi-eng.blogspot.com/2012/11/yuri-molchanov-former-vice-governor-of.html.

7. Joint Judiciary and Government Reform and Oversight Committee, Interview of: George Papadopoulos, US Congress, October 25, 2018, https://www.scribd.com/document/403223382/Papadopoulos-Transcript.

8. *United States of America v. George Papadopoulos*, US Department of Justice, October 5, 2017, https://www.justice.gov/file/1007346/download; David S. Cloud, "Trump Aide Caught in Russia Inquiry withdraws from Consideration for USDA Nomination," *Los Angeles Times*, November 2, 2017, https://www.latimes.com/nation/la-na-pol-trump-clovis-20171102-story.html.

9. Robert S. Mueller III, special counsel, *Report on the Investigation into Russian Interference in the 2016 Presidential Election*, vol. 1 (Washington, DC: US Department of Justice, March 2016), 83.

10. Ibid., 193.

11. *United States of America v. George Papadopoulos.*

12. Katie Zavadski, "Putin's Niece, Olga Polonskaya, Disappears from the Internet," Daily Beast, November 10, 2017, https://www.thedailybeast.com/putins-niece-olga-polonskaya-disappears-from-the-internet.

13. Mueller, *Report on the Investigation into Russian Interference*, vol. 1, 87.

14. *United States of America v. George Papadopoulos.*

15. Alberto Nardelli, "These Are the Contradictions Surrounding the Professor at the Center of the Trump-Russia Probe," Buzzfeed News, November 4, 2017, https://www.buzzfeednews.com/article/albertonardelli/the-professor-identified-in-the-trump-russia-probe-always.

16. Jerry Dunleavy, "Transcript of George Papadopoulos' Private Testimony Released," *Washington Examiner*, March 26, 2019, https://www.washingtonexaminer.com/news/transcript-of-george-papadopoulos-private-testimony-released.

17. Joint Judiciary and Government Reform and Oversight Committee, Interview of: George Papadopoulos, US Congress, October 25, 2018, https://www.scribd.com/document/403223382/Papadopoulos-Transcript.

18. Robert Mueller, *United States of America v. George Papadopoulos*, US Department of Justice, October 5, 2017, https://www.justice.gov/file/1007346/download.

19. Mueller, *Report on the Investigation into Russian Interference*, vol. 1, 88, footnote 458.

20. Natasha Bertrand and Scott Stedman, "Papadopoulos's Russia Ties Continue to Intrigue the FBI," *Atlantic*, November 28, 2018, https://www.theatlantic.com/politics/archive/2018/11/papadopouloss-russia-ties-still-interest-fbi-schiff/576895/.

21. Joint Judiciary and Government Reform and Oversight Committee, Interview of: George Papadopoulos, US Congress, October 25, 2018, https://www.scribd.com/document/403223382/Papadopoulos-Transcript.

22. Mueller, *Report on the Investigation into Russian Interference*, vol. 1, 90.

23. Ibid., 94.

24. Ibid., 95.

25. Joint Judiciary and Government Reform and Oversight Committee, Interview of: George Papadopoulos, US Congress, October 25, 2018, https://www.scribd.com/document/403223382/Papadopoulos-Transcript.

26. Brett Samuels, "Source of Steele Dossier Info Sought Access to Trump Allies in 2016: Report," *Hill* (Washington, DC), January 7, 2019, https://thehill.com/policy/national-security/428905-man-who-was-unwitting-source-of-steele-dossier-info-sought-access-to.

27. Mueller, *Report on the Investigation into Russian Interference*, vol. 1, 92.

28. Joint Judiciary and Government Reform and Oversight Committee, Interview of: George Papadopoulos, US Congress, October 25, 2018, https://www.scribd.com/document/403223382/Papadopoulos-Transcript.

29. Ari Shapiro, "Washington Post' Reporter Discusses FBI Informant Who Met with Trump Campaign," *All Things Considered*, National Public Radio, May 22, 2018, https://www.npr.org/2018/05/22/613449461/washington-post-reporter-discusses-fbi-informant-who-met-with-trump-campaign

30. Luke Harding and Stephanie Kirchgaessner, "The Boss, the Boyfriend, and the FBI: Italian Woman in the Eye of the Trump-Russia Inquiry," *Guardian* (Manchester, UK), January 18, 2018, https://www.theguardian.com/us-news/2018/jan/18/simona-mangiante-trump-russia-joseph-mifsud-george-papadopoulos.

31. Bertrand and Stedman, "Papadopoulos's Russia Ties Continue to Intrigue the FBI."

32. Max de Haldevang, "The Mysterious Work of the Maltese Professor Identified in the FBI's Russia Probe," Quartz, November 1, 2017, https://qz.com/1116571/joseph-mifsud-the-mysterious-maltese-professor-mentioned-by-george-papadopoulos-in-the-fbis-russia-probe-had-a-wealth-of-government-contacts/.

33. Cockburn, "The Different Lives of Simona Manginate Papadopoulos," Spectator USA, December 12, 2018, https://spectator.us/simona-mangiante-papadopoulos/.

34. Ibid.

35. Andrew E. Kramer, "The Master of 'Kompromat' Believed to Be Behind Trump Jr.'s Meeting," *New York Times*, July 17, 2017, https://www.nytimes.com/2017/07/17/world/europe/russia-donald-trump-jr-kompromat-yuri-chaika.html.

36. Nico Hines, "GOP Lawmaker Got Direction from Moscow, Took It Back to D.C.," Daily Beast, July 19, 2017, https://www.thedailybeast.com/gop-lawmaker-got-direction-from-moscow-took-it-back-to-dc.

37. Anastasia Kirilenko, "Gangster Party Candidate: Trump's Ties to Russian Organized Crime," *Insider*, April 7, 2018, https://theins.ru/uncategorized/98190?lang=en.

38. Ashley Feinberg, "Rob Goldstone's Relationship with the Trump's: A Timeline," *Wired*, July 11, 2017, https://www.wired.com/story/rob-goldstone-trump-family-timeline/.

39. Senate Judiciary Committee US Senate, Interview of: Robert Goldstone, December 15, 2017, page 40, https://www.judiciary.senate.gov/imo/media/doc/Goldstone%201%20Transcript_redacted.pdf.

40. Paul Owen, "Full Text of the emails between Donald Trump Jr. and Rob Goldstone," *Guardian* (Manchester, UK), July 11, 2017, https://www.theguardian.com/us-news/2017/jul/11/donald-trump-jr-emails-full-text-russia-rob-goldstone.

41. Neil MacFarquhar and Andrew E. Kramer, "Natalia Veselnitskaya, Lawyer Who Met Trump Jr., Seen as Fearsome Moscow Insider," *New York Times*, July 11,

2017, https://www.nytimes.com/2017/07/11/world/europe/natalia-veselnitskaya-donald-trump-jr-russian-lawyer.html.

42. Brendan Pierson, "U.S. Judge Orders Russian-Owned Company to Pay $6 million Settlement," Reuters, February 2, 2018, https://www.reuters.com/article/us-usa-russia-prevezon/u-s-judge-orders-russian-owned-company-to-pay-6-million-settlement-idUSKBN1FM2FJ.

43. Nico Hines, "Trump Tower Russian Lawyer, Natalia Veselnitskaya, Exposed in Swiss Corruption Case," Daily Beast, January 29, 2018, https://www.thedailybeast.com/trump-tower-russian-lawyer-natalia-veselnitskaya-exposed-in-swiss-corruption-case.

44. Andrew E. Kramer and Sharon LaFraniere, "Lawyer Who Was Said to Have Dirt on Clinton Had Closer Ties to Kremlin Than She Let On," *New York Times*, April 27, 2018, https://www.nytimes.com/2018/04/27/us/natalya-veselnitskaya-trump-tower-russian-prosecutor-general.html.

45. Natasha Bertrand, "New Memo Suggests Russian Lawyer at Trump Tower Meeting Was Acting 'as an Agent' of the Kremlin," *Business Insider*, October 16, 2017, https://www.businessinsider.com/veselnitskaya-memo-trump-tower-russia-meeting-2017-10.

46. Senate Judiciary Committee US Senate, Interview of: Rinat Akhmetshin, November 14, 2017, pages 128–138, https://www.judiciary.senate.gov/imo/media/doc/Akhmetshin%20Transcript_redacted.pdf.

47. Ibid., 19–21.

48. Richard Engeland and Aggelos Petropoulos, "Lawyer Probing Russian Corruption Says His Balcony Fall Was 'No Accident,'" NBC News, July 7, 2017, https://www.nbcnews.com/news/world/lawyer-probing-russian-corruption-says-his-balcony-fall-was-no-n780416

49. Jordan Tama, "What Is the Global Magnitsky Act, and Why Are U.S. Senators Invoking This on Saudi Arabia?" October 12, 2018, *Washington Post*, https://www.washingtonpost.com/news/monkey-cage/wp/2018/10/12/what-is-the-global-magnitsky-act-and-why-are-u-s-senators-invoking-this-on-saudi-arabia/.

50. "The US Global Magnitsky Act," Human Rights Watch, September 13, 2017, https://www.hrw.org/news/2017/09/13/us-global-magnitsky-act.

51. Mueller, *Report on the Investigation into Russian Interference*, vol. 1, 115.

52. Luke Harding, "Why Carter Page Was Worth Watching," Politico, February 3, 2018, https://www.politico.com/magazine/story/2018/02/03/carter-page-nunes-memo-216934

53. Kevin G. Hall, "Why Did FBI Suspect Trump Campaign Adviser Was a Foreign Agent?," McClatchy DC, April 14, 2017, https://www.mcclatchydc.com/news/politics-government/white-house/article144722444.html

54. Ibid.

55. Bess Levin, "Trump Campaign Associate Passed Documents to a Russian Spy Who Thought He Was an Idiot," *Vanity Fair*, April 4, 2017, https://www.vanityfair.com/news/2017/04/carter-page-victor-podobnyy.

56. Ali Watkins, "A Former Trump Adviser Met with a Russian Spy," Buzzfeed News, April 3, 2017, https://www.buzzfeednews.com/article/alimwatkins/a-former-trump-adviser-met-with-a-russian-spy.

57. Mueller, *Report on the Investigation into Russian Interference*, vol. 1, 95–97.

58. Massimo Calabresi and Alana Abramson, "Carter Page Touted Kremlin Contacts in 2013 Letter," *Time*, February 4, 2018, http://time.com/5132126/carter-page-russia-2013-letter/.

59. Watkins, "A Former Trump Adviser Met with a Russian Spy."

60. Massimo Calabresi and Alana Abramson, "Carter Page Touted Kremlin Contacts in 2013 Letter," *Time*, February 4, 2018, http://time.com/5132126/carter-page-russia-2013-letter/.

61. Julia Ioffe, "The Mystery of Donald Trump's Man in Moscow," Politico, September 24, 2016, https://www.politico.eu/article/the-mystery-of-donald-trumps-man-in-moscow-carter-page-phd/.

62. Steven Mufson and Tom Hamburger, "Trump Adviser's Public Comments, Ties to Moscow Stir Unease in Both Parties," *Washington Post*, August 5, 2016, https://www.washingtonpost.com/business/economy/trump-advisers-public-comments-ties-to-moscow-stir-unease-in-both-parties/2016/08/05/2e8722fa-5815-11e6-9aee-8075993d73a2_story.html?utm_term=.88cbb96976c4.

63. Josh Meyer and Kenneth P. Vogel, "Trump Campaign Approved Adviser's Trip to Moscow," Politico, March 7, 2017, https://www.politico.com/story/2017/03/carter-page-russia-trip-trump-corey-lewandowski-235784.

64. Justin Salhani, "The Russian Billionaire Carrying Out Putin's Will across Europe," *Think Progress*, January 4, 2017, https://thinkprogress.org/putins-man-in-europe-a4fe6bb48d76/.

65. Katehon, "The Lecture of Trump's Advisor Carter Page in Moscow," Katehon Think Tank, Katehon Press Relations, July 7, 2016, http://katehon.com/article/lecture-trumps-advisor-carter-page-moscow-watch-live-broadcast.

66. Mueller, *Report on the Investigation into Russian Interference*, vol. 1, 101–102.

67. Patricia Zengerle, "Former Trump Adviser Page Met Russian Officials in 2016 Moscow Trips," Reuters, November 6, 2017, https://www.reuters.com/article/us-usa-trump-russia-page/former-trump-adviser-page-met-russian-officials-in-2016-moscow-trips-idUSKBN1D70CR.

68. Tierney Sneed, "Trump Campaign Adviser Steps Down While Disputing Claims of Russia Ties," Talking Points Memo (blog), September 26, 2016, https://talkingpointsmemo.com/livewire/carter-page-steps-down-from-campaign.

69. Mueller, *Report on the Investigation into Russian Interference*, vol. 1, 95, 101.

Chapter 8—Team Dirty Tricks

1. Guccifer 2, "New Docs from DNC Network: Lots of Financial Reports and Donors' personal data," Guccifer 2.0 (blog), June 18, 2016, https://guccifer2.wordpress.com/2016/06/18/new-docs-from-dnc/.

2. Guccifer 2, "Dossier on Hillary Clinton from DNC," Guccifer 2.0 (blog), June 21, 2016, https://guccifer2.wordpress.com/2016/06/21/hillary-clinton/.

3. *United States v. Viktor Borisovich Netyksho et al.*, No. 1:18-CR-000215 (ABJ) (D. D.C. July 13, 2018), https://www.justice.gov/file/1080281/download.

4. Ibid.

5. WikiLeaks, Twitter, June 28, 2016, https://twitter.com/wikileaks/status/747805878275956737.

6. *United States v. Viktor Borisovich Netyksho et al.*

7. Ibid.

8. Ibid.

9. *United States v. Viktor Borisovich Netyksho, et al.*

10. *United States v. Roger Stone*, No. 1:19-CR-00018 (ABJ) (D. D.C. Jan. 24, 2019), https://www.justice.gov/file/1124706/download; Anna Schechter, "Mueller Has Emails from Stone Pal Corsi about WikiLeaks Dem Email Dump," NBC News, November 27, 2018, https://www.nbcnews.com/politics/justice-department/mueller-has-emails-stone-pal-corsi-about-wikileaks-dem-email-n940611.

11. Mueller, *Report on the Investigation into Russian Interference*, vol. 1.

12. Andrew Kaczynski and Gloria Borger, "Stone, on Day He Sent Assange Dinner Email Also Said, 'Devastating' WikiLeaks Were Forthcoming," CNN, April 4, 2018, https://www.cnn.com/2018/04/04/politics/roger-stone-julian-assange-email-wikileaks/index.html.

13. Roger Stone, "Dear Hillary: DNC Hack Solved, So Now Stop Blaming Russia," Breitbart News, August 5, 2016, https://www.breitbart.com/politics/2016/08/05/dear-hillary-dnc-hack-solved-so-now-stop-blaming-russia/.

14. Tom Hamburger, Josh Dawsey, Carol Leonnig, and Shane Harris, "Roger Stone Claimed Contact with WikiLeaks Founder Julian Assange in 2016, According to Two Associates," *Washington Post*, March 13, 2018, https://www.washingtonpost.com/politics/roger-stone-claimed-contact-with-wikileaks-founder-julian-assange-in-2016-according-to-two-associates/2018/03/13/a263f842-2604-11e8-b79d-f3d931db7f68_story.html.

15. *United States v. Roger Stone.*

16. Ibid.

17. Ibid.

18. Ibid.

19. WikiLeaks, "'Gucifer 2.0' tweets that they have released some files from the Democratic Congressional Campaign Committee," Twitter, August 12, 2016, https://twitter.com/wikileaks/status/764256561539735552.

20. Guccifer 2, "Guccifer 2.0 Hacked DCCC," Guccifer 2.0 (blog), August 12, 2016, https://guccifer2.wordpress.com/2016/08/12/guccifer-2-0-hacked-dccc/.

21. WikiLeaks, "'@ Guccifer_2' has account completely censored by Twitter after publishing some files from Democratic campaign," Twitter, August 13, 2016, https://twitter.com/wikileaks/status/764472143346270208.

22. WikiLeaks, "Washington DC newspaper the *Hill* is publishing some documents it says are from '@Guccifer_2' whose account Twitter censored completely," Twitter, August 13, 2016, https://twitter.com/wikileaks/status/764485057239191552.

23. Roger Stone, "Roger Stone: The Smoking Gun Aims, Fires, Misses," Stone Cold Truth, March 10, 2017, https://stonecoldtruth.com/roger-stone-the-smoking-gun-aims-fires-misses/.

24. Ibid.

25. Ibid.

26. Ibid.

27. Guccifer 2, "DCCC Internal Docs on Primaries in Florida," Guccifer 2.0 (blog), August 15, 2016, https://guccifer2.wordpress.com/2016/08/15/dccc-internal-docs-on-primaries-in-florida/.

28. *United States v. Viktor Borisovich Netyksho, et al.*

29. Anthony Man and Brittany Wallman, "Who Is Aaron Nevins?," *South Florida Sun Sentinel*, July 16, 2018, https://www.sun-sentinel.com/news/politics/fl-reg-aaron-nevins-robert-mueller-russia-elections-20180716-story.html.

30. *United States v. Viktor Borisovich Netyksho, et al.*

31. Roger Stone, "Randy & Me: Truth about Wikileaks," Stone Cold Truth, March 9, 2018, http://www.stonecoldtruth.com/randy-me-truth-about-wikileaks/.

32. *United States v. Roger Stone.*

33. Ibid.

34. Ibid.

35. Ibid.

36. Ibid

37. Roger Stone, Twitter, August 21, 2016, https://twitter.com/RogerJStoneJr/status/767366825743097856 (account suspended).

38. *United States v. Roger Stone.*

39. Stone, "Roger Stone: The Smoking Gun Aims, Fires, Misses."

40. *United States v. Roger Stone.*

41. Ibid.

42. Ibid.

43. Ibid.

44. Ibid.

45. Ibid.

46. Ibid.

47. Sharon Rondeau, "Roger Stone on Alex Jones: Assange Has 'All of the Emails' from Clinton's Private Server," *Post & Email*, October 3, 2016, https://www.thepostemail.com/2016/10/03/roger-stone-on-alex-jones-assange-has-all-of-the-emails-from-clintons-private-server/.

48. Roger Stone, Twitter, October 2, 2016, https://twitter.com/rogerjstonejr/status/782443074874138624 (account suspended).

49. *United States v. Roger Stone.*

50. Michael Schmidt, Mark Mazzetti, Maggie Haberman, and Sharon LaFraniere, "Read the Emails: The Trump Campaign and Roger Stone," *New York Times*, November 1, 2018, https://www.nytimes.com/2018/11/01/us/politics/wikileaks-roger-stone-trump.html.

51. Ibid.

52. Roger Stone, Twitter, October 3, 2016, https://twitter.com/RogerJStoneJr/status/782994854964031489 (account suspended).

53. Schmidt, Mazzetti, Haberman, and LaFraniere, "Read the Emails: The Trump Campaign and Roger Stone."

54. Hallie Jackson, Phil Helsel, Josh Meyer, and Monica Alba, "Roger Stone Calls

Claims of Wikileaks Collusion 'Categorically False,'" NBC News, October 12, 2016, https://www.nbcnews.com/politics/2016-election/roger-stone-calls-claims-wikileaks-collusion-categorically-false-n665441.

55. WikiLeaks, Twitter, October 13, 2016, https://twitter.com/wikileaks/status/786609272729632768?lang=en.

56. Natasha Bertrand, "Roger Stone's Secret Messages with WikiLeaks," *Atlantic*, February 27, 2018, https://www.theatlantic.com/politics/archive/2018/02/roger-stones-secret-messages-with-wikileaks/554432/.

57. Ibid.

58. Mueller, *Report on the Investigation into Russian Interference*, vol. 1, 141.

59. Bertrand, "Roger Stone's Secret Messages with WikiLeaks."

60. Katherine Skiba, David Heinzmann, and Todd Lightly, "Peter W. Smith's Final Day: 'It Seemed Like He Had a Lot on His Mind,'" *Chicago Tribune*, July 14, 2017, https://www.chicagotribune.com/news/local/politics/ct-peter-w-smith-death-met-0716-20170714-story.html.

61. Shane Harris, "GOP Operative Sought Clinton Emails from Hackers, Implied a Connection to Flynn," *Wall Street Journal*, June 29, 2017, https://www.wsj.com/articles/gop-operative-sought-clinton-emails-from-hackers-implied-a-connection-to-flynn-1498770851.

62. Mueller, *Report on the Investigation into Russian Interference*, vol. 1.

63. Ibid.

64. Ben Schreckinger, "GOP Researcher Who Sought Clinton Emails Had Alt-right Help," Politico, July 11, 2017, https://www.politico.com/magazinestory/2017/07/11/gop-researcher-who-sought-clinton-emails-had-alt-right-help-215359.

65. Ibid.

66. Ibid.

67. Matt Tait, "The Time I Got Recruited to Collude with the Russians," Lawfare (blog), June 30, 2017, https://www.lawfareblog.com/time-i-got-recruited-collude-russians.

68. Ibid.

69. Byron Tau, Dustin Volz, and Shelby Holliday, "GOP Operative Secretly Raised at Least $100,000 in Search for Clinton Emails," *Wall Street Journal*, October 7, 2018, https://www.wsj.com/articles/gop-operative-secretly-raised-at-least-100-000-in-search-for-clinton-emails-1538913614.

70. Harris, "GOP Operative Sought Clinton Emails from Hackers."

71. Ibid.

72. Mueller, *Report on the Investigation into Russian Interference*, vol. 1.

73. Ibid.

74. Ibid.

75. Ibid.

76. Skiba, Heinzmann, and Lightly, "Peter W. Smith's Final Day."

77. Joshua Green and Sasha Issenberg, "Inside the Trump Bunker, with Days to Go," *Bloomberg News*, October 27, 2016, https://www.bloomberg.com/news/articles/2016-10-27/inside-the-trump-bunker-with-12-days-to-go.

78. Steven Bertoni, "Exclusive Interview: How Jared Kushner Won Trump the White House," *Forbes*, November 22, 2016, https://www.forbes.com/sites/steven

bertoni/2016/11/22/exclusive-interview-how-jared-kushner-won-trump-the-white-house/.

79. Lois Beckett, "Trump Digital Director Says Facebook Helped Win the White House," *Guardian* (Manchester, UK), October 8, 2017, https://www.theguardian.com/technology/2017/oct/08/trump-digital-director-brad-parscale-facebook-advertising.

80. Ibid.

81. PBS, "Brad Parscale: Trump 2016 Digital Media Director," *Frontline*, PBS, August 8, 2018, https://www.pbs.org/wgbh/frontline/interview/brad-parscale/.

82. Ibid.

83. Lesley Stahl, "Facebook 'Embeds,' Russia and the Trump Campaign's Secret Weapon," CBS News, October 8, 2017, https://www.cbsnews.com/news/facebook-embeds-russia-and-the-trump-campaigns-secret-weapon/.

84. Carol Cadwalladr, "'I Made Steve Bannon's Psychological Warfare Tool': Meet the Data War Whistleblower," *Guardian* (Manchester, UK), March 18, 2018, https://www.theguardian.com/news/2018/mar/17/data-war-whistleblower-christopher-wylie-faceook-nix-bannon-trump.

85. Sean Illing, "Cambridge Analytica: The Shady Data Firm That Might Be a Key Trump-Russia Link, Explained," Vox, April 4, 2018, https://www.vox.com/policy-and-politics/2017/10/16/15657512/cambridge-analytica-facebook-alexander-nix-christopher-wylie.

86. Carole Cadwalladr and Emma Graham-Harrison, "Revealed: 50 million Facebook Profiles Harvested for Cambridge Analytica in Major Data Breach," *Guardian* (Manchester, UK), March 17, 2018, https://www.theguardian.com/news/2018/mar/17/cambridge-analytica-facebook-influence-us-election.

87. Ibid.

88. Shane Harris and Gideon Resnick, "Will Brexit Masterminds Work for Trump?," Daily Beast, July 3, 2016, https://www.thedailybeast.com/will-brexit-masterminds-work-for-trump.

89. Rebecca Savransky, "Cambridge Analytica Exec Says They 'Ran All the Digital Campaign' for Trump: Report," *Hill* (Washington, DC), March 20, 2018, https://thehill.com/homenews/campaign/379368-cambridge-analytica-executives-claim-they-ran-all-the-digital-campaign-for.

90. Ibid.

91. Jackie Schechter, "Cambridge Analytica Brags about Trump Work," Committee to Investigate Russia, March 20, 2018, https://investigaterussia.org/media/2018-03-20/cambridge-analytica-brags-about-trump-work.

92. Ibid.

93. Mark Mazetti, Ronen Bergman, David Kirkpatrick, and Maggie Haberman, "Rick Gates Sought Online Manipulation Plans from Israeli Intelligence Firm for Trump Campaign," *New York Times*, October 8, 2018, https://www.nytimes.com/2018/10/08/us/politics/rick-gates-psy-group-trump.html

94. PsyGroup, *Project "Rome": Campaign Intelligence and Influence Services Proposal*, April 2016, https://int.nyt.com/data/documenthelper/360-trump-project-rome/574d679d1ff58a30836c/optimized/full.pdf.

95. Ibid.

96. Mazetti, Bergman, Kirkpatrick, and Haberman, "Rick Gates Sought Online Manipulation Plans from Israeli Intelligence Firm for Trump Campaign."

97. Michael Riley and Lauren Etter, "Mueller Asked about Money Flows to Israeli Social-Media Firm, Source Says," *Bloomberg News*, May 22, 2018, https://www.bloomberg.com/news/articles/2018-05-22/mueller-targeted-flows-of-money-to-israeli-social-media-company.

Chapter 9—The Worst Presidency in History

1. David Filipov and Andrew Roth, "'Yes We Did': Russia's Establishment Basks in Trump's Victory," *Washington Post*, November 9, 2016, https://www.washingtonpost.com/news/worldviews/wp/2016/11/09/yes-we-did-russias-establishment-basks-in-trumps-victory/?utm_term=.cf9d25751ecb.

2. Andrew Osborn, "Russia Says It Was in Touch with Trump Campaign during Election," Reuters, November 10, 2016, https://www.reuters.com/article/us-usa-election-russia-trump/russia-says-it-was-in-touch-with-trumps-campaign-during-election-idUSKBN1351RJ.

3. Barney Henderson, "Donald Trump and Vladimir Putin Hold First Conversation and Vow New US-Russia Partnership to Tackle International Terrorism," *Telegraph* (London), November 14, 2016, http://www.telegraph.co.uk/news/2016/11/14/donald-trump-and-vladimir-putin-hold-first-conversation-and-vow/.

4. "Donald Trump's *New York Times* Interview: Full Transcript," *New York Times*, November 23, 2016, https://www.nytimes.com/2016/11/23/us/politics/trump-new-york-times-interview-transcript.html?_r=0.

5. Associated Press, "Putin 'Ready for Cooperation' with Trump," Politico, December 1, 2016, https://www.politico.com/story/2016/12/putin-ready-for-cooperation-with-trump-232044.

6. Adam Entous, Ellen Nakashima, and Greg Miller, "Secret CIA Assessment Says Russia Was Trying to Help Trump Win White House," *Washington Post*, December 9, 2016, https://www.washingtonpost.com/world/national-security/obama-orders-review-of-russian-hacking-during-presidential-campaign/2016/12/09/31d6b300-be2a-11e6-94ac-3d324840106c_story.html?utm_term=.f1dd5e869495.

7. Stephen Collinson and Elise Labott, "Donald Trump Takes Aim at Intelligence Community on Russia," CNN, December 11, 2016, http://www.cnn.com/2016/12/10/politics/donald-trump-response-russian-hacking/index.html.

8. Nicholas Fandos, "Trump Links C.I.A. Reports on Russia to Democrats," *New York Times*, December 11, 2016, https://www.nytimes.com/2016/12/11/us/politics/trump-russia-democrats.html.

9. Donald Trump, Twitter, December 12, 2016, https://twitter.com/realdonaldtrump/status/808299841147248640?lang=en.

10. Miriam Valverde, "Pants on Fire! Trump Tweet about White House, Russia Hacking Probe," PolitiFact, December 15, 2016, http://www.politifact.com/truth-o-meter/statements/2016/dec/15/donald-trump/pants-fire-trump-tweet-about-russian-hacking-probe/.

11. Politico staff, "Putin on Trump: 'Nobody Believed He Would Win Except for Us,'" Politico, December 23, 2016, https://www.politico.com/story/2016/12/putin-on-trump-us-democrats-232945.

12. Brooke Seipel, "Social Media Erupts over Trump's Putin Tweet," *Hill* (Washington, DC), December 24, 2016, http://thehill.com/blogs/in-the-know/in-the-know/311751-social-media-erupts-over-trumps-putin-tweet.

13. Graham Lanktree, "Susan Rice Explains Why She Unmasked Trump Officials," *Newsweek*, September 14, 2017, https://www.newsweek.com/susan-rices-explains-why-she-unmasked-trump-officials-664726.

14. Adam Entous, "Israeli, Saudi, and Emirati Officials Privately Pushed for Trump to Start a Grand Bargain with Putin," *New Yorker*, July 9, 2018, https://www.newyorker.com/news/news-desk/israeli-saudi-and-emirati-officials-privately-pushed-for-trump-to-strike-a-grand-bargain-with-putin.

15. Carol Lee and Julia Ainsley, "Mueller Probing Possible Deal between Turks, Flynn during Presidential Transition," NBC News, November 10, 2017, https://www.nbcnews.com/news/us-news/mueller-probing-possible-deal-between-turks-flynn-during-presidential-transition-n819616.

16. Julian Borger, "Ex-Trump Aide Flynn Investigated over Plot to Kidnap Turkish Dissident: Report," *Guardian* (Manchester, UK), November 10, 2017, https://www.theguardian.com/us-news/2017/nov/10/michael-flynn-trump-turkish-dissident-cleric-plot.

17. Nicholas Schmindle, "What Mike Flynn Did for Turkey," *New Yorker*, March 16, 2017, https://www.newyorker.com/news/news-desk/what-mike-flynn-did-for-turkey.

18. Maggie Haberman, Mark Mazzetti, and Matt Apuzzo, "Kushner Is Said to Have Discussed a Secret Channel to Talk to Russia," *New York Times*, May 26, 2017, https://www.nytimes.com/2017/05/26/us/politics/kushner-talked-to-russian-envoy-about-creating-secret-channel-with-kremlin.html.

19. The White House, "Statement by President Obama on U.S. Response to Russian Hacking," *Baltimore Sun*, December 29, 2016, http://www.baltimoresun.com/news/maryland/bal-statement-by-president-obama-on-response-to-russian-hacking-20161229-story.html.

20. Justin Carissimo and Chris Stevenson, "Obama Says He Personally Warned Putin to 'Cut It Out' over Election Hacking," *Independent* (London), December 16, 2016, http://www.independent.co.uk/news/world/americas/us-elections/obama-says-he-personally-told-putin-to-cut-it-out-on-hacking-a7480576.html.

21. The White House, "Statement by President Obama on U.S. response to Russian hacking."

22. Richard Cown, "Asked About Russia Sanctions, Trump Says 'We Ought to Get on with Our Lives,'" Reuters, December 28, 2016, https://www.reuters.com/article/us-usa-trump-russia/asked-about-russia-sanctions-trump-says-we-ought-to-get-on-with-our-lives-idUSKBN14I05A.

23. Melissa Quinn, "Jared Kushner Directed Michael Flynn to Contact Russian Government in Dec. 2016: Report," *Washington Examiner*, December 1, 2017, http://www.washingtonexaminer.com/jared-kushner-directed-michael-flynn-to-contact-russian-government-in-dec-2016-report/article/2642306.

24. Jennifer Rubin, "Michael Flynn Wasn't Entrapped," *Washington Post*, December 18, 2018, https://www.washingtonpost.com/opinions/2018/12/18/flynn-wasnt-entrapped/?utm_term=.b65cbe8df5d8.

25. Robert S. Mueller III, special counsel, *Report on the Investigation into Russian Interference in the 2016 Presidential Election,* vol. 1 (Washington, DC: US Department of Justice, March 2016), 167–168.

26. Ibid., 168–173.

27. Caroline Kenny and Kevin Liptak, "Trump: Putin 'Very Smart' for Decision to Withhold Sanctions," CNN, December 30, 2016, http://www.cnn.com/2016/12/30/politics/trump-putin-very-smart-for-decision-to-withhold-sanctions/index.html.

28. Adam Goldman and Matt Apuzzo, "FBI Warned Hope Hicks about Emails from Russian Operatives," *New York Times,* December 8, 2017, https://www.nytimes.com/2017/12/08/us/politics/hope-hicks-russia-trump-fbi.html?_r=0.

29. Michael D. Shear, "Donald Trump, after Dismissing Hacking, Agrees to an Intelligence Briefing," *New York Times,* December 29, 2016, https://www.nytimes.com/2016/12/29/us/politics/donald-trump-russia-hack.html.

30. Guccifer 2, "Here I am Again, My Friends," Guccifer 2.0 (blog), January 12, 2017, https://guccifer2.wordpress.com/2017/01/12/fake-evidence/.

31. Ibid.

Chapter 10—Masters of Fake News

1. Michael D. Shear and David E. Sanger, "Putin Led a Complex Cyberattack Scheme to Aid Trump, Report Finds," *New York Times,* January 6, 2017, https://www.nytimes.com/2017/01/06/us/politics/donald-trump-wall-hack-russia.html.

2. "Donald Trump's Statement after Intelligence Briefing on Hacking," *New York Times,* January 6, 2017, https://www.nytimes.com/2017/01/06/us/politics/donald-trump-statement-hack-intelligence-briefing.html.

3. Steve Benen, "Donald Trump Asks, 'Are We Living in Nazi Germany'?," MSNBC Maddow (blog), January 11, 2017, http://www.msnbc.com/rachel-maddow-show/donald-trump-asks-are-we-living-nazi-germany.

4. Eugene Scott, "Trump: Only 'Stupid' People Think Warm Ties with Russia Are a Bad Thing," CNN, January 7, 2016, https://www.cnn.com/2017/01/07/politics/donald-trump-russia-relationship/index.html.

5. Scott Shane, Adam Goldman, and Matthew Rosenberg, "Trump Received Unsubstantiated Report That Russia Had Damaging Information about Him," *New York Times,* January 10, 2017, https://www.nytimes.com/2017/01/10/us/politics/donald-trump-russia-intelligence.html; and Ken Bensinger, Miriam Elder, and Mark Schoofs, "These Reports Allege Trump Had Deep Ties to Russia," BuzzFeed News, January 10, 2016, https://www.buzzfeed.com/kenbensinger/these-reports-allege-trump-has-deep-ties-to-russia?utm_term=.wddoGo577#.ekzo3oLgg.

6. Tina Nguyen, "Donald Trump Just Offered Putin Exactly What He Wants," *Vanity Fair,* January 16, 2017. https://www.vanityfair.com/news/2017/01/donald-trump-nato-russia-interview.

7. Michael S. Schmidt, Matthew Rosenberg, Adam Goldman, and Matt Apuzzo, "Intercepted Communications Part of Inquiry into Trump Associates," *New York Times*, January 19, 2017, https://www.nytimes.com/2017/01/19/us/politics/trump-russia-associates-investigation.html.

8. Donald J. Trump, "The Inaugural Address," The White House, US government, January 20, 2017, www.whitehouse.gov/briefings-statements/the-inaugural-address/.

9. Elephants in the Room Contributors, "Trump's First Year in Review: Views from the Republican Bench," *Foreign Policy*, December 29, 2017, foreignpolicy.com/2017/12/29/trumps-first-year-in-review-views-from-the-republican-bench/.

10. Brooke Seipel, "Report: Bush Called Trump's Inauguration Speech 'Some Weird S--t,'" *Hill* (Washington, DC), March 29, 2017, http://thehill.com/blogs/blog-briefing-room/news/326438-george-bush-after-inauguration-that-was-some-weird-s-t-report.

11. "The Billionaire Oligarchs behind Alfa-Access-Renova (AAR)," *Guardian* (Manchester, UK), May 17, 2011, https://www.theguardian.com/business/2011/may/17/aar-billionaire-oligarchs.

12. Stephanie Baker, Irina Rezik, and Katya Kazakina, "Billionaire Ally of Putin Socialized with Kushner, Ivanka Trump," *Bloomberg News*, August 18, 2017, https://www.bloomberg.com/news/articles/2017-08-18/billionaire-ally-of-putin-socialized-with-kushner-ivanka-trump.

13. Sarah Farolfi, IRPI, and Stelios Orphanides, "Russian Billionaire Linked to Trump, Manafort Has New Cyprus Passport," Organized Crime and Corruption Reporting Project (OCCRP), March 5, 2018, https://www.occrp.org/en/goldforvisas/russian-billionaire-linked-to-trump-manafort-has-new-cyprus-passport.

14. Robert Windrem, "Guess Who Came to Dinner with Flynn and Putin," NBC News, April 18, 2017, https://www.nbcnews.com/news/world/guess-who-came-dinner-flynn-putin-n742696.

15. Shimon Prokupecz, Kara Scannell, and Jeremy Herb, "Russian Oligarch Met with Michael Cohen at Trump Tower during Transition," CNN May 26, 2018, https://www.cnn.com/2018/05/25/politics/viktor-vekselberg-trump-tower-michael-cohen-meeting/index.html.

16. Adam Goldman, Ben Protess, and William K. Rashbaum, "Viktor Vekselberg, Russian Billionaire, Was Questioned by Mueller's Investigators," *New York Times*, May 4, 2018, https://www.nytimes.com/2018/05/04/us/politics/viktor-vekselberg-mueller-investigation.html.

17. Brenna Hughes Neghaiwi, "U.S. Sanctions on Vekselberg Have $1.5–$2 Billion Assets Frozen: Sources," Reuters, April 21, 2018, https://www.reuters.com/article/us-usa-russia-sanctions-renova/u-s-sanctions-on-vekselberg-have-1-5-2-billion-assets-frozen-sources-idUSKBN1HS0FB.

18. Yulia Bushuyeva and Kirill Koryukin, "TNK Rival Claims CIA Spied on Kukes," *Moscow Times*, December 15, 2003, http://old.themoscowtimes.com/news/article/tmt/234052.html.

19. Simon Kukes Contributions, 2016, Federal Election Commission, https://www.fec.gov/data/receipts/individualcontributions/?two_year_transaction_

period=2016&contributor_name=simon+kukes&min_date=01%2F01%2F2015&max_date=12%2F31%2F2016.

20. Ibid.

21. Luke Harding, "Russian-US Tycoon Boasted of 'Active' Involvement in Trump Election Campaign," *Guardian* (Manchester, UK), September 28, 2018, https://www.theguardian.com/us-news/2018/sep/28/russian-us-tycoon-boasted-of-active-involvement-in-trump-election-campaign-simon-kukes.

22. JTA and Ron Kampeas, "Know Your Oligarch: A Guide to the Jewish Billionaires in the Trump-Russia Probe," *Haaretz*, May 23, 2018, https://www.haaretz.com/us-news/know-your-oligarch-a-guide-to-the-jewish-machers-in-the-russia-probe-1.6113189.

23. Caroline Kelly, "WNYC: Ivanka Trump Involved in Negotiations for Trump Hotel Rentals during Inauguration," CNN, December 14, 2018, https://www.cnn.com/2018/12/14/politics/trump-inaugural-committee-ivanka-trump-hotel/index.html.

24. Laura Smith-Spark, "Protesters Rally Worldwide in Solidarity with Washington March," CNN, January 27, 2017, www.cnn.com/2017/01/21/politics/trump-women-march-on-washington/index.html.

25. Politico staff, "Transcript of White House Press Secretary Statement to the Media," Politico, January 21, 2017, www.politico.com/story/2017/01/transcript-press-secretary-sean-spicer-media-233979.

26. Stephen Collinson, "On Day Two, Trump Prayed, Met the CIA and Attacked the Press," CNN, January 21, 2017, http://www.cnn.com/2017/01/21/politics/trump-presidency-day-two/index.html.

27. Noah Bierman and Brian Bennett, "Trump Boasts and Attacks the Media in Solemn CIA Setting," *Los Angeles Times*, January 21, 2017, http://www.latimes.com/politics/la-na-pol-trump-cia-20170121-story.html.

28. Andrea Mitchell and Ken Dilanian, "Ex-CIA Boss Brennan, Others Rip Trump Speech in Front of Memorial," NBC News, January 21, 2017, https://www.nbcnews.com/news/us-news/ex-cia-boss-brennan-others-rip-trump-speech-front-memorial-n710366.

29. David Ignatius, "CIA Officers Give Mixed Reviews of Trump's Strange Visit," *Washington Post*, January 22, 2017, https://www.washingtonpost.com/blogs/post-partisan/wp/2017/01/22/cia-officers-give-mixed-reviews-of-trumps-strange-visit/?utm_term=.87167d36cb15.

30. Politico staff, "Transcript of White House Press Secretary Statement to the Media."

31. Donald Trump, Twitter, January 16, 2016, https://twitter.com/realDonaldTrump/status/820789938887294977.

Chapter 11—The Good Guys

1. Rachel Maddow, "The FBI Secretly Investigated Russian Spies for Years," *The Rachel Maddow Show*, MSNBC, July 11, 2018, http://www.msnbc.com/transcripts/rachel-maddow-show/2018-07-11.

2. Ibid.

3. Ibid.

4. Laura Jarrett and Evan Perez, "FBI Agent Dismissed from Mueller Probe Changed Comey's Description of Clinton to 'Extremely Careless,'" CNN, December 4, 2017, https://www.cnn.com/2017/12/04/politics/peter-strzok-james-comey/index.html.

5. Maddow, "The FBI Secretly Investigated Russian Spies for Years."

6. John Kruzel, "No Evidence FBI Officials' Texts Deliberately Erased, as Donald Trump Says," PolitiFact, December 19, 2019, https://www.politifact.com/truth-o-meter/statements/2018/dec/19/donald-trump/no-evidence-fbi-officials-texts-deliberately-erase/.

7. Matt Apuzzo, Adam Goldman, and Nicholas Fandos, "Code Name Crossfire Hurricane: The Secret Origins of the Trump Investigation," *New York Times*, May 16, 2018, https://www.nytimes.com/2018/05/16/us/politics/crossfire-hurricane-trump-russia-fbi-mueller-investigation.html.

8. David Corn, "A Veteran Spy Has Given the FBI Information Alleging a Russian Operation to Cultivate Donald Trump," *Mother Jones*, October 31, 2016, https://www.motherjones.com/politics/2016/10/veteran-spy-gave-fbi-info-alleging-russian-operation-cultivate-donald-trump/.

9. Apuzzo, Goldman, and Fandos, "Code Name Crossfire Hurricane."

10. Devlin Barrett, "'I Expect Loyalty,' Trump Told Comey, According to Written Testimony," *Washington Post*, June 7, 2017, https://www.washingtonpost.com/world/national-security/i-expect-loyalty-trump-told-comey-according-to-written-testimony/2017/06/07/46413298-4bab-11e7-a186-60c031eab644_story.html.

11. Matt Apuzzo and Emmarie Huetteman, "Sally Yates Tells Senators She Warned Trump about Michael Flynn," *New York Times*, May 8, 2017, https://www.nytimes.com/2017/05/08/us/politics/michael-flynn-sally-yates-hearing.htm.

12. Nicole Scanga, "Sally Yates Talks about Her 10 Days as Acting Attorney General," CBS News, May 20, 2018, https://www.cbsnews.com/news/sally-yates-talks-about-her-10-days-as-acting-attorney-general/.

13. Sally Q. Yates, "Letter from Sally Yates on Unlawful Immigration Ban," *New York Times*, January 30, 2017, https://www.nytimes.com/2017/01/30/us/politics/attorney-general-civil-rights-refugee.html.

14. Rosenberg Habermann, Matt Apuzzo, and Glen Thrush, "Michael Flynn Resigns as National Security Adviser," *New York Times*, February 13, 2017, https://www.nytimes.com/2017/02/13/us/politics/donald-trump-national-security-adviser-michael-flynn.html.

15. Ibid.

16. Donald Trump, Twitter, March 4, 2017, https://twitter.com/realdonaldtrump/status/837989835818287106?lang=en.

17. Matt Apuzzo, Matthew Rosenberg, and Emmarie Hueteman, "F.B.I. Is Investigating Trump's Russia Ties, Comey Confirms," *New York Times*, March 20, 2017, https://www.nytimes.com/2017/03/20/us/politics/fbi-investigation-trump-russia-comey.html.

18. Ibid.

19. Associated Press, "FBI Director Comey Corrects Trump's Tweets in Real Time," *Times-Republican* (Marshalltown, IA), March 22, 2017, https://www.timesrepublican.com/news/todays-news/2017/03/fbi-director-comey-corrects-trumps-tweets-in-real-time/.

20. Jana Heigl, "A Timeline of Donald Trump's False Wiretapping Charge," PolitiFact, March 21, 2017, http://www.politifact.com/truth-o-meter/article/2017/mar/21/timeline-donald-trumps-false-wiretapping-charge/.

21. Chris Wilson, "FBI Chief Comey on Trump Wiretapping Claims: 'I Have No Information That Supports Those Tweets,'" Yahoo News, March 20, 2017, https://www.yahoo.com/news/fbi-chief-comey-on-trump-wiretapping-claims-i-have-no-information-that-supports-those-tweets-151721645.html.

22. Kevin Johnson, "Intel Chair Nunes Met Source of New Surveillance Documents at White House," *USA Today*, March 27, 2017, https://www.usatoday.com/story/news/politics/2017/03/27/intel-chair-nunes-met-source-new-surveillance-documents-white-house/99685382/.

23. Veronica Stracqualursi and Adam Kelsey, "A Timeline of President Trump's Unsubstantiated Wiretapping Claims," ABC News, April 6, 2017, http://abcnews.go.com/Politics/timeline-president-trumps-unsubstantiated-wiretapping-claims/story?id=46198888.

24. Michael S. Schmidt, "Comey Memo Says Trump Asked Him to End Flynn Investigation," *New York Times*, May 16, 2017, https://www.nytimes.com/2017/05/16/us/politics/james-comey-trump-flynn-russia-investigation.html.

25. James Comey, "Statement for the Record Senate Select Committee on Intelligence," June 8, 2017, https://www.intelligence.senate.gov/sites/default/files/documents/os-jcomey-060817.pdf.

26. Ibid.

27. Michael D. Shear and Matt Apuzzo, "F.B.I. Director James Comey Is Fired by Trump," *New York Times*, May 9, 2017, https://www.nytimes.com/2017/05/09/us/politics/james-comey-fired-fbi.html.

28. Ibid.

29. Ibid.

30. Andrew McCabe, *The Threat: How the FBI Protects America in the Age of Terrorism and Trump* (New York: Simon and Schuster, 2019), 222.

31. Andrew Prokop, "Trump Has Now Admitted He Fired Comey Because of the Russia Investigation," Vox, May 11, 2017, https://www.vox.com/2017/5/11/15628276/trump-comey-fired-russia.

32. McCabe, *The Threat*, 40.

33. Ibid., 14.

34. Robert S. Mueller III, special counsel, *Report on the Investigation into Russian Interference in the 2016 Presidential Election*, vol. 2 (Washington, DC: US Department of Justice, March 2016), 78.

35. Ibid.

36. Natasha Bertrand and Scott Stedman, "Papadopoulos's Russia Ties Continue to Intrigue the FBI," *Atlantic*, November 28, 2018, https://www.theatlantic.com/politics/archive/2018/11/papadopouloss-russia-ties-still-interest-fbi-schiff/576895/.

37. *United States of America v. George Papadopoulos*, US Department of Justice, October 5, 2017, https://www.justice.gov/file/1007346/download.

38. Raphael Satter, "Malta Academic in Trump Probe Has History of Vanishing Acts," Associated Press, October 22, 2018, https://apnews.com/800354d636af47f3afbd19338a377887?utm_medium=AP&utm_source=Twitter&utm_campaign=SocialFlow.

39. Evan Perez, Shimon Prokupecz, and Pamela Brown, "Exclusive: US government Wiretapped Trump Campaign Chairman," CNN, September 18, 2017, http://edition.cnn.com/2017/09/18/politics/paul-manafort-government-wiretapped-fisa-russians/.

40. *U.S. v. Paul J. Manafort, Jr.* (1:17-cr-201, District of Columbia), "Superseding Criminal Information," September 14, 2018, https://www.justice.gov/file/1094141/download.

41. Issie Lapowsky, "Facebook May Have More Russian Troll Farms to Worry About," *Wired*, September 8, 2017, https://www.wired.com/story/facebook-may-have-more-russian-troll-farms-to-worry-about/.

Chapter 12—All the (Russian) President's Men

1. Adam Entous, Ellen Nakashima, and Greg Miller, "Sessions Met with Russian Envoy Twice Last Year, Encounters He Later Did Not Disclose, *Washington Post*, March 1, 2017, https://www.washingtonpost.com/world/national-security/sessions-spoke-twice-with-russian-ambassador-during-trumps-presidential-campaign-justice-officials-say/2017/03/01/77205eda-feac-11e6-99b4-9e613afeb09f_story.html?utm_term=.cec55cf460bd.

2. "Lindsey Graham Dismisses Obama's 'Pebble' Thrown at Russia: 'I'm Ready to Throw a Rock,'" *Week*, January 5, 2017, https://theweek.com/speedreads/671338/lindsey-graham-dismisses-obamas-pebble-thrown-russia-im-ready-throw-rock.

3. Kristen Mitchell, "Lindsey Graham, John McCain Share Concerns on Russia," GW Today, March 2, 2017, https://gwtoday.gwu.edu/lindsey-graham-john-mccain-share-concerns-russia.

4. Lissette Rodriguez, "Lindsey Graham Says Campaign Account Hacked by Russia," ABC News, December 14, 2016, https://abcnews.go.com/Politics/lindsey-graham-campaign-account-hacked-russia/story?id=44199574.

5. Manu Raju, "Graham Encouraged McCain to Turn Trump-Russia Dossier Over to FBI," CNN, March 25, 2019, https://www.cnn.com/2019/03/25/politics/lindsey-graham-john-mccain-dossier-fbi/index.html.

6. Ruth May, "How Putin's Oligarchs Funneled Millions into GOP Campaigns," *Dallas Morning News*, May 8, 2018, https://www.dallasnews.com/opinion/commentary/2017/12/15/putins-proxies-helped-funnel-millions-gop-campaigns.

7. Isaac Arnsdorf and Benjamin Oreskes, "Putin's Favorite Congressman," Politico, November 23, 2016, https://www.politico.com/story/2016/11/putin-congress-rohrabacher-trump-231775.

8. John Rabe and Kitty Felde, "Rep. Dana Rohrabacher: I Arm Wrestled Vladimir Putin . . . and Lost!," KPCC, September 12, 2013, https://www.scpr.org/programs

/offramp/2013/09/12/33692/congressman-dana-rohrabacher-i-arm-wrestled-vladim/.

9. Arnsdorf and Oreskes, "Putin's Favorite Congressman."

10. Jordan Graham, "California GOP Congressman Met with Accused Russian Agent Maria Butina in St. Petersburg," *Mercury News* (San Jose, CA), July 18, 2018, https://www.mercurynews.com/2018/07/18/orange-county-congressman-rohrabacher-met-with-accused-spy-in-russia/.

11. Ashley May, "Pro-Russia Dana Rohrabacher Set to Lose to Harley Rouda in California Congressional Race," *USA Today*, November 7, 2018, https://www.usatoday.com/story/news/politics/elections/2018/11/07/election-results-2018-dana-rohrabacher-harvey-rouda/1917374002/.

12. Ryan Evans, Twitter, December 25, 2017, https://twitter.com/Usefulnotes_/status/945691334844788737.

13. Andrew Desiderio, "GOP Senators Tell Contradictory Stories about Moscow Trip," Daily Beast, July 10, 2018, https://www.thedailybeast.com/gop-senators-tell-contradictory-stories-about-moscow-trip.

14. Jordain Carney, "McCain: Rand Paul 'Working for Vladimir Putin,'" *Hill* (Washington, DC), March 15, 2017, https://thehill.com/blogs/floor-action/senate/324182-mccain-rand-paul-working-for-vladimir-putin.

15. Jennifer Hansler, "Rand Paul Wants Trump to Lift US Travel Sanctions on Some Russian Lawmakers," CNN, August 17, 2018, https://www.cnn.com/2018/08/17/politics/rand-paul-russian-lawmakers-sanctions/index.html.

16. Eli Watkins, "WaPo: Trump Hasn't Signed Off on Russia Sanctions Haley Announced," CNN, April 17, 2018, https://www.cnn.com/2018/04/16/politics/nikki-haley-trump-russia/index.html.

17. Congress.gov, "H.R.1677-Caesar Syria Civilian Protection Act of 2018," https://www.congress.gov/bill/115th-congress/house-bill/1677.

18. Rebecca Morin, "Rand Paul Delivers Letter from Trump to Putin," Politico, August 8, 2018, https://www.politico.com/story/2018/08/08/rand-paul-delivers-letter-to-trump-from-putin-766743.

19. Tina Nguyen, "Rand Paul Is Trump's Perfect Russia Stooge," *Vanity Fair*, August 7, 2018, https://www.vanityfair.com/news/2018/08/rand-paul-donald-trump-perfect-russia-stooge.

20. Ibid.

21. Joe Gould, "Here's Why 22 Republicans Voted against Blocking Trump from NATO Pullout," *Defense News*, January 24, 2019, https://www.defensenews.com/congress/2019/01/25/heres-why-22-republicans-voted-against-blocking-trump-from-nato-pullout/.

22. "Final Vote Results for Roll Call 44," H R 676: NATO Support Act, House of Representatives, January 22, 2019, http://clerk.house.gov/evs/2019/roll044.xml.

23. George Washington to Lafayette, 7 February 1788, Founders Online, National Archives, https://founders.archives.gov/documents/Washington/04-06-02-0079.

24. Mark Slater, Twitter, February 26, 2019, https://twitter.com/MarkSalter55/status/1100597999607209990?s=20.

25. Editorial board, "Cohen in the Colosseum," *Wall Street Journal*, February 27, 2019, https://www.wsj.com/articles/cohen-in-the-colosseum-11551314328.

Chapter 13—The Trump Doctrine: Buying This American, Buys America

1. Brian Fung, "What Does Teddy Roosevelt's 'Big Stick' Line Really Mean, Anyway?," *Atlantic*, September 24, 2012, https://www.theatlantic.com/politics/archive/2012/09/what-does-teddy-roosevelts-big-stick-line-really-mean-anyway/262579/.

2. Shane Harris, Carol Leonnig, Greg Jaffe, and Josh Dawsey, "Kushner's Overseas Contacts Raise Concerns as Foreign Officials Seek Leverage," *Washington Post*, February 27, 2018, https://www.washingtonpost.com/world/national-security/kushners-overseas-contacts-raise-concerns-as-foreign-officials-seek-leverage/2018/02/27/16bbc052-18c3-11e8-942d-16a950029788_story.html.

3. Suzanne Craig, Jo Becker, and Jesse Drucker, "Jared Kushner, a Trump In-Law and Adviser, Chases a Chinese Deal," *New York Times*, January 7, 2017, https://www.nytimes.com/2017/01/07/us/politics/jared-kushner-trump-business.html.

4. Charles Bagli and Kate Kelly, "Deal Gives Kushners Cash Infusion on 666 Fifth Avenue," *New York Times*, August 3, 2018, https://www.nytimes.com/2018/08/03/nyregion/kushners-building-fifth-avenue-brookfield-lease.html.

5. Adam Entous, Greg Miller, Kevin Sieff, and Karen DeYoung, "Blackwater Founder Held Secret Seychelles Meeting to Establish Trump-Putin Back Channel," *Washington Post*, April 3, 2017, https://www.washingtonpost.com/world/national-security/blackwater-founder-held-secret-seychelles-meeting-to-establish-trump-putin-back-channel/2017/04/03/95908a08-1648-11e7-ada0-1489b735b3a3_story.html?utm_term=.00e5f18a97ae.

6. Jen Kirby, "Erik Prince May Have Lied to Congress about His Seychelles Meeting," Vox, May 10, 2018, https://www.vox.com/2018/3/10/17097692/seychelles-erik-prince-congress-mueller.

7. Eric Levitz, "Report: UAE Orchestrated Qatari Feud by Spreading Fake News," *New York Magazine*, July 17, 2017, http://nymag.com/intelligencer/2017/07/report-uae-orchestrated-qatar-feud-by-spreading-fake-news.html.

8. Bess Levin, "Qatar Shocked to Learn It Accidentally Bailed Out Jared Kushner," *New York Magazine*, February 12, 2019, https://www.vanityfair.com/news/2019/02/qatar-666-5th-ave-jared-kushner.

9. Will Parker, "Brookfield Closes Largest Piece of Refinancing at 666 Fifth, Formerly Kushner's Crown Jewel," The Real Deal: New York Real Estate News, January 3, 2019, https://therealdeal.com/2019/01/03/brookfield-closes-largest-piece-of-666-fifth-refinancing/.

10. Levin, "Qatar Shocked to Learn It Accidentally Bailed Out Jared Kushner."

11. Edward Luce, "Jared Kushner and the Triumph of Saudi Arabia," *Financial Times*, February 21, 2019, https://www.ft.com/content/90d98374-3528-11e9-bb0c-42459962a812.

12. Alex Emmons, Ryan Grim, and Clayton Swisher, "Saudi Crown Prince Boasted That Jared Kushner Was 'in His Pocket,'" The Intercept, March 21, 2018, https://theintercept.com/2018/03/21/jared-kushner-saudi-crown-prince-mohammed-bin-salman/.

13. Javier C. Hernández, Cao Li, and Jesse Drucker, "Jared Kushner's Sister Highlights Family Ties in Pitch to Chinese Investors," *New York Times,* May 6, 2017, https://www.nytimes.com/2017/05/06/world/asia/jared-kushner-sister-nicole-meyer-china-investors.html.

14. Al Jazeera, "Trump Arrives in Saudi Arabia in First Foreign Visit," Al Jazeera, May 20, 2017, https://www.aljazeera.com/news/2017/05/trump-arrives-saudi-arabia-foreign-trip-170520063253596.html.

15. Merrit Kennedy, "In Saudi Arabia, Trump Says Fight against Terrorism, a 'Battle between Good and Evil,'" NPR, May 21, 2017, https://www.npr.org/sections/thetwoway/2017/05/21/529378735/in-saudi-arabia-trump-says-fight-against-terrorism-a-battle-between-good-and-evil.

16. BBC News, "Khashoggi Murder: Body 'Dissolved in Acid,'" BBC News, November 2, 2018, https://www.bbc.com/news/world-middle-east-46070087.

17. Nicole Gaoulette, "As Cohen Rivets Washington, White House Announces Kushner Met with Saudi Crown Prince," CNN, February 27, 2019, https://www.cnn.com/2019/02/27/politics/kushner-saudi-prince-visit-khashoggi/index.html.

18. "Trump Says Khashoggi Murder 'Worst Cover-up in History,'" BBC News, Ocotber 24, 2018, https://www.bbc.com/news/world-us-canada-45960865.

19. "Trump Says Standing by Saudi Crown Prince Despite Pleas from Senate," Reuters, December 11, 2018, https://www.cnbc.com/2018/12/12/donald-trump-supports-saudi-crown-prince-mohammed-bin-salman.html.

20. Martin Pengelly, "Trump: CIA 'Didn't Conclude' Saudi Crown Prince Ordered Khashoggi Death," *Guardian* (Manchester, UK), November 22, 2018, https://www.theguardian.com/us-news/2018/nov/22/trump-cia-saudi-crown-prince-jamal-khashoggi-murder.

21. Warren Strobel, Nathan Layne, and Jonathan Landay, "Exclusive: Mideast Nuclear Plan Backers Bragged of Support of Top Trump Aide Flynn," Reuters, December 1, 2017, https://www.reuters.com/article/us-usa-trump-flynn-nuclear-exclusive/exclusive-mideast-nuclear-plan-backers-bragged-of-support-of-top-trump-aide-flynn-idUSKBN1DV5Z6.

22. Ibid.

23. *Times of Israel* staff, "Netanyahu Said to Ask Trump Not to Sell Saudis Nuclear Reactors," *Times of Israel,* March 9, 2018, https://www.timesofisrael.com/netanyahu-said-to-ask-trump-not-to-supply-nuclear-reactors-to-saudi-arabia/.

24. Interim Staff Report, House Oversight Committee, *Whistleblowers Raise Grave Concerns with Trump Administration's Efforts to Transfer Sensitive Nuclear Technology to Saudi Arabia,* US House of Representatives, February 2019, https://www.documentcloud.org/documents/5743767-House-Oversight-Whistleblowers-Saudi-Nuclear.html.

25. "MBS: Saudis Will Pursue Nuclear Weapons If Iran Does," Al Jazeera, March 15, 2018, https://www.aljazeera.com/news/2018/03/mbs-saudis-pursue-nuclear-weapons-iran-180315152433732.html.

26. "Workshop on Russian Nuclear Technologies Held in Saudi Arabia," Press Service of Rusatom International Network, Rosatom, December 6, 2018, https://www.rosatom.ru/en/press-centre/news/workshop-on-russian-nuclear-technologies-held-in-saudi-arabia/.

27. Bushehr Nuclear Power Plant (BNPP), Iran country profile, Nuclear Threat Initiative (NTI), July 10, 2017, https://www.nti.org/learn/facilities/184/.

28. Anna Borshchevskaya, "The Tactical Side of Russia's Arms Sales to the Middle East," Jamestown Foundation, December 20, 2017, https://jamestown.org/program/tactical-side-russias-arms-sales-middle-east/.

29. Elisabeth Dyck, "IAEA Delivers Report on Nuclear Power Infrastructure Development to Saudi Arabia," International Atomic Energy Agency, January 25, 2019, https://www.iaea.org/newscenter/news/iaea-delivers-report-on-nuclear-power-infrastructure-development-to-saudi-arabia.

30. Asharq al-Awsat, "Saudi Arabia Receives Offers from Five Countries to Build Two Nuclear Reactors," *Asharq al-Awsat* (London), January 23, 2019, https://aawsat.com/english/home/article/1558606/saudi-arabia-receives-offers-5-countries-build-2-nuclear-reactors.

31. "Bin Salman Launches Saudi Arabia's First Nuclear Plant Project," Al Jazeera, November 5, 2018, https://www.aljazeera.com/news/2018/11/bin-salman-launches-saudi-arabia-nuclear-plant-project-181105192827938.html.

Chapter 14—Hydra 2.0: Destroying America's Security from Within

1. Alexander Dugin, "Dugin's Guideline; American Hegemony; The Dragon Is Wounded," Katehon Think Tank, YouTube video, 8:43, July 22, 2016, https://www.youtube.com/watch?v=KqTqnaB7hRM.

2. Aileen Graef, "Chuck Hagel: Trump 'an Embarrassment,'" CNN, January 15, 2017, http://www.cnn.com/2018/01/14/politics/chuck-hagel-donald-trump/index.html.

3. Daniel Politi, "Former Joint Chiefs Head: 'Never Been Closer to Nuclear War with North Korea,'" Slate, December 31, 2017, https://slate.com/news-and-politics/2017/12/former-joint-chiefs-head-weve-never-been-closer-to-nuclear-war-with-north-korea.html.

4. Chris Tomlinson, "Trump's Right Hand Man in Europe Rick Grenell Wants to 'Empower' European Conservatives," Breitbart News, June 3, 2018, https://www.breitbart.com/europe/2018/06/03/trumps-right-hand-man-in-europe-wants-to-empower-european-anti-establishment-conservatives/.

5. Greg Miller, "Trump Has Concealed Details of His Face-to-Face Encounters with Putin from Senior Officials in Administration," *Washington Post*, January 13, 2019, https://www.washingtonpost.com/world/national-security/trump-has-concealed-details-of-his-face-to-face-encounters-with-putin-from-senior-officials-in-administration/2019/01/12/65f6686c-1434-11e9-b6ad-9cfd62dbb0a8_story.html.

6. Ibid.

7. Jennie Neufeld, "Read the Full Transcript of the Helsinki Press Conference," Vox, July 17, 2018, https://www.vox.com/2018/7/16/17576956/transcript-putin-trump-russia-helsinki-press-conference.

8. Ibid.

9. Ibid.

10. Ibid.

11. Ibid.

12. Ibid.

13. Ibid.

14. Jon Greenberg, "Putin's Pants-on-Fire Claim about $400 Million Donation to Clinton from Bill Browder Partners," PolitiFact, July 16, 2018, https://www.politifact.com/truth-o-meter/statements/2018/jul/16/vladimir-putin/putins-pants-fire-claim-about-400-million-donation/.

15. Neufeld, "Read the Full Transcript of the Helsinki Press Conference."

16. Kevin Poulsen, "Trump's 'Missing DNC Server' Is Neither Missing, Nor a Server," Daily Beast, July 16, 2018, https://www.thedailybeast.com/trumps-missing-dnc-server-is-neither-missing-nor-a-server.

17. Neufeld, "Read the Full Transcript of the Helsinki Press Conference."

18. Dan Mangan, "Sen. John McCain Says Trump Gave 'One of the Most Disgraceful Performances by an American President' at Putin Summit," CNBC, July 16, 2018, https://www.cnbc.com/2018/07/16/john-mccain-says-trump-abased-himself-before-putin-at-summit.html.

19. Douglas E. Schoen, "Putin Eats Trump's Lunch in Helsinki: This Is No Way to Win against Russia," Fox News, July 16, 2018, https://www.foxnews.com/opinion/putin-eats-trumps-lunch-in-helsinki-this-is-no-way-to-win-against-russia.

20. Philip Bump, "Where the U.S. Has Considered Leaving or Left International Agreements under Trump," *Washington Post*, June 29, 2018, https://www.washingtonpost.com/news/politics/wp/2018/06/29/where-the-u-s-has-considered-leaving-or-left-international-agreements-under-trump/?utm_term=.a42e26e419b9.

21. Priyanka Boghani, "The US and North Korea on the Brink: A Timeline," PBS, February 28, 2019, https://www.pbs.org/wgbh/frontline/article/the-u-s-and-north-korea-on-the-brink-a-timeline/.

22. Meghan Keneally, "From 'Fire and Fury' to 'Rocket Man,' the Various Barbs Traded Between Trump and Kim Jong Un," ABC News, June 12, 2018, https://abcnews.go.com/International/fire-fury-rocket-man-barbs-traded-trump-kim/story?id=53634996.

23. Boghani, "The US and North Korea on the Brink: A Timeline."

24. Phil McCausland, "Kim Jong Un Calls President Trump 'Dotard' and 'Frightened Dog,'" NBC News, September 21, 2017, https://www.nbcnews.com/news/world/north-korea-s-kim-jong-un-calls-president-trump-frightened-n803631.

25. Keneally, "From 'Fire and Fury' to 'Rocket Man.'"

26. Justin McCurry and Julian Borger, "North Korea Missile Launch: Regime Says New Rocket Can Hit Anywhere in US," *Guardian* (Manchester, UK), November 29, 2017, https://www.theguardian.com/world/2017/nov/28/north-korea-has-fired-ballistic-missile-say-reports-in-south-korea.

27. Geoff Brumfiel, "North Korea Has Miniaturized a Nuclear Warhead, U.S. Intelligence Says," NPR, August 8, 2017, https://www.npr.org/2017/08/08/542286036/north-korea-has-miniaturized-a-nuclear-warhead-u-s-intelligence-says.

28. Yaron Steinbuch, "US Preparing 'Bloody Nose' Attack on North Korea," *New York Post*, December 21, 2017, https://nypost.com/2017/12/21/us-preparing-bloody-nose-attack-on-north-korea/.

29. Keneally, "From 'Fire and Fury' to 'Rocket Man.'"

30. Ibid.

31. "Trump Kim Summit: US and North Korean Leaders Hold Historic Talks," BBC News, June 12, 2018, https://www.bbc.com/news/world-asia-44435035.

32. "Trump and Kim in Quotes: From a Bitter Rivalry to Unlikely Bromance," Al Jazeera, February 27, 2019, https://www.aljazeera.com/news/2019/02/trump-kim-quotes-bitter-rivalry-bromance-190228004711797.html.

33. Hannah Ellis-Petersen and Benjamin Hass, "How North Korea Got Away with the Assassination of Kim Jong-nam," *Guardian* (Manchester, UK), April 1, 2019, https://www.theguardian.com/world/2019/apr/01/how-north-korea-got-away-with-the-assassination-of-kim-jong-nam.

34. "Trump and Kim in Quotes."

35. Andrew McCabe, *The Threat: How the FBI Protects America in the Age of Terrorism and Trump* (New York: St. Martin's Press, 2018), 156.

36. Maggie Haberman, Michael S Schmidt, Adam Goldman, and Annie Karni, "Trump Ordered Officials to Give Jared Kushner a Security Clearance," *New York Times*, February 28, 2019, https://www.cnn.com/2019/03/01/us/five-things-march-1-trnd/index.html.

37. Stephen Collinson, "Kushner, Russia Bombshells Rock the White House," CNN, updated February 28, 2018, https://www.cnn.com/2018/02/28/politics/donald-trump-jared-kushner-investigations/index.html.

38. Dan Merica, "Officials from Four Countries Discussed Exploiting Jared Kushner," CNN, updated February 28, 2018, https://www.cnn.com/2018/02/27/politics/jared-kushner-manipulation-mexico-israel-china-uae/index.html.

39. Susan Murray and Jeremy Diamond, "Source: Some White House Staff Worry Kushner Security Clearance in Jeopardy," CNN, July 18, 2017, https://www.cnn.com/2017/07/18/politics/jared-kushner-security-clearance/index.html.

40. Mark Lander and Maggie Haberman, "With Glare on Trump Children, Political Gets Personal for President," *New York Times*, July 12, 2017, https://www.nytimes.com/2017/07/12/us/politics/trump-says-son-is-innocent-amid-reports-of-russia-meeting.html.

41. Christian Berthelsel, "Russia Laundering Probe Puts Trump Tower Meeting in New Light," *Bloomberg News*, September 15, 2017, https://www.bloomberg.com/news/articles/2017-09-15/russia-laundering-probe-puts-trump-tower-meeting-in-new-light.

42. Darla Cameraon, Amy Brittain, and Jonathan O'Connell, "What Jared Kushner Still Owns," *Washington Post*, May 21, 2017, https://www.washingtonpost.com/graphics/politics/kushner-conflicts/?utm_term=.c3810b941e5d.

43. Committee Staff, "Summary of Interview with White House Whistleblower on Security Clearances" (memorandum), Committee on Oversight and Reform, US House of Representatives, April 1, 2019, https://www.politico.com/f/?id=00000169-d8ff-dc59-a16d-feff50910001.

44. Chris Cillizza, "Here's What Ivanka Trump Still Doesn't Get about Her Email Problems," CNN, November 28, 2018, https://www.cnn.com/2018/11/28/politics/ivanka-trump-emails-gma/index.html.

45. Rebecca Morin, "Trump Pulls Security Clearance of Ex-CIA Director John Brennan," Politico, August 15, 2018, https://www.politico.com/story/2018/08/15/trump-pulls-security-clearance-of-ex-cia-director-brennan-778791.

46. William McRaven, "Revoke My Security Clearance, Too, Mr. President," *Washington Post*, August 16, 2018, https://www.washingtonpost.com/opinions/revoke-my-security-clearance-too-mr-president/2018/08/16/8b149b02-a178-11e8-93e3-24d1703d2a7a_story.html.

Chapter 15—The Asteroid of Awfulness

1. NPR, Twitter, July 4, 2017, https://twitter.com/NPR/status/882316829301116928.

2. Josh Dawsey, Isaac Arnsdorf, et al., "Trump's Team Nixed Ethics Course for White House Staff," Politico, March 2, 2017, www.politico.com/story/2017/03/trump-ethics-white-house-235586.

3. Minority staff report, *Putin's Asymmetric Assault on Democracy in Russia and Europe: Implications for U.S. National Security*, Committee on Foreign Relations, US Senate, 115th Congress, Second Session (Washington, DC: US GPO, 2018), https://www.govinfo.gov/content/pkg/CPRT-115SPRT28110/html/CPRT-115SPRT28110.htm.

4. McFaul, Ambassador Michael, Twitter @McFaul, https://twitter.com/McFaul?ref_src-twsrc965Egoogle967Ctwcamp965Exerp967Ctwgr965Eauthor.

5. Michael M. Grynbaum, "Trump Strategist Stephen Bannon Says Media Should 'Keep Its Mouth Shut,'" *New York Times*, January 26, 2017, www.nytimes.com/2017/01/26/business/media/stephen-bannon-trump-news-media.html.

6. Sara Fischer, "Journalists Keep Getting in Trouble for Tweeting," Axios, June 5, 2017, https://www.axios.com/journalists-keep-getting-in-trouble-for-tweeting-1513302760-ec8fc61f-243e-47e6-b7e9-81e071bf30fe.html.

7. Eric Wemple, "To Discredit and to Demean: Trump Bragged about His Media-Bashing Strategy," *Washington Post*, May 22, 2018, https://www.washingtonpost.com/blogs/erik-wemple/wp/2018/05/22/to-discredit-and-to-demean-trump-bragged-about-his-media-bashing-strategy/?utm_term=.f708b9db550d.

8. Alex Ward, "Trump Laments That US Troops Can't Get 'Rough' with Migrants at the Border," Vox, April 19, 2019, https://www.vox.com/policy-and-politics/2019/4/10/18305175/trump-border-immigration-military-texas.

9. Paul Brandus, "President Trump Makes Citizenship Hard Work, but Don't Give Up on America," *USA Today*, December 29, 2017, https://www.usatoday.com/story/opinion/2017/12/29/trump-reminds-americans-every-day-citizenship-hard-work-but-dont-give-up-paul-brandus-column/985917001/.

10. Ezra Klein, Twitter, December 29, 2017.

11. Andrew McCabe, *The Threat: How the FBI Protects America in the Age of Terror and Trump* (New York: Simon and Schuster, 2019), 217.

12. Ibid.

13. Fiona Hill and Clifford Gaddy, *Mr. Putin: Operative in the Kremlin* (Washington, DC: Brookings Institution Press, 2013), 13.

14. Garry Kasparov, Twitter, December 27, 2017, https://twitter.com/kasparov63/status/946125063312551938?lang=en.

15. Carl Reiner, Twitter, https://twitter.com/carlreiner?lang=en.

16. George Washington to President Reed, July 29, 1775, Revolutionary War and Beyond, http://www.revolutionary-war-and-beyond.com/george-washington-letter-to-joseph-reed-january-4-1776.html.

17. Alex Morales, "Trump Is an 'Asteroid of Awfulness,' U.K. Labour Party Says," *Bloomberg News*, January 14, 2018, https://www.bloomberg.com/news/articles/2018-01-14/trump-branded-asteroid-of-awfulness-by-u-k-labour-party.

Chapter 16—"The End of My Presidency . . ."

1. Matthew Whitaker, "Mueller's Investigation into Trump Is Going Too Far," CNN, November 7, 2018, https://www.cnn.com/2017/08/06/opinions/rosenstein-should-curb-mueller-whittaker-opinion/index.html.

2. Jeremy Herb and Jeff Zeleny, "Whitaker Was Campaign Chairman for Mueller Witness," CNN, November 7, 2018, https://www.cnn.com/2018/11/07/politics/whitaker-sessions-mueller-clovis/index.html.

3. George Bush, CIA Director, draft letter to Senator Mike Mansfield, re: records destruction moratorium, May 20, 1976, https://assets.documentcloud.org/documents/5912516/CIA-RDP77M00144R000800070004-6.pdf.

4. Kim Ellis, "READ: Bill Barr's 19-Page Memo Ripping Mueller Probe," *National Law Journal*, December 20, 2018, https://www.law.com/nationallawjournal/2018/12/20/read-bill-barrs-19-page-memo-ripping-mueller-probe/?slreturn=20190316231011; "William P. Barr Oral History" (transcript), Miller Center, University of Virginia, interview date April 5, 2001, https://millercenter.org/the-presidency/presidential-oral-histories/william-p-barr-oral-history.

5. Ibid.

6. Christina Maza, "Should William Barr Recuse Himself from Mueller Report? Legal Experts Say Attorney General's Ties to Russia Are Troubling," *Newsweek*, April 15, 2019, https://www.newsweek.com/so-many-conflicts-so-little-time-1396435.

7. Ibid.

8. Ibid.

9. Committee of the Judiciary, US Senate, "Testimony of Natalia Veselnitskaya," November 20, 2017, https://www.judiciary.senate.gov/imo/media/doc/2017-11-20%20Veselnitskaya%20to%20CEG%20(June%209%20Meeting).pdf.

10. Maza, "Should William Barr Recuse Himself from Mueller Report?"

11. William Barr, "Trump Was Right to Fire Sally Yates," *Washington Post*, February 1, 2017, https://www.washingtonpost.com/opinions/former-attorney-general-trump-was-right-to-fire-sally-yates/2017/02/01/5981d890-e809-11e6-80c2-30e57e57e05d_story.html.

12. Ibid.

13. Matt Zapotosky, "As Mueller Builds His Russia Special-Counsel Team, Every Hire Is Under Scrutiny," July 5, 2017, *Washington Post*, https://www.washingtonpost

.com/news/post-politics/wp/2017/07/05/as-mueller-grows-his-russia-special-counsel-team-every-hire-is-under-scrutiny/.

14. Peter Baker, "Lock Her Up Becomes More Than Slogan," *New York Times*, November 14, 2017, https://www.nytimes.com/2017/11/14/us/politics/trump-pressure-clinton-investigation.html.

15. Aaron Blake, "William Barr Tries to Clean Up His Clinton Comments—but Stumbles into a New Mueller Problem," *Washington Post*, January 16, 2019, https://www.washingtonpost.com/politics/2019/01/16/william-barr-tries-clean-up-his-clinton-comments-stumbles-into-new-mueller-problem/?utm_term=.7bb684073f2d.

16. Ellis, "Read: Bill Barr's 19-Page Memo Ripping Mueller Probe."

17. Sharon LaFraniere and Katie Benner, "Mueller Delivers Report on Trump-Russia Investigation to Attorney General," *New York Times*, March 22, 2019, https://www.nytimes.com/2019/03/22/us/politics/mueller-report.html.

18. "Read Attorney General William Barr's Summary of the Mueller Report," *New York Times*, March 24, 2019, https://www.nytimes.com/interactive/2019/03/24/us/politics/barr-letter-mueller-report.html.

19. Lawrence Tribe, "Yes, the Constitution Allows Indictment of the President," Lawfare, December 20, 2018, https://www.lawfareblog.com/yes-constitution-allows-indictment-president.

20. Department of Justice, "Attorney General William P. Barr Delivers Remarks on the Release of the Report on the Investigation into Russian Interference in the 2016 Presidential Election," April 18, 2019, https://www.justice.gov/opa/speech/attorney-general-william-p-barr-delivers-remarks-release-report-investigation-russian.

21. Ibid.

22. Josh Gerstein, "Judge: Barr Sowing Public Mistrust with Mueller Report Handling," Politico, April 16, 2019, https://www.politico.com/story/2019/04/16/judge-barr-mistrust-mueller-1278030.

23. Robert S. Mueller III, special counsel, *Report on the Investigation into Russian Interference in the 2016 Presidential Election*, Vol. 1 (Washington, DC: US Department of Justice, March 2016), 1.

24. Ibid., 2.

25. Ibid., 10.

26. Matt Apuzzo, Adam Goldman, and Nicholas Fandos, "Code Name Crossfire Hurricane: The Secret Origins of the Trump Investigation," *New York Times*, May 16, 2018, https://www.nytimes.com/2018/05/16/us/politics/crossfire-hurricane-trump-russia-fbi-mueller-investigation.html.

27. Ibid.

28. Georgetown University Institute of Politics and Public Service, "Justice & Law: A Conversation w/Former U.S. Dep AG Sally Yates," YouTube video, 1:06:01, April 4, 2018, https://www.youtube.com/watch?v=SpRp7natc20.

29. Robert S. Mueller III, special counsel, *Report on the Investigation into Russian Interference in the 2016 Presidential Election*, Vol. 2 (Washington, DC: US Department of Justice, March 2016), 7.

30. Mueller, *Report on the Investigation into Russian Interference*, 1:188.

31. Ibid.

32. Mueller, *Report on the Investigation into Russian Interference*, 2:12.

33. Ibid.

34. Ibid., 3.

35. Ibid.

36. Ibid., 4

37. Ibid.

38. Ibid., 5.

39. Ibid.

40. Ibid.

41. Ibid.

42. Ibid.

43. Issac Stanley-Becker, "Calling Michael Cohen a 'Rat,' Trump Brings 'American Underworld' Lingo to the White House," *Washington Post*, December 17, 2018, https://www.washingtonpost.com/nation/2018/12/17/calling-michael-cohen-rat-trump-brings-american-underworld-lingo-white-house/.

44. Mueller, *Report on the Investigation into Russian Interference*, 2:7.

45. Ibid., 8.

46. Ibid., 2.

47. Mueller, *Report on the Investigation into Russian Interference*, 1:10.

48. Camilo Montoya-Galvez, "Justice Department Offers Mueller Docs If House Intel Drops Barr Contempt Threat," CBS, May 21, 2019, https://www.cbsnews.com/news/justice-department-offers-mueller-docs-if-house-dems-drop-barr-contempt-threat/.

49. Robert S. Mueller III, Special Counsel, to Attorney General William P. Barr, RE: Report of the Special Counsel on the Investigation into Russian Interference in the 2016 Presidential Election and Obstruction of Justice (March 2019), March 27, 2019, https://www.documentcloud.org/documents/5984397-Letter-32719.html#document/p1.

50. "William Barr Testifies on Mueller Report Before Senate Judiciary Committee," CSPAN, May 1, 2019, https://www.c-span.org/video/?459922-1/william-barr-testifies-mueller-report-senate-judiciary-committee.

51. Ibid.

52. Felicia Sonmez, "In Reversal, Trump Says Mueller 'Should Not Testify' Before Congress," *Washington Post*, May 5, 2019, https://www.washingtonpost.com/politics/house-democrat-says-mueller-and-judiciary-committee-tentatively-agree-on-may-15-for-his-testimony-on-russia-investigation/2019/05/05/576dabae-6f45-11e9-8be0-ca575670e91c_story.html?utm_term=.281cec867773.

53. Stephen Collinson, Laura Jarrett, and Veronica Stracqualursi, "Trump Invokes Executive Privilege over Mueller Report," CNN, May 8, 2019, https://www.cnn.com/2019/05/08/politics/trump-mueller-report-executive-privilege/index.html.

54. Jeremy Herb and Manu Raju, "House Committee Votes to Hold Barr in Contempt After Trump Invokes Executive Privilege," CNN, May 8, 2019, https://www.cnn.com/2019/05/08/politics/barr-contempt-vote-house-judiciary-committee/index.html.

55. Eric Lutz, "William Barr Hits Back at Democrats, Buries the Rest of the Mueller Report," *Vanity Fair*, May 8, 2019, https://www.vanityfair.com/news/2019/05/william-barr-hits-back-at-democrats-buries-the-rest-of-the-mueller-report-executive-privilege.

56. Matthew Kahn, "Document: Justice Department Letter to Nadler Invoking Executive Privilege over Unredacted Mueller Report," Lawfare, May 8, 2019, https://www.lawfareblog.com/document-justice-department-letter-nadler-invoking-executive-privilege-over-unredacted-mueller.

57. Caitlin Oprysko, "Trump Backs Off Statement That Mueller Shouldn't Testify," Politico, May 9, 2019, https://www.politico.com/story/2019/05/09/trump-mueller-testify-congress-1314257.

58. Sadie Gurman and Aruna Viswanatha, "Barr Says Review of Origins of Russia Probe Could Lead to Rule Changes," *Wall Street Journal*, May 17, 2019, https://www.wsj.com/articles/barr-review-of-origins-of-fbis-trump-russia-probe-could-lead-to-rule-changes-11558090803.

59. Caitlin Oprysko, "Barr: The Allegation I Lied to Congress Is 'Laughable,'" Politico, May 17, 2019, https://www.politico.com/story/2019/05/17/william-barr-congress-1330116.

60. Gregg Jarrett, *The Russia Hoax: The Illicit Scheme to Clear Hillary Clinton and Frame Donald Trump* (New York: Broadside Books, 2018).

61. Jack Holmes, "Trump Suggested His Pet Attorney General May Prosecute His Enemies for 'Treason,'" *Esquire*, May 21, 2019, https://www.esquire.com/news-politics/a27541034/donald-trump-william-barr-lock-them-up-democrats-fbi/.

62. Ryan Teague Beckwith, "President Trump Said Democrats Who Didn't Clap at the State of the Union Were 'Treasonous,'" *Time*, February 6, 2018, https://time.com/5134150/donald-trump-state-union-democrats-treasonous/.

63. Greg Sargent, "Trump: You Wouldn't Like My Supporters in the Military If They Got Angry," Plum Line (blog), *Washington Post*, March 14, 2019, https://www.washingtonpost.com/opinions/2019/03/14/trump-you-wouldnt-like-my-supporters-military-if-they-got-angry/?utm_term=.6476534613e8.

64. Tom Embury-Dennis, "Trump Refuses to Rule Out Opponents Being Executed for Treason," *The Independent*, May 24, 2019, https://www.independent.co.uk/news/world/americas/us-politics/trump-treason-comey-mccabe-strzok-page-white-house-a8928556.html?ref=hvper.com.

65. Daniel Chaitin, "Corey Lewandowski: Joe Biden 'Has Gotten a Pass' on Trump-Russia Investigation," *Washington Examiner*, May 24, 2019, https://www.washingtonexaminer.com/news/corey-lewandowski-joe-biden-has-gotten-a-pass-on-trump-russia-investigation.

66. "Special Counsel Robert Mueller Statement on Russia Investigation," CSPAN, May 29, 2019, https://www.c-span.org/video/?461196-1/special-counsel-robert-mueller-doj-policy-prohibited-indictment-president.

67. "Nadler: Mueller Clearly Demonstrated That Trump Is Lying," CNN, May 29, 2019, https://www.cnn.com/videos/politics/2019/05/29/jerry-nadler-statement-robert-mueller-response-sot-nr-vpx.cnn.

68. "Rep. Nadler After Mueller's Statement: It Falls to Congress to Deal with Trump," MSNBC, May 29, 2019, https://www.msnbc.com/msnbc/watch/rep

-nadler-after-mueller-s-statement-it-falls-to-congress-to-deal-with-trump-60505157597.

69. US Embassy in Ukraine, "Readout of Vice President Biden's Meeting with President of Ukraine Petro Poroshenko," January 21, 2016, https://ua.usembassy.gov/readout-vice-president-bidens-meeting-president-ukraine-petro-poroshenko-012116/.

70. Glenn Thrush and Kenneth Vogel, "What Joe Biden Actually Did in Ukraine," *New York Times*, November 10, 2019, updated March 6, 2020, https://www.nytimes.com/2019/11/10/us/politics/joe-biden-ukraine.html.

71. Council on Foreign Relations, "Foreign Affairs Issue Launch with Former Vice President Joe Biden," January 23, 2018, https://www.cfr.org/event/foreign-affairs-issue-launch-former-vice-president-joe-biden.

72. Donald Trump (@realDonaldTrump), "Ukrainian efforts to sabotage Trump campaign—'quietly working to boost Clinton,'" Twitter, July 25, 2017, 4:03 a.m., https://twitter.com/realDonaldTrump/status/889788202172780544.

73. Vicki Ward, "Exclusive: After Private White House Meeting, Giuliani Associate Lev Parnas Said He Was on a 'Secret Mission' for Trump, Sources Say," CNN, November 16, 2019, https://www.cnn.com/2019/11/15/politics/parnas-trump-special-mission-ukraine/index.html.

74. John Solomon, "As Russia Collusion Fades, Ukrainian Plot to Help Clinton Emerges," *The Hill*, March 30, 2019, https://thehill.com/opinion/campaign/435029-as-russia-collusion-fades-ukrainian-plot-to-help-clinton-emerges.

75. John Solomon, "US Embassy Pressed Ukraine to Drop Probe of George Soros Group During 2016 Election," *The Hill*, March 26, 2019, https://thehill.com/opinion/campaign/435906-us-embassy-pressed-ukraine-to-drop-probe-of-george-soros-group-during-2016.

76. Natasha Bertrand (@NatashaBertrand), "Here's the page from the packet that @ErinBanco shared yesterday (with emails blacked out by me)," Twitter, October 3, 2019, 7:57 a.m., https://twitter.com/NatashaBertrand/status/1179757424921718789/photo/1.

77. *Opening Statement Before the House Permanent Select Committee on Intelligence*, November 13, 2019 (statement of George P. Kent, Deputy Assistant Secretary, Bureau of European and Eurasian Affairs, US Department of State), https://intelligence.house.gov/uploadedfiles/kent_impeachment_testimony_final_clean.pdf.

78. John Solomon, "As Russia Collusion Fades, Ukrainian Plot to Help Clinton Emerges," *The Hill*, March 30, 2019, https://thehill.com/opinion/campaign/435029-as-russia-collusion-fades-ukrainian-plot-to-help-clinton-emerges.

79. Serhiy Leshchenko, "Rudy Giuliani Accused Me of Exposing Paul Manafort's Ukraine Deals to Help U.S. Democrats. That's a Lie," *Washington Post*, September 21, 2019, https://www.washingtonpost.com/opinions/2019/09/21/why-is-rudy-giuliani-trying-drag-my-countrys-president-into-trumps-reelection-campaign/.

80. Daryna Krasnolutska, Kateryna Choursina, and Stephanie Baker, "Ukraine Prosecutor Says No Evidence of Wrongdoing by Bidens," Bloomberg, May 16, 2019, https://www.bloomberg.com/news/articles/2019-05-16/ukraine-prosecutor-says-no-evidence-of-wrongdoing-by-bidens.

81. Leigh Ann Caldwell, Kristen Welker, Heidi Przybyla, Josh Lederman, and Abigail Williams, "Giuliani Says State Dept Vowed to Investigate After He Gave Ukraine Docs to Pompeo," NBC News, October 3, 2019, https://www.nbcnews.com/politics/trump-impeachment-inquiry/giuliani-says-state-dept-vowed-investigate-after-he-gave-ukraine-n1061931.

82. Karoun Demirjian, Josh Dawsey, Ellen Nakashima, and Carol Leonnig, "Trump Ordered Hold on Military Aid Days Before Calling Ukrainian President, Officials Say," *Washington Post*, September 23, 2019, https://www.washingtonpost.com/national-security/trump-ordered-hold-on-military-aid-days-before-calling-ukrainian-president-officials-say/2019/09/23/df93a6ca-de38-11e9-8dc8-498eabc129a0_story.html.

83. Justin Sink, "Russia Says President Trump Initiated Long Phone Call with Vladimir Putin," *Time*, May 4, 2019, https://time.com/5583327/trump-intiated-putin-long-phone-call/.

84. "George Kent Testimony: Key Excerpts from the Impeachment Inquiry Transcripts," *New York Times*, November 7, 2019, https://www.nytimes.com/2019/11/07/us/politics/george-kent-impeachment-testimony.html.

85. Adam Goldman, Charlie Savage, and Michael Schmidt, "Barr Assigns U.S. Attorney in Connecticut to Review Origins of Russia Inquiry," *New York Times*, May 13, 2019, https://www.nytimes.com/2019/05/13/us/politics/russia-investigation-justice-department-review.html.

86. Rudy Giuliani (@RudyGuiliani), "This is a test for the Pres.-elect," Twitter, May 18, 2019, https://twitter.com/RudyGiuliani/status/1129761369660841984?s=20.

87. Peter Baker and Nicholas Fandos, "Trump Is Assailed for Saying He Would Take Campaign Help from Russia," *New York Times*, June 13, 2019, https://www.nytimes.com/2019/06/13/us/politics/trump-russia-campaign-help.html.

88. White House, "Telephone Conversation with President Zelensky of Ukraine," memorandum of telephone conversation, July 25, 2019, declassified September 24, 2019, https://www.whitehouse.gov/wp-content/uploads/2019/09/Unclassified09.2019.pdf.

89. Greg Miller, Ellen Nakashima, and Shane Harris, "Trump's Communications with Foreign Leader Are Part of Whistleblower Complaint That Spurred Standoff Between Spy Chief and Congress, Former Officials Say," *Washington Post*, September 18, 2019, https://www.washingtonpost.com/national-security/trumps-communications-with-foreign-leader-are-part-of-whistleblower-complaint-that-spurred-standoff-between-spy-chief-and-congress-former-officials-say/2019/09/18/df651aa2-da60-11e9-bfb1-849887369476_story.html.

90. Eliot L. Engel, Adam Schiff, and Elijah E. Cummings, letter to Mike Pompeo, Secretary of State, US Congress, September 27, 2019, https://int.nyt.com/data/documenthelper/1857-engel-pompeo-supboena-letter/bf07096b8980914250ba/optimized/full.pdf.

91. Ellen Cranley, "Secretary of State Pompeo Said He Approves of Giuliani's Push for Ukraine to Investigate Joe Biden," *Business Insider*, September 22, 2019, https://www.businessinsider.com/pompeo-rudy-giuliani-calling-ukraine-investigate-biden-2019-9.

92. Peter Baker, "Trump Ousts John Bolton as National Security Adviser," *New York Times,* September 10, 2019, https://www.nytimes.com/2019/09/10/us/politics/john-bolton-national-security-adviser-trump.html.

93. Alan Cullison, Rebecca Ballhaus, and Dustin Volz, "Trump Repeatedly Pressed Ukraine President to Investigate Biden's Son," *Wall Street Journal,* September 21, 2019, https://www.wsj.com/articles/trump-defends-conversation-with-ukraine-leader-11568993176.

94. Allan Smith, "Trump Admits to Discussing Biden in Scrutinized Talk with Ukrainian Leader," NBC News, September 22, 2019, https://www.nbcnews.com/politics/donald-trump/trump-claims-no-quid-pro-quo-when-he-discussed-biden-n1057376.

95. Amita Kelly, "READ: White House Account of President Trump's Call with Ukraine's Leader," National Public Radio, September 25, 2019, https://www.npr.org/2019/09/25/764052120/read-transcript-of-president-trumps-call-with-ukraine-s-leader.

96. Nicholas Fandos, "Panel Approves Impeachment Articles and Sends Charges for a House Vote," *New York Times,* December 13, 2019, https://www.nytimes.com/2019/12/13/us/politics/impeachment-vote.html.

97. Jeremy Herb and Clare Foran, "House Sends Two Articles of Impeachment to the Senate," CNN, January 15, 2020, https://www.cnn.com/2020/01/15/politics/pelosi-naming-impeachment-managers/index.html.

98. "Read Adam Schiff's Opening Argument at Senate Impeachment Trial," Politico, January 22, 2020, https://www.politico.com/news/2020/01/22/adam-schiff-opening-argument-trump-impeachment-trial-102202.

99. Yelena Dzhanova and Christina Wilkie, "Trump Impeachment Trial: Defense Wraps Up Oral Arguments, Urges Senate to Acquit the President," CNBC, January 28, 2020, https://www.cnbc.com/2020/01/28/trump-impeachment-trial-defense-wraps-up-case-for-acquittal.html.

100. Nicholas Fandos, "Trump Acquitted of Two Impeachment Charges in Near Party-Line Vote," *New York Times,* February 5, 2020, https://www.nytimes.com/2020/02/05/us/politics/trump-acquitted-impeachment.html.

Chapter 17—Fixing a Fractured Democracy

1. Dave R. Palmer, *George Washington and Benedict Arnold: A Tale of Two Patriots* (Washington, DC: Regnery Press, 2004).

2. Joshua Lawrence Chamberlain, "Chamberlain's Address for the 20th Maine Monument at Gettysburg" (speech), October 3, 1889, https://www.battlefields.org/learn/primary-sources/chamberlains-address-20th-maine-monument-gettysburg.

3. Steven Beschloss, "One day we'll have a president again who's not a demagogue," Twitter, March 29, 2019, 6:46 p.m., https://twitter.com/StevenBeschloss/status/1111791725872218112.

4. Ale Russian, "Trump Boasted of Avoiding STDs While Dating: Vaginas Are 'Landmines... It Is My Personal Vietnam,'" *People Magazine,* October 28, 2016,

https://people.com/politics/trump-boasted-of-avoiding-stds-while-dating-vaginas-are-landmines-it-was-my-personal-vietnam/.

5. Adam Goldman and Michael S. Schmidt, "Rod Rosenstein Suggested Secretly Recording Trump and Discussed 25th Amendment," *New York Times*, September 21, 2018, https://www.nytimes.com/2018/09/21/us/politics/rod-rosenstein-wear-wire-25th-amendment.html.

6. Nina Khrushcheva, "Donald Trump's Not Quite Joseph Stalin. But His 'Fake News Awards' Should Scare Us," MSNBC, January 17, 2018, https://www.nbcnews.com/think/opinion/donald-trump-s-not-quite-joseph-stalin-his-fake-news-ncna838456.

7. Jonathan McCullough, phone call with author, December 12, 2018.

8. Franklin Delano Roosevelt, Franklin Roosevelt's Address Announcing the Second New Deal, October 31, 1936, Roosevelt Presidential Library, Marist University, http://docs.fdrlibrary.marist.edu/od2ndst.html.

9. Nina Jankowicz, "The Disinformation Vaccination," *Wilson Quarterly*, Winter 2018, https://wilsonquarterly.com/quarterly/the-disinformation-age/the-disinformation-vaccination/.

10. Ibid.

11. Ibid.

12. Christian Caryle, "Europe Is Sending Us a Warning for 2020. Will We Listen?" *Washington Post*, May 23, 2019, https://www.washingtonpost.com/opinions/2019/05/23/europe-is-sending-us-warning-will-we-listen.

13. Jankowicz, "The Disinformation Vaccination."

14. Ibid.

15. Ibid.

16. Sean Gallagher, "Web Tool Tracks Russian 'Influence Ops' on Twitter," ArsTechnica, August 2, 2017, https://arstechnica.com/gadgets/2017/08/new-web-tool-tracks-russian-influence-ops-on-twitter/.

17. Reinhold Niebuhr, *The Irony of American History* (Chicago: University of Chicago Press, 1952), 174.

18. Karen Tumulty and Ed O'Keefe, "Michelle Obama's Convention Speech Proves to Be Shining Moment," *Washington Post*, September 5, 2012, https://www.washingtonpost.com/politics/michelle-obamas-convention-speech-proves-to-be-shining-moment/2012/09/05/c6618e5e-f779-11e1-8b93-c4f4ab1c8d13_story.html?utm_term=.23f0894785bb.

19. Joy Reid (@JoyAnnReid), "4. Trump thinks he is still the star of a TV show," Twitter, December 28, 2017, https://twitter.com/JoyAnnReid/status/946597543173066752?s=20.

20. Thomas Paine, "The Crisis," December 23, 1776, http://www.ushistory.org/Paine/crisis/c-01.htm.

Epilogue—Benedict Arnold Vindicated

1. Glenn Kessler, Salvador Rizzi, and Meg Kelly, "President Trump Made 19,127 False or Misleading Claims in 1,226 Days," *Washington Post*, https://www

.washingtonpost.com/politics/2020/06/01/president-trump-made-19127-false-or-misleading-claims-1226-days/.

2. Charles Lee, "The Lee Papers...1754–[1811], Vol. 5," in *Collections of the New-York Historical Society for the Year 1872* (New York: New-York Historical Society, 1872), 303, https://archive.org/details/leepapersooleegoog.

3. "From Alexander Hamilton to Elias Boudinot" (letter), July 5, 1778, https://founders.archives.gov/documents/Hamilton/01-01-02-0499.

4. Dave R. Palmer, *George Washington and Benedict Arnold: A Tale of Two Patriots* (Washington, DC: Regnery Press, 2004), 377.

Index